HARLEY QUINN and the BIRDS OF PREY

THE HUNT FOR HARLEY

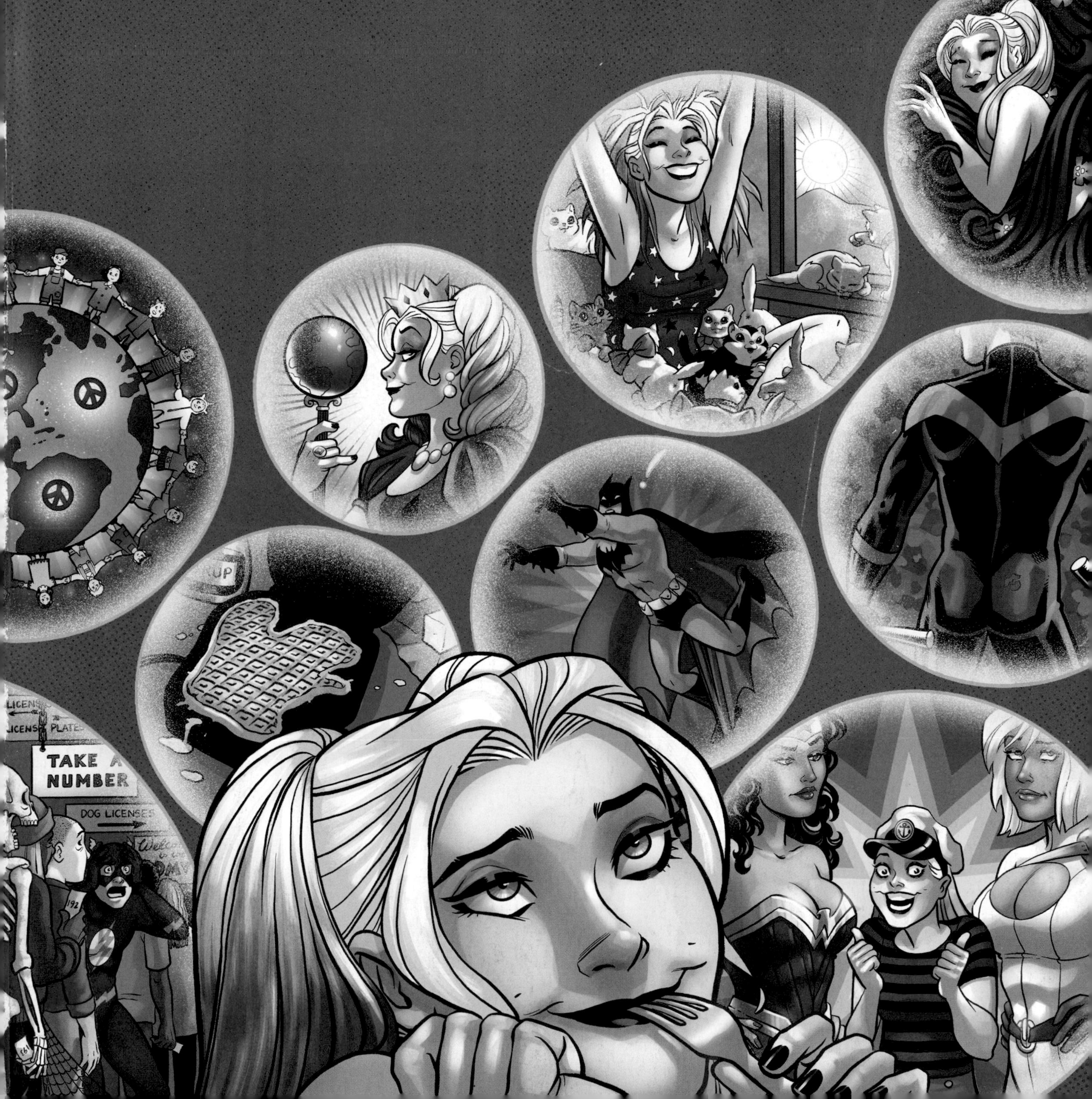
TAKE A
NUMBER
DOG LICENSES

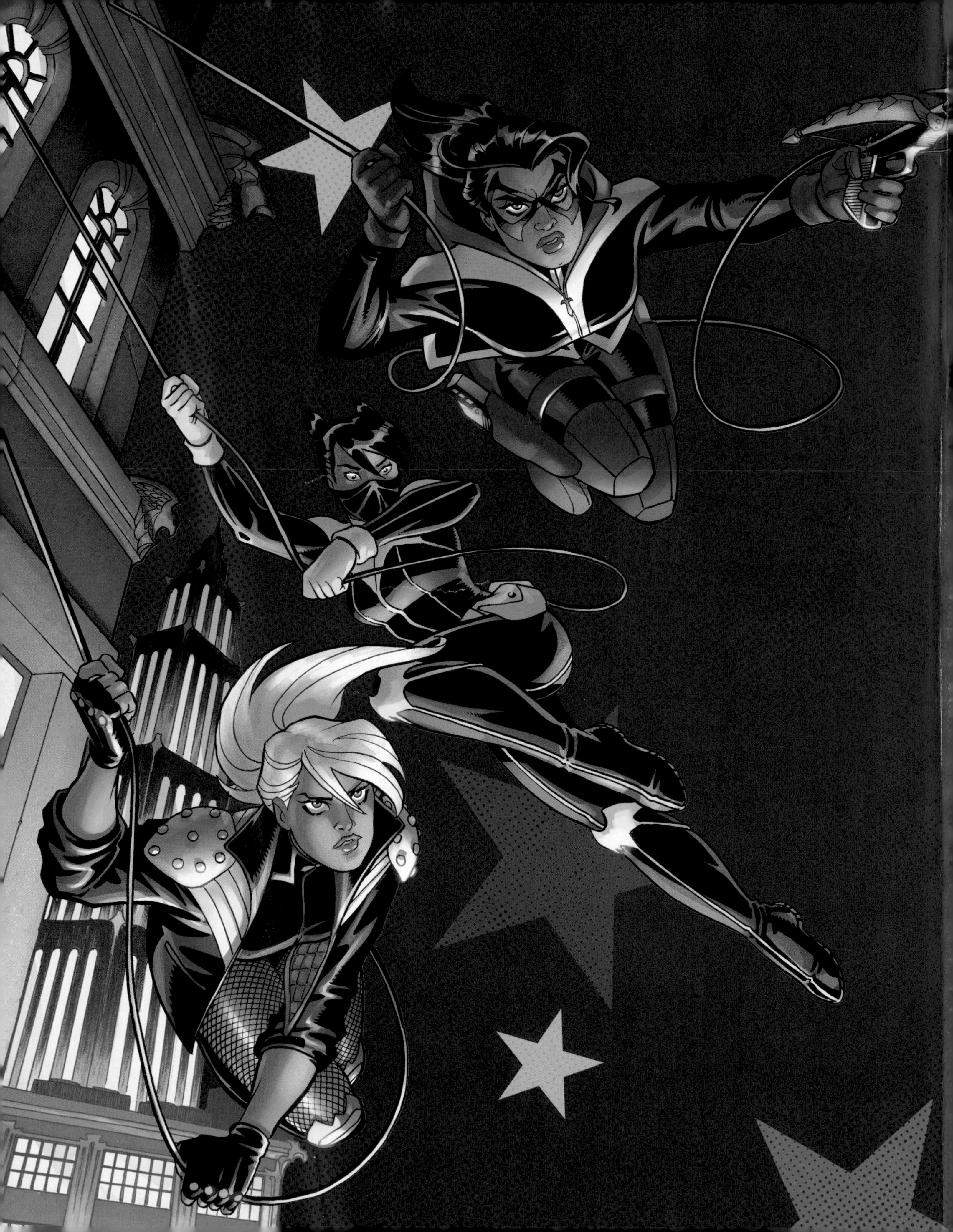

HARLEY QUINN
and the BIRDS OF PREY
THE HUNT FOR HARLEY

◆ ◆ ◆ ◆ ◆ ◆ ◆ ◆

AMANDA CONNER & JIMMY PALMIOTTI
writers

AMANDA CONNER
CHAD HARDIN
artists

ALEX SINCLAIR
PAUL MOUNTS   ENRICA EREN ANGIOLINI
colorists

JOHN J. HILL
DAVE SHARPE
letterers

AMANDA CONNER & PAUL MOUNTS
collection and issue #1 cover artists

AMANDA CONNER & ALEX SINCLAIR
issues #2-4 cover artists

HARLEY QUINN created by PAUL DINI & BRUCE TIMM

CHRIS CONROY Editor – Original Series & Collected Edition
MAGGIE HOWELL, AMEDEO TURTURRO Associate Editors – Original Series
STEVE COOK Design Director – Books
MEGEN BELLERSEN Publication Design
SUZANNAH ROWNTREE Publication Production

MARIE JAVINS Editor-in-Chief, DC Comics

DANIEL CHERRY III Senior VP – General Manager
JIM LEE Publisher & Chief Creative Officer
DON FALLETTI VP – Manufacturing Operations & Workflow Management
LAWRENCE GANEM VP – Talent Services
ALISON GILL Senior VP – Manufacturing & Operations
NICK J. NAPOLITANO VP – Manufacturing Administration & Design
NANCY SPEARS VP – Revenue
MICHELE R. WELLS VP & Executive Editor, Young Reader

HARLEY QUINN & THE BIRDS OF PREY: THE HUNT FOR HARLEY

DC Comics, 2900 West Alameda Ave., Burbank, CA 91505
Printed by Transcontinental Interglobe, Beauceville, QC, Canada. 2/12/21. First Printing.
ISBN: 978-1-77950-449-4

Library of Congress Cataloging-in-Publication Data is available.

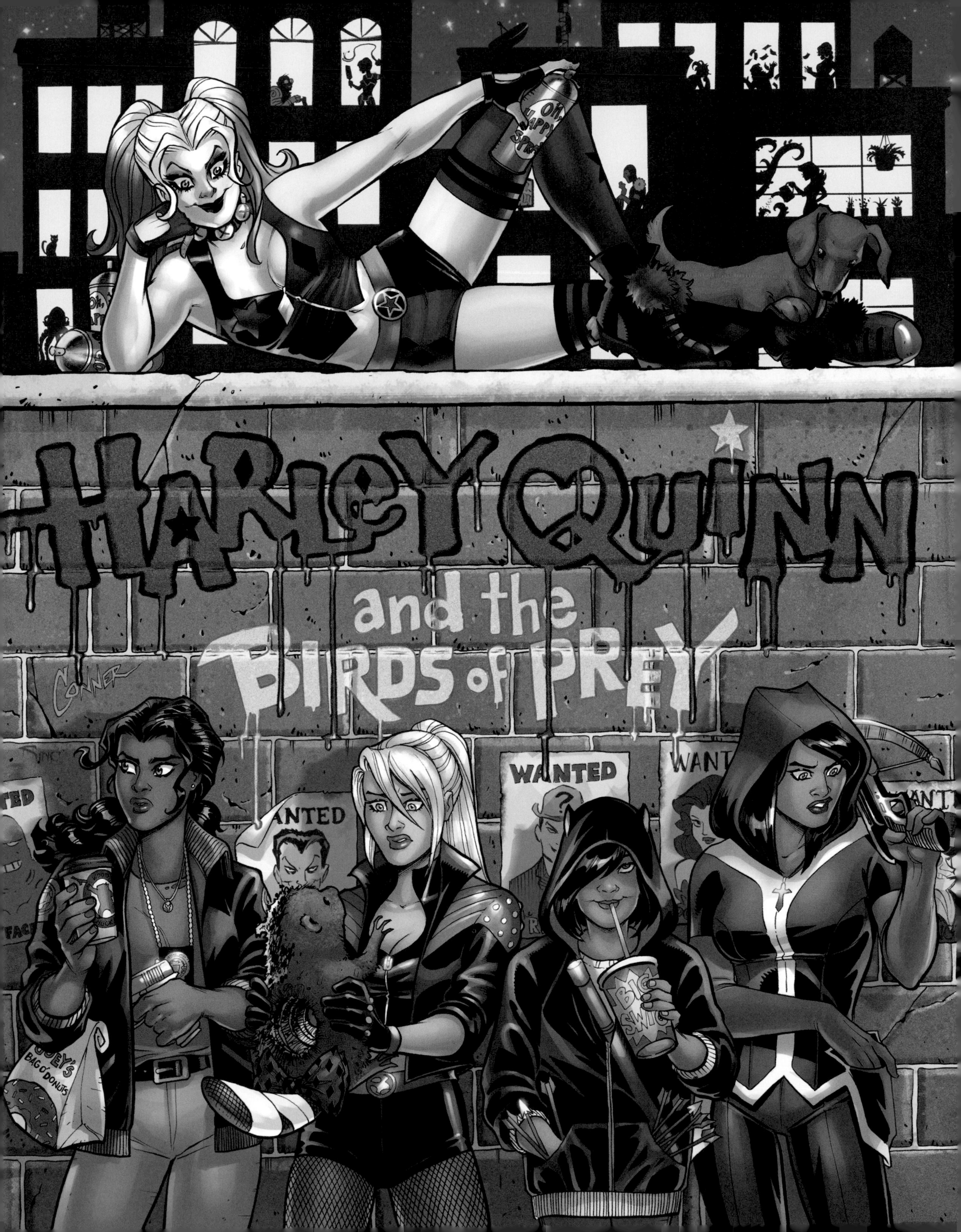
HARLEY QUINN
and the
BIRDS OF PREY
CONNER
WANTED
WANTED
JOEY'S
BAG O' DONUTS
BIG SWIG

BOOK ONE
NO SLEEP TILL...GOTHAM!

"I got some PERSONAL BUSINESS that needs my attention..."

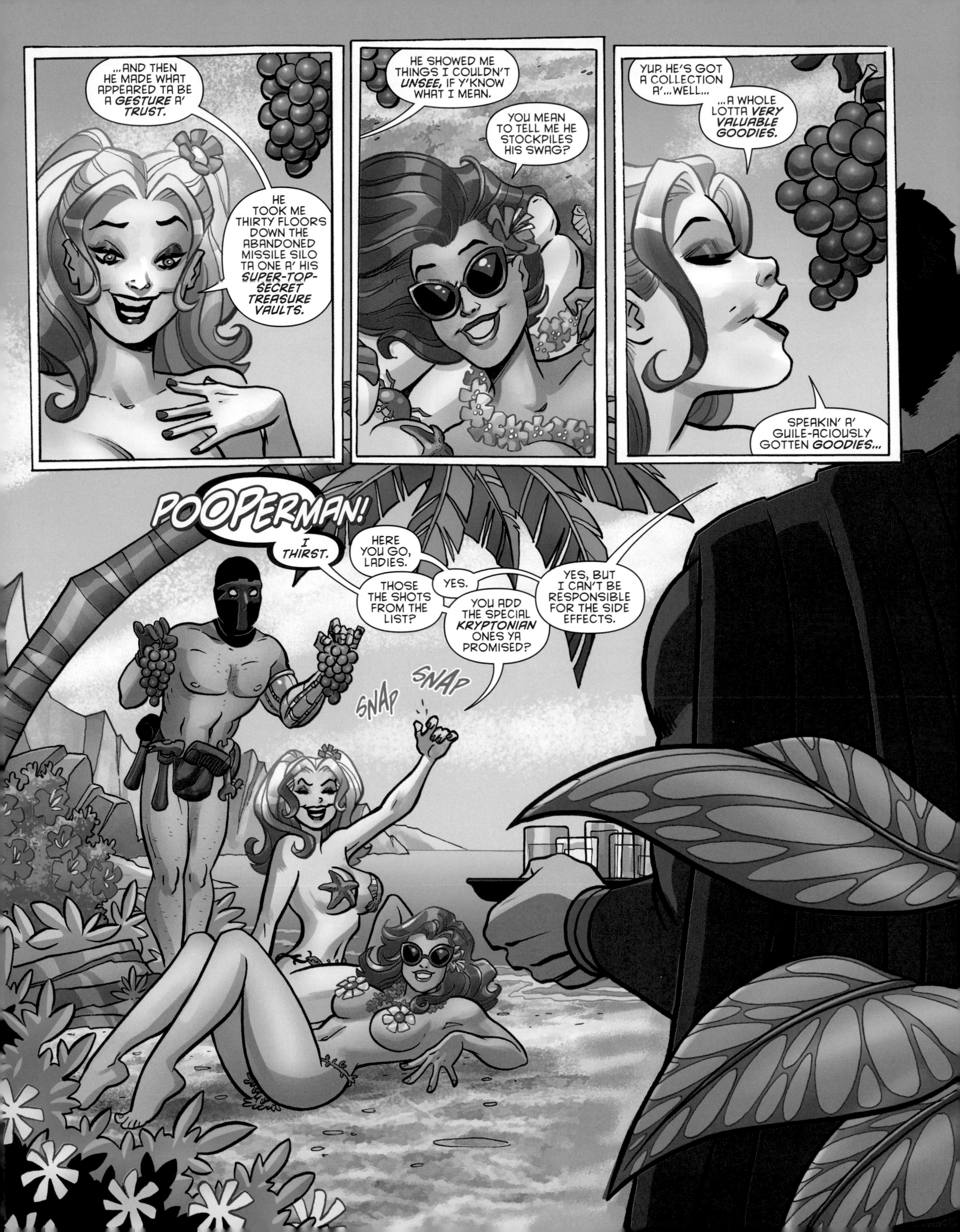

...AND THEN HE MADE WHAT APPEARED TA BE A GESTURE A' TRUST.
HE TOOK ME THIRTY FLOORS DOWN THE ABANDONED MISSILE SILO TA ONE A' HIS SUPER-TOP-SECRET TREASURE VAULTS.
HE SHOWED ME THINGS I COULDN'T UNSEE, IF Y'KNOW WHAT I MEAN.
YOU MEAN TO TELL ME HE STOCKPILES HIS SWAG?
YUP. HE'S GOT A COLLECTION A'...WELL...
...A WHOLE LOTTA VERY VALUABLE GOODIES.
SPEAKIN' A' GUILE-ACIOUSLY GOTTEN GOODIES...
POOPERMAN!
I THIRST.
HERE YOU GO, LADIES.
THOSE THE SHOTS FROM THE LIST?
YES.
YOU ADD THE SPECIAL KRYPTONIAN ONES YA PROMISED?
YES, BUT I CAN'T BE RESPONSIBLE FOR THE SIDE EFFECTS.
SNAP
SNAP

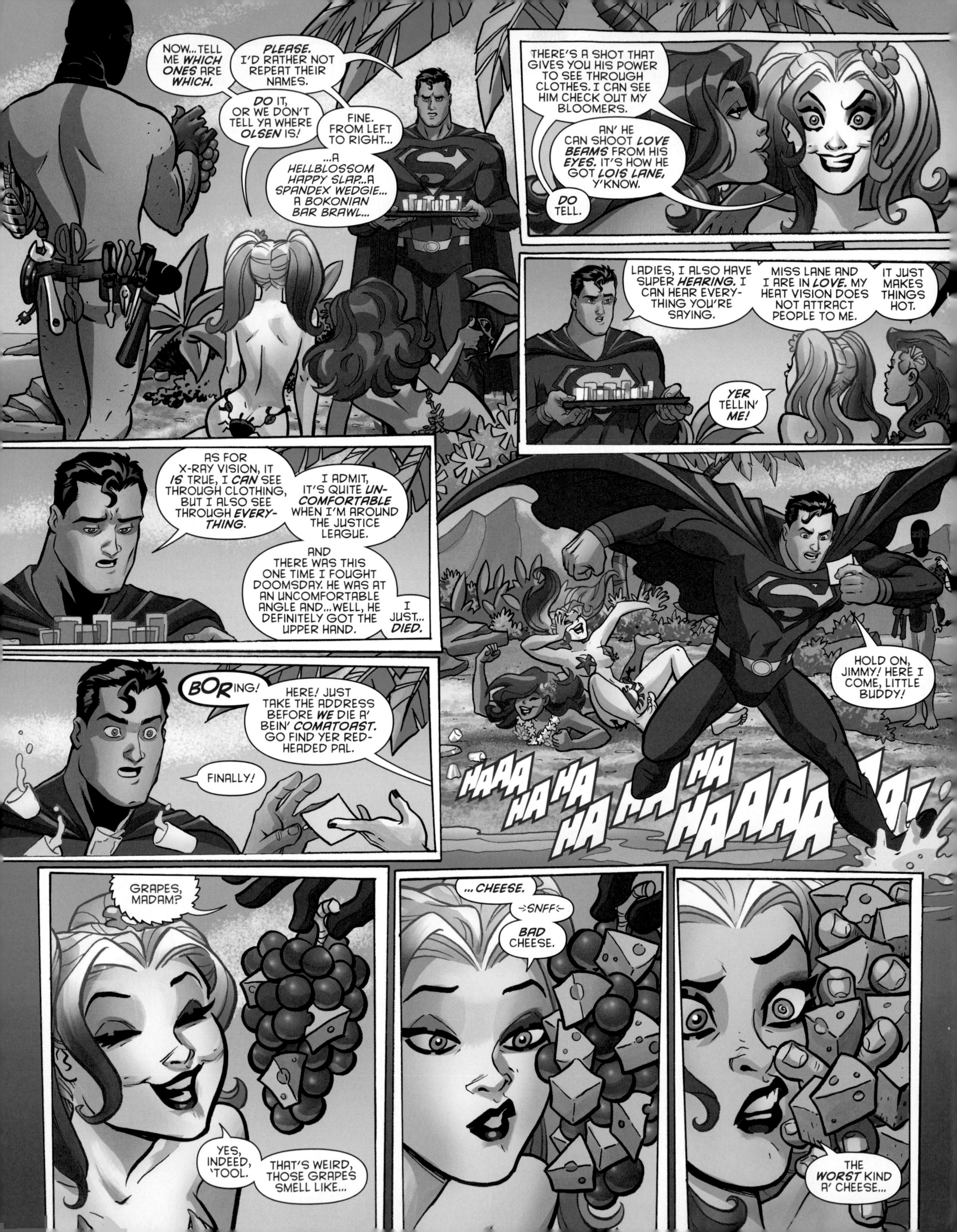
NOW...TELL ME WHICH ONES ARE WHICH.
PLEASE. I'D RATHER NOT REPEAT THEIR NAMES.
DO IT, OR WE DON'T TELL YA WHERE OLSEN IS!
FINE. FROM LEFT TO RIGHT...
...A HELLBLOSSOM HAPPY SLAP...A SPANDEX WEDGIE... A BOKONIAN BAR BRAWL...
THERE'S A SHOT THAT GIVES YOU HIS POWER TO SEE THROUGH CLOTHES. I CAN SEE HIM CHECK OUT MY BLOOMERS.
AN' HE CAN SHOOT LOVE BEAMS FROM HIS EYES. IT'S HOW HE GOT LOIS LANE, Y'KNOW.
DO TELL.
LADIES, I ALSO HAVE SUPER HEARING. I CAN HEAR EVERYTHING YOU'RE SAYING.
MISS LANE AND I ARE IN LOVE. MY HEAT VISION DOES NOT ATTRACT PEOPLE TO ME.
IT JUST MAKES THINGS HOT.
YER TELLIN' ME!
AS FOR X-RAY VISION, IT IS TRUE, I CAN SEE THROUGH CLOTHING, BUT I ALSO SEE THROUGH EVERYTHING.
I ADMIT, IT'S QUITE UNCOMFORTABLE WHEN I'M AROUND THE JUSTICE LEAGUE.
AND THERE WAS THIS ONE TIME I FOUGHT DOOMSDAY. HE WAS AT AN UNCOMFORTABLE ANGLE AND...WELL, HE DEFINITELY GOT THE UPPER HAND.
I JUST... DIED.
BORING!
HERE! JUST TAKE THE ADDRESS BEFORE WE DIE A' BEIN' COMATOAST. GO FIND YER RED-HEADED PAL.
FINALLY!
HOLD ON, JIMMY! HERE I COME, LITTLE BUDDY!
HAAA HA HA HA HA HA HAAAAA!
GRAPES, MADAM?
YES, INDEED, 'TOOL.
THAT'S WEIRD, THOSE GRAPES SMELL LIKE...
...CHEESE.
SNFF
BAD CHEESE.
THE WORST KIND A' CHEESE...

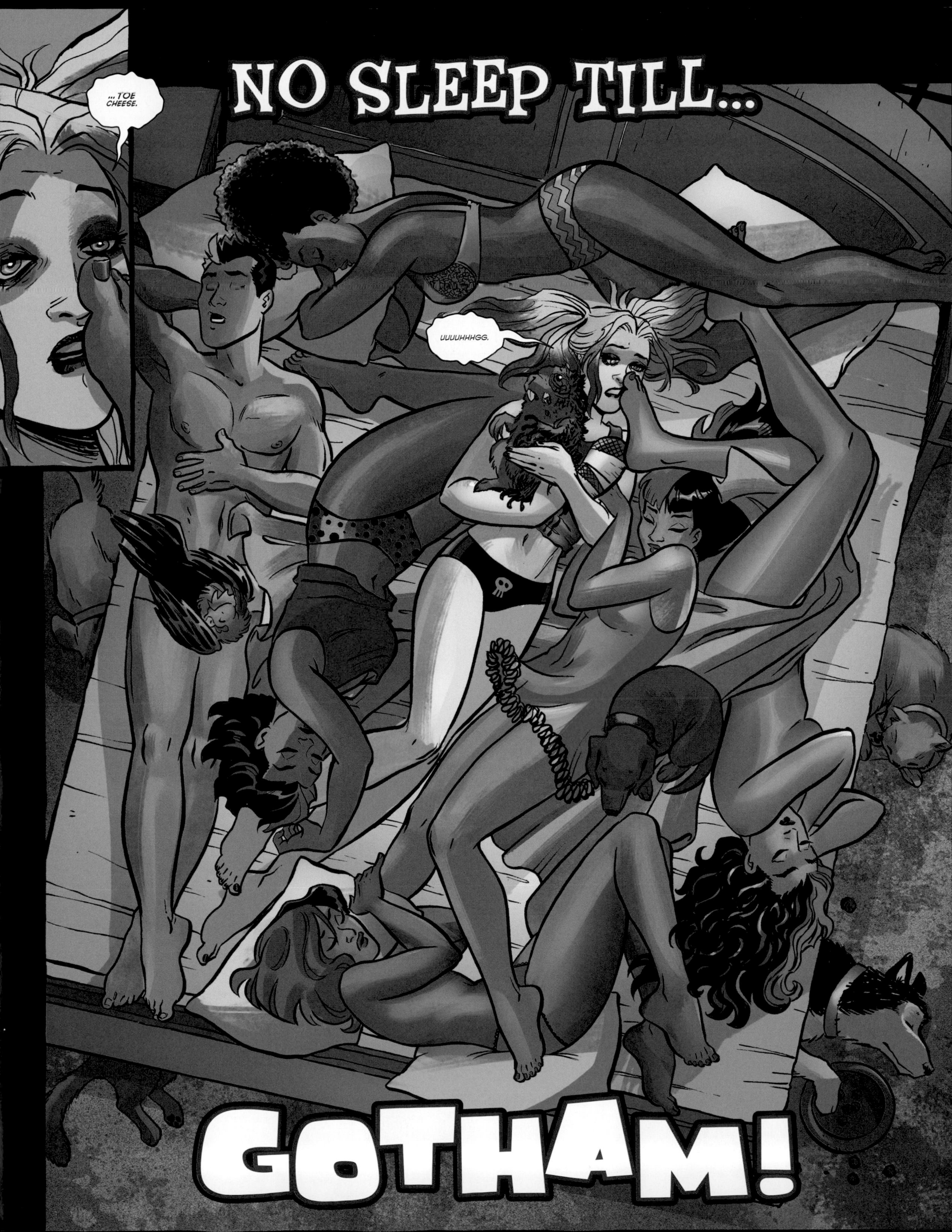
...TOE CHEESE.
NO SLEEP TILL...
UUUUHHHGG.
GOTHAM!

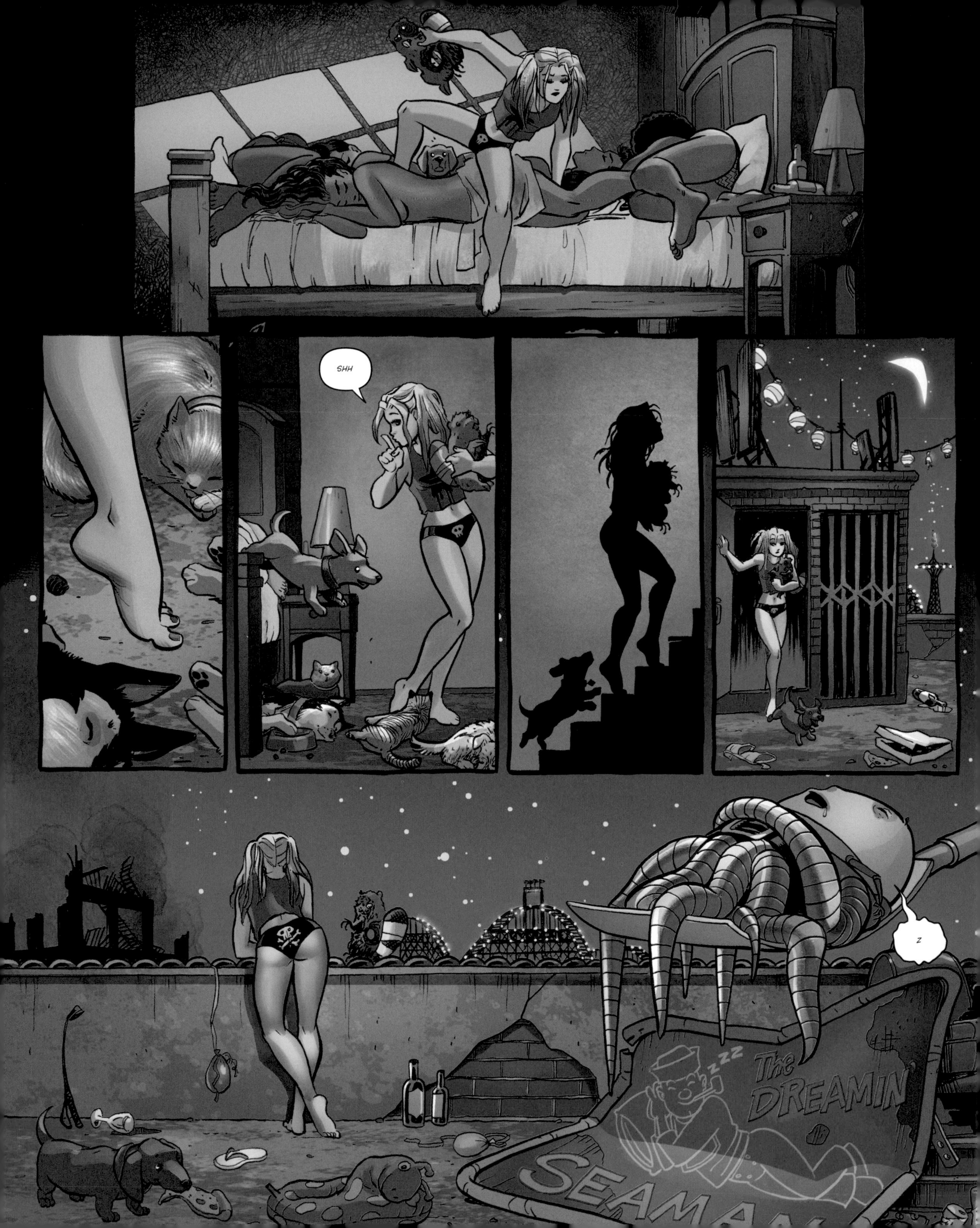
SHH
Z
The DREAMIN
SEAMA

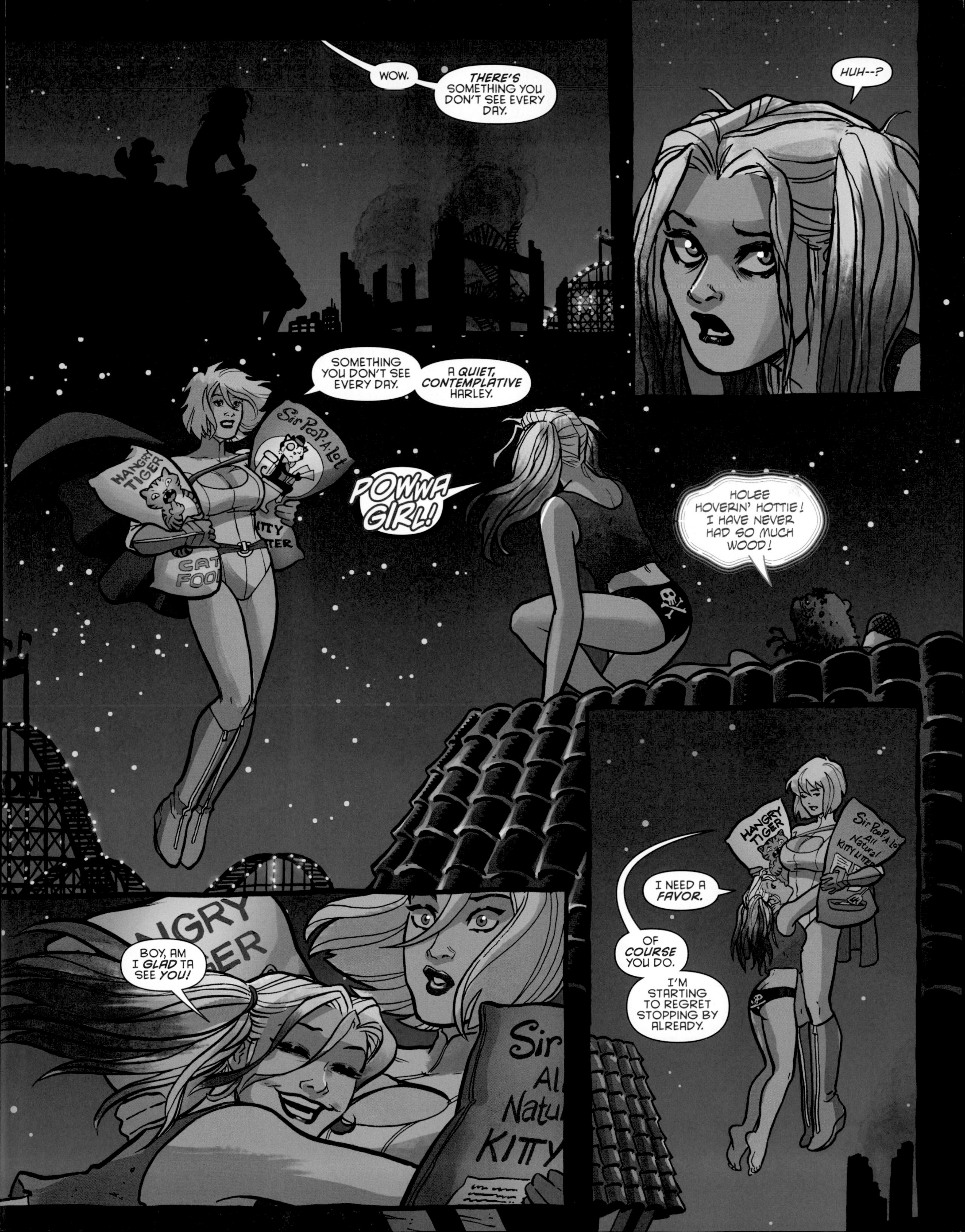
WOW.
THERE'S SOMETHING YOU DON'T SEE EVERY DAY.
HUH--?
SOMETHING YOU DON'T SEE EVERY DAY.
A QUIET, CONTEMPLATIVE HARLEY.
POWWA GIRL!
HOLEE HOVERIN' HOTTIE! I HAVE NEVER HAD SO MUCH WOOD!
HANGRY TIGER
CAT FOOD
Sir Poop-A-Lot
KITTY LITTER
BOY, AM I GLAD TA SEE YOU!
I NEED A FAVOR.
OF COURSE YOU DO.
I'M STARTING TO REGRET STOPPING BY ALREADY.

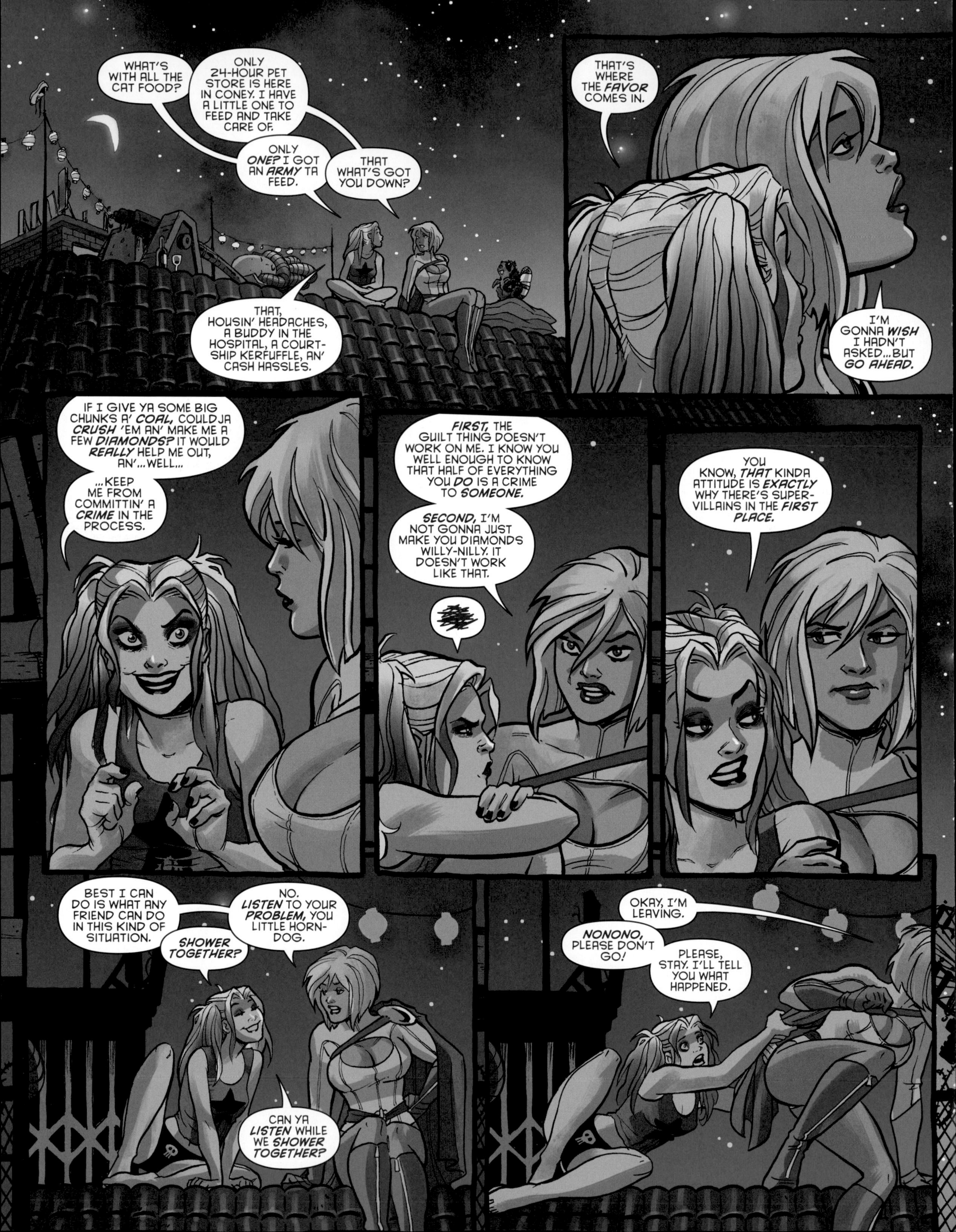
WHAT'S WITH ALL THE CAT FOOD?
ONLY 24-HOUR PET STORE IS HERE IN CONEY. I HAVE A LITTLE ONE TO FEED AND TAKE CARE OF.
ONLY ONE? I GOT AN ARMY TA FEED.
THAT WHAT'S GOT YOU DOWN?
THAT, HOUSIN' HEADACHES, A BUDDY IN THE HOSPITAL, A COURT-SHIP KERFUFFLE, AN' CASH HASSLES.
THAT'S WHERE THE FAVOR COMES IN.
I'M GONNA WISH I HADN'T ASKED...BUT GO AHEAD.
IF I GIVE YA SOME BIG CHUNKS A' COAL, COULDJA CRUSH 'EM AN' MAKE ME A FEW DIAMONDS? IT WOULD REALLY HELP ME OUT, AN'...WELL...
...KEEP ME FROM COMMITTIN' A CRIME IN THE PROCESS.
FIRST, THE GUILT THING DOESN'T WORK ON ME. I KNOW YOU WELL ENOUGH TO KNOW THAT HALF OF EVERYTHING YOU DO IS A CRIME TO SOMEONE.
SECOND, I'M NOT GONNA JUST MAKE YOU DIAMONDS WILLY-NILLY. IT DOESN'T WORK LIKE THAT.
YOU KNOW, THAT KINDA ATTITUDE IS EXACTLY WHY THERE'S SUPER-VILLAINS IN THE FIRST PLACE.
BEST I CAN DO IS WHAT ANY FRIEND CAN DO IN THIS KIND OF SITUATION.
SHOWER TOGETHER?
NO. LISTEN TO YOUR PROBLEM, YOU LITTLE HORN-DOG.
CAN YA LISTEN WHILE WE SHOWER TOGETHER?
OKAY, I'M LEAVING.
NONONO, PLEASE DON'T GO!
PLEASE, STAY. I'LL TELL YOU WHAT HAPPENED.

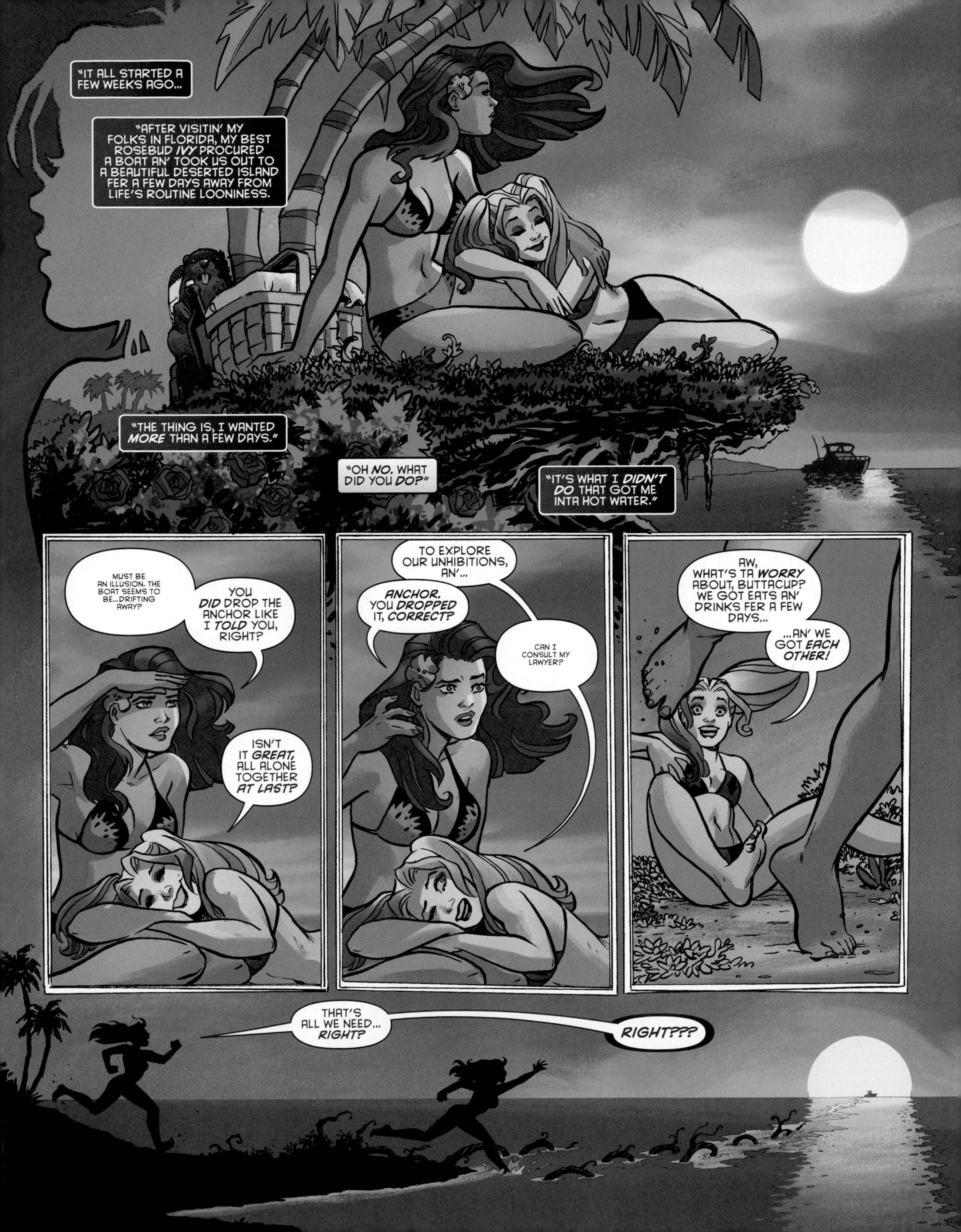
"IT ALL STARTED A FEW WEEKS AGO...
"AFTER VISITIN' MY FOLKS IN FLORIDA, MY BEST ROSEBUD IVY PROCURED A BOAT AN' TOOK US OUT TO A BEAUTIFUL DESERTED ISLAND FER A FEW DAYS AWAY FROM LIFE'S ROUTINE LOONINESS.
"THE THING IS, I WANTED MORE THAN A FEW DAYS."
"OH NO. WHAT DID YOU DO?"
"IT'S WHAT I DIDN'T DO THAT GOT ME INTA HOT WATER."
MUST BE AN ILLUSION. THE BOAT SEEMS TO BE...DRIFTING AWAY?
YOU DID DROP THE ANCHOR LIKE I TOLD YOU, RIGHT?
ISN'T IT GREAT, ALL ALONE TOGETHER AT LAST?
TO EXPLORE OUR UNHIBITIONS, AN'...
ANCHOR. YOU DROPPED IT, CORRECT?
CAN I CONSULT MY LAWYER?
AW, WHAT'S TA WORRY ABOUT, BUTTACUP? WE GOT EATS AN' DRINKS FER A FEW DAYS...
...AN' WE GOT EACH OTHER!
THAT'S ALL WE NEED... RIGHT?
RIGHT???

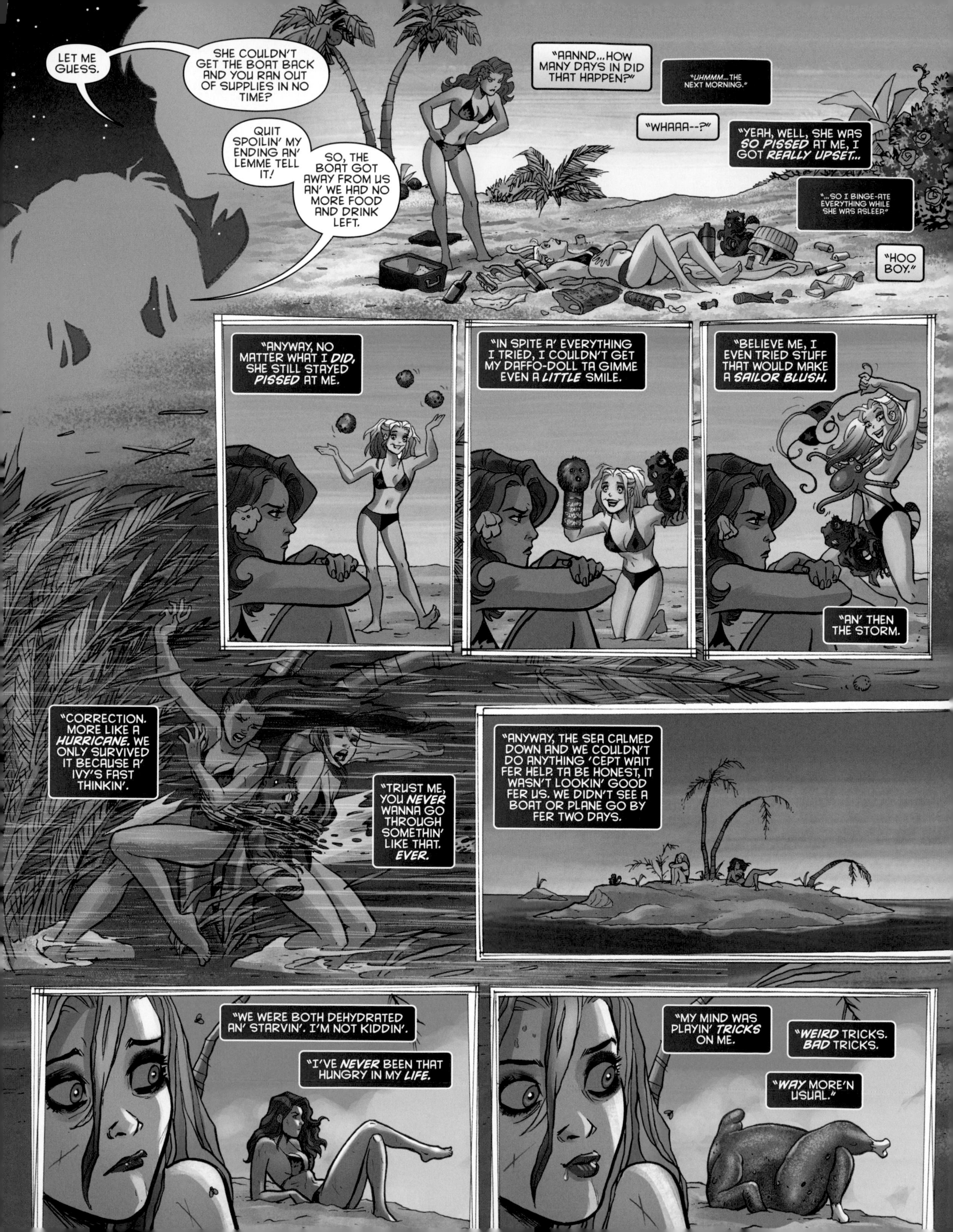
LET ME GUESS.
SHE COULDN'T GET THE BOAT BACK AND YOU RAN OUT OF SUPPLIES IN NO TIME?
QUIT SPOILIN' MY ENDING AN' LEMME TELL IT!
SO, THE BOAT GOT AWAY FROM US AN' WE HAD NO MORE FOOD AND DRINK LEFT.
"AANND...HOW MANY DAYS IN DID THAT HAPPEN?"
"UHMMM...THE NEXT MORNING."
"WHAAA--?"
"YEAH, WELL, SHE WAS SO PISSED AT ME, I GOT REALLY UPSET...
"...SO I BINGE-ATE EVERYTHING WHILE SHE WAS ASLEEP."
"HOO BOY."
"ANYWAY, NO MATTER WHAT I DID, SHE STILL STAYED PISSED AT ME.
"IN SPITE A' EVERYTHING I TRIED, I COULDN'T GET MY DAFFO-DOLL TA GIMME EVEN A LITTLE SMILE.
"BELIEVE ME, I EVEN TRIED STUFF THAT WOULD MAKE A SAILOR BLUSH.
"AN' THEN THE STORM.
"CORRECTION. MORE LIKE A HURRICANE. WE ONLY SURVIVED IT BECAUSE A' IVY'S FAST THINKIN'.
"TRUST ME, YOU NEVER WANNA GO THROUGH SOMETHIN' LIKE THAT. EVER.
"ANYWAY, THE SEA CALMED DOWN AND WE COULDN'T DO ANYTHING 'CEPT WAIT FER HELP. TA BE HONEST, IT WASN'T LOOKIN' GOOD FER US. WE DIDN'T SEE A BOAT OR PLANE GO BY FER TWO DAYS.
"WE WERE BOTH DEHYDRATED AN' STARVIN'. I'M NOT KIDDIN'.
"I'VE NEVER BEEN THAT HUNGRY IN MY LIFE.
"MY MIND WAS PLAYIN' TRICKS ON ME.
"WEIRD TRICKS. BAD TRICKS.
"WAY MORE'N USUAL."

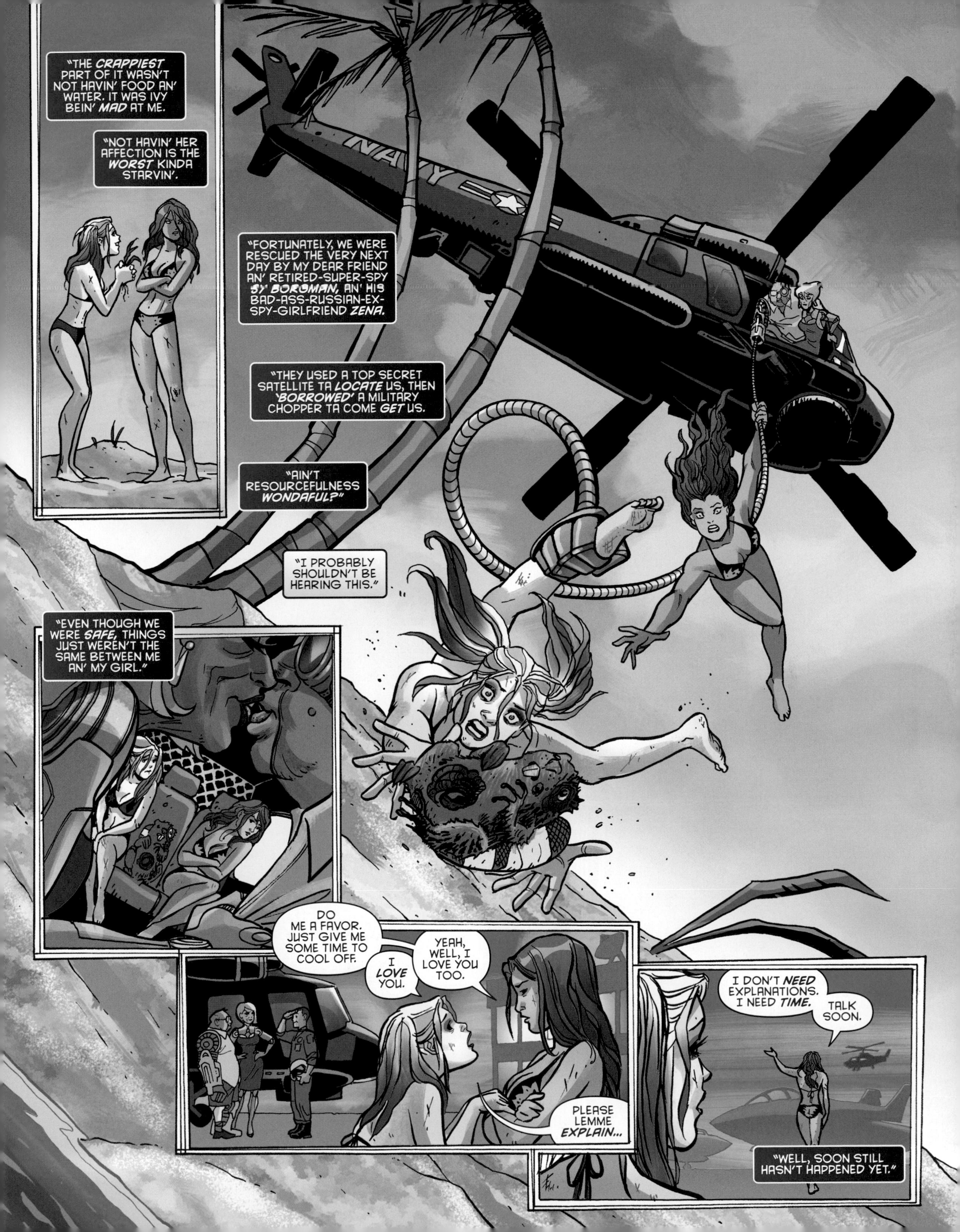
"THE CRAPPIEST PART OF IT WASN'T NOT HAVIN' FOOD AN' WATER. IT WAS IVY BEIN' MAD AT ME.
"NOT HAVIN' HER AFFECTION IS THE WORST KINDA STARVIN'.
NAVY
"FORTUNATELY, WE WERE RESCUED THE VERY NEXT DAY BY MY DEAR FRIEND AN' RETIRED-SUPER-SPY SY BORGMAN, AN' HIS BAD-ASS-RUSSIAN-EX-SPY-GIRLFRIEND ZENA.
"THEY USED A TOP SECRET SATELLITE TA LOCATE US, THEN 'BORROWED' A MILITARY CHOPPER TA COME GET US.
"AIN'T RESOURCEFULNESS WONDAFUL?"
"I PROBABLY SHOULDN'T BE HEARING THIS."
"EVEN THOUGH WE WERE SAFE, THINGS JUST WEREN'T THE SAME BETWEEN ME AN' MY GIRL."
DO ME A FAVOR. JUST GIVE ME SOME TIME TO COOL OFF.
I LOVE YOU.
YEAH, WELL, I LOVE YOU TOO.
PLEASE LEMME EXPLAIN...
I DON'T NEED EXPLANATIONS. I NEED TIME.
TALK SOON.
"WELL, SOON STILL HASN'T HAPPENED YET."

IVY MAD AT ME IS MISERABLE ENOUGH, BUT *HERE...*

...HERE I *REALLY* SCREWED UP, AN' MY FRIENDS GOT HURT. I DIDN'T KEEP UP WITH THE MORTGAGE ON THE DREAMIN' SEAMAN HOTEL. MY RIGHT-HAND MAN *TONY* TOOK THE *BRUNT* A' THAT MISTAKE.

WHAT HAPPENED? DID YOU HAVE TO PAY *PENALTIES* ON THE LOAN?

I THINK THAT ONLY HAPPENS WHEN YA GET A MORTGAGE FROM A *LEGITIMATE* COMPANY, BUT I COULDN'T GET ONE FER THE HOTEL, SO I WENT TA...

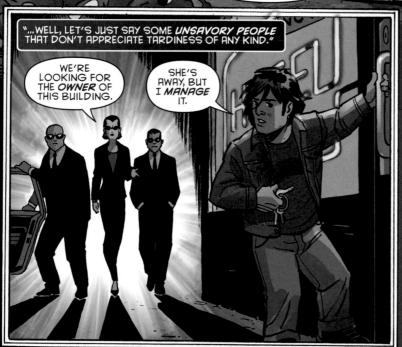

"...WELL, LET'S JUST SAY SOME *UNSAVORY* PEOPLE THAT DON'T APPRECIATE TARDINESS OF ANY KIND."

WE'RE LOOKING FOR THE *OWNER* OF THIS BUILDING.

SHE'S AWAY, BUT I *MANAGE* IT.

CAN I HELP YOU?

WE'RE WITH THE *DEFEO MORTGAGE COMPANY.*

SEEMS YOU AND YOUR BOSS HAVEN'T PAID YOUR MORTGAGE IN A WHILE.

THAT'S *UNACCEPT-ABLE.*

"NEEDLESS TA SAY, THEY MADE AN *EXAMPLE* OUTTA MY POOR TONY."

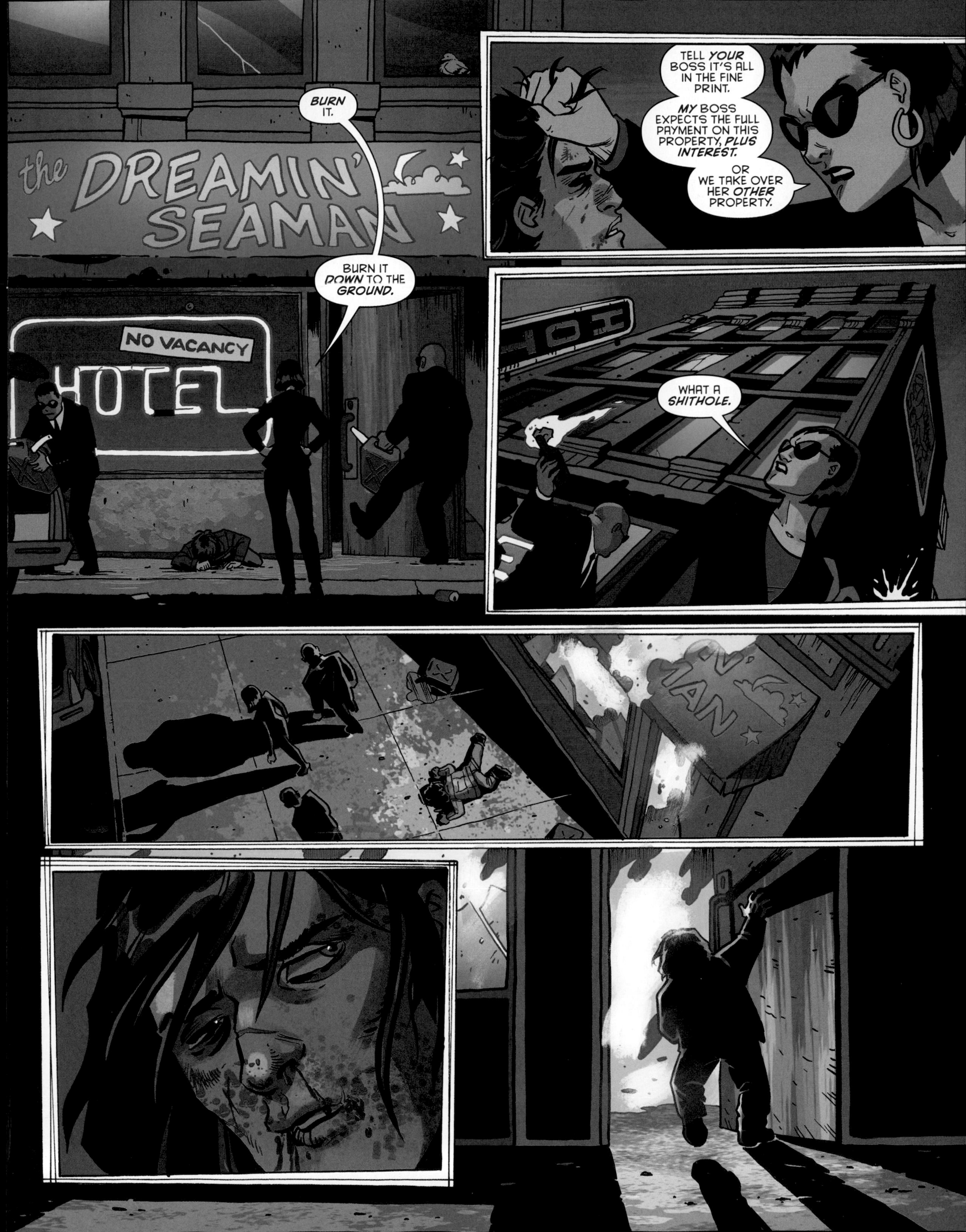
the DREAMIN' SEAMAN
NO VACANCY
HOTEL
BURN IT.
BURN IT DOWN TO THE GROUND.
TELL YOUR BOSS IT'S ALL IN THE FINE PRINT.
MY BOSS EXPECTS THE FULL PAYMENT ON THIS PROPERTY, PLUS INTEREST.
OR WE TAKE OVER HER OTHER PROPERTY.
WHAT A SHITHOLE.

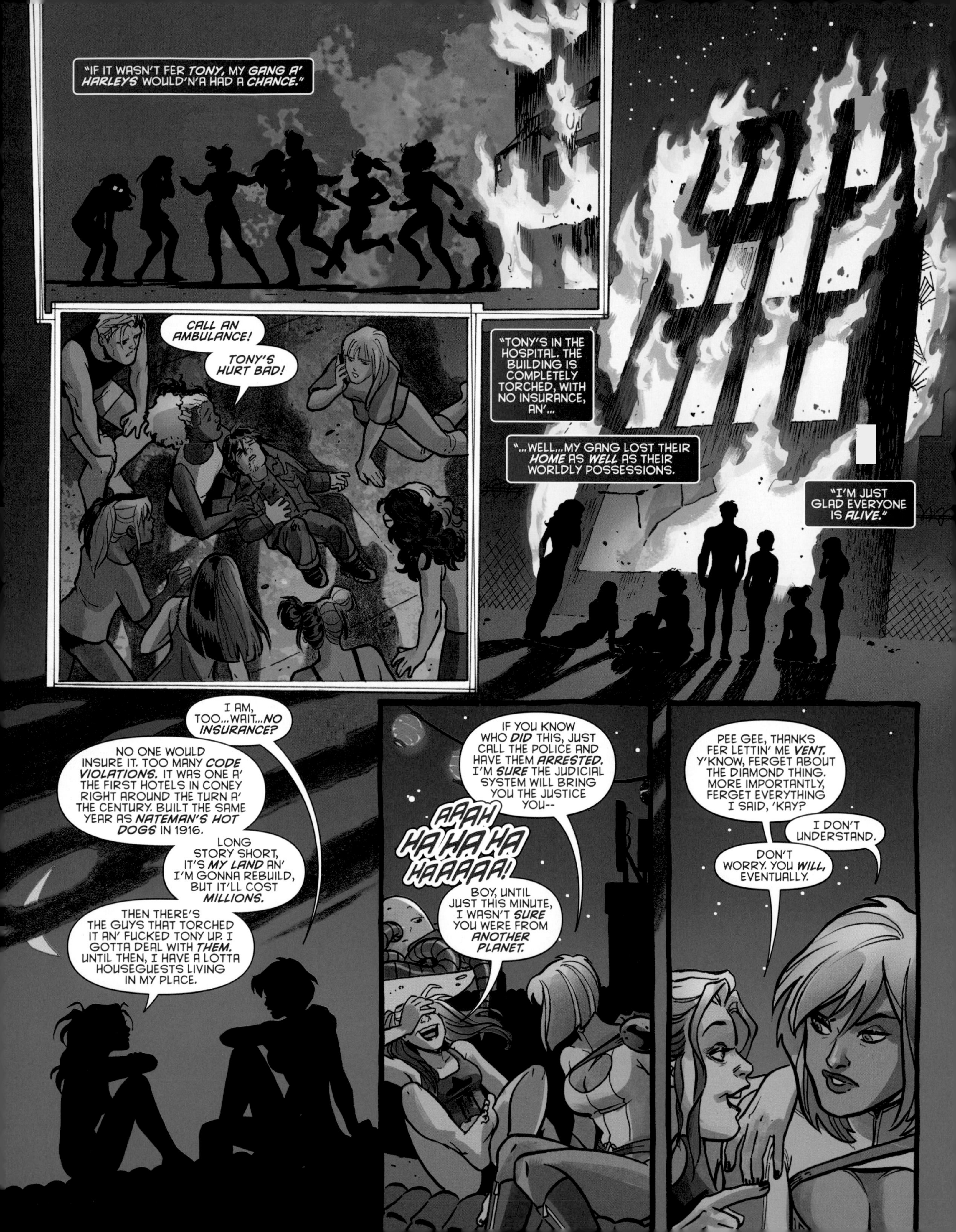
"IF IT WASN'T FER TONY, MY GANG A' HARLEY'S WOULD'N'A HAD A CHANCE."
CALL AN AMBULANCE!
TONY'S HURT BAD!
"TONY'S IN THE HOSPITAL. THE BUILDING IS COMPLETELY TORCHED, WITH NO INSURANCE, AN'...
"...WELL...MY GANG LOST THEIR HOME AS WELL AS THEIR WORLDLY POSSESSIONS.
"I'M JUST GLAD EVERYONE IS ALIVE."
I AM, TOO...WAIT...NO INSURANCE?
NO ONE WOULD INSURE IT. TOO MANY CODE VIOLATIONS. IT WAS ONE A' THE FIRST HOTELS IN CONEY RIGHT AROUND THE TURN A' THE CENTURY. BUILT THE SAME YEAR AS NATEMAN'S HOT DOGS IN 1916.
LONG STORY SHORT, IT'S MY LAND AN' I'M GONNA REBUILD, BUT IT'LL COST MILLIONS.
THEN THERE'S THE GUYS THAT TORCHED IT AN' FUCKED TONY UP. I GOTTA DEAL WITH THEM. UNTIL THEN, I HAVE A LOTTA HOUSEGUESTS LIVING IN MY PLACE.
IF YOU KNOW WHO DID THIS, JUST CALL THE POLICE AND HAVE THEM ARRESTED. I'M SURE THE JUDICIAL SYSTEM WILL BRING YOU THE JUSTICE YOU--
AAAH HA HA HA HAAAAA!
BOY, UNTIL JUST THIS MINUTE, I WASN'T SURE YOU WERE FROM ANOTHER PLANET.
PEE GEE, THANKS FER LETTIN' ME VENT. Y'KNOW, FERGET ABOUT THE DIAMOND THING. MORE IMPORTANTLY, FERGET EVERYTHING I SAID, 'KAY?
I DON'T UNDERSTAND.
DON'T WORRY. YOU WILL, EVENTUALLY.

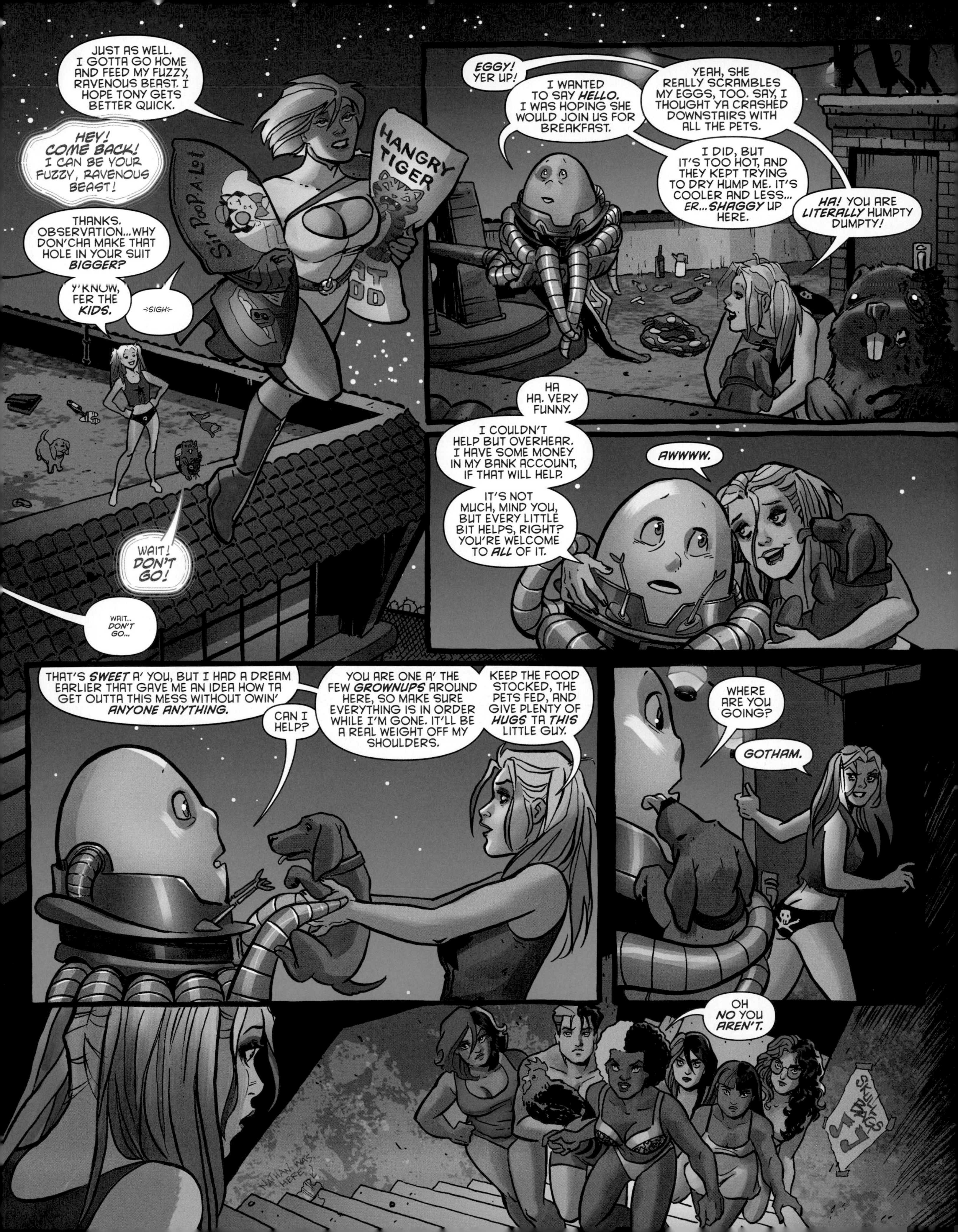
JUST AS WELL. I GOTTA GO HOME AND FEED MY FUZZY, RAVENOUS BEAST. I HOPE TONY GETS BETTER QUICK.
HEY! COME BACK! I CAN BE YOUR FUZZY, RAVENOUS BEAST!
HANGRY TIGER
THANKS. OBSERVATION...WHY DON'CHA MAKE THAT HOLE IN YOUR SUIT BIGGER?
Y'KNOW, FER THE KIDS.
SIGH
WAIT! DON'T GO!
WAIT... DON'T GO...
EGGY! YER UP!
I WANTED TO SAY HELLO. I WAS HOPING SHE WOULD JOIN US FOR BREAKFAST.
YEAH, SHE REALLY SCRAMBLES MY EGGS, TOO. SAY, I THOUGHT YA CRASHED DOWNSTAIRS WITH ALL THE PETS.
I DID, BUT IT'S TOO HOT, AND THEY KEPT TRYING TO DRY HUMP ME. IT'S COOLER AND LESS... ER...SHAGGY UP HERE.
HA! YOU ARE LITERALLY HUMPTY DUMPTY!
HA HA. VERY FUNNY.
I COULDN'T HELP BUT OVERHEAR. I HAVE SOME MONEY IN MY BANK ACCOUNT, IF THAT WILL HELP.
AWWWW.
IT'S NOT MUCH, MIND YOU, BUT EVERY LITTLE BIT HELPS, RIGHT? YOU'RE WELCOME TO ALL OF IT.
THAT'S SWEET A' YOU, BUT I HAD A DREAM EARLIER THAT GAVE ME AN IDEA HOW TA GET OUTTA THIS MESS WITHOUT OWIN' ANYONE ANYTHING.
CAN I HELP?
YOU ARE ONE A' THE FEW GROWNUPS AROUND HERE, SO MAKE SURE EVERYTHING IS IN ORDER WHILE I'M GONE. IT'LL BE A REAL WEIGHT OFF MY SHOULDERS.
KEEP THE FOOD STOCKED, THE PETS FED, AND GIVE PLENTY OF HUGS TA THIS LITTLE GUY.
WHERE ARE YOU GOING?
GOTHAM.
OH NO YOU AREN'T.
NATHAN WAS HERE

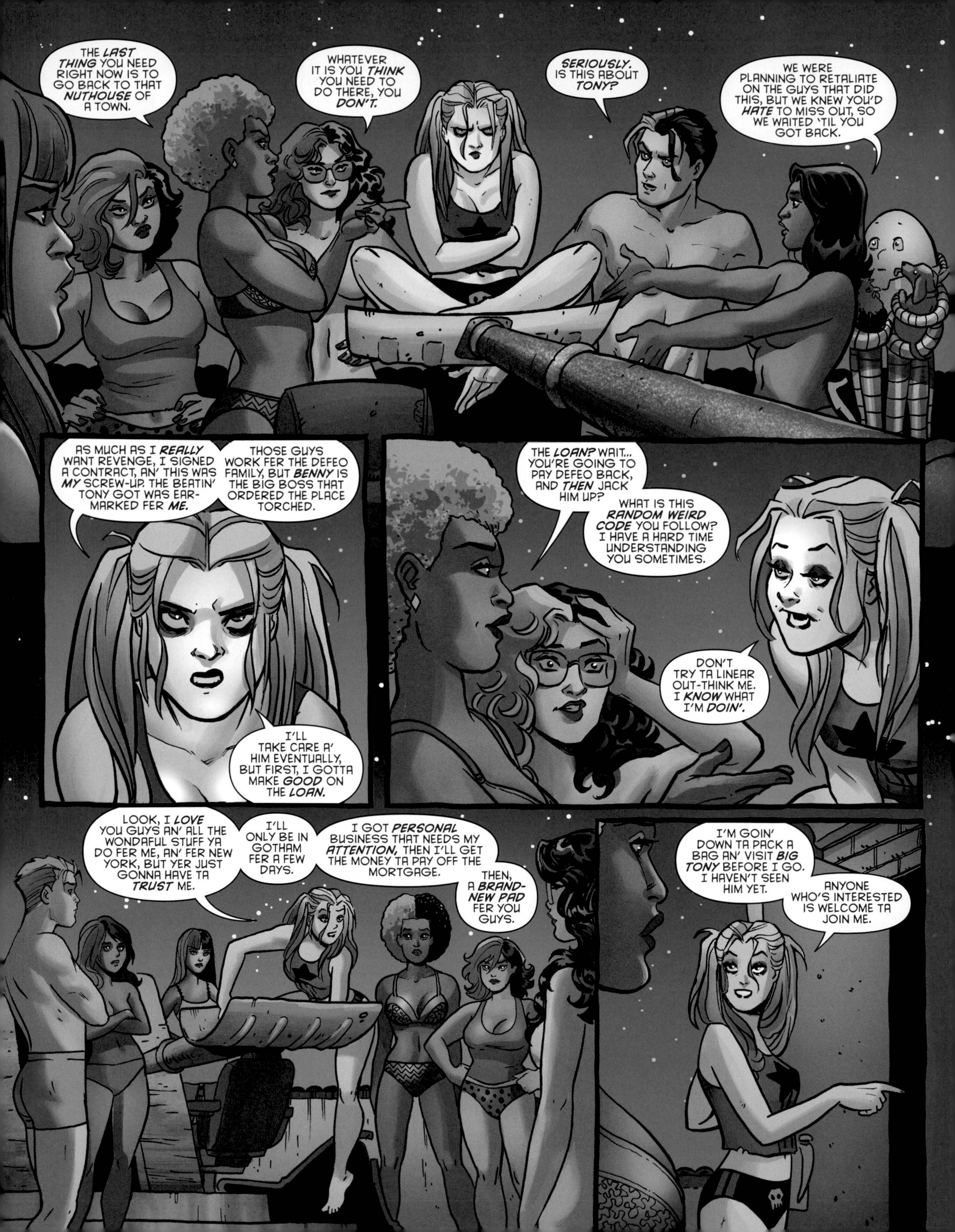
THE LAST THING YOU NEED RIGHT NOW IS TO GO BACK TO THAT NUTHOUSE OF A TOWN.
WHATEVER IT IS YOU THINK YOU NEED TO DO THERE, YOU DON'T.
SERIOUSLY. IS THIS ABOUT TONY?
WE WERE PLANNING TO RETALIATE ON THE GUYS THAT DID THIS, BUT WE KNEW YOU'D HATE TO MISS OUT, SO WE WAITED 'TIL YOU GOT BACK.
AS MUCH AS I REALLY WANT REVENGE, I SIGNED A CONTRACT, AN' THIS WAS MY SCREW-UP. THE BEATIN' TONY GOT WAS EAR-MARKED FER ME.
THOSE GUYS WORK FER THE DEFEO FAMILY, BUT BENNY IS THE BIG BOSS THAT ORDERED THE PLACE TORCHED.
I'LL TAKE CARE A' HIM EVENTUALLY, BUT FIRST, I GOTTA MAKE GOOD ON THE LOAN.
THE LOAN? WAIT... YOU'RE GOING TO PAY DEFEO BACK, AND THEN JACK HIM UP?
WHAT IS THIS RANDOM WEIRD CODE YOU FOLLOW? I HAVE A HARD TIME UNDERSTANDING YOU SOMETIMES.
DON'T TRY TA LINEAR OUT-THINK ME. I KNOW WHAT I'M DOIN'.
LOOK, I LOVE YOU GUYS AN' ALL THE WONDAFUL STUFF YA DO FER ME, AN' FER NEW YORK, BUT YER JUST GONNA HAVE TA TRUST ME.
I'LL ONLY BE IN GOTHAM FER A FEW DAYS.
I GOT PERSONAL BUSINESS THAT NEEDS MY ATTENTION, THEN I'LL GET THE MONEY TA PAY OFF THE MORTGAGE.
THEN, A BRAND-NEW PAD FER YOU GUYS.
I'M GOIN' DOWN TA PACK A BAG AN' VISIT BIG TONY BEFORE I GO. I HAVEN'T SEEN HIM YET.
ANYONE WHO'S INTERESTED IS WELCOME TA JOIN ME.

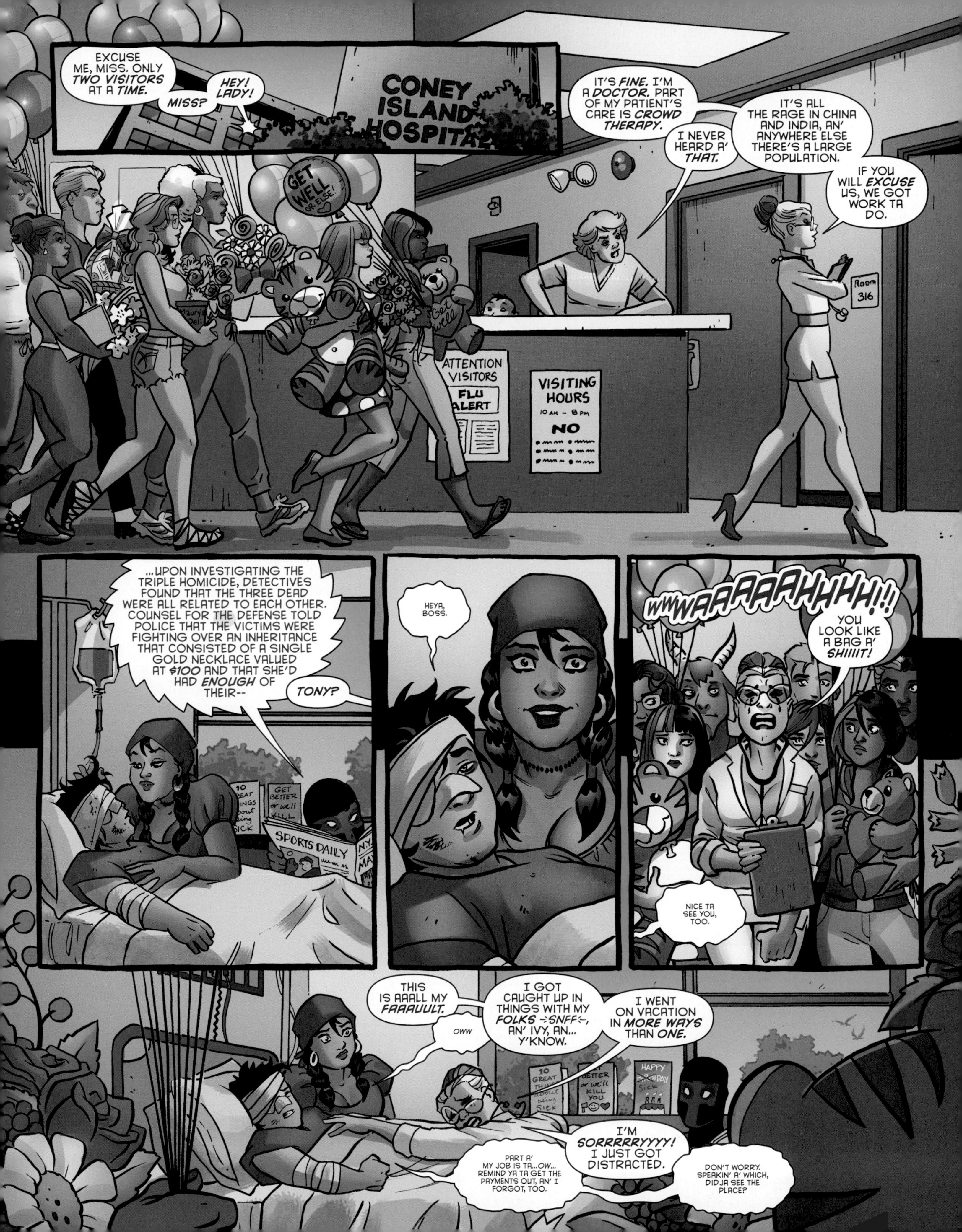

EXCUSE ME, MISS. ONLY TWO VISITORS AT A TIME.
MISS?
HEY! LADY!
CONEY ISLAND HOSPITAL
IT'S FINE. I'M A DOCTOR. PART OF MY PATIENT'S CARE IS CROWD THERAPY.
I NEVER HEARD A' THAT.
IT'S ALL THE RAGE IN CHINA AND INDIA, AN' ANYWHERE ELSE THERE'S A LARGE POPULATION.
IF YOU WILL EXCUSE US, WE GOT WORK TA DO.
GET WELL OR ELSE!
ATTENTION VISITORS
FLU ALERT
VISITING HOURS
10 AM - 8 PM
NO
Room 316
...UPON INVESTIGATING THE TRIPLE HOMICIDE, DETECTIVES FOUND THAT THE THREE DEAD WERE ALL RELATED TO EACH OTHER. COUNSEL FOR THE DEFENSE TOLD POLICE THAT THE VICTIMS WERE FIGHTING OVER AN INHERITANCE THAT CONSISTED OF A SINGLE GOLD NECKLACE VALUED AT $100 AND THAT SHE'D HAD ENOUGH OF THEIR--
TONY?
SPORTS DAILY
HEYA, BOSS.
WWWAAAAAAHHHH!!!
YOU LOOK LIKE A BAG A' SHIIIIT!
NICE TA SEE YOU, TOO.
THIS IS AAALL MY FAAAUULT.
OWW
I GOT CAUGHT UP IN THINGS WITH MY FOLKS -SNFF-, AN' IVY, AN... Y'KNOW.
I WENT ON VACATION IN MORE WAYS THAN ONE.
10 GREAT THINGS about being SICK
GET BETTER or we'll KILL YOU
HAPPY BIRTHDAY Sick
I'M SORRRRRYYYY! I JUST GOT DISTRACTED.
PART A' MY JOB IS TA...OW... REMIND YA TA GET THE PAYMENTS OUT, AN' I FORGOT, TOO.
DON'T WORRY. SPEAKIN' A' WHICH, DIDJA SEE THE PLACE?

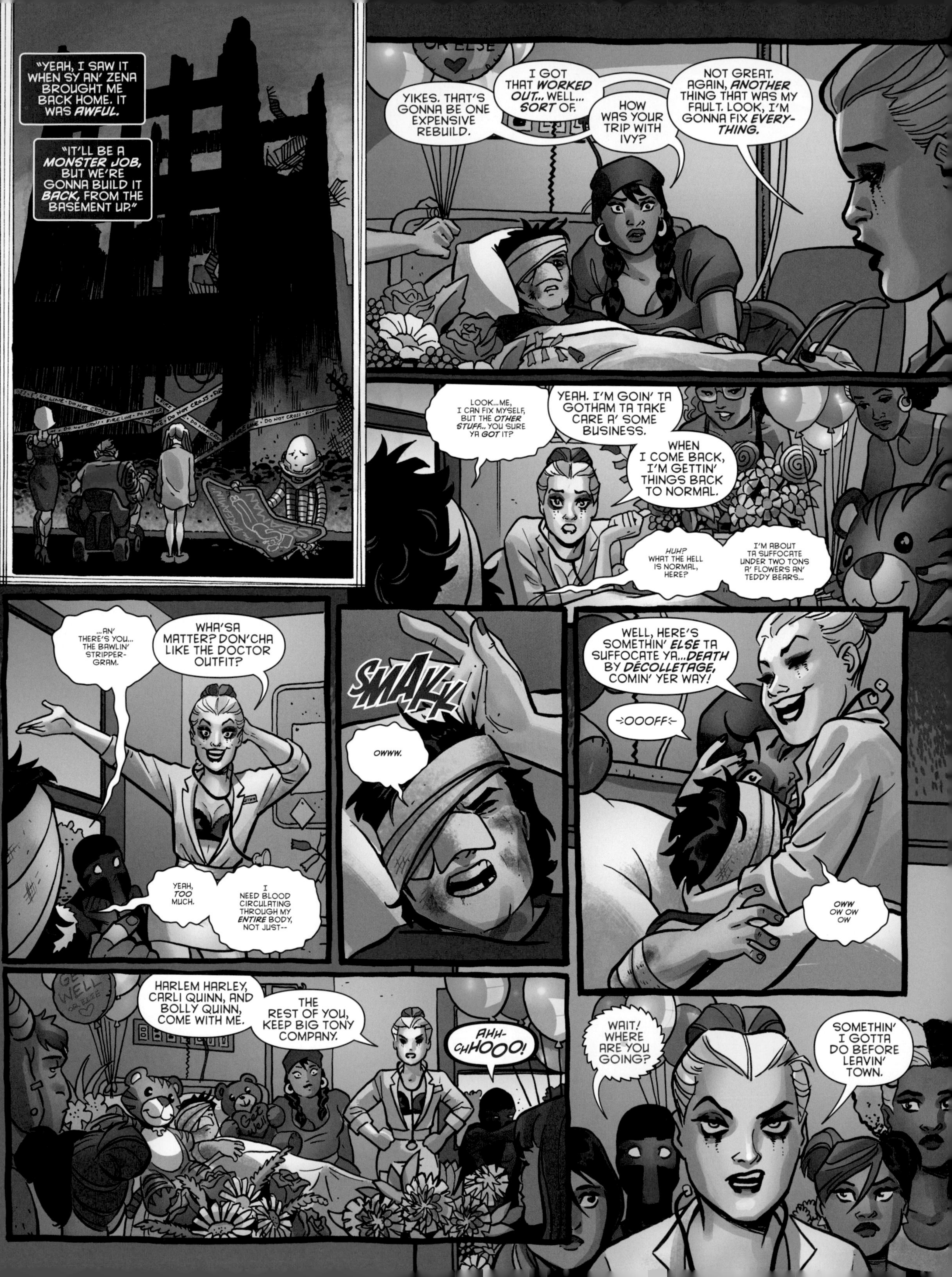
"YEAH, I SAW IT WHEN SY AN' ZENA BROUGHT ME BACK HOME. IT WAS *AWFUL.*
"IT'LL BE A *MONSTER JOB,* BUT WE'RE GONNA BUILD IT *BACK,* FROM THE BASEMENT UP."
FIRE LINE · DO NOT CROSS
YIKES. THAT'S GONNA BE ONE EXPENSIVE REBUILD.
I GOT THAT *WORKED OUT*... WELL... *SORT* OF.
HOW WAS YOUR TRIP WITH IVY?
NOT GREAT. AGAIN, *ANOTHER* THING THAT WAS MY FAULT. LOOK, I'M GONNA FIX *EVERY-THING.*
LOOK...ME, I CAN FIX MYSELF, BUT THE *OTHER STUFF*... YOU SURE YA *GOT* IT?
YEAH. I'M GOIN' TA GOTHAM TA TAKE CARE A' SOME BUSINESS.
WHEN I COME BACK, I'M GETTIN' THINGS BACK TO NORMAL.
HUH? WHAT THE HELL IS NORMAL, HERE?
I'M ABOUT TA SUFFOCATE UNDER TWO TONS A' FLOWERS AN' TEDDY BEARS...
...AN' THERE'S YOU... THE BAWLIN' STRIPPER-GRAM.
WHA'SA MATTER? DON'CHA LIKE THE DOCTOR OUTFIT?
YEAH, *TOO* MUCH.
I NEED BLOOD CIRCULATING THROUGH MY *ENTIRE* BODY, NOT JUST--
SMAKK
OWWW.
WELL, HERE'S SOMETHIN' *ELSE* TA SUFFOCATE YA...*DEATH* BY *DÉCOLLETAGE,* COMIN' YER WAY!
OOOFF
OWW OW OW OW
GET WELL OR ELSE
HARLEM HARLEY, CARLI QUINN, AND BOLLY QUINN, COME WITH ME.
THE REST OF YOU, KEEP BIG TONY COMPANY.
AHH-CHHOOO!
WAIT! WHERE ARE YOU GOING?
SOMETHIN' I GOTTA DO BEFORE LEAVIN' TOWN.

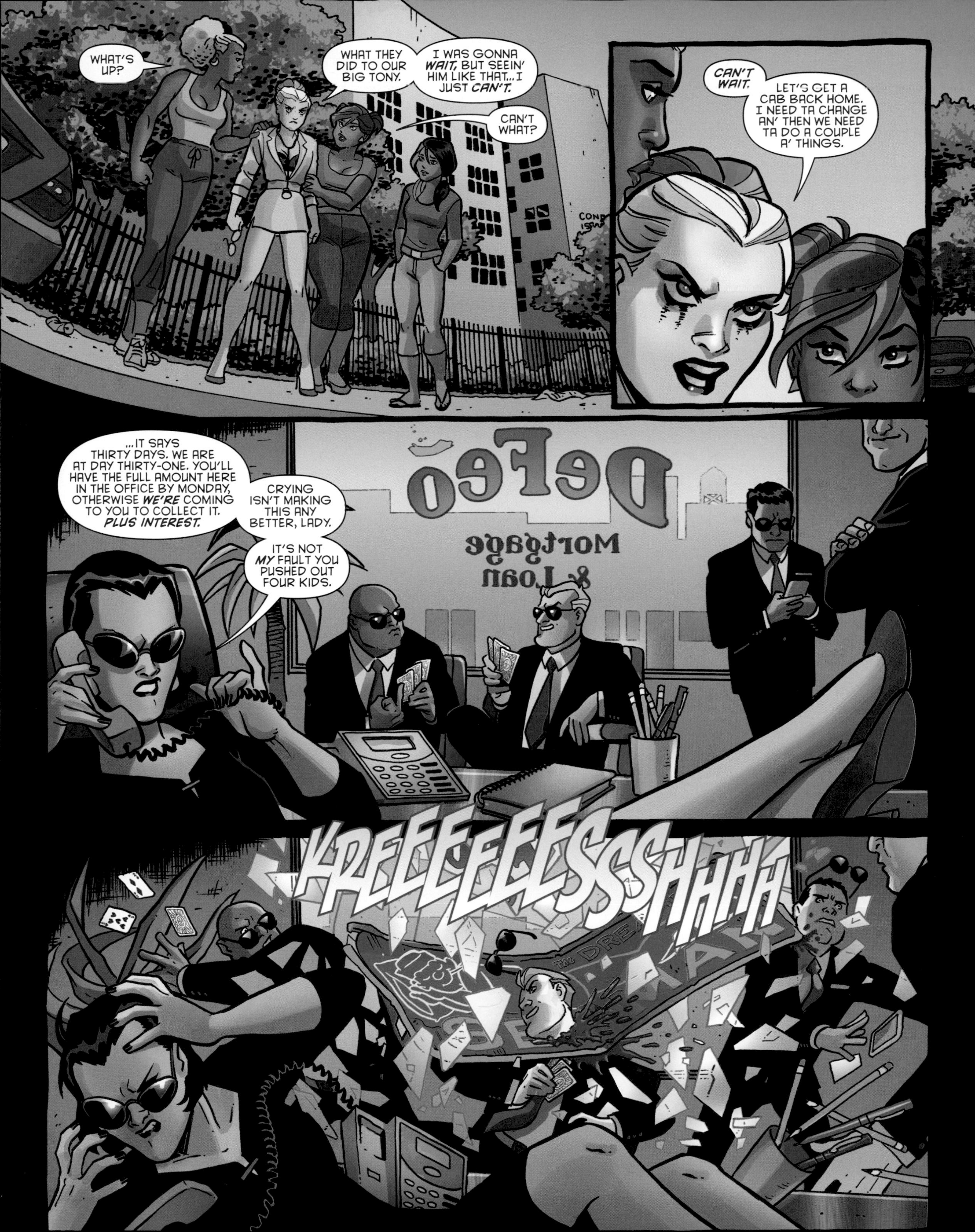

WHAT'S UP?
WHAT THEY DID TO OUR BIG TONY.
I WAS GONNA WAIT, BUT SEEIN' HIM LIKE THAT... I JUST CAN'T.
CAN'T WHAT?
CAN'T WAIT.
LET'S GET A CAB BACK HOME. I NEED TA CHANGE AN' THEN WE NEED TA DO A COUPLE A' THINGS.
DeFeo Mortgage & Loan
...IT SAYS THIRTY DAYS. WE ARE AT DAY THIRTY-ONE. YOU'LL HAVE THE FULL AMOUNT HERE IN THE OFFICE BY MONDAY, OTHERWISE WE'RE COMING TO YOU TO COLLECT IT. PLUS INTEREST.
CRYING ISN'T MAKING THIS ANY BETTER, LADY.
IT'S NOT MY FAULT YOU PUSHED OUT FOUR KIDS.
KREEEEEESSSHHHH

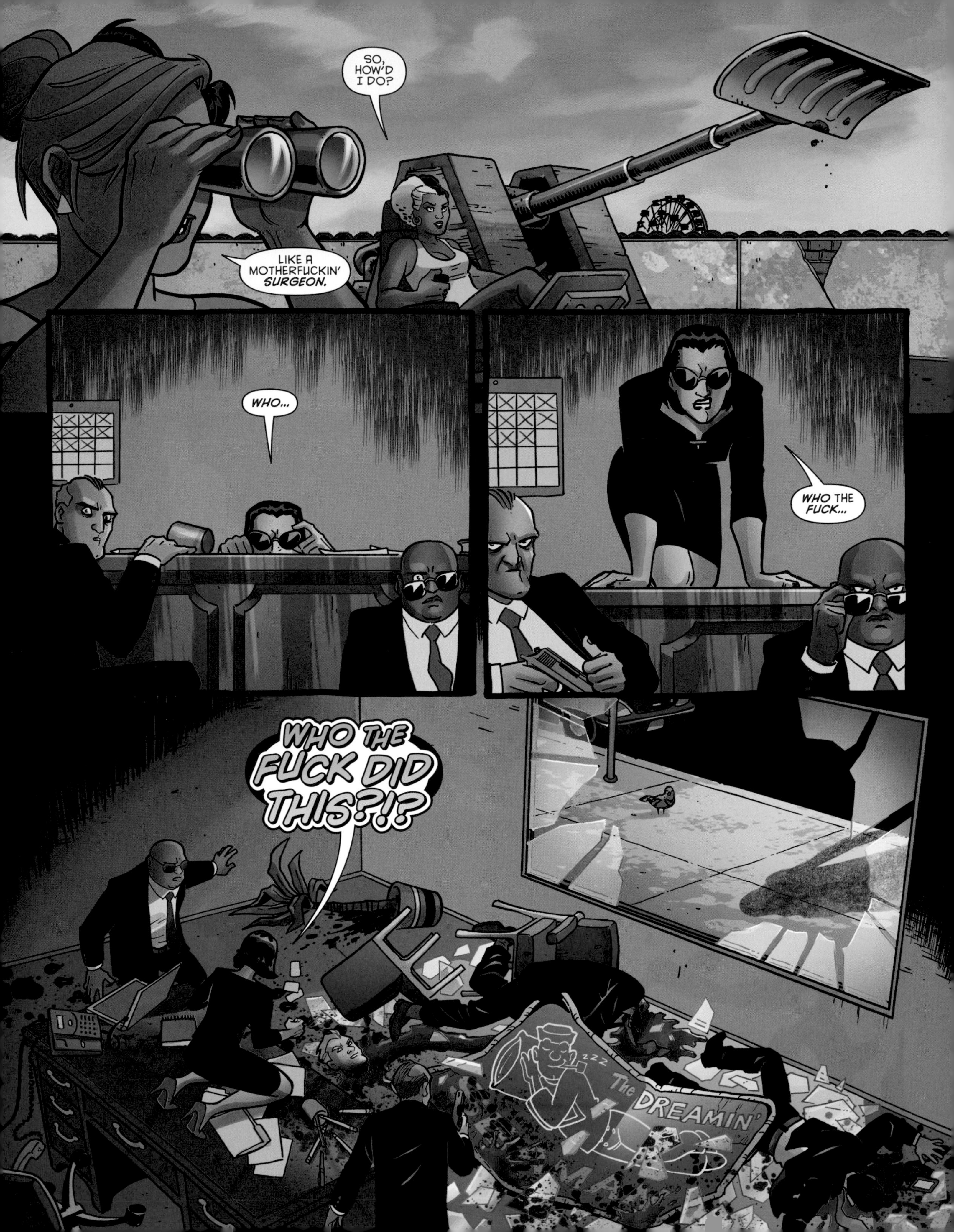
SO, HOW'D I DO?
LIKE A MOTHERFUCKIN' SURGEON.
WHO...
WHO THE FUCK...
WHO THE FUCK DID THIS?!?
The DREAMIN'

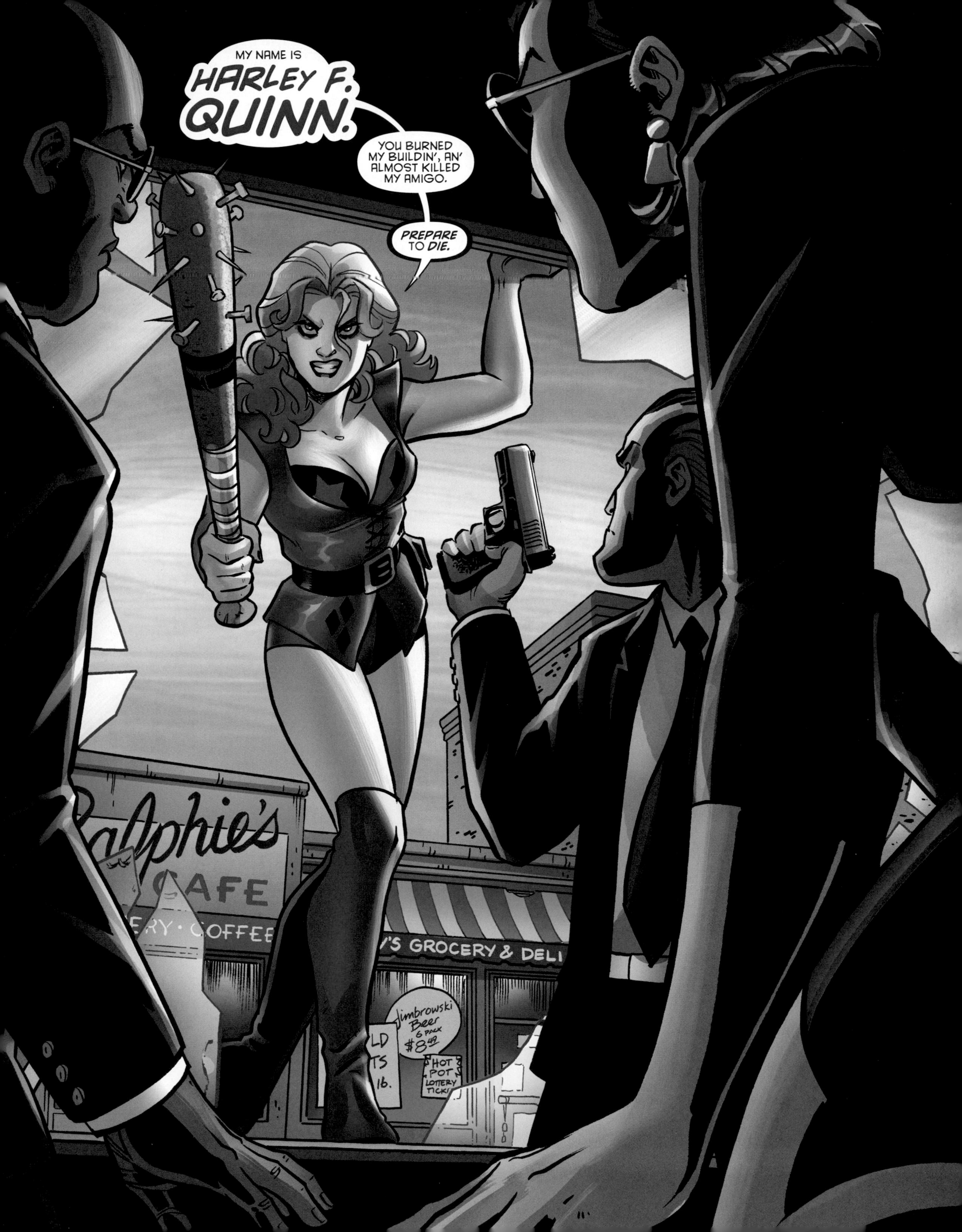
MY NAME IS HARLEY F. QUINN.
YOU BURNED MY BUILDIN', AN' ALMOST KILLED MY AMIGO.
PREPARE TO DIE.
CAFE
GROCERY & DELI
Jimbrowski Beer 6 PACK $8.49
HOT POT

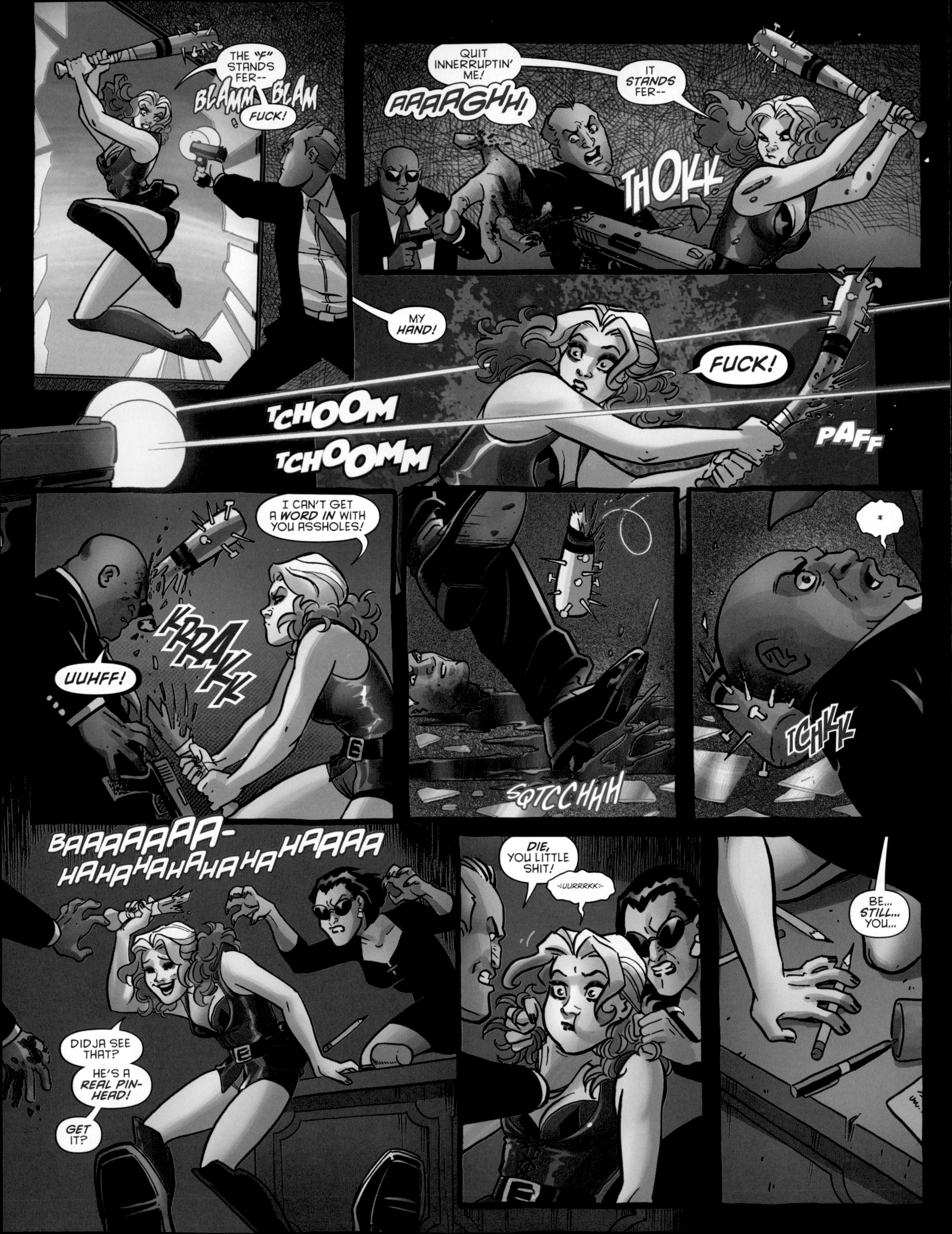
THE "F" STANDS FER--
BLAMM BLAM
FUCK!
QUIT INNERRUPTIN' ME!
AAAAGHH!
IT STANDS FER--
THOKK
MY HAND!
FUCK!
TCHOOM
TCHOOMM
PAFF
I CAN'T GET A WORD IN WITH YOU ASSHOLES!
UUHFF!
KRRAKK
SQTCCHHH
*
TCHKK
BAAAAAAA-HAHAHAHAHAHAHAAAAA
DIDJA SEE THAT?
HE'S A REAL PIN-HEAD!
GET IT?
DIE, YOU LITTLE SHIT!
UURRRKK
BE... STILL... YOU...

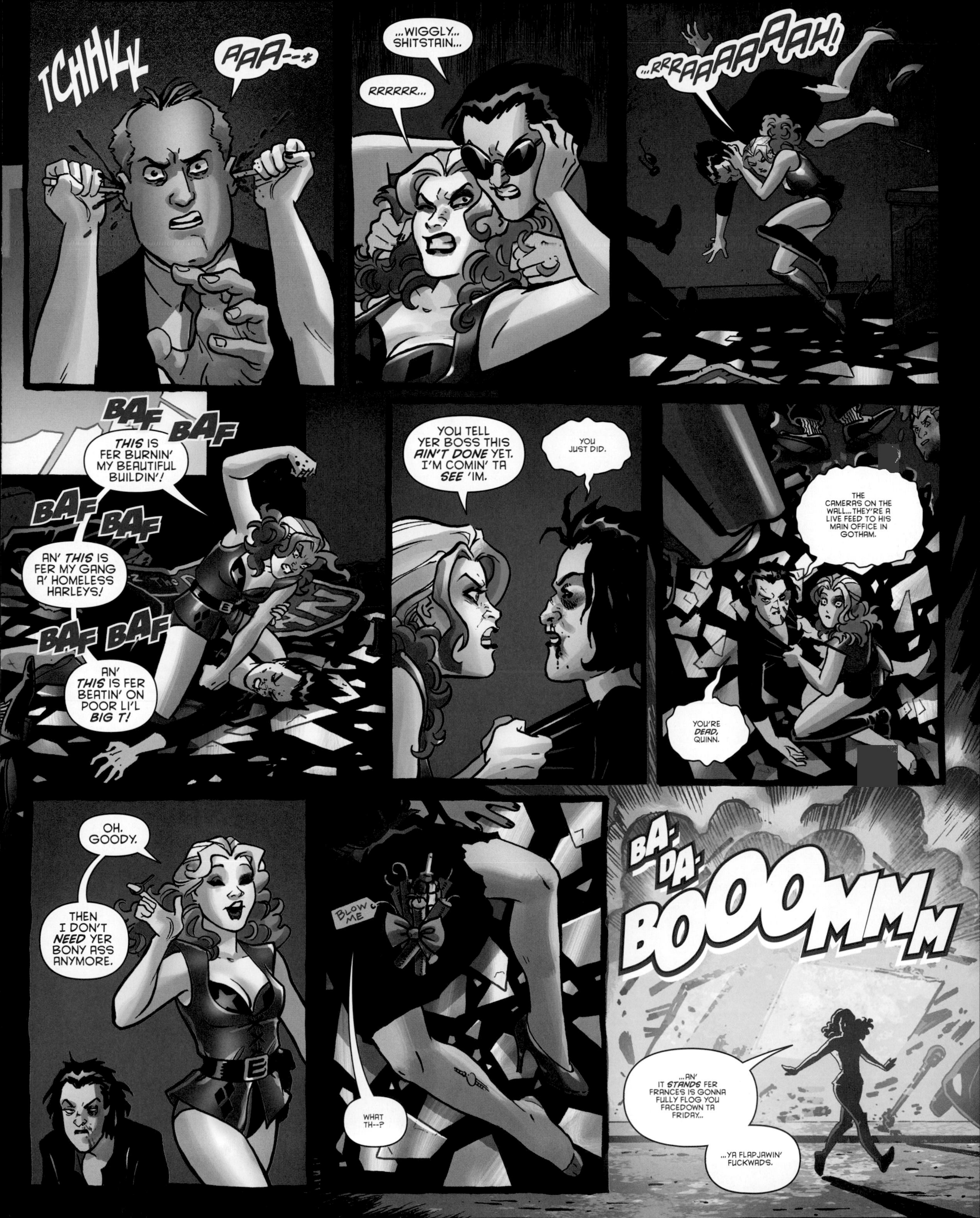
TCHHKK
AAA--*
...WIGGLY... SHITSTAIN...
RRRRRR...
...RRRAAAAAAAAH!
BAF BAF
THIS IS FER BURNIN' MY BEAUTIFUL BUILDIN'!
BAF BAF
AN' THIS IS FER MY GANG A' HOMELESS HARLEYS!
BAF BAF
AN' THIS IS FER BEATIN' ON POOR LI'L BIG T!
YOU TELL YER BOSS THIS AIN'T DONE YET. I'M COMIN' TA SEE 'IM.
YOU JUST DID.
THE CAMERAS ON THE WALL...THEY'RE A LIVE FEED TO HIS MAIN OFFICE IN GOTHAM.
YOU'RE DEAD, QUINN.
OH. GOODY.
THEN I DON'T NEED YER BONY ASS ANYMORE.
BLOW ME
WHAT TH--?
BA-DA-BOOOMMMM
...AN' IT STANDS FER FRANCES IS GONNA FULLY FLOG YOU FACEDOWN TA FRIDAY...
...YA FLAPJAWIN' FUCKWAD'S.

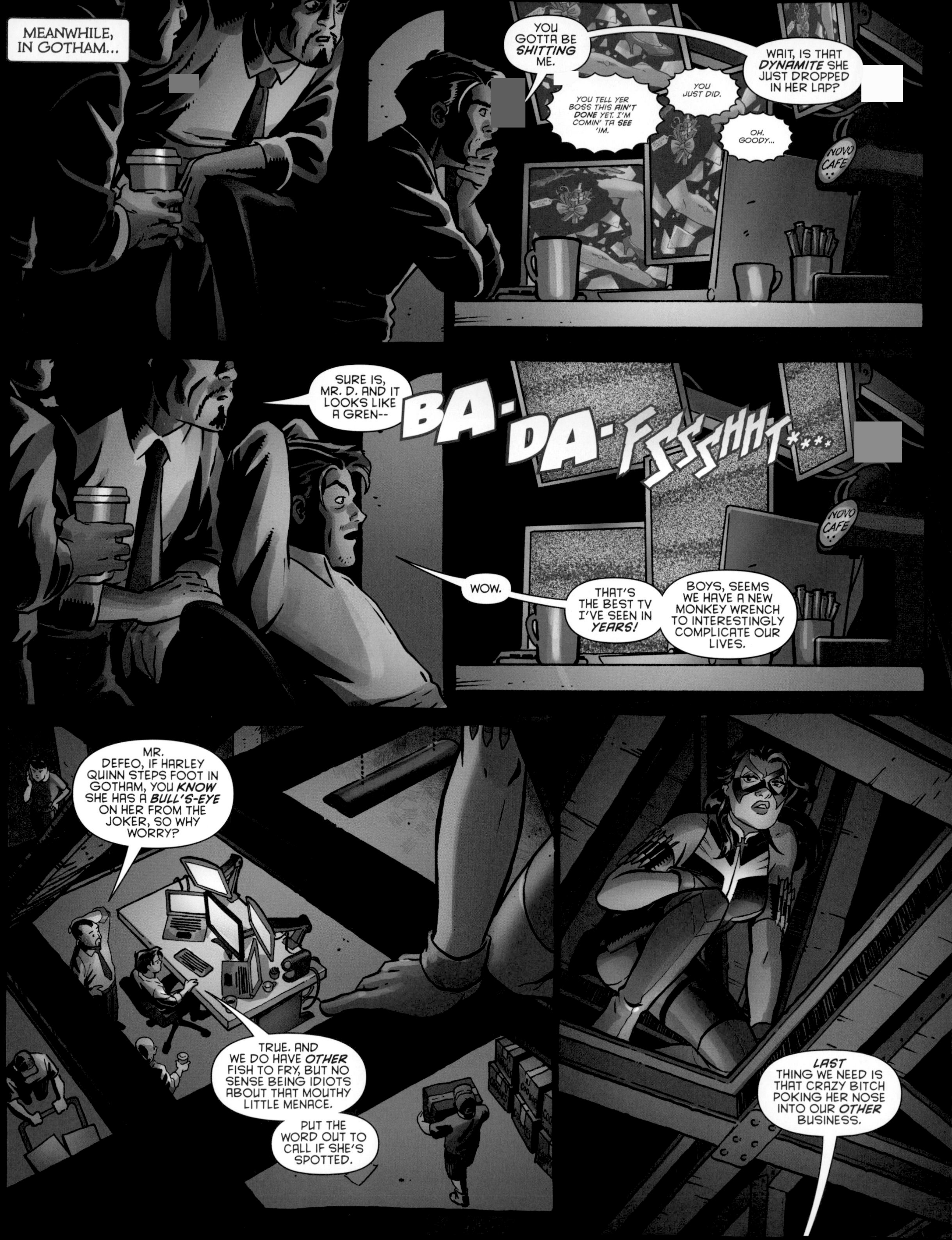
MEANWHILE, IN GOTHAM...
YOU GOTTA BE SHITTING ME.
WAIT, IS THAT DYNAMITE SHE JUST DROPPED IN HER LAP?
YOU TELL YER BOSS THIS AIN'T DONE YET. I'M COMIN' TA SEE 'IM.
YOU JUST DID.
OH. GOODY...
NOVO CAFE
SURE IS, MR. D. AND IT LOOKS LIKE A GREN--
BA-DA-FSSSHHT*...
NOVO CAFE
WOW.
THAT'S THE BEST TV I'VE SEEN IN YEARS!
BOYS, SEEMS WE HAVE A NEW MONKEY WRENCH TO INTERESTINGLY COMPLICATE OUR LIVES.
MR. DEFEO, IF HARLEY QUINN STEPS FOOT IN GOTHAM, YOU KNOW SHE HAS A BULL'S-EYE ON HER FROM THE JOKER, SO WHY WORRY?
TRUE. AND WE DO HAVE OTHER FISH TO FRY, BUT NO SENSE BEING IDIOTS ABOUT THAT MOUTHY LITTLE MENACE.
PUT THE WORD OUT TO CALL IF SHE'S SPOTTED.
LAST THING WE NEED IS THAT CRAZY BITCH POKING HER NOSE INTO OUR OTHER BUSINESS.

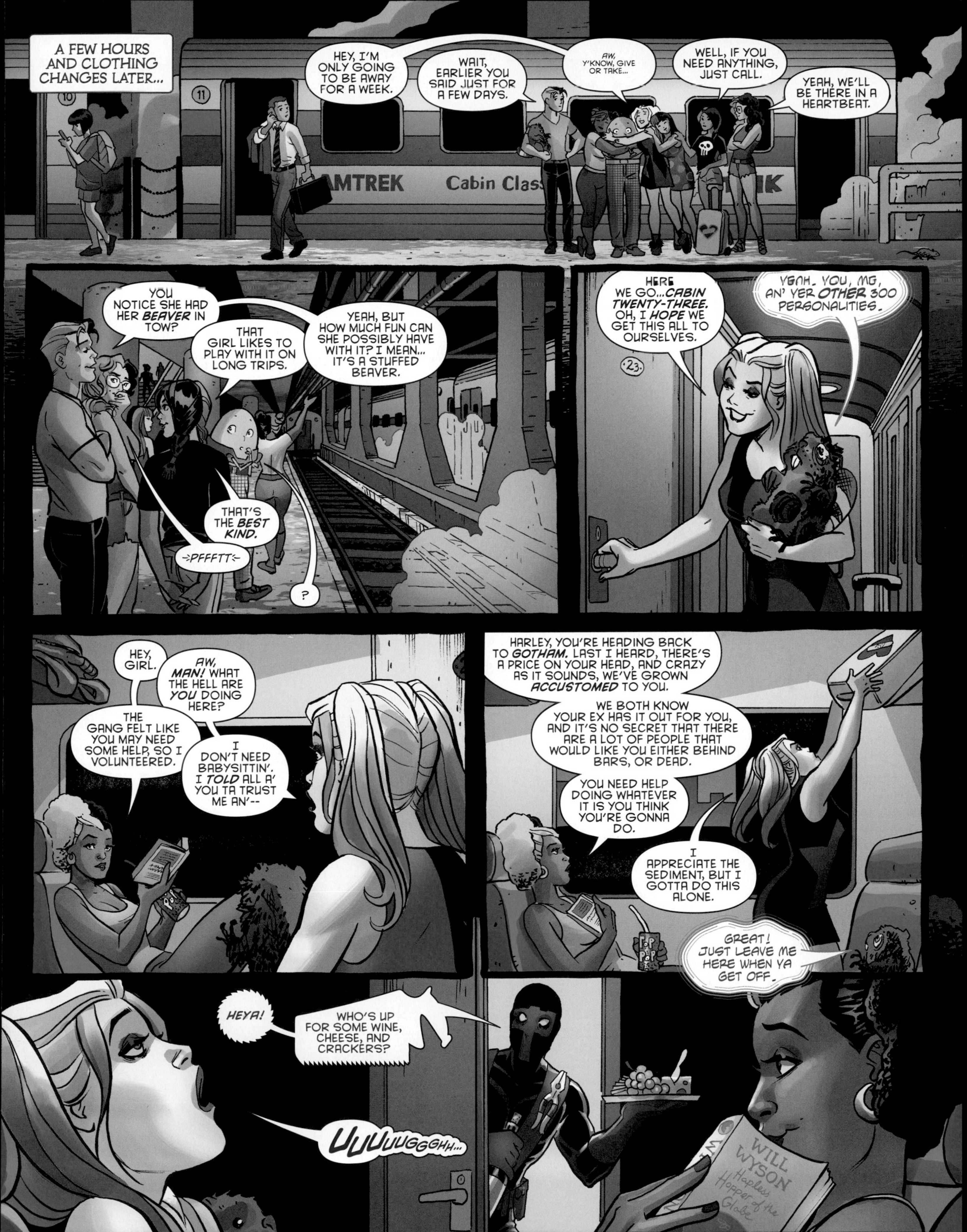
A FEW HOURS AND CLOTHING CHANGES LATER...
HEY, I'M ONLY GOING TO BE AWAY FOR A WEEK.
WAIT, EARLIER YOU SAID JUST FOR A FEW DAYS.
AW, Y'KNOW, GIVE OR TAKE...
WELL, IF YOU NEED ANYTHING, JUST CALL.
YEAH, WE'LL BE THERE IN A HEARTBEAT.
AMTREK Cabin Class
YOU NOTICE SHE HAD HER BEAVER IN TOW?
THAT GIRL LIKES TO PLAY WITH IT ON LONG TRIPS.
YEAH, BUT HOW MUCH FUN CAN SHE POSSIBLY HAVE WITH IT? I MEAN... IT'S A STUFFED BEAVER.
THAT'S THE BEST KIND.
PFFFTT
?
HERE WE GO...CABIN TWENTY-THREE. OH, I HOPE WE GET THIS ALL TO OURSELVES.
YEAH. YOU, ME, AN' YER OTHER 300 PERSONALITIES.
HEY, GIRL.
AW, MAN! WHAT THE HELL ARE YOU DOING HERE?
THE GANG FELT LIKE YOU MAY NEED SOME HELP, SO I VOLUNTEERED.
I DON'T NEED BABYSITTIN'. I TOLD ALL A' YOU TA TRUST ME AN'--
HARLEY, YOU'RE HEADING BACK TO GOTHAM. LAST I HEARD, THERE'S A PRICE ON YOUR HEAD, AND CRAZY AS IT SOUNDS, WE'VE GROWN ACCUSTOMED TO YOU.
WE BOTH KNOW YOUR EX HAS IT OUT FOR YOU, AND IT'S NO SECRET THAT THERE ARE A LOT OF PEOPLE THAT WOULD LIKE YOU EITHER BEHIND BARS, OR DEAD.
YOU NEED HELP DOING WHATEVER IT IS YOU THINK YOU'RE GONNA DO.
I APPRECIATE THE SEDIMENT, BUT I GOTTA DO THIS ALONE.
GREAT! JUST LEAVE ME HERE WHEN YA GET OFF.
HEYA!
WHO'S UP FOR SOME WINE, CHEESE, AND CRACKERS?
UUUUUGGGHH...
WILL WYSON Hapless Hopper of the Globe

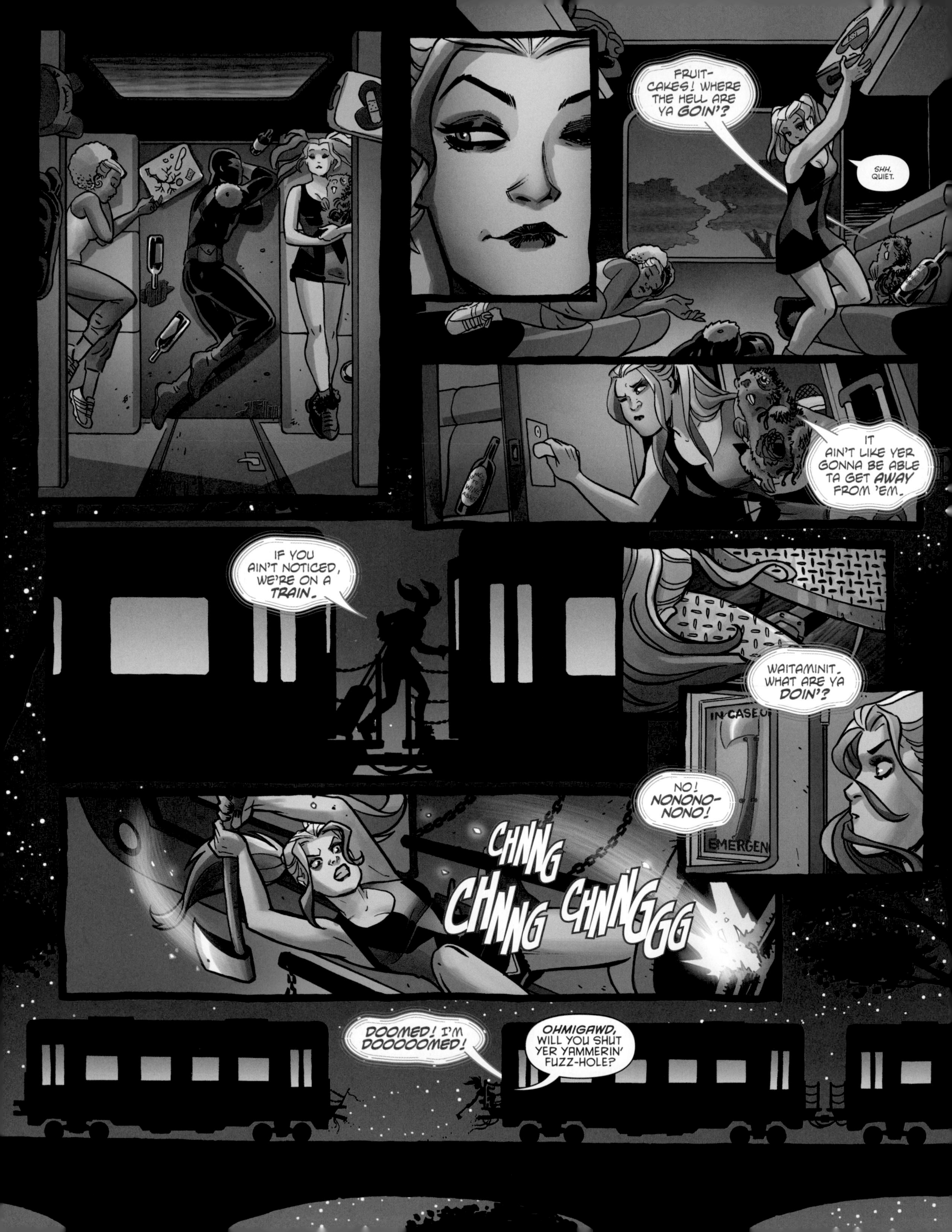
FRUIT-CAKES! WHERE THE HELL ARE YA GOIN'?
SHH. QUIET.
IT AIN'T LIKE YER GONNA BE ABLE TA GET AWAY FROM 'EM.
IF YOU AIN'T NOTICED, WE'RE ON A TRAIN.
WAITAMINIT. WHAT ARE YA DOIN'?
IN CASE O
EMERGEN
NO! NONONO-NONO!
CHNNG CHNNG CHNNGGG
DOOMED! I'M DOOOOOMED!
OHMIGAWD, WILL YOU SHUT YER YAMMERIN' FUZZ-HOLE?

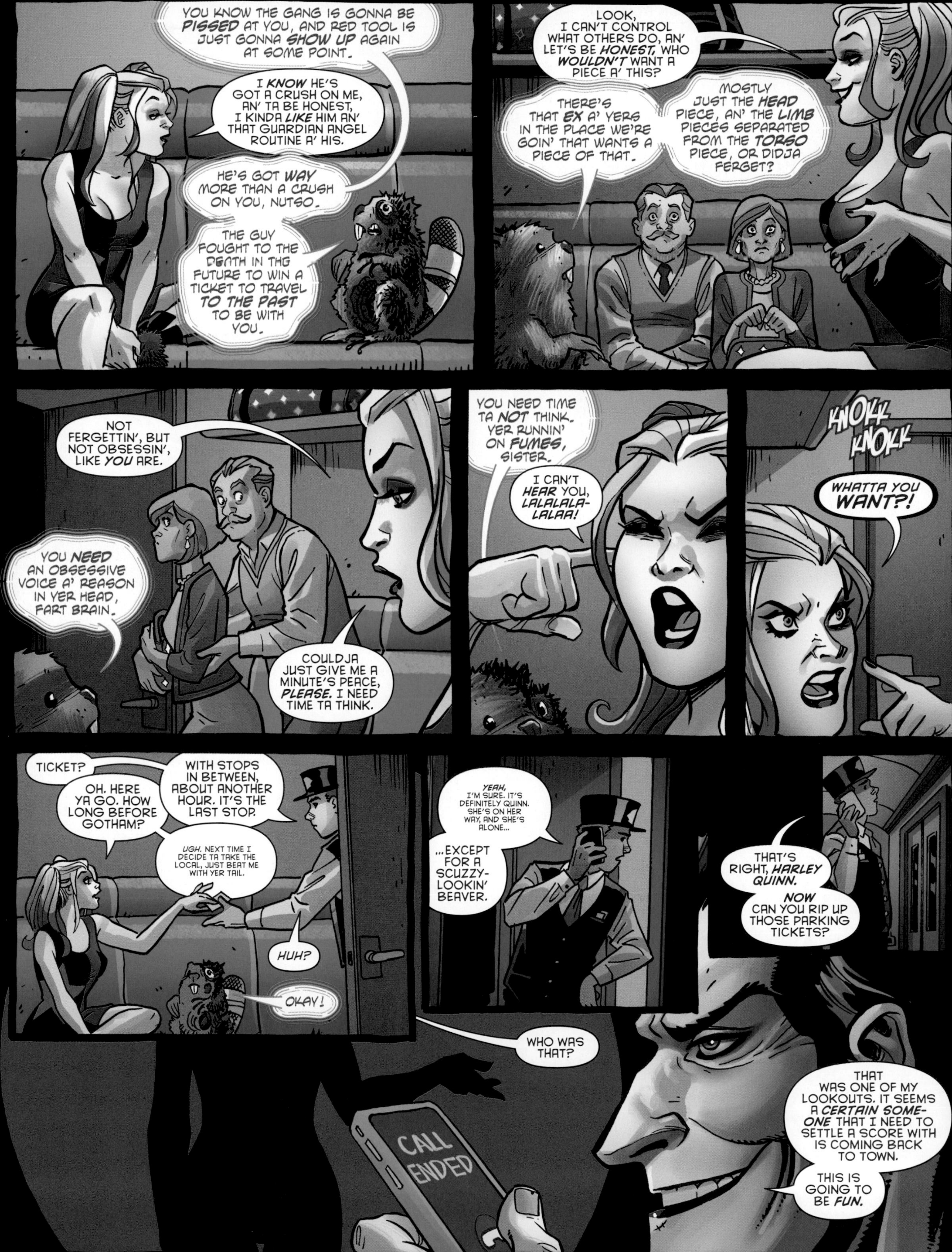

YOU KNOW THE GANG IS GONNA BE PISSED AT YOU, AND RED TOOL IS JUST GONNA SHOW UP AGAIN AT SOME POINT.
I KNOW HE'S GOT A CRUSH ON ME, AN' TA BE HONEST, I KINDA LIKE HIM AN' THAT GUARDIAN ANGEL ROUTINE A' HIS.
HE'S GOT WAY MORE THAN A CRUSH ON YOU, NUTSO.
THE GUY FOUGHT TO THE DEATH IN THE FUTURE TO WIN A TICKET TO TRAVEL TO THE PAST TO BE WITH YOU.
LOOK, I CAN'T CONTROL WHAT OTHERS DO, AN' LET'S BE HONEST, WHO WOULDN'T WANT A PIECE A' THIS?
THERE'S THAT EX A' YERS IN THE PLACE WE'RE GOIN' THAT WANTS A PIECE OF THAT.
MOSTLY JUST THE HEAD PIECE, AN' THE LIMB PIECES SEPARATED FROM THE TORSO PIECE, OR DIDJA FERGET?
NOT FERGETTIN', BUT NOT OBSESSIN', LIKE YOU ARE.
YOU NEED AN OBSESSIVE VOICE A' REASON IN YER HEAD, FART BRAIN.
COULDJA JUST GIVE ME A MINUTE'S PEACE, PLEASE. I NEED TIME TA THINK.
YOU NEED TIME TA NOT THINK. YER RUNNIN' ON FUMES, SISTER.
I CAN'T HEAR YOU, LALALALA-LALAA!
KNOKK KNOKK
WHATTA YOU WANT?!
TICKET?
OH. HERE YA GO. HOW LONG BEFORE GOTHAM?
WITH STOPS IN BETWEEN, ABOUT ANOTHER HOUR. IT'S THE LAST STOP.
UGH. NEXT TIME I DECIDE TA TAKE THE LOCAL, JUST BEAT ME WITH YER TAIL.
HUH?
OKAY!
YEAH, I'M SURE. IT'S DEFINITELY QUINN. SHE'S ON HER WAY, AND SHE'S ALONE...
...EXCEPT FOR A SCUZZY-LOOKIN' BEAVER.
THAT'S RIGHT, HARLEY QUINN.
NOW CAN YOU RIP UP THOSE PARKING TICKETS?
WHO WAS THAT?
CALL ENDED
THAT WAS ONE OF MY LOOKOUTS. IT SEEMS A CERTAIN SOMEONE THAT I NEED TO SETTLE A SCORE WITH IS COMING BACK TO TOWN.
THIS IS GOING TO BE FUN.

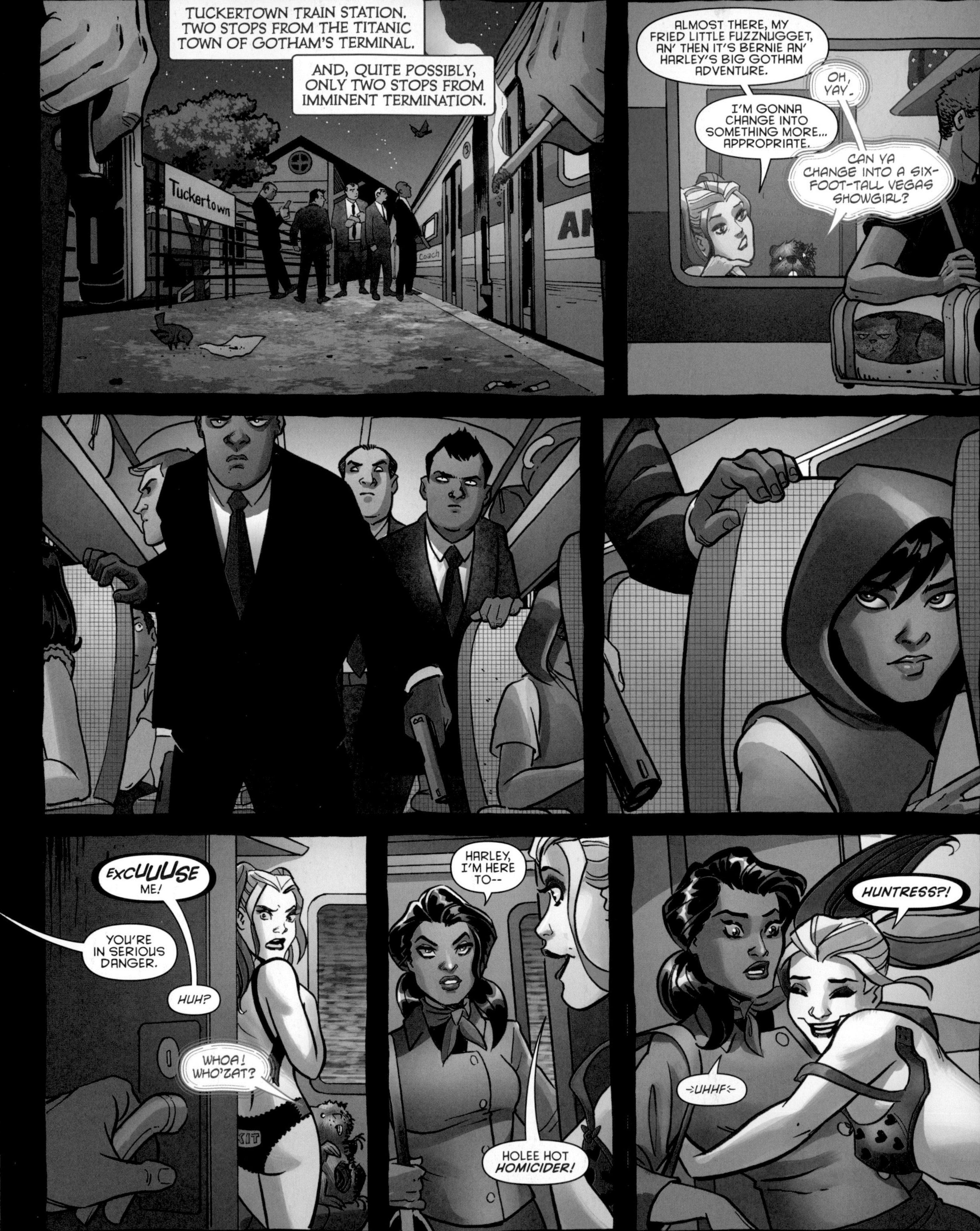
TUCKERTOWN TRAIN STATION. TWO STOPS FROM THE TITANIC TOWN OF GOTHAM'S TERMINAL.
AND, QUITE POSSIBLY, ONLY TWO STOPS FROM IMMINENT TERMINATION.
Tuckertown
Coach
ALMOST THERE, MY FRIED LITTLE FUZZNUGGET, AN' THEN IT'S BERNIE AN' HARLEY'S BIG GOTHAM ADVENTURE.
OH, YAY.
I'M GONNA CHANGE INTO SOMETHING MORE... APPROPRIATE.
CAN YA CHANGE INTO A SIX-FOOT-TALL VEGAS SHOWGIRL?
EXCUUUSE ME!
YOU'RE IN SERIOUS DANGER.
HUH?
WHOA! WHO'ZAT?
HARLEY, I'M HERE TO--
HOLEE HOT HOMICIDER!
HUNTRESS?!
UHHF

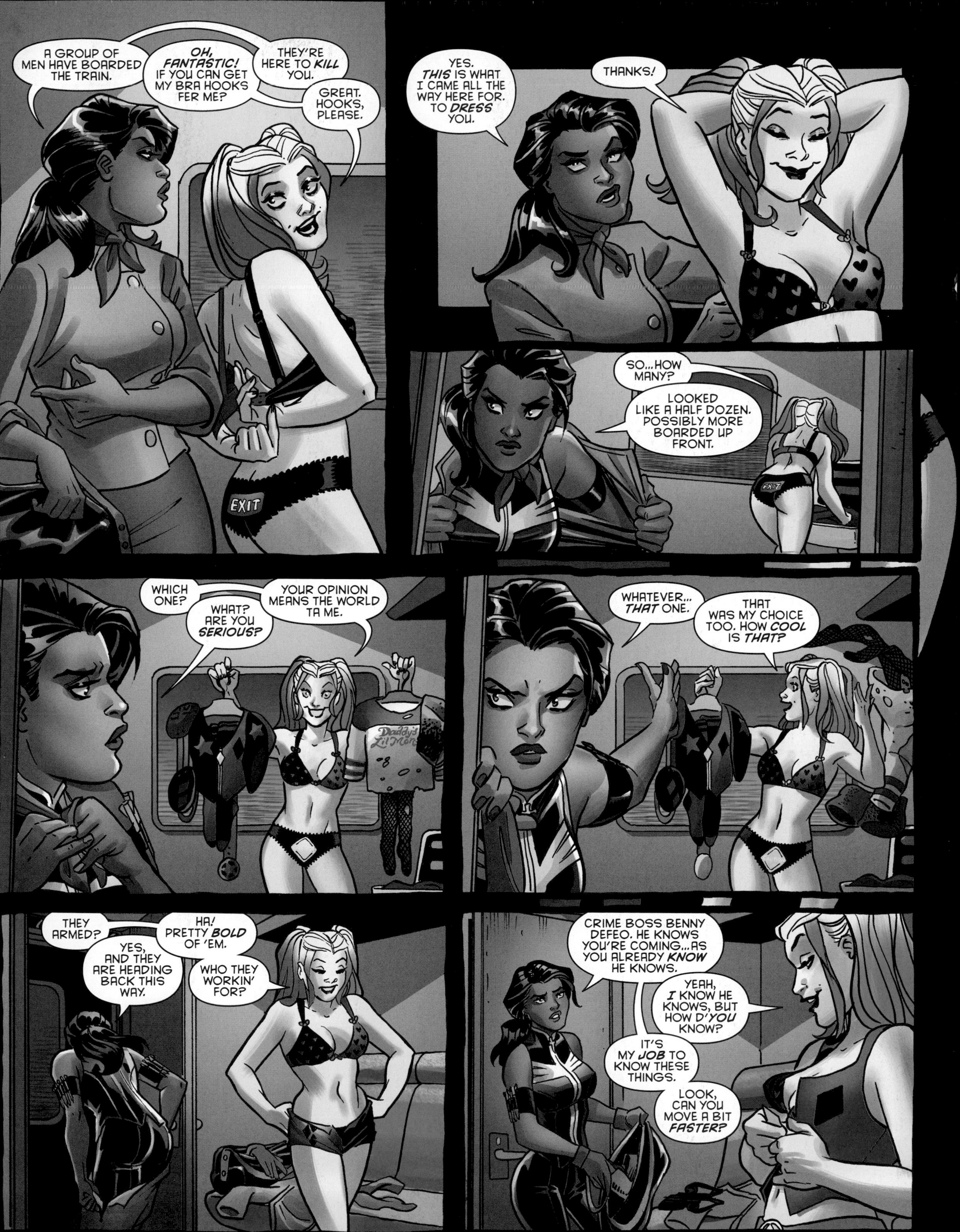
A GROUP OF MEN HAVE BOARDED THE TRAIN.
OH, FANTASTIC! IF YOU CAN GET MY BRA HOOKS FER ME?
THEY'RE HERE TO KILL YOU.
GREAT. HOOKS, PLEASE.
YES. THIS IS WHAT I CAME ALL THE WAY HERE FOR. TO DRESS YOU.
THANKS!
SO...HOW MANY?
LOOKED LIKE A HALF DOZEN. POSSIBLY MORE BOARDED UP FRONT.
EXIT
WHICH ONE?
WHAT? ARE YOU SERIOUS?
YOUR OPINION MEANS THE WORLD TA ME.
WHATEVER... THAT ONE.
THAT WAS MY CHOICE TOO. HOW COOL IS THAT?
THEY ARMED?
YES, AND THEY ARE HEADING BACK THIS WAY.
HA! PRETTY BOLD OF 'EM.
WHO THEY WORKIN' FOR?
CRIME BOSS BENNY DEFEO. HE KNOWS YOU'RE COMING...AS YOU ALREADY KNOW HE KNOWS.
YEAH, I KNOW HE KNOWS, BUT HOW D'YOU KNOW?
IT'S MY JOB TO KNOW THESE THINGS.
LOOK, CAN YOU MOVE A BIT FASTER?

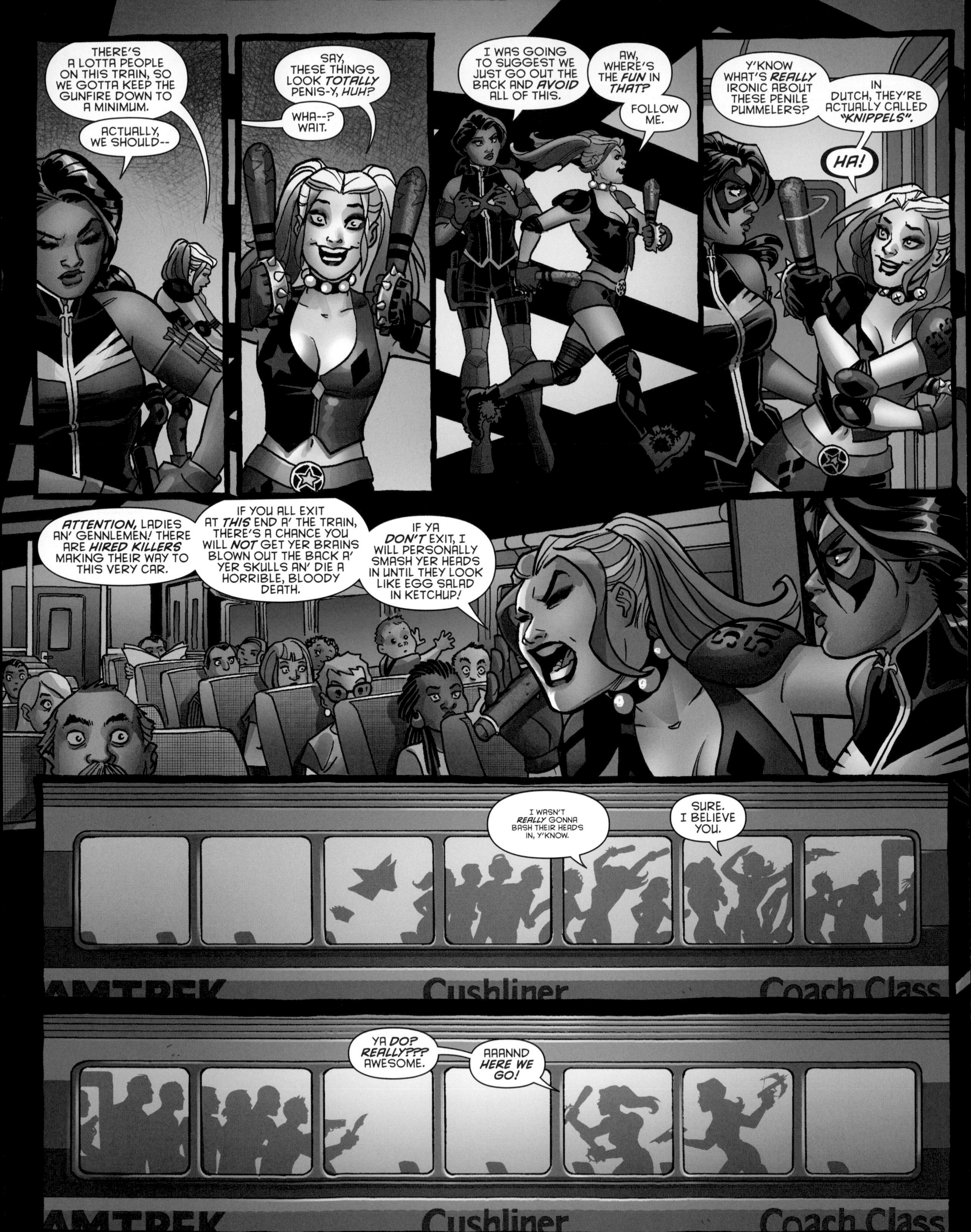
THERE'S A LOTTA PEOPLE ON THIS TRAIN, SO WE GOTTA KEEP THE GUNFIRE DOWN TO A MINIMUM.
ACTUALLY, WE SHOULD--
SAY, THESE THINGS LOOK TOTALLY PENIS-Y, HUH?
WHA--? WAIT.
I WAS GOING TO SUGGEST WE JUST GO OUT THE BACK AND AVOID ALL OF THIS.
AW, WHERE'S THE FUN IN THAT?
FOLLOW ME.
Y'KNOW WHAT'S REALLY IRONIC ABOUT THESE PENILE PUMMELERS?
IN DUTCH, THEY'RE ACTUALLY CALLED "KNIPPELS".
HA!
ATTENTION, LADIES AN' GENNLEMEN! THERE ARE HIRED KILLERS MAKING THEIR WAY TO THIS VERY CAR.
IF YOU ALL EXIT AT THIS END A' THE TRAIN, THERE'S A CHANCE YOU WILL NOT GET YER BRAINS BLOWN OUT THE BACK A' YER SKULLS AN' DIE A HORRIBLE, BLOODY DEATH.
IF YA DON'T EXIT, I WILL PERSONALLY SMASH YER HEADS IN UNTIL THEY LOOK LIKE EGG SALAD IN KETCHUP!
I WASN'T REALLY GONNA BASH THEIR HEADS IN, Y'KNOW.
SURE. I BELIEVE YOU.
Cushliner
Coach Class
YA DO? REALLY??? AWESOME.
AAAAND HERE WE GO!
Cushliner
Coach Class

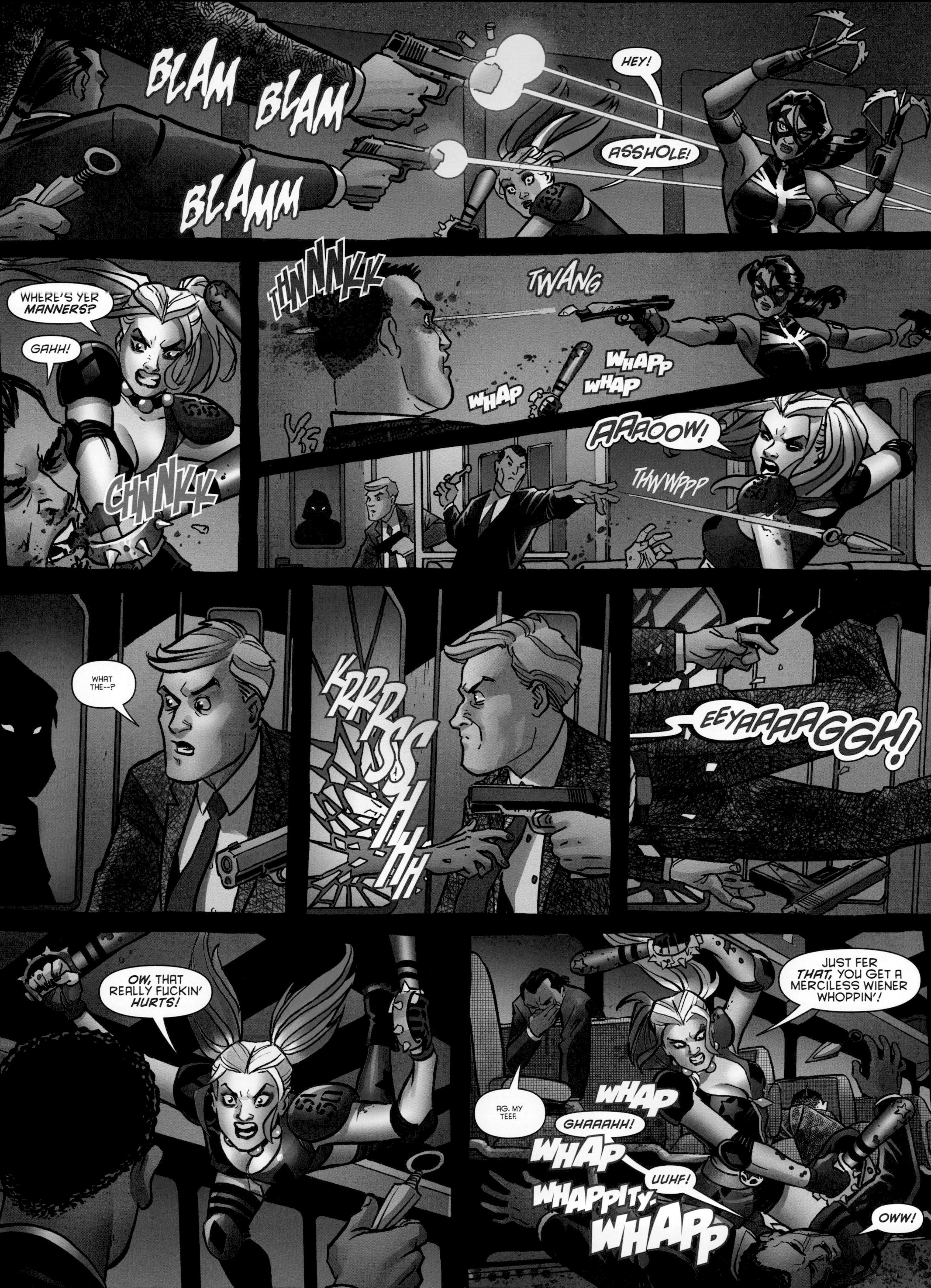
BLAM BLAM
BLAMM
HEY!
ASSHOLE!
WHERE'S YER MANNERS?
GAHH!
CHNKK
THNNKK
TWANG
WHAP
WHAPP WHAP
AAAOOW!
THWPPP
WHAT THE--?
KRRRSSHHH
EEYAAAAAGGH!
OW, THAT REALLY FUCKIN' HURTS!
JUST FER THAT, YOU GET A MERCILESS WIENER WHOPPIN'!
AG. MY TEEF.
WHAP
GHAAAHH!
WHAP
UUHF!
WHAPPITY-WHAPP
OWW!

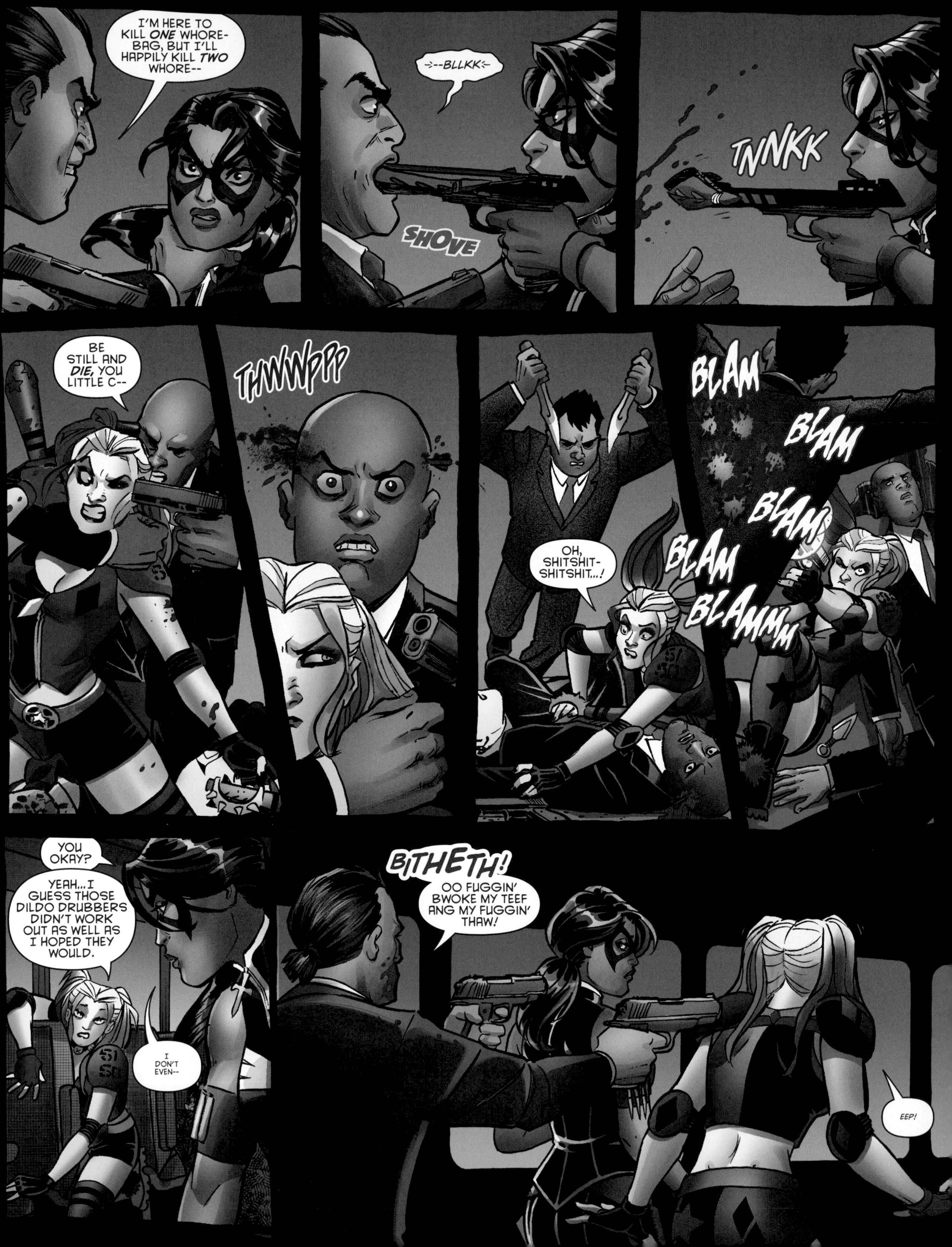
I'M HERE TO KILL ONE WHORE-BAG, BUT I'LL HAPPILY KILL TWO WHORE--
--BLLKK--
SHOVE
TNNKK
BE STILL AND DIE, YOU LITTLE C--
THWWPPP
OH, SHITSHIT-SHITSHIT...!
BLAM
BLAM
BLAM
BLAM
BLAMMM
YOU OKAY?
YEAH...I GUESS THOSE DILDO DRUBBERS DIDN'T WORK OUT AS WELL AS I HOPED THEY WOULD.
I DON'T EVEN--
BITHETH!
OO FUGGIN' BWOKE MY TEEF ANG MY FUGGIN' THAW!
EEP!

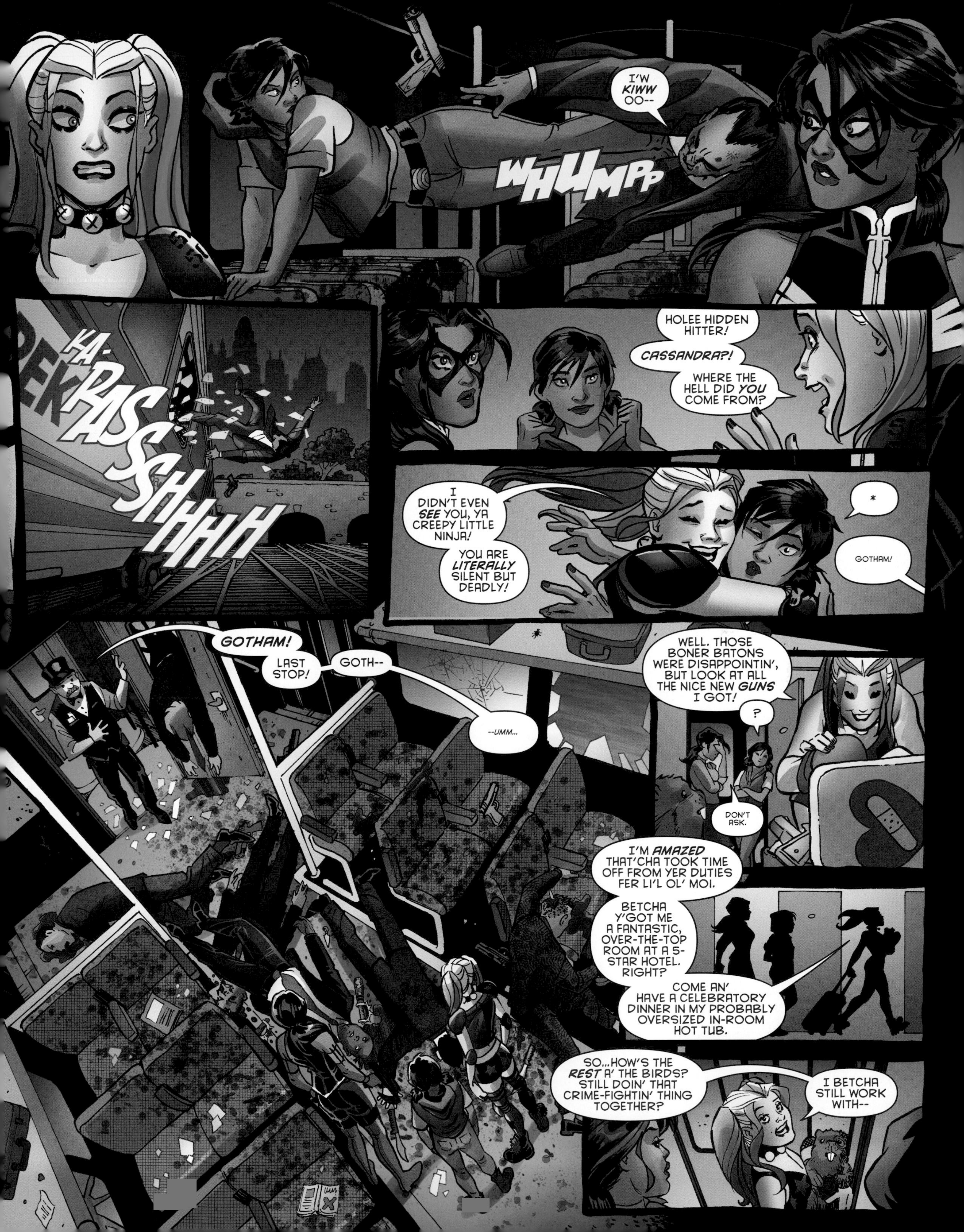
I'W KIWW OO--
WHUMPP
KA-PEKRASSHHHH
HOLEE HIDDEN HITTER!
CASSANDRA?!
WHERE THE HELL DID YOU COME FROM?
I DIDN'T EVEN SEE YOU, YA CREEPY LITTLE NINJA!
YOU ARE LITERALLY SILENT BUT DEADLY!
*
GOTHAM!
GOTHAM!
LAST STOP!
GOTH--
--UMM...
WELL. THOSE BONER BATONS WERE DISAPPOINTIN', BUT LOOK AT ALL THE NICE NEW GUNS I GOT!
?
DON'T ASK.
I'M AMAZED THAT'CHA TOOK TIME OFF FROM YER DUTIES FER LI'L OL' MOI.
BETCHA Y'GOT ME A FANTASTIC, OVER-THE-TOP ROOM AT A 5-STAR HOTEL. RIGHT?
COME AN' HAVE A CELEBRATORY DINNER IN MY PROBABLY OVERSIZED IN-ROOM HOT TUB.
SO...HOW'S THE REST A' THE BIRDS? STILL DOIN' THAT CRIME-FIGHTIN' THING TOGETHER?
I BETCHA STILL WORK WITH--

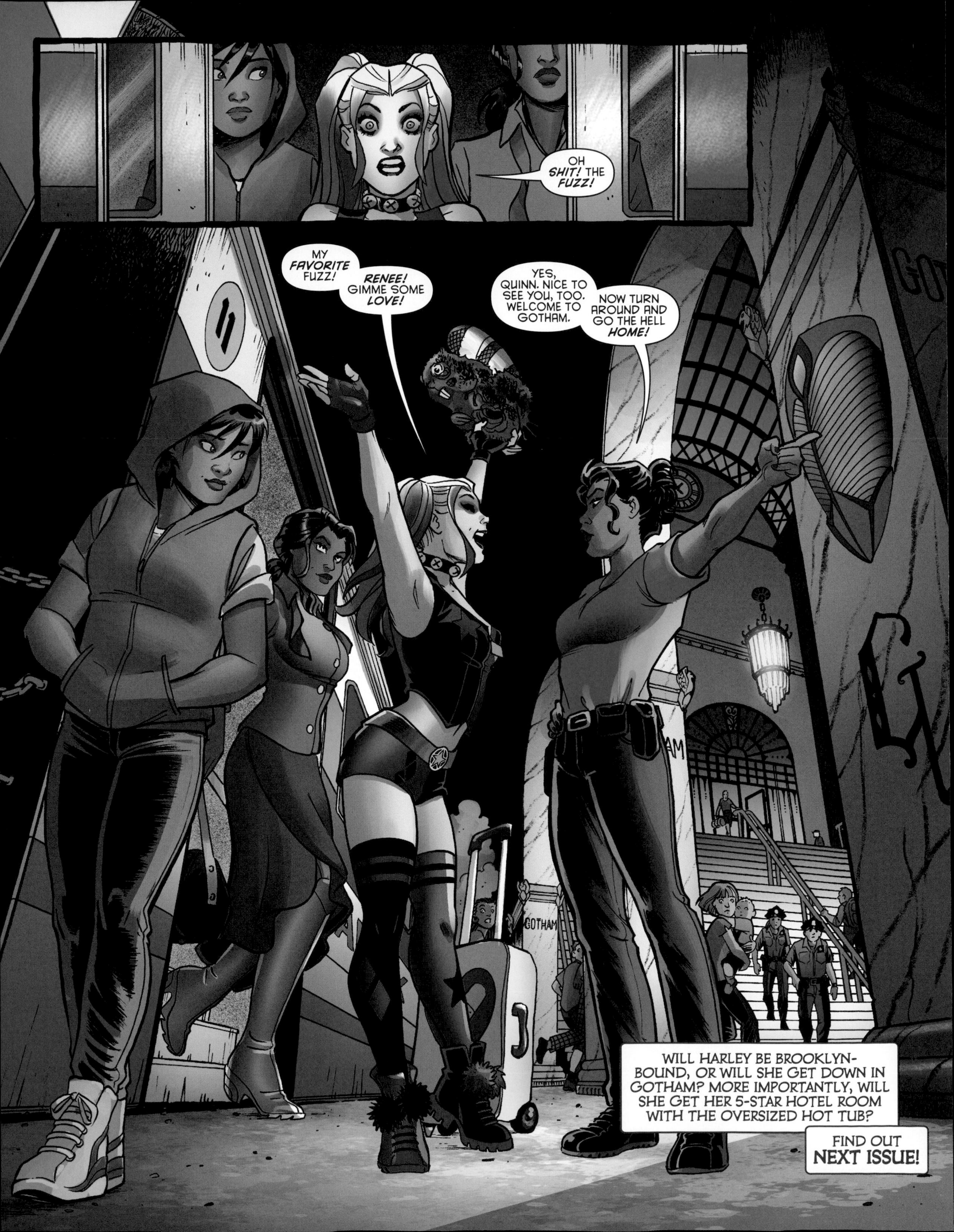

OH SHIT! THE FUZZ!
MY FAVORITE FUZZ!
RENEE! GIMME SOME LOVE!
YES, QUINN. NICE TO SEE YOU, TOO. WELCOME TO GOTHAM.
NOW TURN AROUND AND GO THE HELL HOME!
GOTHAM
WILL HARLEY BE BROOKLYN-BOUND, OR WILL SHE GET DOWN IN GOTHAM? MORE IMPORTANTLY, WILL SHE GET HER 5-STAR HOTEL ROOM WITH THE OVERSIZED HOT TUB?
FIND OUT NEXT ISSUE!

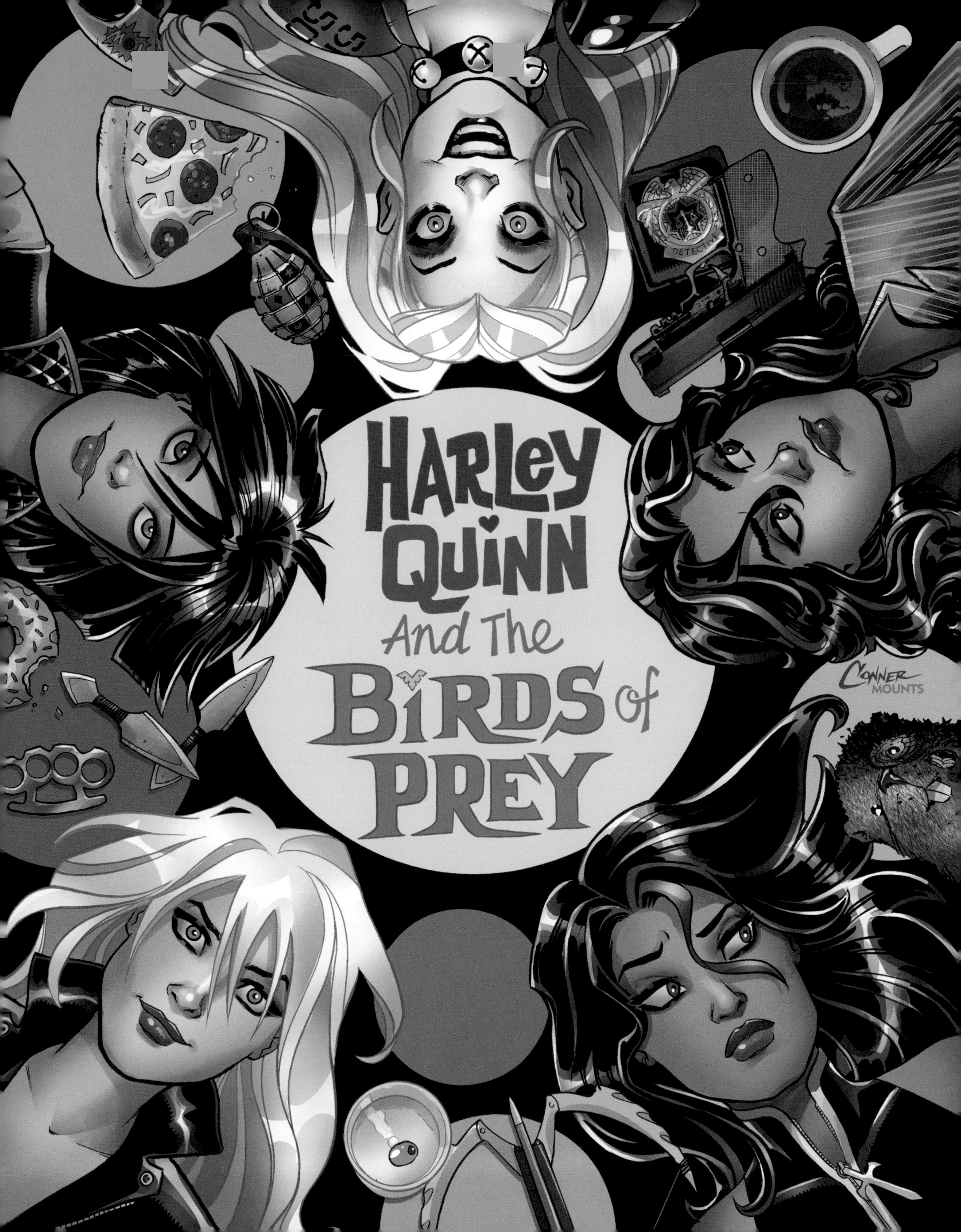
HARLEY QUINN
And The
BIRDS of
PREY
DETECTIVE
CONNER
MOUNTS

BOOK TWO
BELOW & BEYOND THE CALL OF DOODY

"Let me handle this MY way, in MY town."

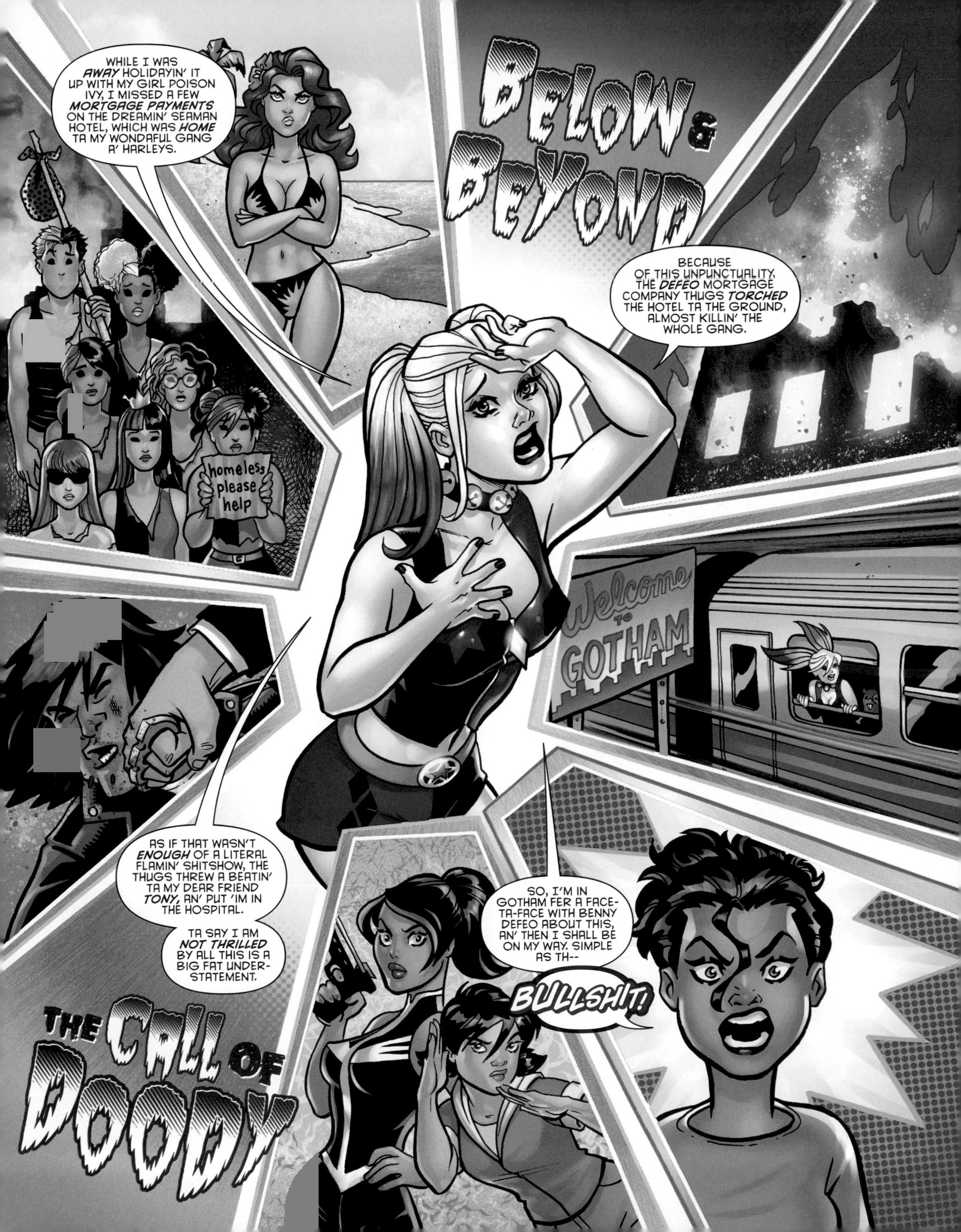

BELOW & BEYOND
WHILE I WAS AWAY HOLIDAYIN' IT UP WITH MY GIRL POISON IVY, I MISSED A FEW MORTGAGE PAYMENTS ON THE DREAMIN' SEAMAN HOTEL, WHICH WAS HOME TA MY WONDAFUL GANG A' HARLEYS.
homeless please help
BECAUSE OF THIS UNPUNCTUALITY, THE DEFEO MORTGAGE COMPANY THUGS TORCHED THE HOTEL TA THE GROUND, ALMOST KILLIN' THE WHOLE GANG.
Welcome TO GOTHAM
AS IF THAT WASN'T ENOUGH OF A LITERAL FLAMIN' SHITSHOW, THE THUGS THREW A BEATIN' TA MY DEAR FRIEND TONY, AN' PUT 'IM IN THE HOSPITAL.
TA SAY I AM NOT THRILLED BY ALL THIS IS A BIG FAT UNDER-STATEMENT.
SO, I'M IN GOTHAM FER A FACE-TA-FACE WITH BENNY DEFEO ABOUT THIS, AN' THEN I SHALL BE ON MY WAY. SIMPLE AS TH--
BULLSHIT!
THE CALL OF DOODY

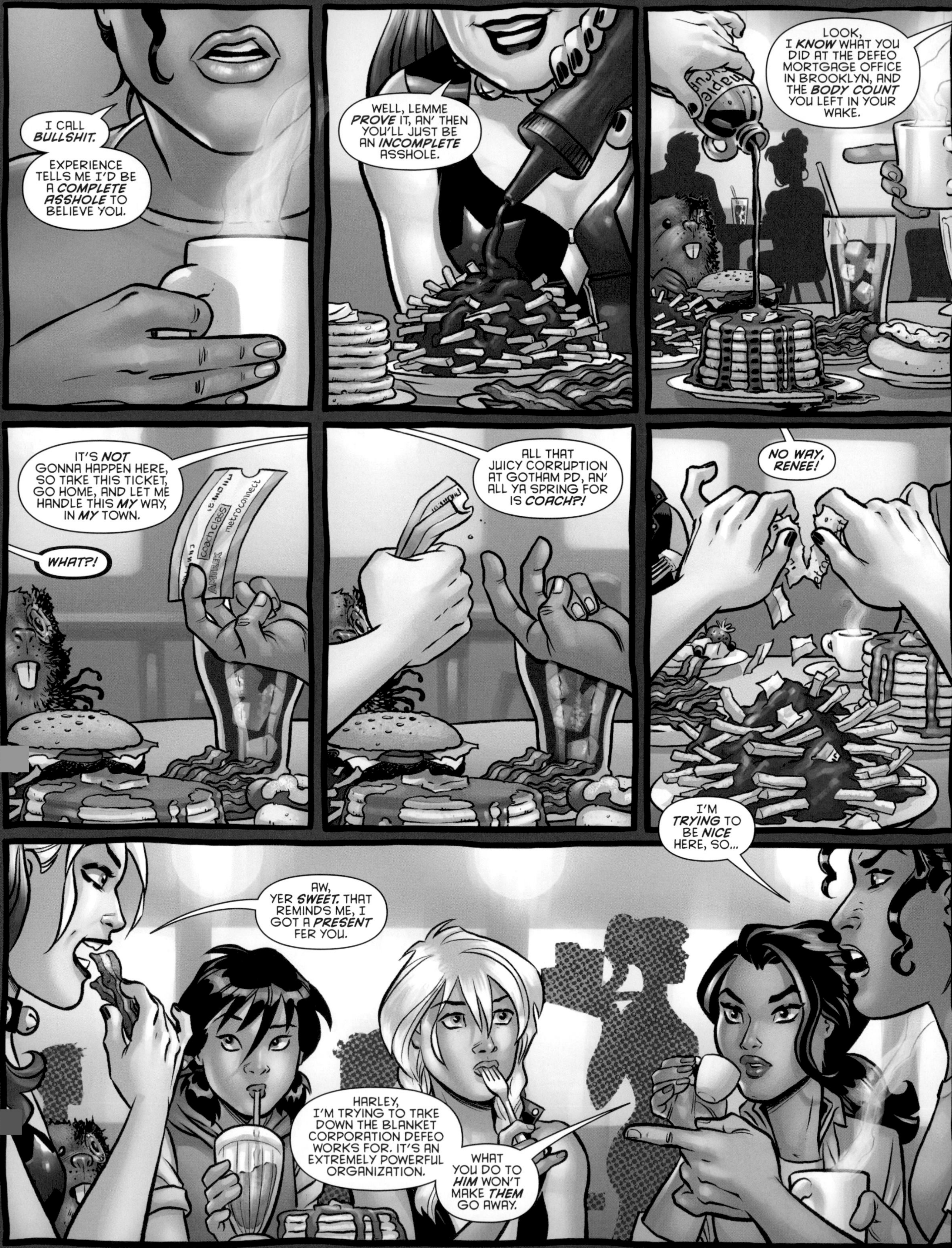
I CALL BULLSHIT.
EXPERIENCE TELLS ME I'D BE A COMPLETE ASSHOLE TO BELIEVE YOU.
WELL, LEMME PROVE IT, AN' THEN YOU'LL JUST BE AN INCOMPLETE ASSHOLE.
maple syrup
LOOK, I KNOW WHAT YOU DID AT THE DEFEO MORTGAGE OFFICE IN BROOKLYN, AND THE BODY COUNT YOU LEFT IN YOUR WAKE.
IT'S NOT GONNA HAPPEN HERE, SO TAKE THIS TICKET, GO HOME, AND LET ME HANDLE THIS MY WAY, IN MY TOWN.
AMTRAK coach class metroconnect
WHAT?!
ALL THAT JUICY CORRUPTION AT GOTHAM PD, AN' ALL YA SPRING FOR IS COACH?!
NO WAY, RENEE!
I'M TRYING TO BE NICE HERE, SO...
AW, YER SWEET. THAT REMINDS ME, I GOT A PRESENT FER YOU.
HARLEY, I'M TRYING TO TAKE DOWN THE BLANKET CORPORATION DEFEO WORKS FOR. IT'S AN EXTREMELY POWERFUL ORGANIZATION.
WHAT YOU DO TO HIM WON'T MAKE THEM GO AWAY.

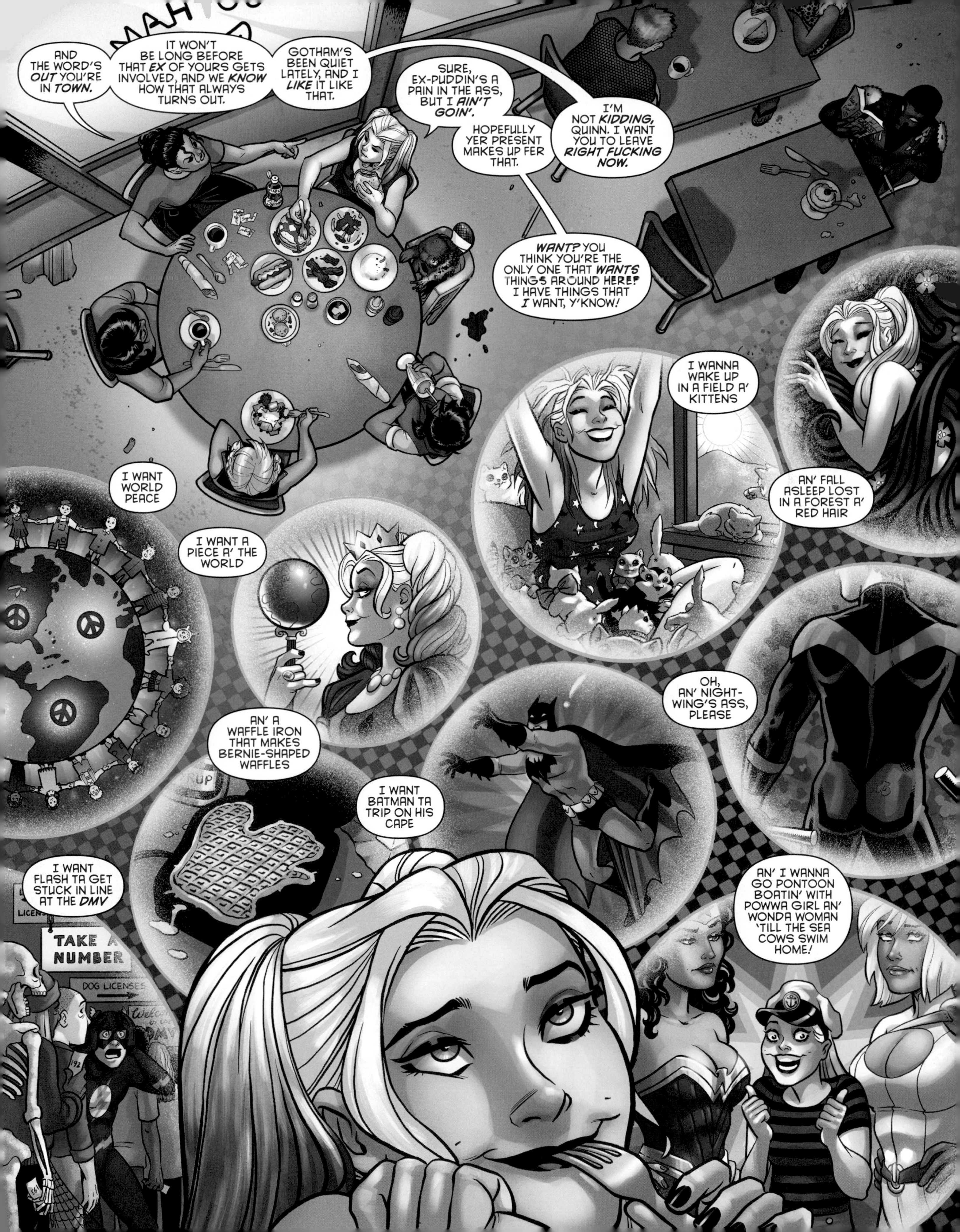
MAH
AND THE WORD'S OUT YOU'RE IN TOWN.
IT WON'T BE LONG BEFORE THAT EX OF YOURS GETS INVOLVED, AND WE KNOW HOW THAT ALWAYS TURNS OUT.
GOTHAM'S BEEN QUIET LATELY, AND I LIKE IT LIKE THAT.
SURE, EX-PUDDIN'S A PAIN IN THE ASS, BUT I AIN'T GOIN'.
HOPEFULLY YER PRESENT MAKES UP FER THAT.
I'M NOT KIDDING, QUINN. I WANT YOU TO LEAVE RIGHT FUCKING NOW.
WANT? YOU THINK YOU'RE THE ONLY ONE THAT WANTS THINGS AROUND HERE? I HAVE THINGS THAT I WANT, Y'KNOW!
I WANNA WAKE UP IN A FIELD A' KITTENS
AN' FALL ASLEEP LOST IN A FOREST A' RED HAIR
I WANT WORLD PEACE
I WANT A PIECE A' THE WORLD
OH, AN' NIGHT-WING'S ASS, PLEASE
AN' A WAFFLE IRON THAT MAKES BERNIE-SHAPED WAFFLES
I WANT BATMAN TA TRIP ON HIS CAPE
I WANT FLASH TA GET STUCK IN LINE AT THE DMV
TAKE A NUMBER
DOG LICENSES
AN' I WANNA GO PONTOON BOATIN' WITH POWWA GIRL AN' WONDA WOMAN 'TILL THE SEA COWS SWIM HOME!

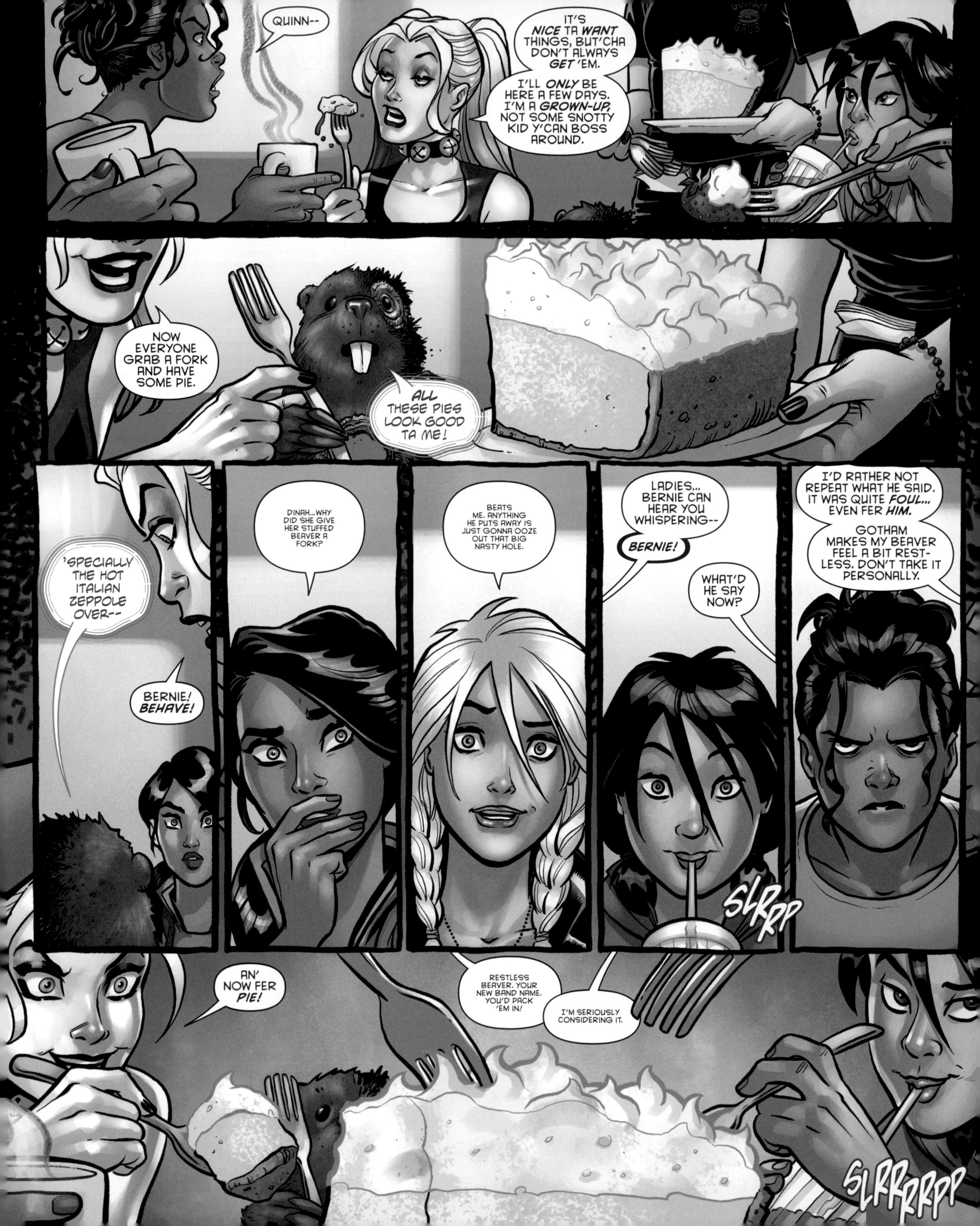
QUINN--
IT'S NICE TA WANT THINGS, BUT'CHA DON'T ALWAYS GET 'EM.
I'LL ONLY BE HERE A FEW DAYS. I'M A GROWN-UP, NOT SOME SNOTTY KID Y'CAN BOSS AROUND.
NOW EVERYONE GRAB A FORK AND HAVE SOME PIE.
ALL THESE PIES LOOK GOOD TA ME!
'SPECIALLY THE HOT ITALIAN ZEPPOLE OVER--
BERNIE! BEHAVE!
DINAH...WHY DID SHE GIVE HER STUFFED BEAVER A FORK?
BEATS ME. ANYTHING HE PUTS AWAY IS JUST GONNA OOZE OUT THAT BIG NASTY HOLE.
LADIES... BERNIE CAN HEAR YOU WHISPERING--
BERNIE!
WHAT'D HE SAY NOW?
SLRRP
I'D RATHER NOT REPEAT WHAT HE SAID. IT WAS QUITE FOUL... EVEN FER HIM.
GOTHAM MAKES MY BEAVER FEEL A BIT REST-LESS. DON'T TAKE IT PERSONALLY.
AN' NOW FER PIE!
RESTLESS BEAVER. YOUR NEW BAND NAME. YOU'D PACK 'EM IN!
I'M SERIOUSLY CONSIDERING IT.
SLRRRRPP

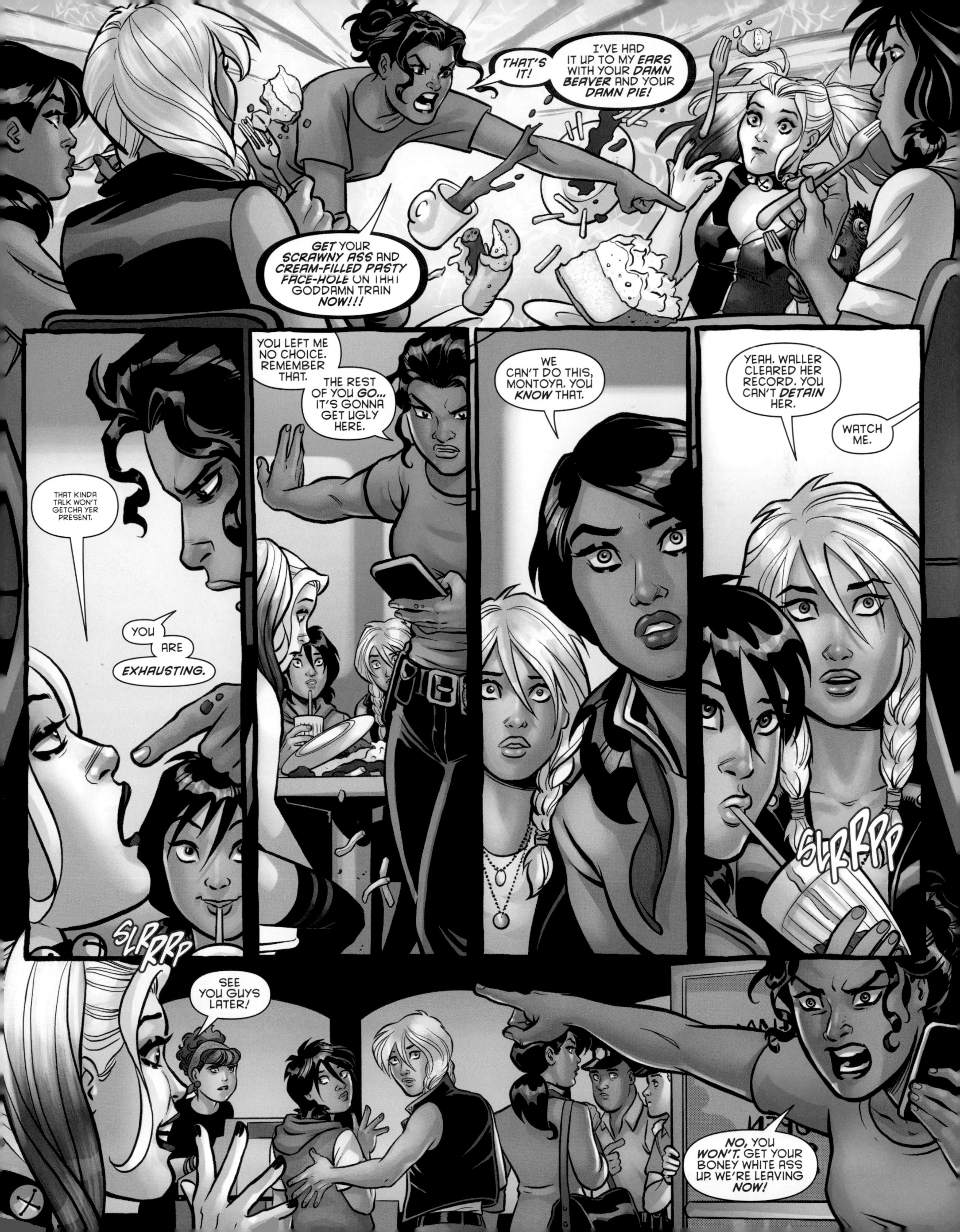

THAT'S IT!
I'VE HAD IT UP TO MY EARS WITH YOUR DAMN BEAVER AND YOUR DAMN PIE!
GET YOUR SCRAWNY ASS AND CREAM-FILLED PASTY FACE-HOLE ON THAT GODDAMN TRAIN NOW!!!
THAT KINDA TALK WON'T GETCHA YER PRESENT.
YOU
ARE
EXHAUSTING.
SLRRRP
YOU LEFT ME NO CHOICE. REMEMBER THAT.
THE REST OF YOU GO... IT'S GONNA GET UGLY HERE.
WE CAN'T DO THIS, MONTOYA. YOU KNOW THAT.
YEAH. WALLER CLEARED HER RECORD. YOU CAN'T DETAIN HER.
WATCH ME.
SLRRPP
SEE YOU GUYS LATER!
NO, YOU WON'T. GET YOUR BONEY WHITE ASS UP. WE'RE LEAVING NOW!

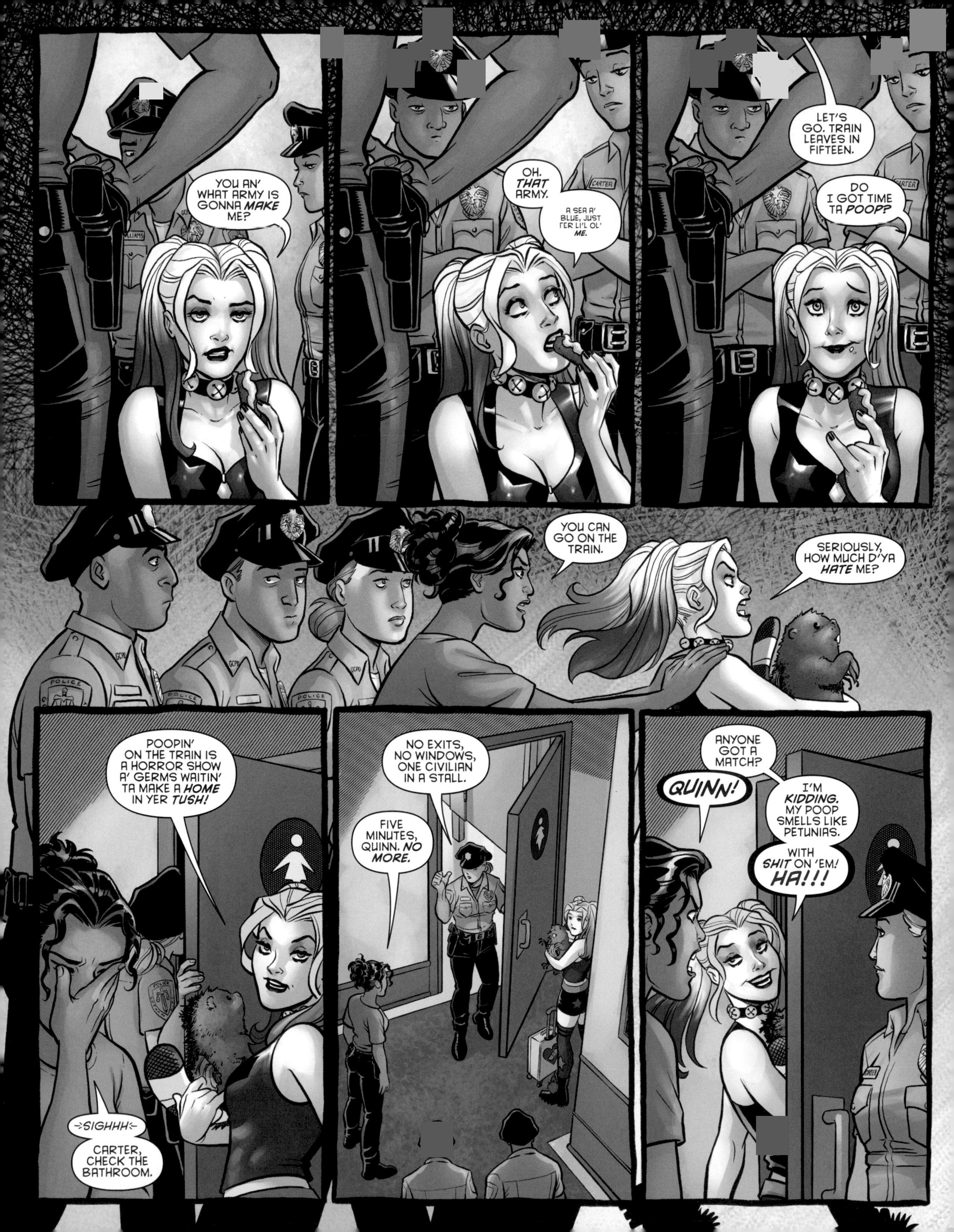
YOU AN' WHAT ARMY IS GONNA *MAKE* ME?
OH. *THAT* ARMY.
A SEA A' BLUE, JUST FER LI'L OL' *ME.*
LET'S GO. TRAIN LEAVES IN FIFTEEN.
DO I GOT TIME TA *POOP?*
YOU CAN GO ON THE TRAIN.
SERIOUSLY, HOW MUCH D'YA *HATE* ME?
POOPIN' ON THE TRAIN IS A HORROR SHOW A' GERMS WAITIN' TA MAKE A *HOME* IN YER *TUSH!*
SIGHHH
CARTER, CHECK THE BATHROOM.
NO EXITS, NO WINDOWS, ONE CIVILIAN IN A STALL.
FIVE MINUTES, QUINN. *NO MORE.*
ANYONE GOT A MATCH?
QUINN!
I'M *KIDDING.* MY POOP SMELLS LIKE PETUNIAS.
WITH *SHIT* ON 'EM! *HA!!!*

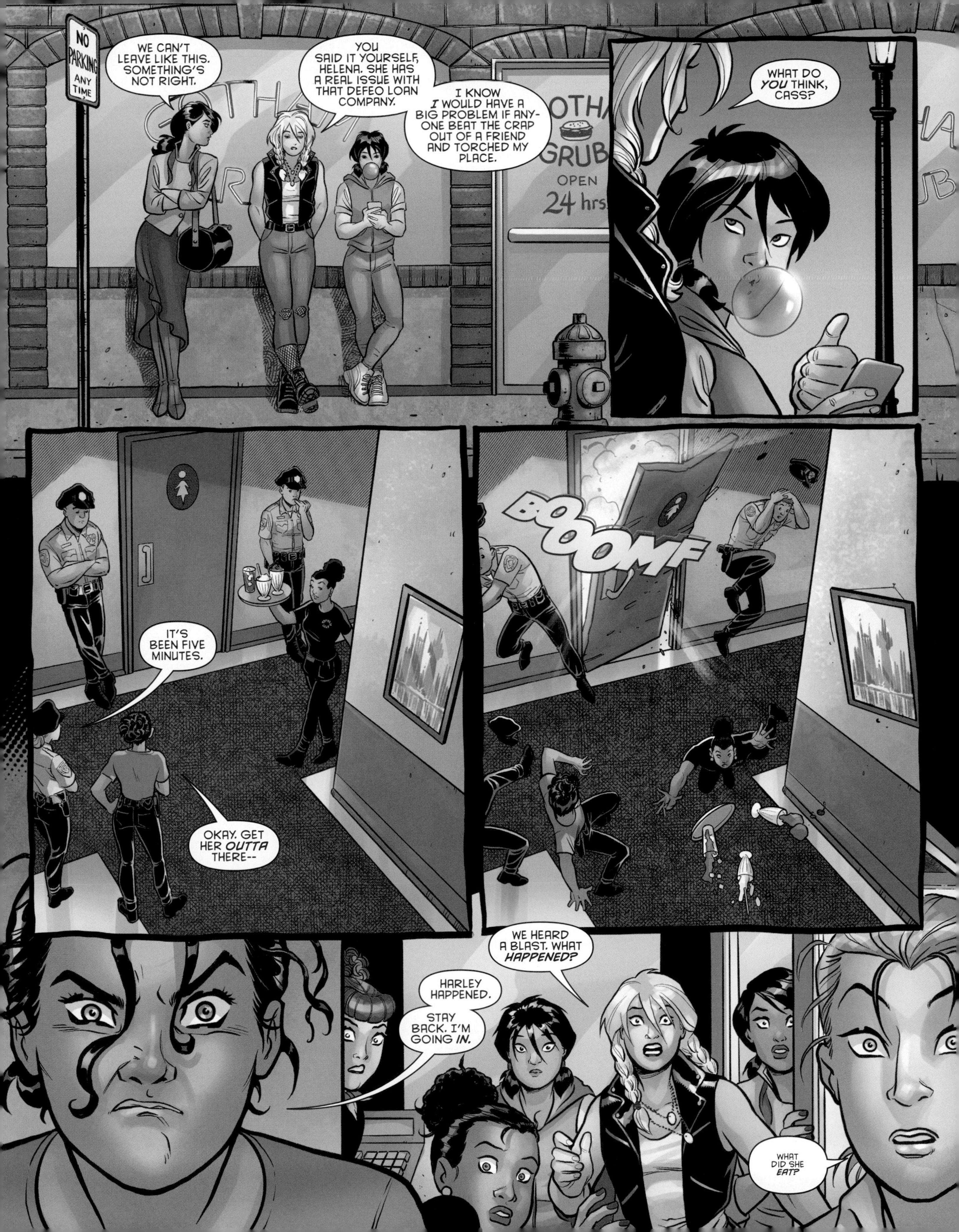
NO PARKING ANY TIME
WE CAN'T LEAVE LIKE THIS. SOMETHING'S NOT RIGHT.
YOU SAID IT YOURSELF, HELENA. SHE HAS A REAL ISSUE WITH THAT DEFEO LOAN COMPANY.
I KNOW *I* WOULD HAVE A BIG PROBLEM IF ANY-ONE BEAT THE CRAP OUT OF A FRIEND AND TORCHED MY PLACE.
GRUB
OPEN 24 hrs.
WHAT DO *YOU* THINK, CASS?
IT'S BEEN FIVE MINUTES.
OKAY. GET HER *OUTTA* THERE--
BOOOMF
WE HEARD A BLAST. WHAT *HAPPENED?*
HARLEY HAPPENED.
STAY BACK. I'M GOING *IN.*
WHAT DID SHE *EAT?*

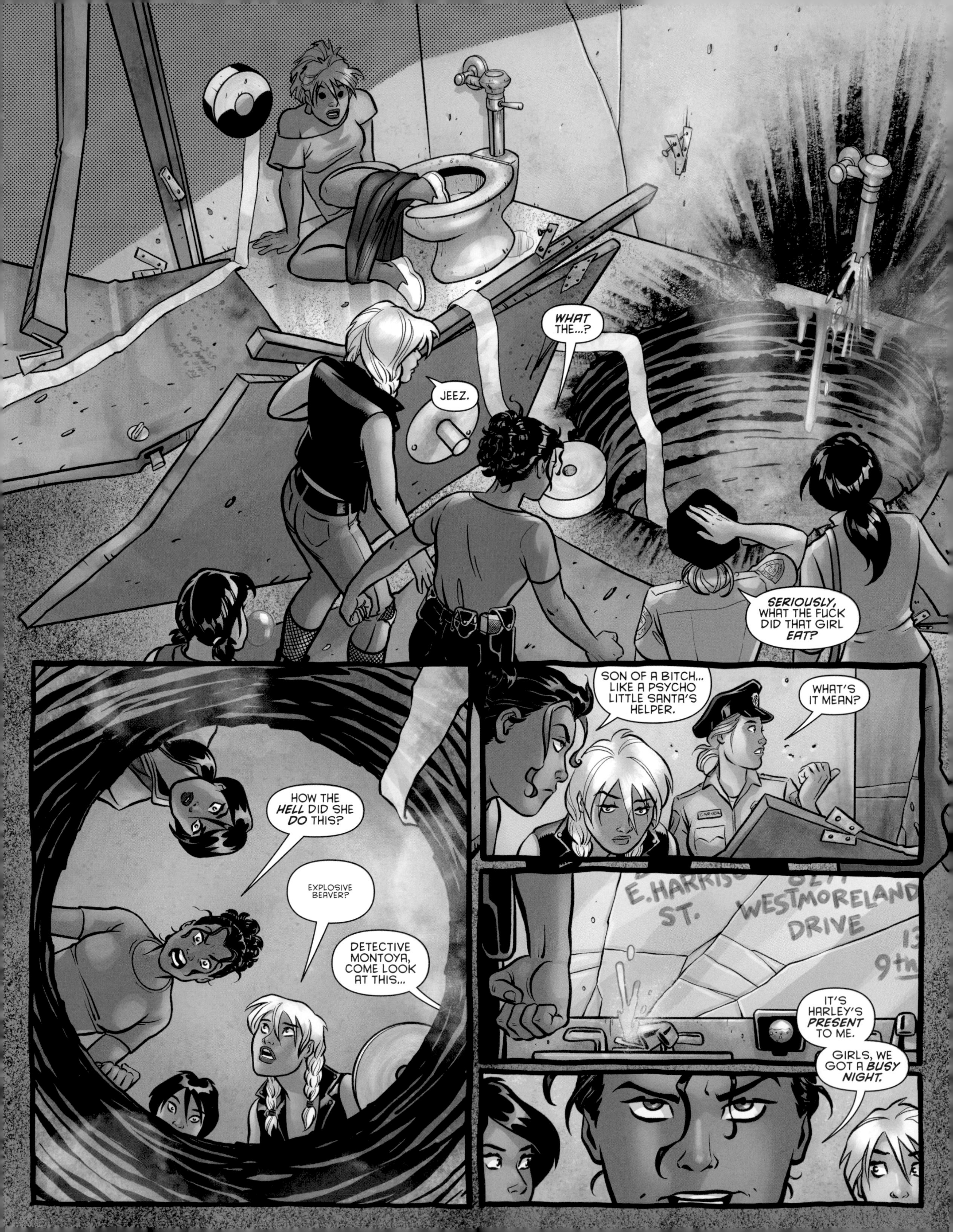
WHAT THE...?
JEEZ.
SERIOUSLY, WHAT THE FUCK DID THAT GIRL EAT?
HOW THE HELL DID SHE DO THIS?
EXPLOSIVE BEAVER?
DETECTIVE MONTOYA, COME LOOK AT THIS...
SON OF A BITCH... LIKE A PSYCHO LITTLE SANTA'S HELPER.
WHAT'S IT MEAN?
E.HARRIS
ST.
WESTMORELAND DRIVE
IT'S HARLEY'S PRESENT TO ME.
GIRLS, WE GOT A BUSY NIGHT.

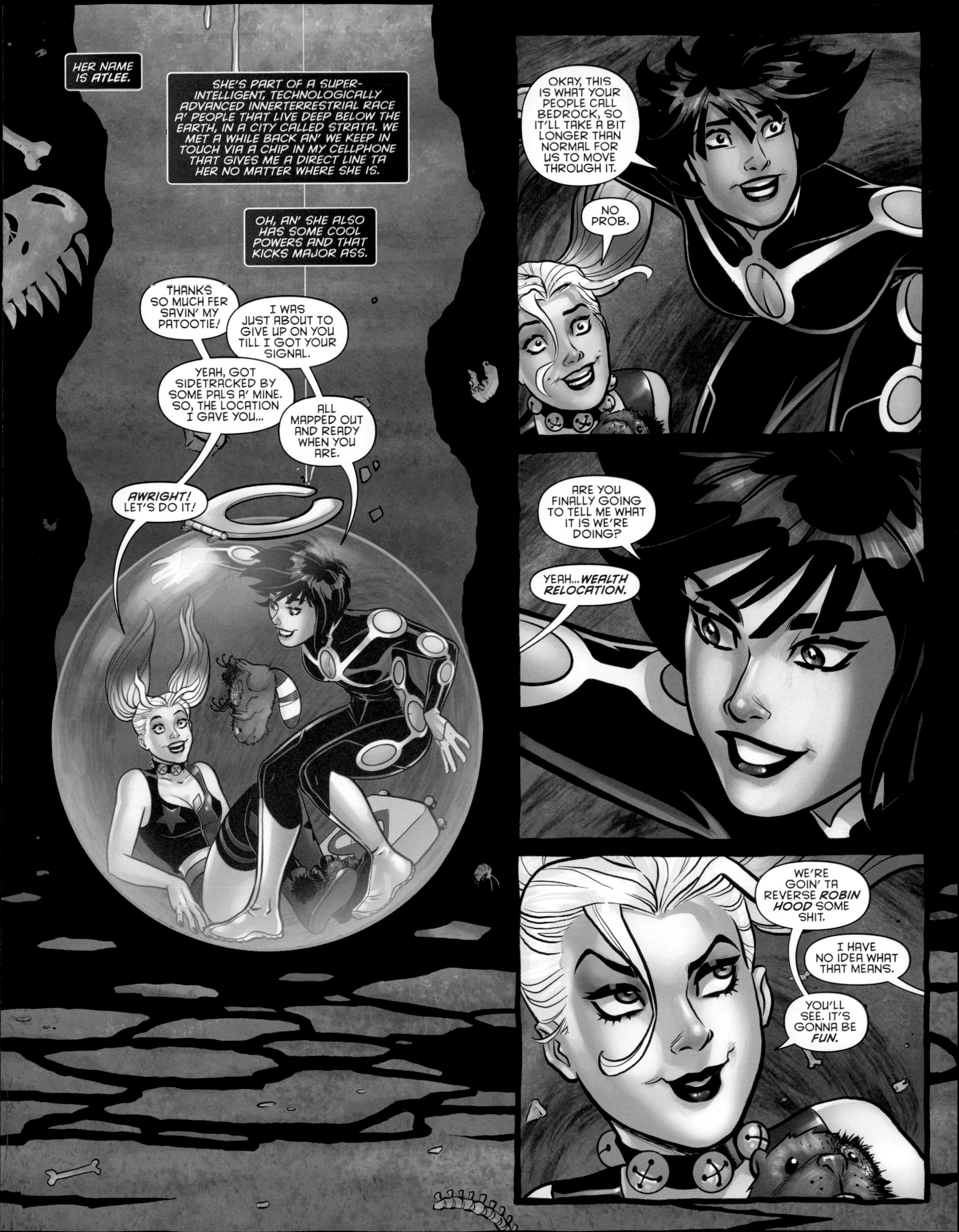
HER NAME IS ATLEE.
SHE'S PART OF A SUPER-INTELLIGENT, TECHNOLOGICALLY ADVANCED INNERTERRESTRIAL RACE A' PEOPLE THAT LIVE DEEP BELOW THE EARTH, IN A CITY CALLED STRATA. WE MET A WHILE BACK AN' WE KEEP IN TOUCH VIA A CHIP IN MY CELLPHONE THAT GIVES ME A DIRECT LINE TA HER NO MATTER WHERE SHE IS.
OH, AN' SHE ALSO HAS SOME COOL POWERS AND THAT KICKS MAJOR ASS.
THANKS SO MUCH FER SAVIN' MY PATOOTIE!
I WAS JUST ABOUT TO GIVE UP ON YOU TILL I GOT YOUR SIGNAL.
YEAH, GOT SIDETRACKED BY SOME PALS A' MINE. SO, THE LOCATION I GAVE YOU...
ALL MAPPED OUT AND READY WHEN YOU ARE.
AWRIGHT! LET'S DO IT!
OKAY, THIS IS WHAT YOUR PEOPLE CALL BEDROCK, SO IT'LL TAKE A BIT LONGER THAN NORMAL FOR US TO MOVE THROUGH IT.
NO PROB.
ARE YOU FINALLY GOING TO TELL ME WHAT IT IS WE'RE DOING?
YEAH... WEALTH RELOCATION.
WE'RE GOIN' TA REVERSE ROBIN HOOD SOME SHIT.
I HAVE NO IDEA WHAT THAT MEANS.
YOU'LL SEE. IT'S GONNA BE FUN.

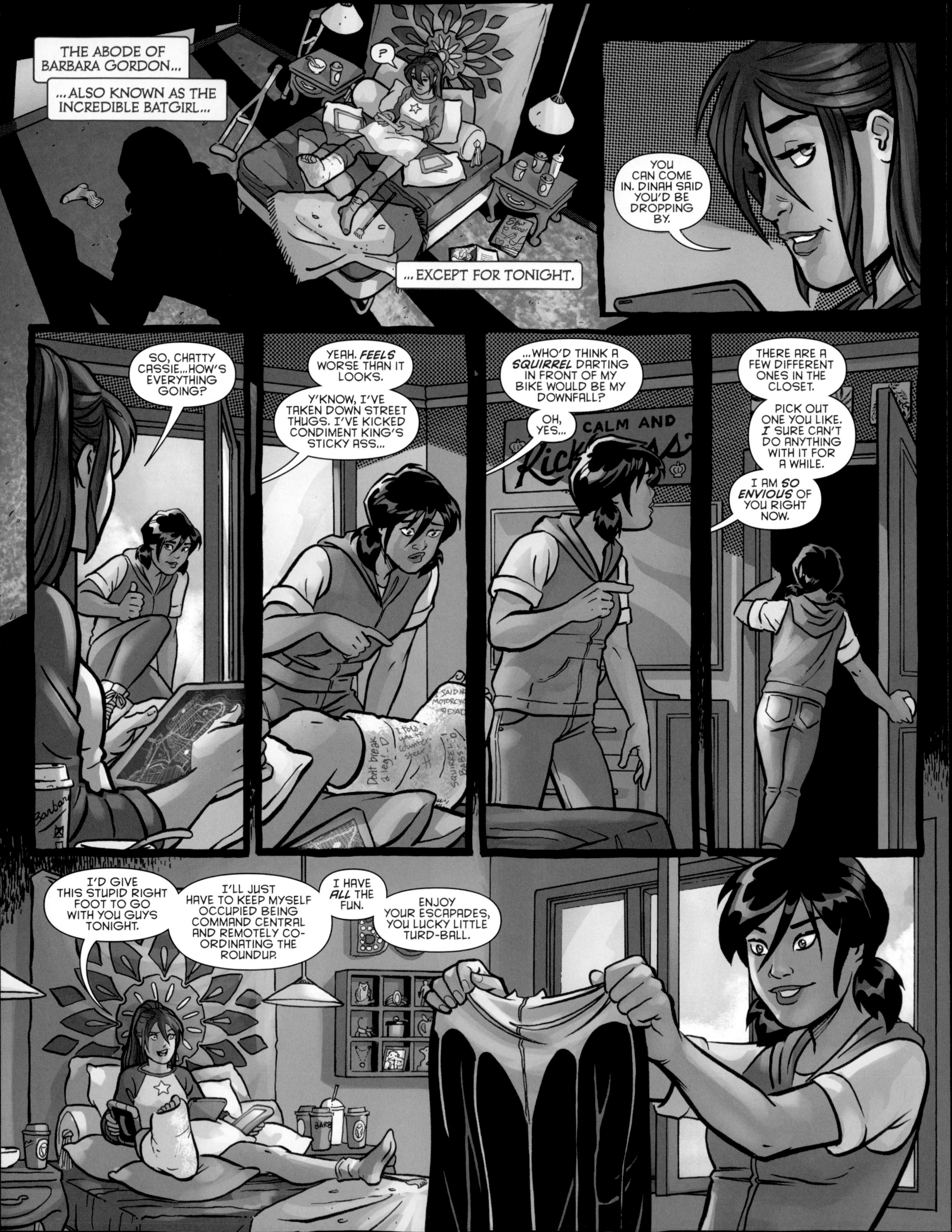
THE ABODE OF BARBARA GORDON...
...ALSO KNOWN AS THE INCREDIBLE BATGIRL...
?
...EXCEPT FOR TONIGHT.
YOU CAN COME IN. DINAH SAID YOU'D BE DROPPING BY.
SO, CHATTY CASSIE...HOW'S EVERYTHING GOING?
YEAH. FEELS WORSE THAN IT LOOKS.
Y'KNOW, I'VE TAKEN DOWN STREET THUGS. I'VE KICKED CONDIMENT KING'S STICKY ASS...
...WHO'D THINK A SQUIRREL DARTING IN FRONT OF MY BIKE WOULD BE MY DOWNFALL?
OH, YES...
CALM AND
THERE ARE A FEW DIFFERENT ONES IN THE CLOSET.
PICK OUT ONE YOU LIKE. I SURE CAN'T DO ANYTHING WITH IT FOR A WHILE.
I AM SO ENVIOUS OF YOU RIGHT NOW.
I'D GIVE THIS STUPID RIGHT FOOT TO GO WITH YOU GUYS TONIGHT.
I'LL JUST HAVE TO KEEP MYSELF OCCUPIED BEING COMMAND CENTRAL AND REMOTELY CO-ORDINATING THE ROUNDUP.
I HAVE ALL THE FUN.
ENJOY YOUR ESCAPADES, YOU LUCKY LITTLE TURD-BALL.

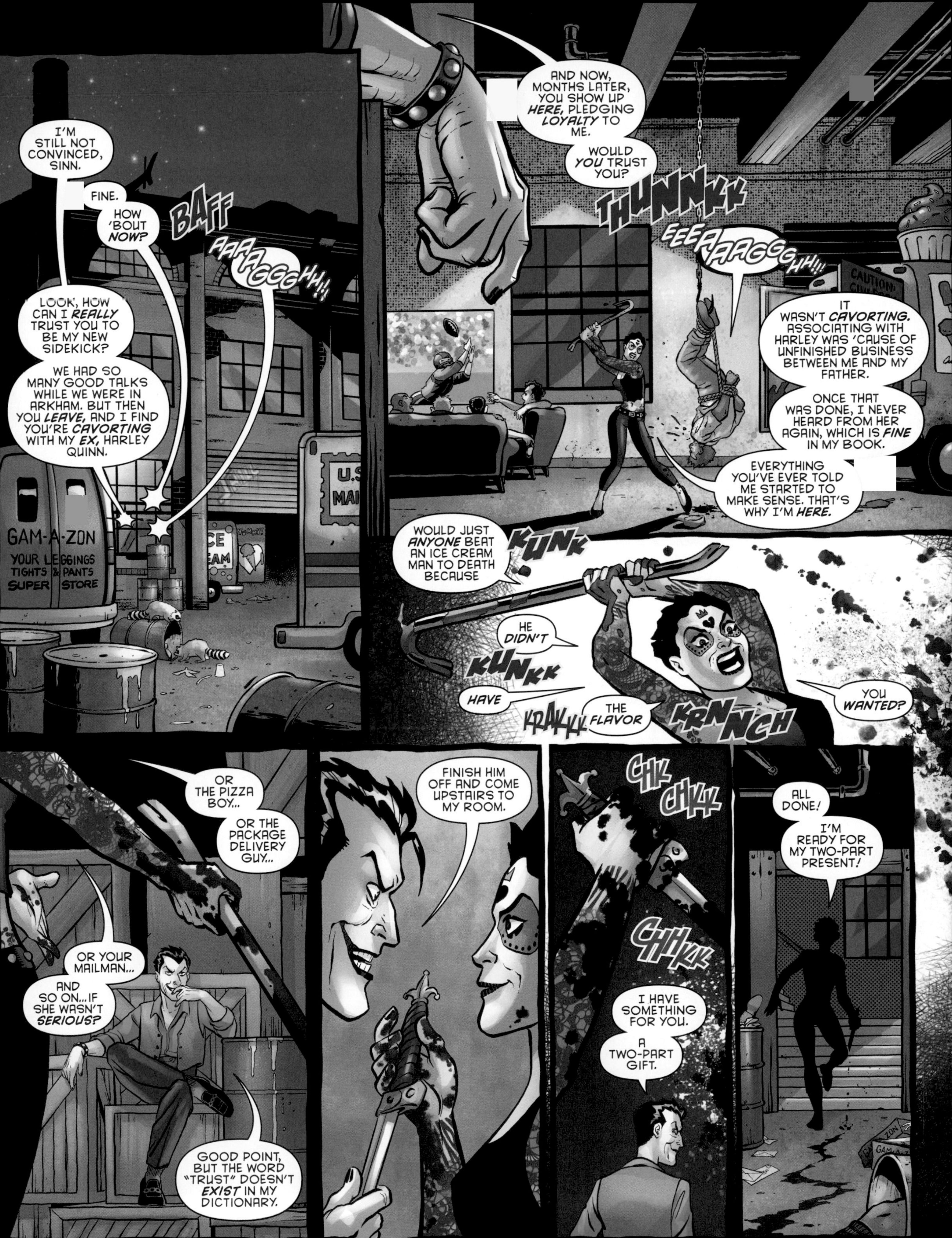
I'M STILL NOT CONVINCED, SINN.
FINE.
HOW 'BOUT NOW?
BAFF
AAAAGGGHH!!
LOOK, HOW CAN I REALLY TRUST YOU TO BE MY NEW SIDEKICK?
WE HAD SO MANY GOOD TALKS WHILE WE WERE IN ARKHAM. BUT THEN YOU LEAVE, AND I FIND YOU'RE CAVORTING WITH MY EX, HARLEY QUINN.
GAM-A-ZON YOUR LEGGINGS TIGHTS & PANTS SUPER STORE
AND NOW, MONTHS LATER, YOU SHOW UP HERE, PLEDGING LOYALTY TO ME.
WOULD YOU TRUST YOU?
THUNNKK
EEEAAAGGGHH!!
IT WASN'T CAVORTING. ASSOCIATING WITH HARLEY WAS 'CAUSE OF UNFINISHED BUSINESS BETWEEN ME AND MY FATHER.
ONCE THAT WAS DONE, I NEVER HEARD FROM HER AGAIN, WHICH IS FINE IN MY BOOK.
EVERYTHING YOU'VE EVER TOLD ME STARTED TO MAKE SENSE. THAT'S WHY I'M HERE.
WOULD JUST ANYONE BEAT AN ICE CREAM MAN TO DEATH BECAUSE
KUNK
HE DIDN'T
KUNKK
HAVE
KRAKKK
THE FLAVOR
KRNNCH
YOU WANTED?
OR THE PIZZA BOY...
OR THE PACKAGE DELIVERY GUY...
OR YOUR MAILMAN...
AND SO ON...IF SHE WASN'T SERIOUS?
GOOD POINT, BUT THE WORD "TRUST" DOESN'T EXIST IN MY DICTIONARY.
FINISH HIM OFF AND COME UPSTAIRS TO MY ROOM.
CHK
CHKK
CHHKK
I HAVE SOMETHING FOR YOU.
A TWO-PART GIFT.
ALL DONE!
I'M READY FOR MY TWO-PART PRESENT!

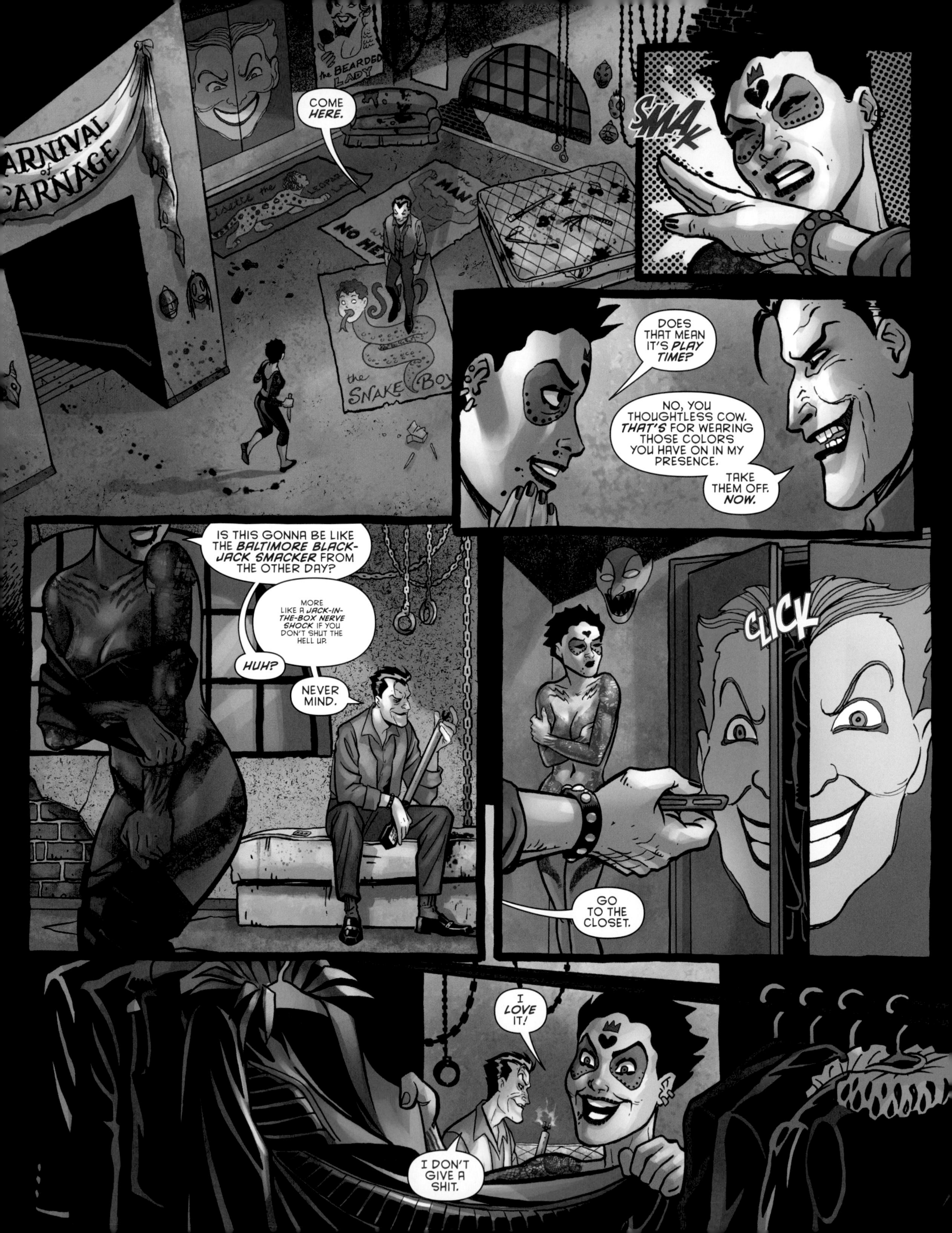
ARNIVAL of CARNAGE
the BEARDED LADY
COME HERE.
the SNAKE BOY
SMAK
DOES THAT MEAN IT'S PLAY TIME?
NO, YOU THOUGHTLESS COW. THAT'S FOR WEARING THOSE COLORS YOU HAVE ON IN MY PRESENCE.
TAKE THEM OFF. NOW.
IS THIS GONNA BE LIKE THE BALTIMORE BLACK-JACK SMACKER FROM THE OTHER DAY?
MORE LIKE A JACK-IN-THE-BOX NERVE SHOCK IF YOU DON'T SHUT THE HELL UP.
HUH?
NEVER MIND.
CLICK
GO TO THE CLOSET.
I LOVE IT!
I DON'T GIVE A SHIT.

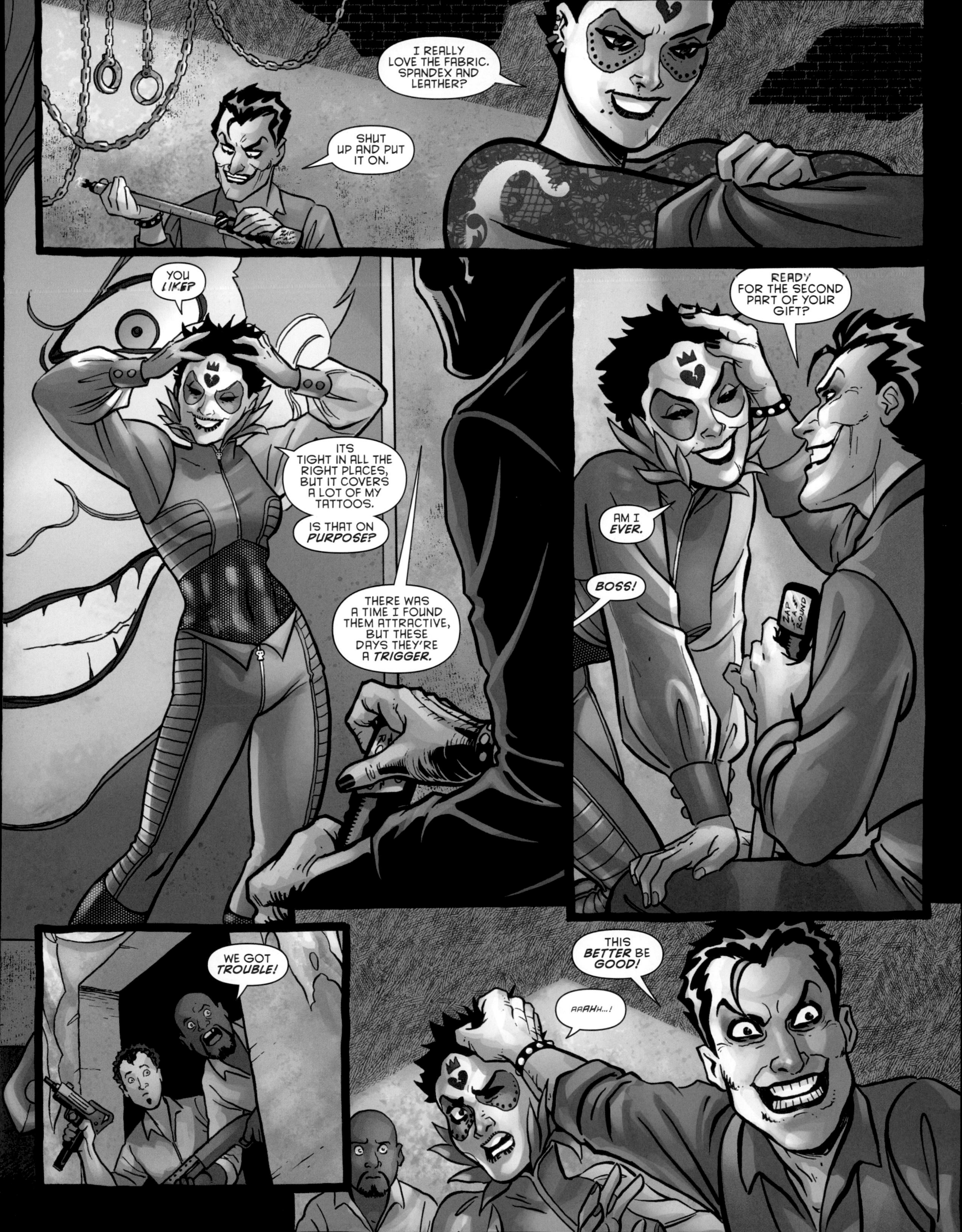
I REALLY LOVE THE FABRIC. SPANDEX AND LEATHER?
SHUT UP AND PUT IT ON.
ZAP A ROUND
YOU LIKE?
ITS TIGHT IN ALL THE RIGHT PLACES, BUT IT COVERS A LOT OF MY TATTOOS.
IS THAT ON PURPOSE?
THERE WAS A TIME I FOUND THEM ATTRACTIVE, BUT THESE DAYS THEY'RE A TRIGGER.
READY FOR THE SECOND PART OF YOUR GIFT?
AM I EVER.
BOSS!
ZAP A ROUND
WE GOT TROUBLE!
THIS BETTER BE GOOD!
AAAHH...!

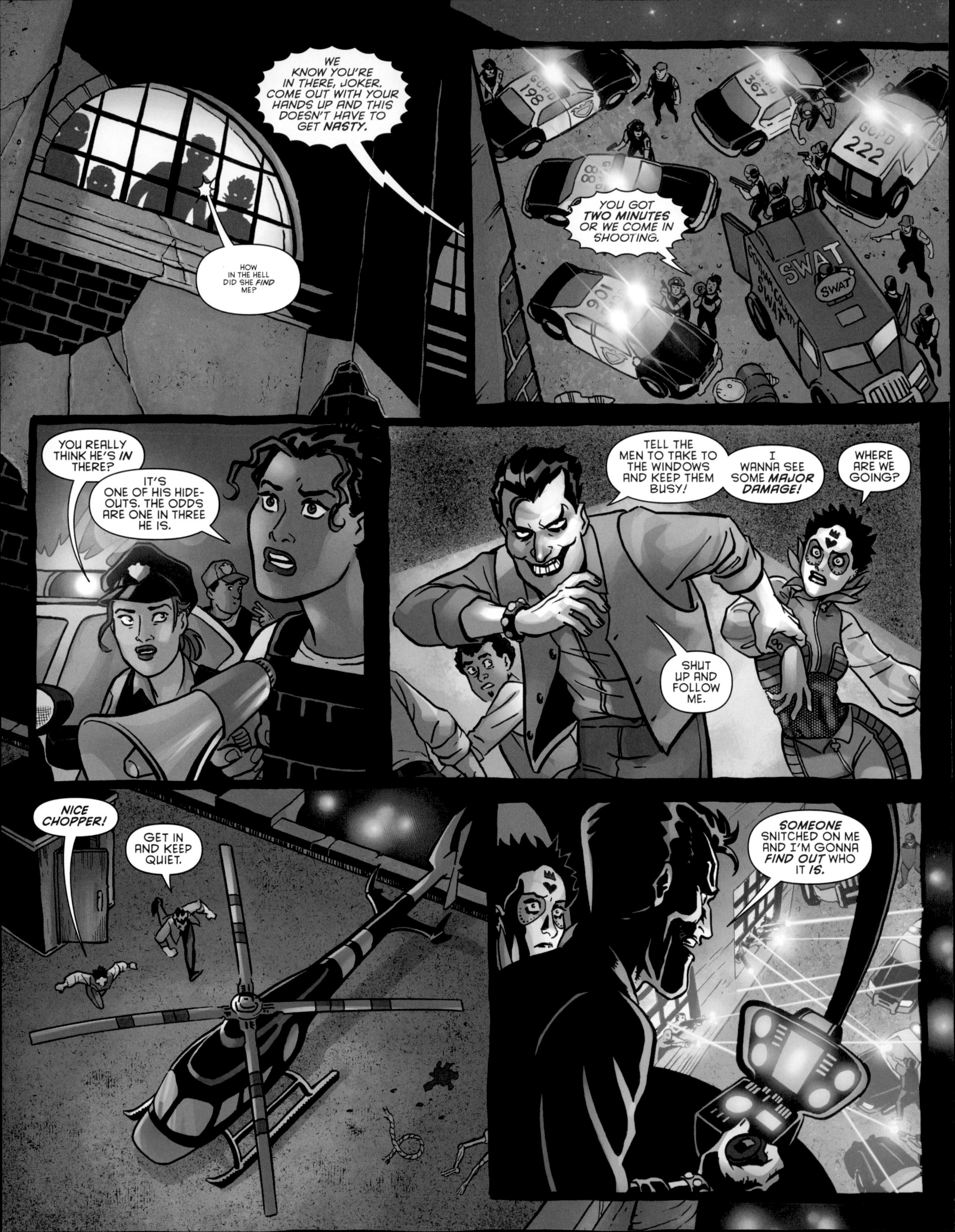
WE KNOW YOU'RE IN THERE, JOKER. COME OUT WITH YOUR HANDS UP AND THIS DOESN'T HAVE TO GET *NASTY.*
HOW IN THE HELL DID SHE *FIND* ME?
YOU GOT *TWO MINUTES* OR WE COME IN SHOOTING.
YOU REALLY THINK HE'S *IN* THERE?
IT'S ONE OF HIS HIDE-OUTS. THE ODDS ARE ONE IN THREE HE IS.
TELL THE MEN TO TAKE TO THE WINDOWS AND KEEP THEM BUSY!
I WANNA SEE SOME *MAJOR DAMAGE!*
WHERE ARE WE GOING?
SHUT UP AND FOLLOW ME.
NICE CHOPPER!
GET IN AND KEEP QUIET.
SOMEONE SNITCHED ON ME AND I'M GONNA *FIND OUT* WHO IT *IS.*

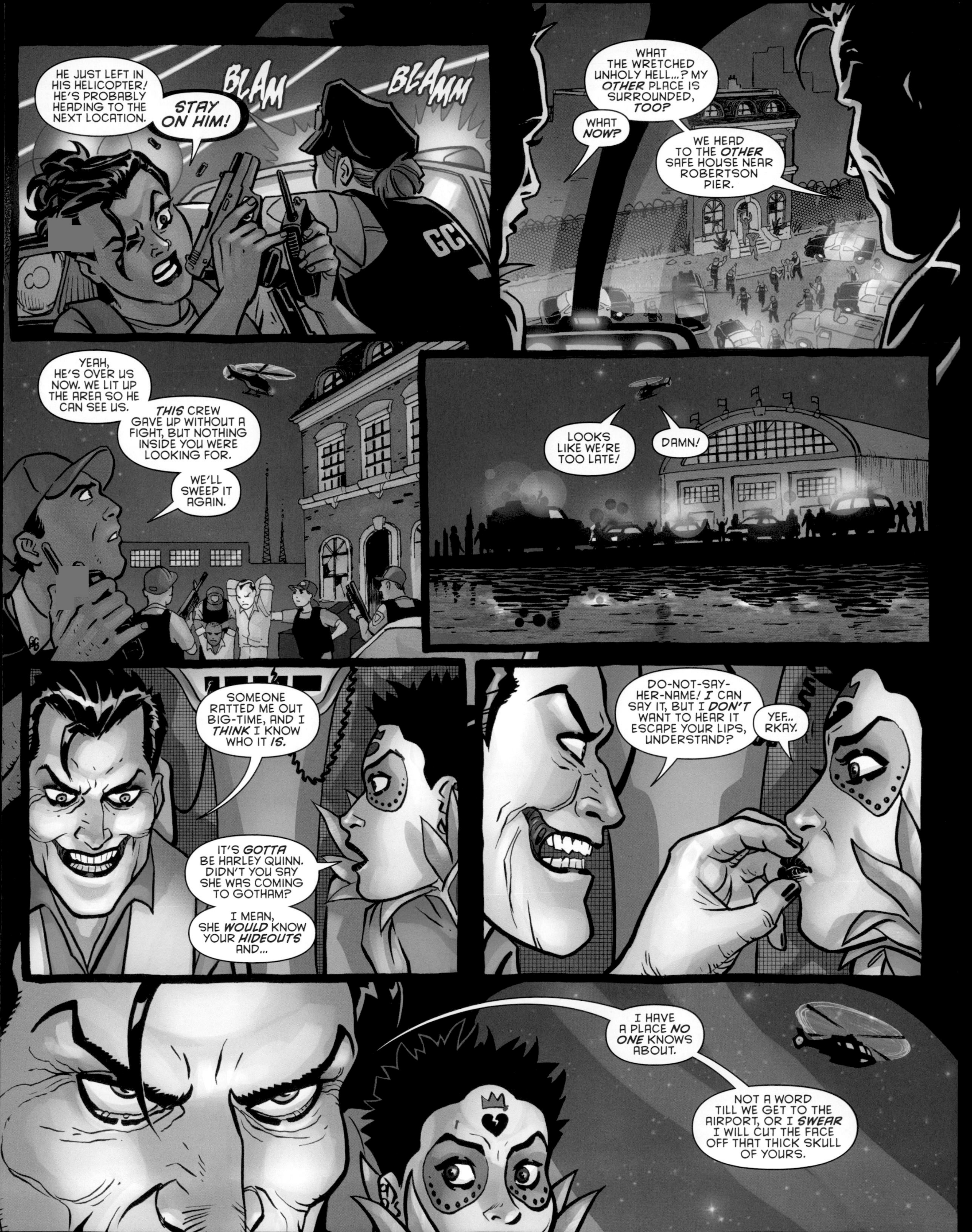
HE JUST LEFT IN HIS HELICOPTER! HE'S PROBABLY HEADING TO THE NEXT LOCATION.
BLAM
STAY ON HIM!
BLAMM
WHAT THE WRETCHED UNHOLY HELL...? MY OTHER PLACE IS SURROUNDED, TOO?
WHAT NOW?
WE HEAD TO THE OTHER SAFE HOUSE NEAR ROBERTSON PIER.
YEAH, HE'S OVER US NOW. WE LIT UP THE AREA SO HE CAN SEE US.
THIS CREW GAVE UP WITHOUT A FIGHT, BUT NOTHING INSIDE YOU WERE LOOKING FOR.
WE'LL SWEEP IT AGAIN.
LOOKS LIKE WE'RE TOO LATE!
DAMN!
SOMEONE RATTED ME OUT BIG-TIME, AND I THINK I KNOW WHO IT IS.
IT'S GOTTA BE HARLEY QUINN. DIDN'T YOU SAY SHE WAS COMING TO GOTHAM?
I MEAN, SHE WOULD KNOW YOUR HIDEOUTS AND...
DO-NOT-SAY-HER-NAME! I CAN SAY IT, BUT I DON'T WANT TO HEAR IT ESCAPE YOUR LIPS, UNDERSTAND?
YEF... RKAY.
I HAVE A PLACE NO ONE KNOWS ABOUT.
NOT A WORD TILL WE GET TO THE AIRPORT, OR I SWEAR I WILL CUT THE FACE OFF THAT THICK SKULL OF YOURS.

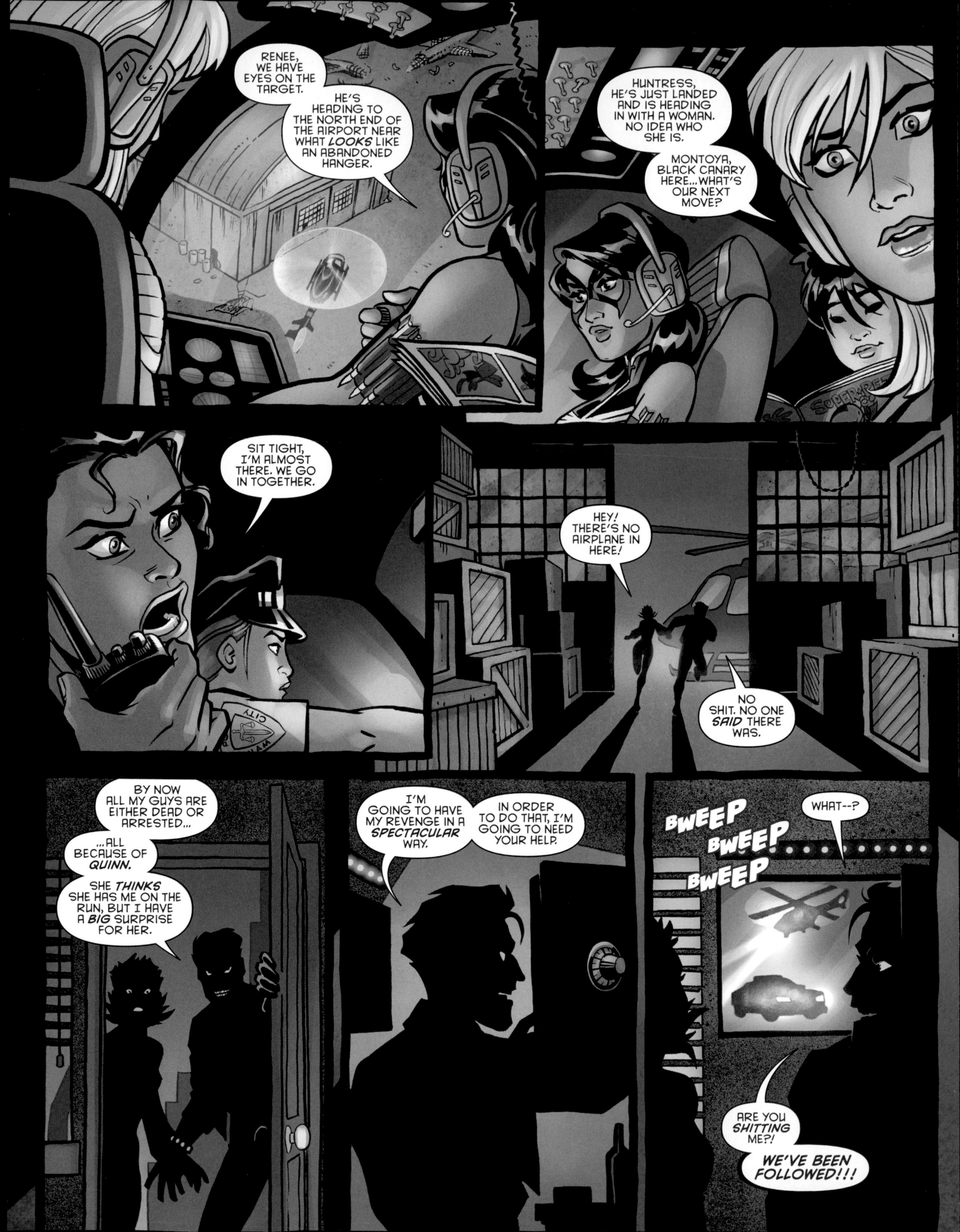
RENEE, WE HAVE EYES ON THE TARGET.
HE'S HEADING TO THE NORTH END OF THE AIRPORT NEAR WHAT *LOOKS* LIKE AN ABANDONED HANGER.
HUNTRESS, HE'S JUST LANDED AND IS HEADING IN WITH A WOMAN. NO IDEA WHO SHE IS.
MONTOYA, BLACK CANARY HERE... WHAT'S OUR NEXT MOVE?
SIT TIGHT, I'M ALMOST THERE. WE GO IN TOGETHER.
HEY! THERE'S NO AIRPLANE IN HERE!
NO SHIT. NO ONE *SAID* THERE WAS.
BY NOW ALL MY GUYS ARE EITHER DEAD OR ARRESTED...
...ALL BECAUSE OF *QUINN.*
SHE *THINKS* SHE HAS ME ON THE RUN, BUT I HAVE A *BIG* SURPRISE FOR HER.
I'M GOING TO HAVE MY REVENGE IN A *SPECTACULAR* WAY.
IN ORDER TO DO THAT, I'M GOING TO NEED YOUR HELP.
BWEEP
BWEEP
BWEEP
WHAT--?
ARE YOU *SHITTING* ME?!
WE'VE BEEN FOLLOWED!!!

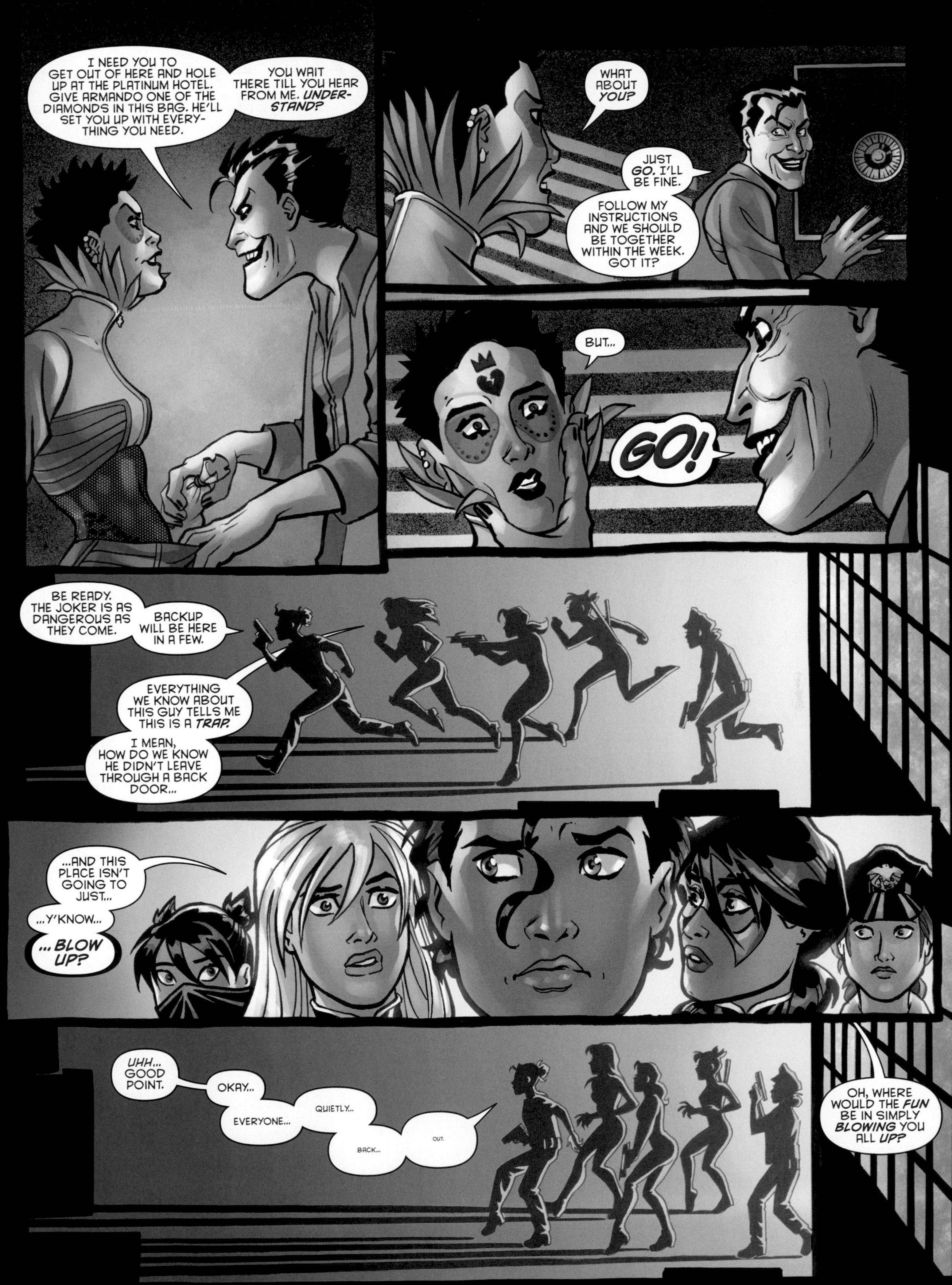
I NEED YOU TO GET OUT OF HERE AND HOLE UP AT THE PLATINUM HOTEL. GIVE ARMANDO ONE OF THE DIAMONDS IN THIS BAG. HE'LL SET YOU UP WITH EVERYTHING YOU NEED.
YOU WAIT THERE TILL YOU HEAR FROM ME. UNDERSTAND?
WHAT ABOUT YOU?
JUST GO. I'LL BE FINE.
FOLLOW MY INSTRUCTIONS AND WE SHOULD BE TOGETHER WITHIN THE WEEK. GOT IT?
BUT...
GO!
BE READY. THE JOKER IS AS DANGEROUS AS THEY COME.
BACKUP WILL BE HERE IN A FEW.
EVERYTHING WE KNOW ABOUT THIS GUY TELLS ME THIS IS A TRAP.
I MEAN, HOW DO WE KNOW HE DIDN'T LEAVE THROUGH A BACK DOOR...
...AND THIS PLACE ISN'T GOING TO JUST...
...Y'KNOW...
...BLOW UP?
UHH... GOOD POINT.
OKAY...
EVERYONE...
QUIETLY...
BACK...
OUT.
OH, WHERE WOULD THE FUN BE IN SIMPLY BLOWING YOU ALL UP?

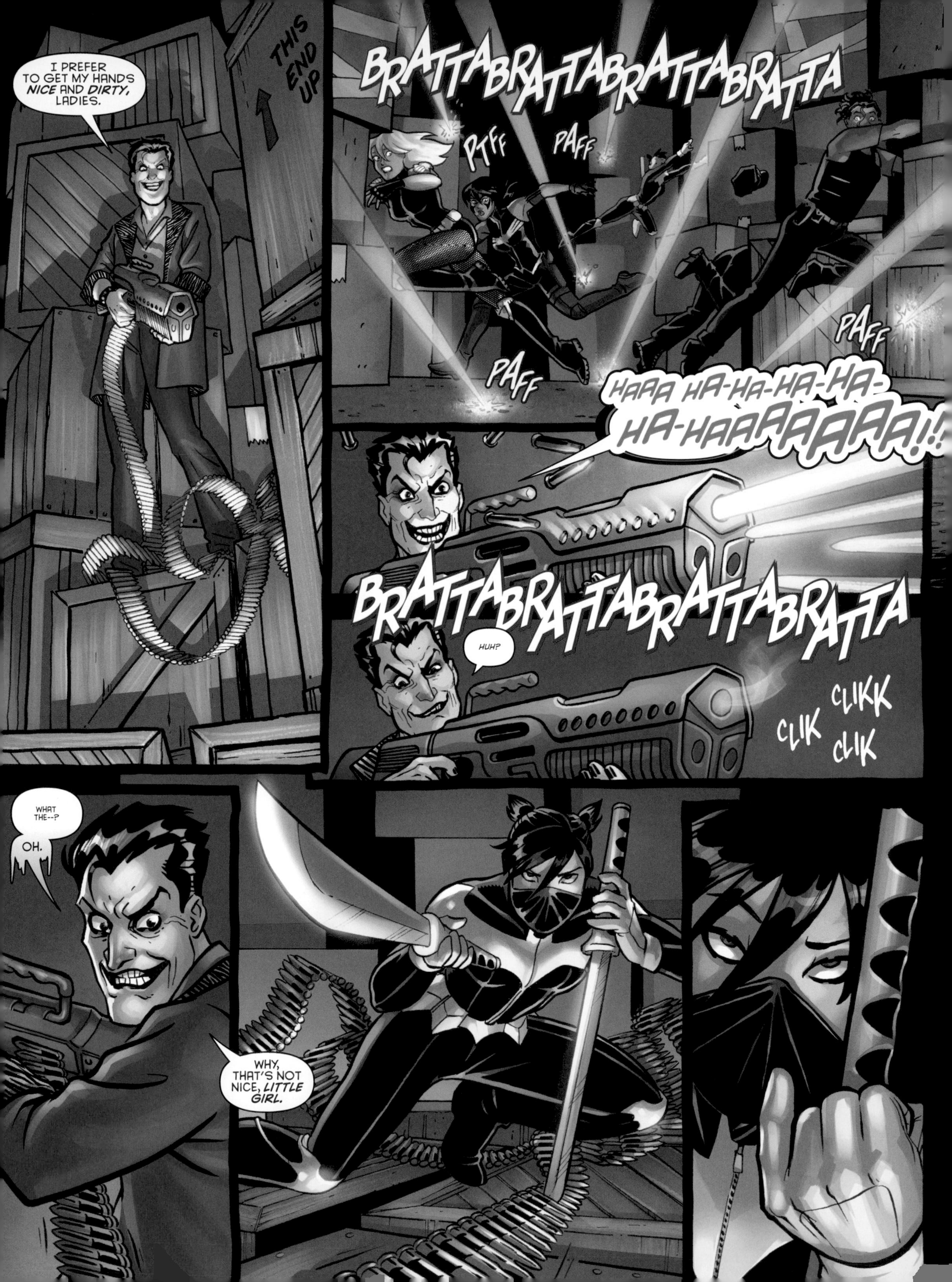

THIS END UP
I PREFER TO GET MY HANDS *NICE* AND *DIRTY,* LADIES.
BRATTABRATTABRATTABRATTA
PTFF
PAFF
PAFF
PAFF
HAAA HA-HA-HA-HA-HA-HAAAAAAAA!!
BRATTABRATTABRATTABRATTA
HUH?
CLIK
CLIKK
CLIK
WHAT THE--?
OH.
WHY, THAT'S NOT NICE, *LITTLE GIRL.*

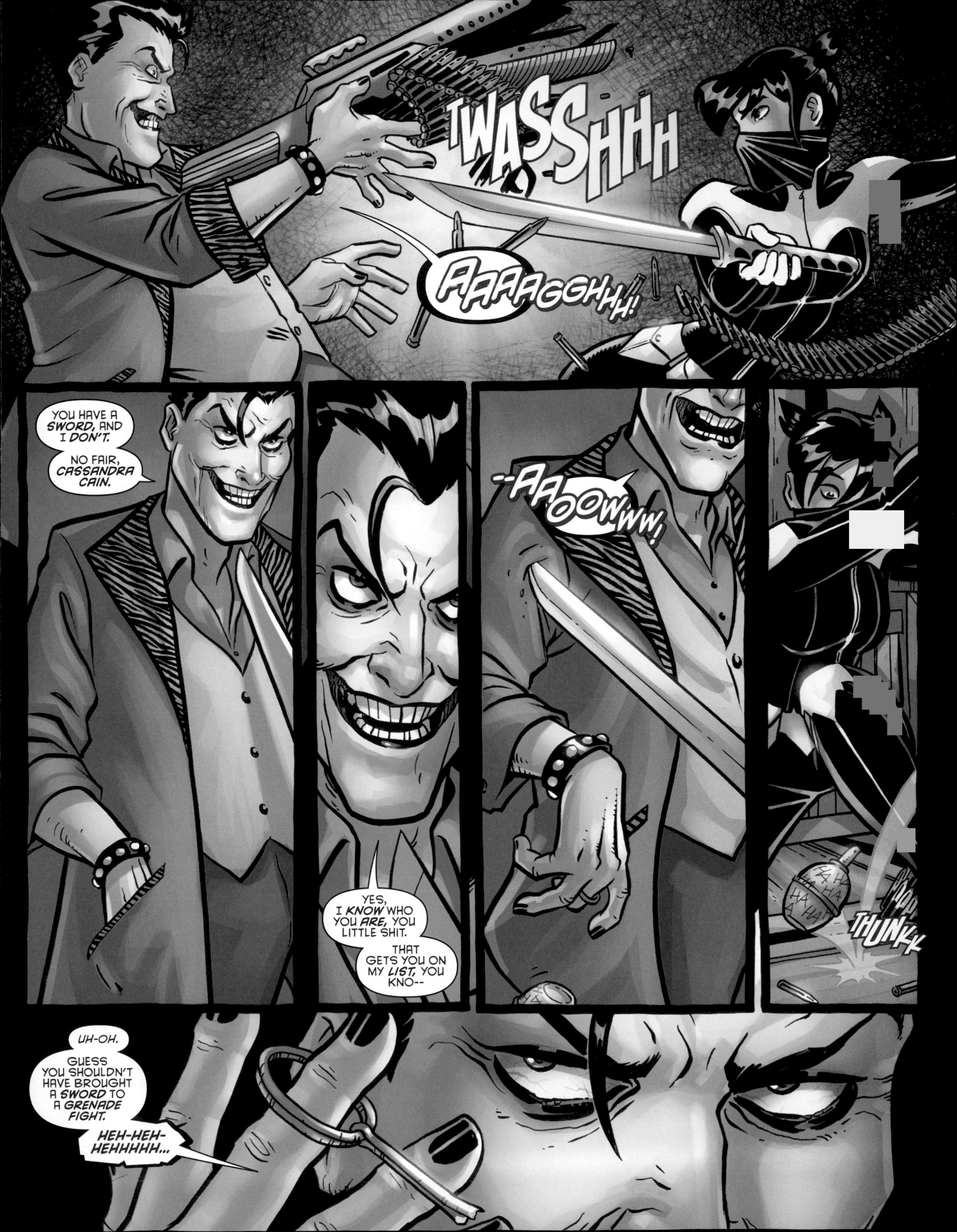
TWASSHHH
AAAAGGHHH!
YOU HAVE A SWORD, AND I DON'T.
NO FAIR, CASSANDRA CAIN.
YES, I KNOW WHO YOU ARE, YOU LITTLE SHIT.
THAT GETS YOU ON MY LIST, YOU KNO--
--AAOOWWW!
THUNKK
UH-OH.
GUESS YOU SHOULDN'T HAVE BROUGHT A SWORD TO A GRENADE FIGHT.
HEH-HEH-HEHHHHH...

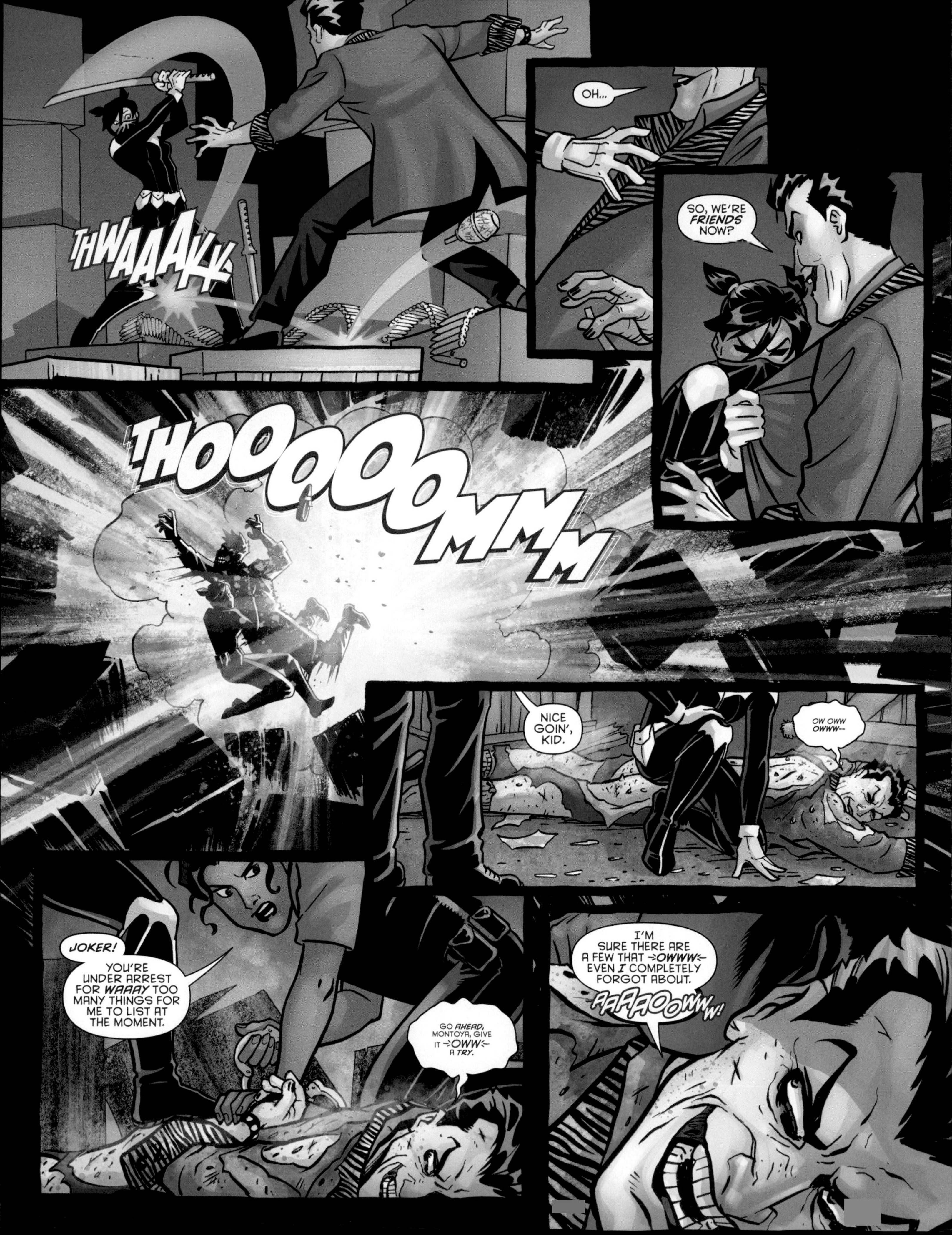
THWAAAKK
OH...
SO, WE'RE FRIENDS NOW?
THOOOOOOMMMM
NICE GOIN', KID.
OW OWW OWWW--
JOKER!
YOU'RE UNDER ARREST FOR WAAAY TOO MANY THINGS FOR ME TO LIST AT THE MOMENT.
GO AHEAD, MONTOYA, GIVE IT -OWW- A TRY.
I'M SURE THERE ARE A FEW THAT -OWWW- EVEN I COMPLETELY FORGOT ABOUT.
AAAAOOWWW!

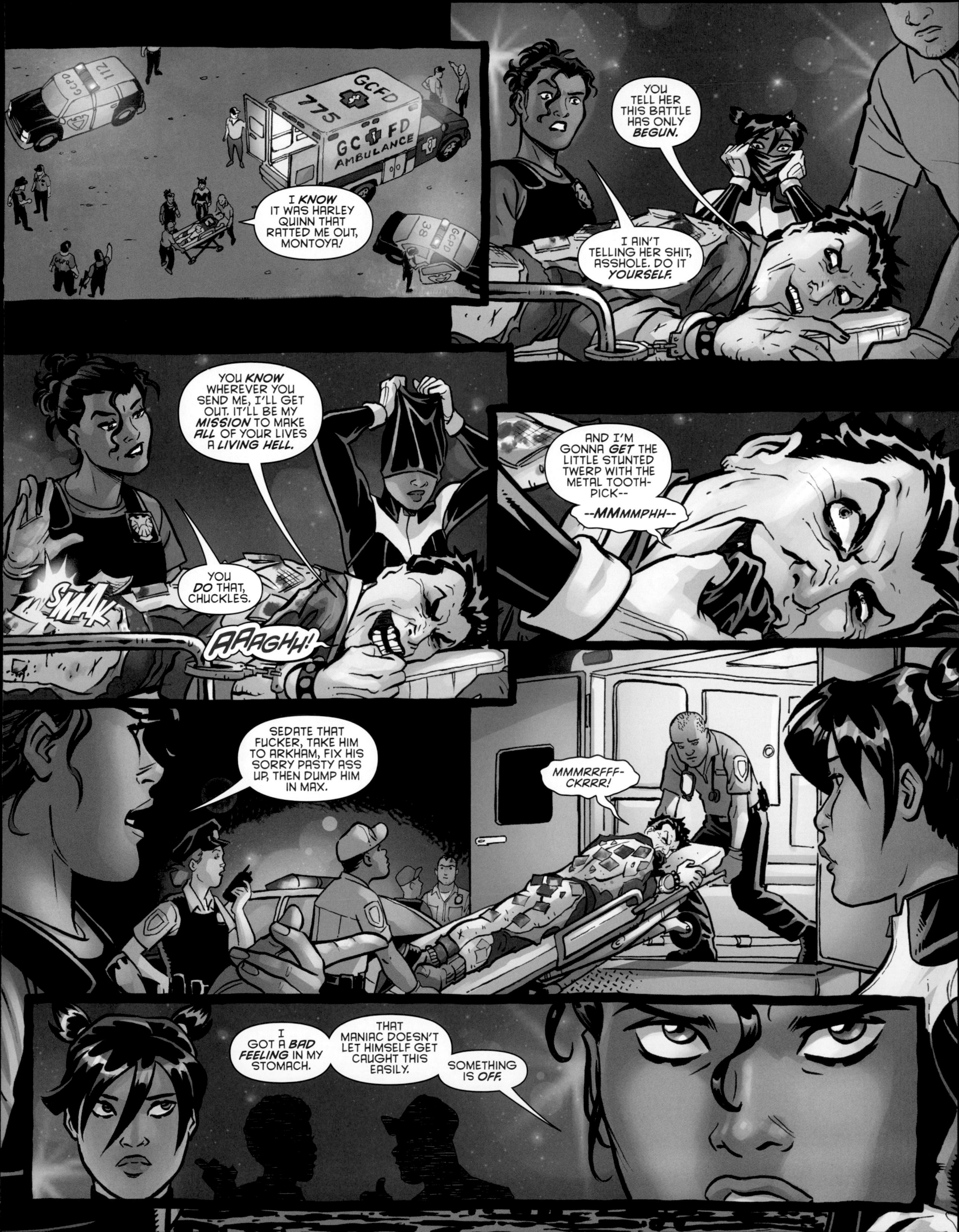
I KNOW IT WAS HARLEY QUINN THAT RATTED ME OUT, MONTOYA!
YOU TELL HER THIS BATTLE HAS ONLY BEGUN.
I AIN'T TELLING HER SHIT, ASSHOLE. DO IT YOURSELF.
YOU KNOW WHEREVER YOU SEND ME, I'LL GET OUT. IT'LL BE MY MISSION TO MAKE ALL OF YOUR LIVES A LIVING HELL.
YOU DO THAT, CHUCKLES.
SMAK
AAAGHH!
AND I'M GONNA GET THE LITTLE STUNTED TWERP WITH THE METAL TOOTH-PICK--
--MMMMPHH--
SEDATE THAT FUCKER, TAKE HIM TO ARKHAM, FIX HIS SORRY PASTY ASS UP, THEN DUMP HIM IN MAX.
MMMRRFFF-CKRRR!
I GOT A BAD FEELING IN MY STOMACH.
THAT MANIAC DOESN'T LET HIMSELF GET CAUGHT THIS EASILY.
SOMETHING IS OFF.

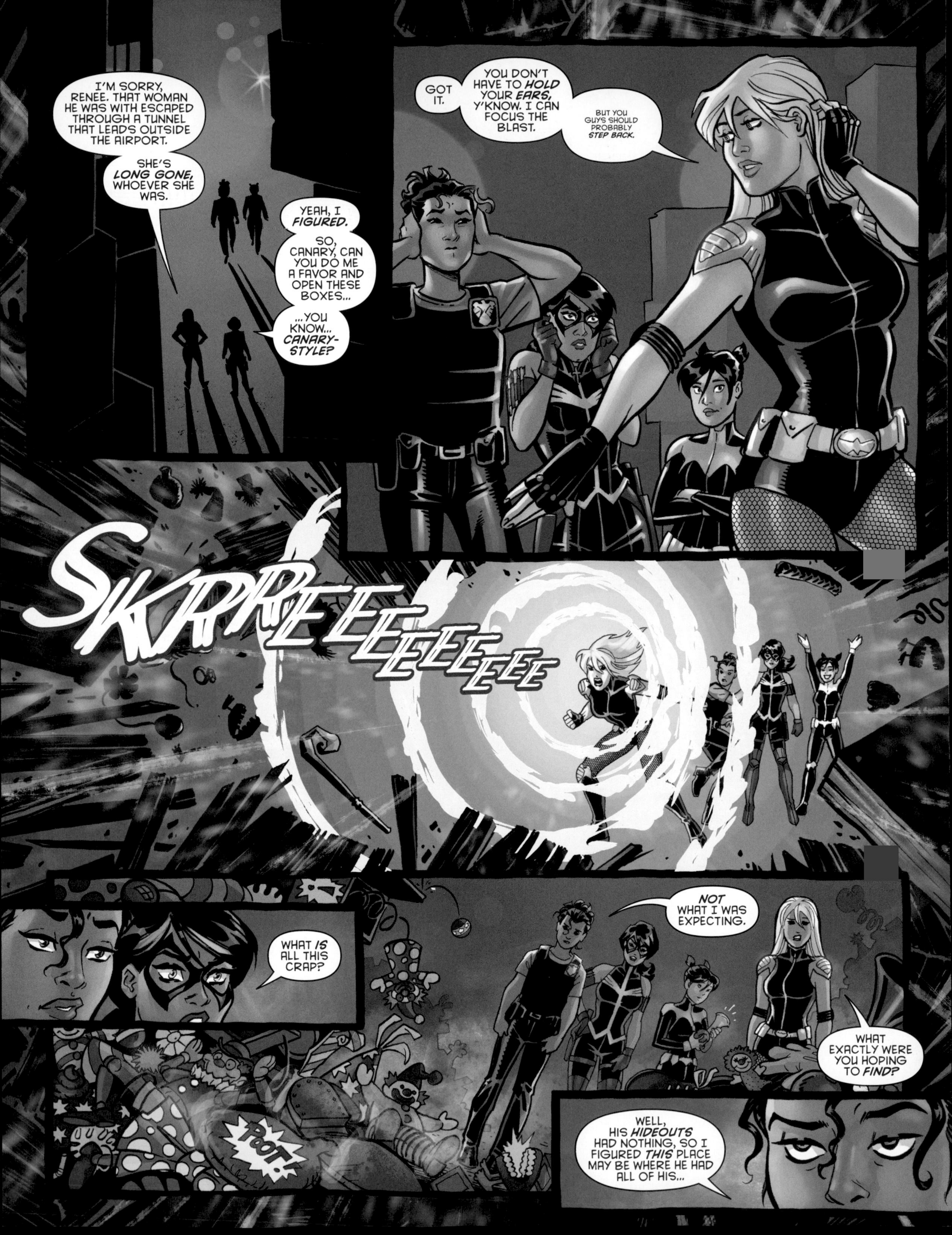
I'M SORRY, RENEE. THAT WOMAN HE WAS WITH ESCAPED THROUGH A TUNNEL THAT LEADS OUTSIDE THE AIRPORT.
SHE'S LONG GONE, WHOEVER SHE WAS.
YEAH, I FIGURED.
SO, CANARY, CAN YOU DO ME A FAVOR AND OPEN THESE BOXES...
...YOU KNOW... CANARY-STYLE?
GOT IT.
YOU DON'T HAVE TO HOLD YOUR EARS, Y'KNOW. I CAN FOCUS THE BLAST.
BUT YOU GUYS SHOULD PROBABLY STEP BACK.
SKRREEEEEEEEEE
WHAT IS ALL THIS CRAP?
NOT WHAT I WAS EXPECTING.
WHAT EXACTLY WERE YOU HOPING TO FIND?
POOT!
WELL, HIS HIDEOUTS HAD NOTHING, SO I FIGURED THIS PLACE MAY BE WHERE HE HAD ALL OF HIS...

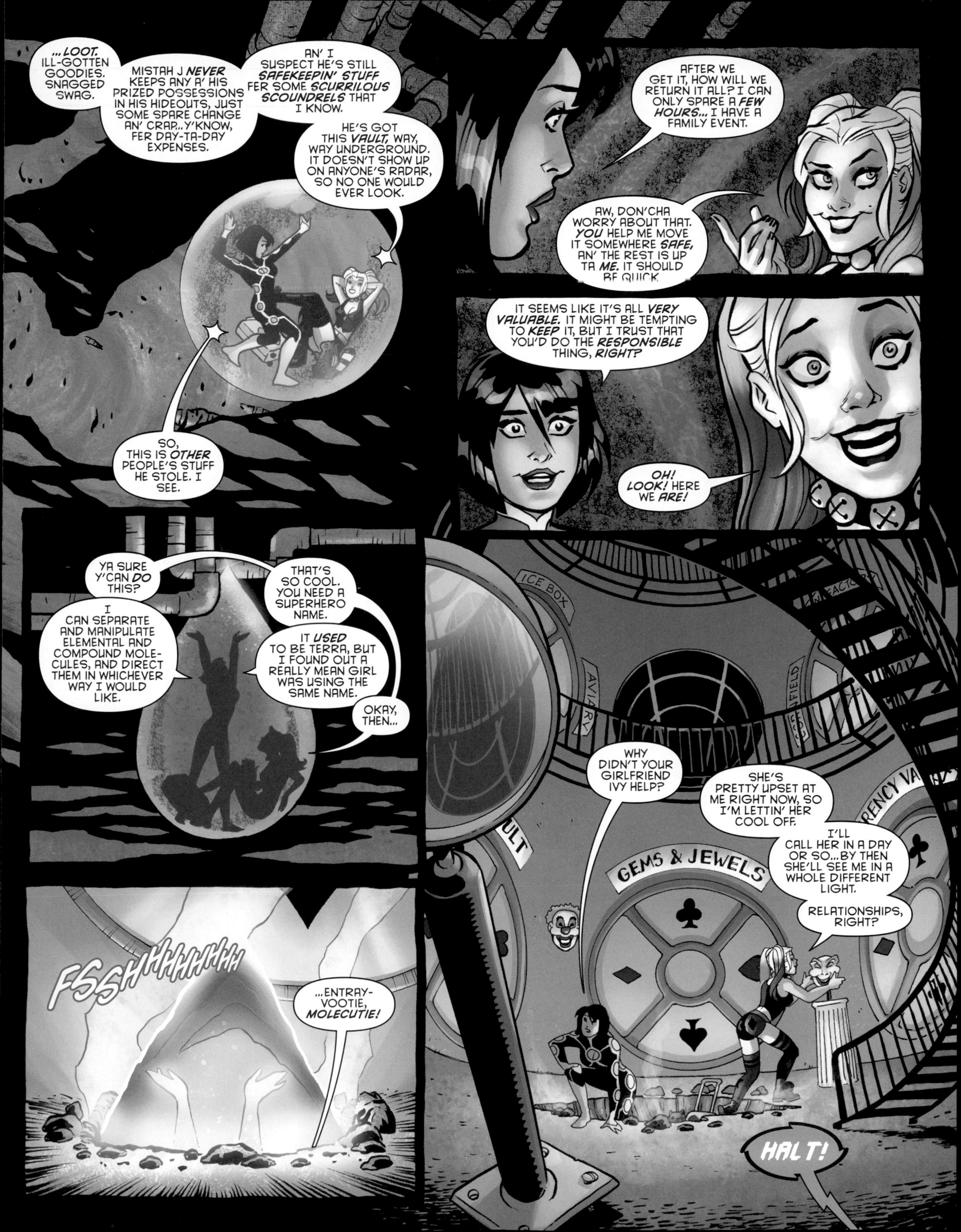
...LOOT. ILL-GOTTEN GOODIES. SNAGGED SWAG.
MISTAH J NEVER KEEPS ANY A' HIS PRIZED POSSESSIONS IN HIS HIDEOUTS, JUST SOME SPARE CHANGE AN' CRAP...Y'KNOW, FER DAY-TA-DAY EXPENSES.
AN' I SUSPECT HE'S STILL SAFEKEEPIN' STUFF FER SOME SCURRILOUS SCOUNDRELS THAT I KNOW.
HE'S GOT THIS VAULT, WAY, WAY UNDERGROUND. IT DOESN'T SHOW UP ON ANYONE'S RADAR, SO NO ONE WOULD EVER LOOK.
SO, THIS IS OTHER PEOPLE'S STUFF HE STOLE. I SEE.
AFTER WE GET IT, HOW WILL WE RETURN IT ALL? I CAN ONLY SPARE A FEW HOURS... I HAVE A FAMILY EVENT.
AW, DON'CHA WORRY ABOUT THAT. YOU HELP ME MOVE IT SOMEWHERE SAFE, AN' THE REST IS UP TA ME. IT SHOULD BE QUICK.
IT SEEMS LIKE IT'S ALL VERY VALUABLE. IT MIGHT BE TEMPTING TO KEEP IT, BUT I TRUST THAT YOU'D DO THE RESPONSIBLE THING, RIGHT?
OH! LOOK! HERE WE ARE!
YA SURE Y'CAN DO THIS?
I CAN SEPARATE AND MANIPULATE ELEMENTAL AND COMPOUND MOLECULES, AND DIRECT THEM IN WHICHEVER WAY I WOULD LIKE.
THAT'S SO COOL. YOU NEED A SUPERHERO NAME.
IT USED TO BE TERRA, BUT I FOUND OUT A REALLY MEAN GIRL WAS USING THE SAME NAME.
OKAY, THEN...
FSSHHHHHHHH
...ENTRAY-VOOTIE, MOLECUTIE!
ICE BOX
AVIARY
GEMS & JEWELS
WHY DIDN'T YOUR GIRLFRIEND IVY HELP?
SHE'S PRETTY UPSET AT ME RIGHT NOW, SO I'M LETTIN' HER COOL OFF.
I'LL CALL HER IN A DAY OR SO...BY THEN SHE'LL SEE ME IN A WHOLE DIFFERENT LIGHT.
RELATIONSHIPS, RIGHT?
HALT!

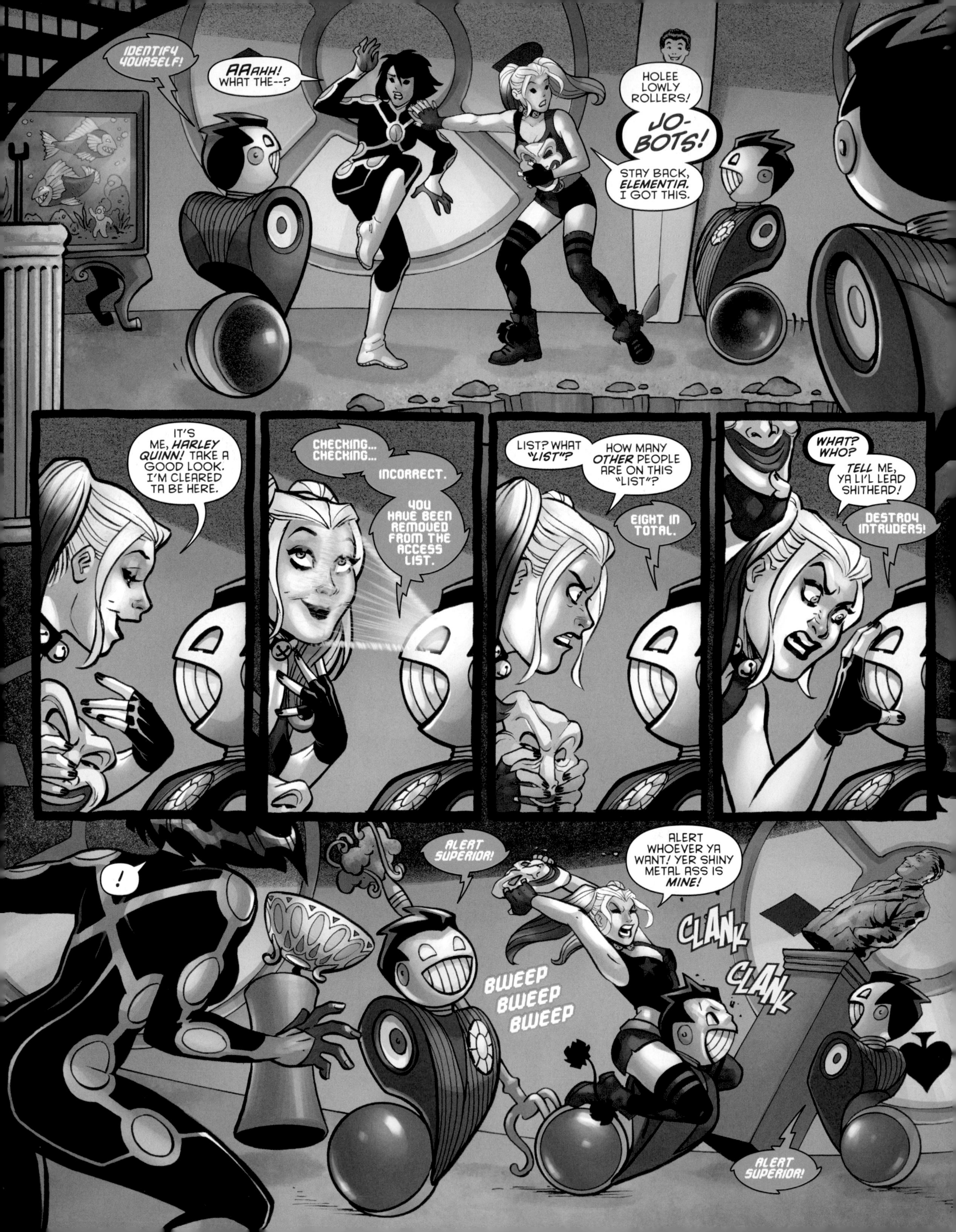

IDENTIFY YOURSELF!
AAAHH! WHAT THE--?
HOLEE LOWLY ROLLERS!
JO-BOTS!
STAY BACK, ELEMENTIA. I GOT THIS.
IT'S ME, HARLEY QUINN! TAKE A GOOD LOOK. I'M CLEARED TA BE HERE.
CHECKING... CHECKING...
INCORRECT.
YOU HAVE BEEN REMOVED FROM THE ACCESS LIST.
LIST? WHAT "LIST"?
HOW MANY OTHER PEOPLE ARE ON THIS "LIST"?
EIGHT IN TOTAL.
WHAT? WHO?
TELL ME, YA LI'L LEAD SHITHEAD!
DESTROY INTRUDERS!
!
ALERT SUPERIOR!
ALERT WHOEVER YA WANT! YER SHINY METAL ASS IS MINE!
CLANK
CLANK
BWEEP BWEEP BWEEP
ALERT SUPERIOR!

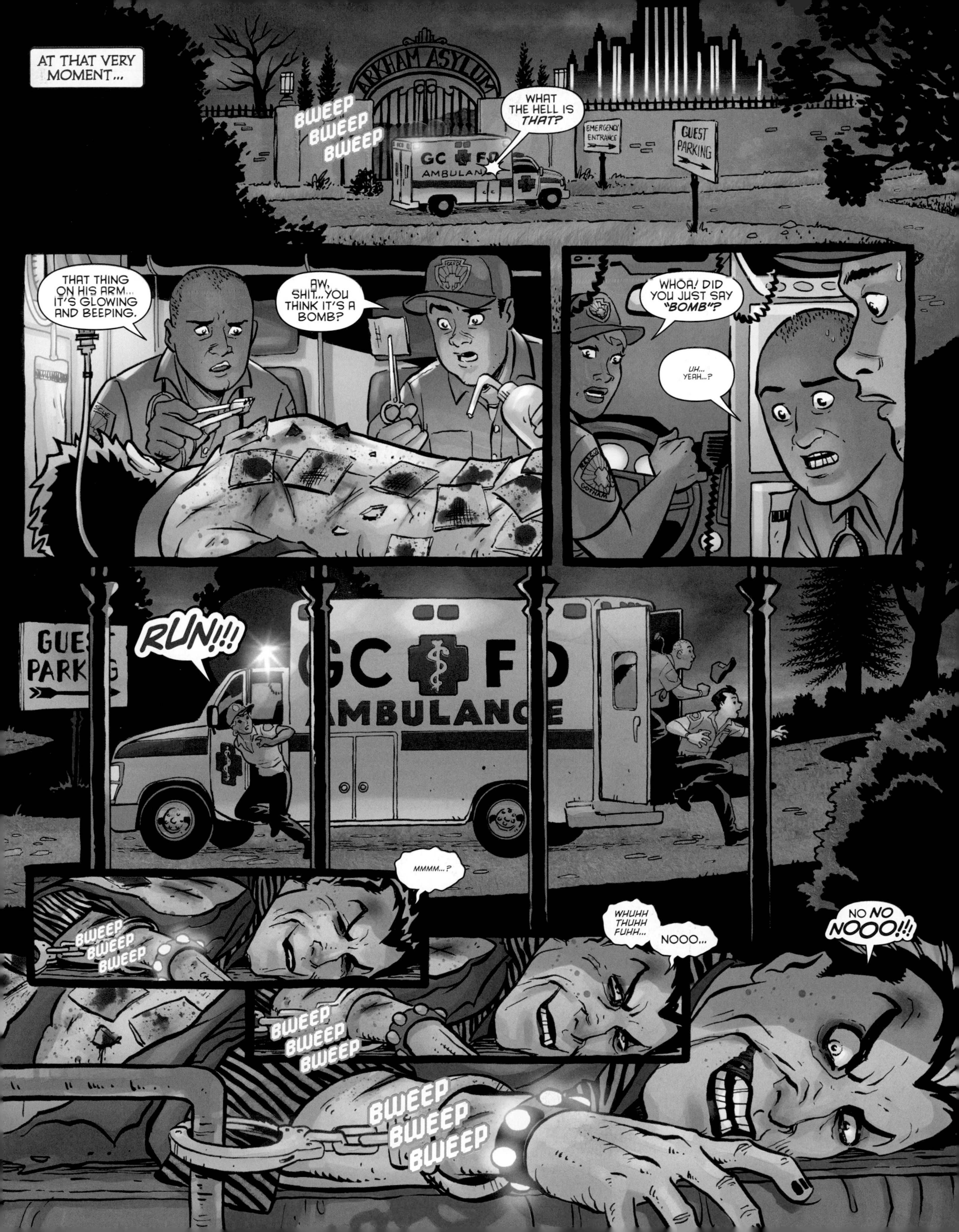
AT THAT VERY MOMENT...
ARKHAM ASYLUM
BWEEP BWEEP BWEEP
WHAT THE HELL IS THAT?
GC FD AMBULANCE
EMERGENCY ENTRANCE
GUEST PARKING
THAT THING ON HIS ARM... IT'S GLOWING AND BEEPING.
AW, SHIT...YOU THINK IT'S A BOMB?
WHOA! DID YOU JUST SAY "BOMB"?
UH... YEAH...?
GUEST PARKING
RUN!!!
GC FD
AMBULANCE
MMMM...?
BWEEP BWEEP BWEEP
WHUHH THUHH FUHH...
NOOO...
NO NO NOOO!!!
BWEEP BWEEP BWEEP
BWEEP BWEEP BWEEP

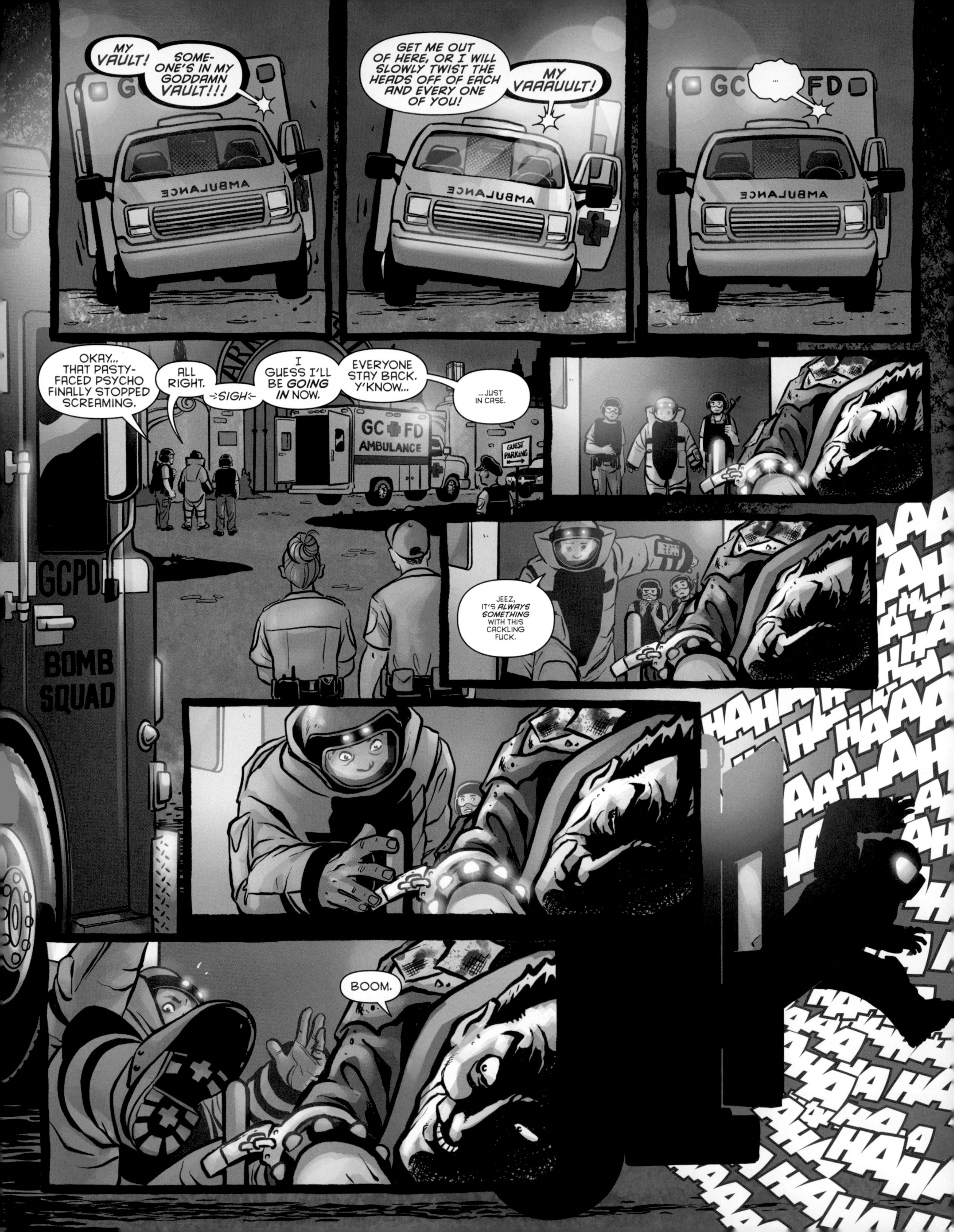
MY VAULT!
SOME-ONE'S IN MY GODDAMN VAULT!!!
AMBULANCE
GET ME OUT OF HERE, OR I WILL SLOWLY TWIST THE HEADS OFF OF EACH AND EVERY ONE OF YOU!
MY VAAAUUULT!
...
GC FD
OKAY... THAT PASTY-FACED PSYCHO FINALLY STOPPED SCREAMING.
ALL RIGHT.
-SIGH-
I GUESS I'LL BE GOING IN NOW.
EVERYONE STAY BACK. Y'KNOW...
...JUST IN CASE.
GC FD AMBULANCE
GUEST PARKING
GCPD
BOMB SQUAD
JEEZ, IT'S ALWAYS SOMETHING WITH THIS CACKLING FUCK.
BOOM.
HAHAHAHAHAHAHAHAHAHA

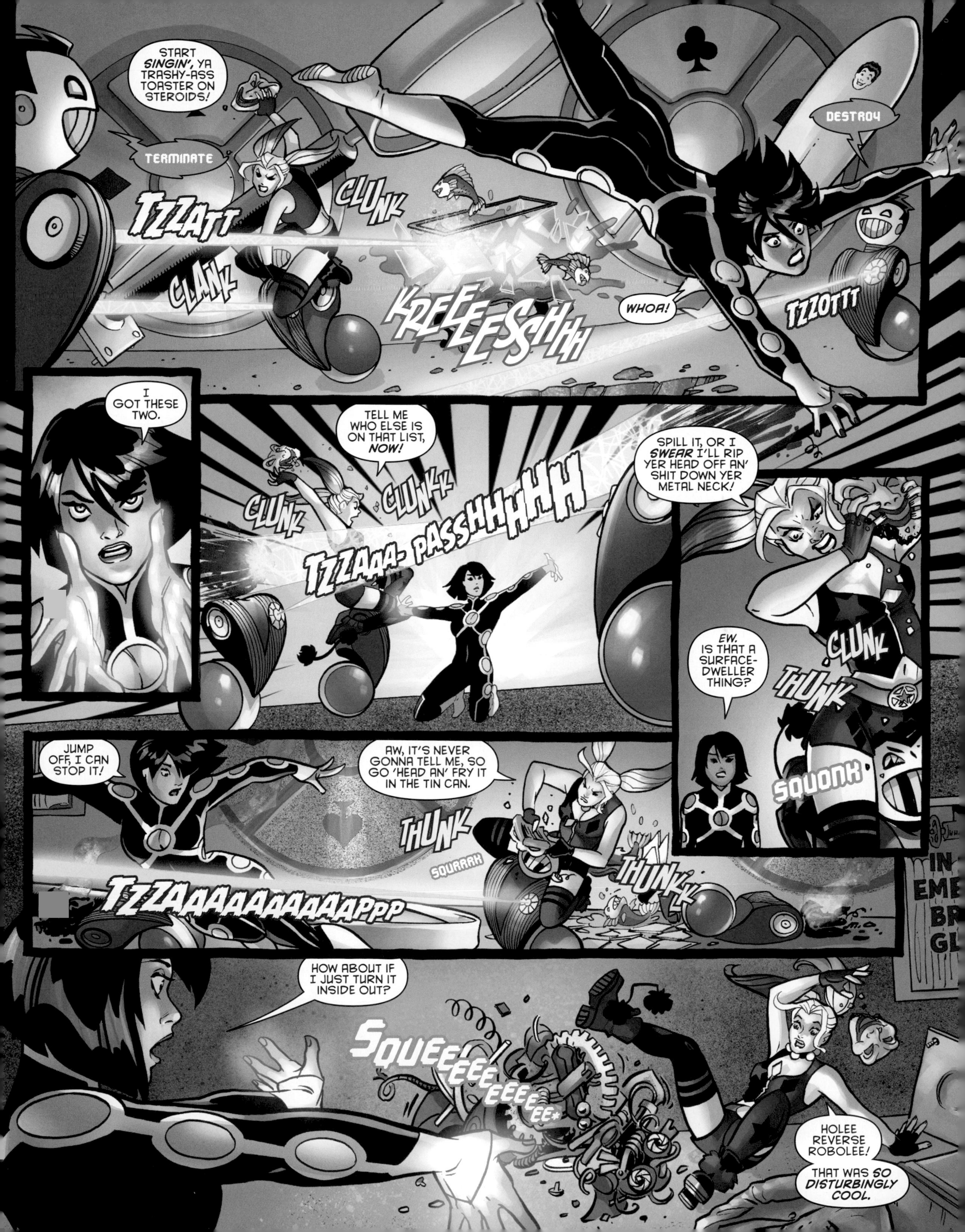
START *SINGIN'*, YA TRASHY-ASS TOASTER ON STEROIDS!
TERMINATE
TZZATT
CLUNK
CLANK
DESTROY
KREEEESHHHH
WHOA!
TZZOTTT
I GOT THESE TWO.
TELL ME WHO ELSE IS ON THAT LIST, *NOW!*
CLUNK
CLUNKK
TZZAAA- PASSHHHHHH
SPILL IT, OR I *SWEAR* I'LL RIP YER HEAD OFF AN' SHIT DOWN YER METAL NECK!
EW. IS THAT A SURFACE-DWELLER THING?
CLUNK
THUNK
SQUONK
JUMP OFF, I CAN STOP IT!
AW, IT'S NEVER GONNA TELL ME, SO GO 'HEAD AN' FRY IT IN THE TIN CAN.
THUNK
SQURRRK
THUNKK
TZZAAAAAAAAAAAPPP
HOW ABOUT IF I JUST TURN IT INSIDE OUT?
SQUEEEEEEEEEEEE*
HOLEE REVERSE ROBOLEE!
THAT WAS *SO DISTURBINGLY* COOL.

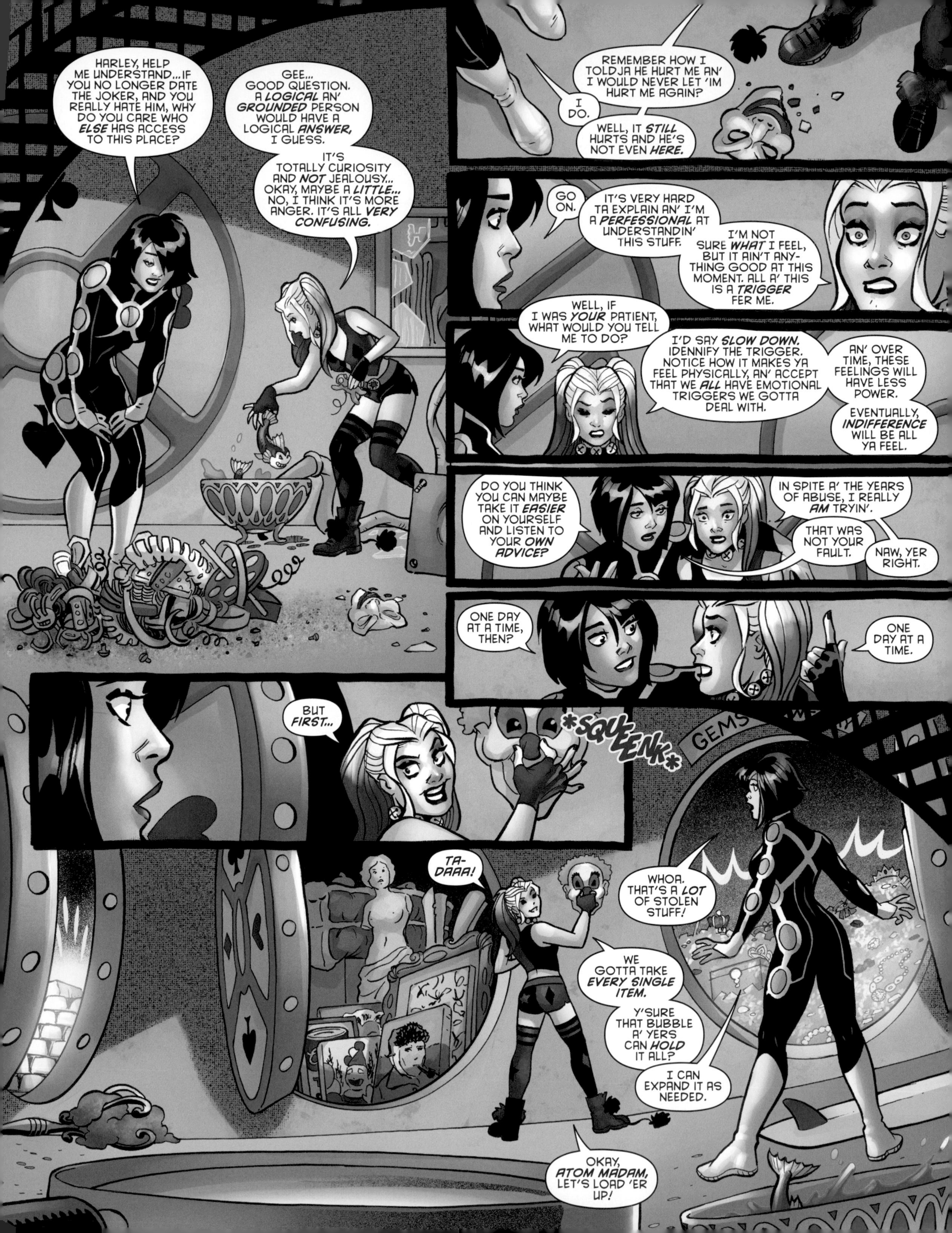
HARLEY, HELP ME UNDERSTAND... IF YOU NO LONGER DATE THE JOKER, AND YOU REALLY HATE HIM, WHY DO YOU CARE WHO *ELSE* HAS ACCESS TO THIS PLACE?
GEE... GOOD QUESTION. A *LOGICAL* AN' *GROUNDED* PERSON WOULD HAVE A LOGICAL *ANSWER,* I GUESS.
IT'S TOTALLY CURIOSITY AND *NOT* JEALOUSY... OKAY, MAYBE A *LITTLE...* NO, I THINK IT'S MORE ANGER. IT'S ALL *VERY CONFUSING.*
REMEMBER HOW I TOLDJA HE HURT ME AN' I WOULD NEVER LET 'IM HURT ME AGAIN?
I DO.
WELL, IT *STILL* HURTS AND HE'S NOT EVEN *HERE.*
GO ON.
IT'S VERY HARD TA EXPLAIN AN' I'M A *PERFESSIONAL* AT UNDERSTANDIN' THIS STUFF.
I'M NOT SURE *WHAT* I FEEL, BUT IT AIN'T ANY-THING GOOD AT THIS MOMENT. ALL A' THIS IS A *TRIGGER* FER ME.
WELL, IF I WAS *YOUR* PATIENT, WHAT WOULD YOU TELL ME TO DO?
I'D SAY *SLOW DOWN.* IDENNIFY THE TRIGGER. NOTICE HOW IT MAKES YA FEEL PHYSICALLY, AN' ACCEPT THAT WE *ALL* HAVE EMOTIONAL TRIGGERS WE GOTTA DEAL WITH.
AN' OVER TIME, THESE FEELINGS WILL HAVE LESS POWER.
EVENTUALLY, *INDIFFERENCE* WILL BE ALL YA FEEL.
DO YOU THINK YOU CAN MAYBE TAKE IT *EASIER* ON YOURSELF AND LISTEN TO YOUR *OWN ADVICE?*
IN SPITE A' THE YEARS OF ABUSE, I REALLY *AM* TRYIN'.
THAT WAS NOT YOUR FAULT.
NAW, YER RIGHT.
ONE DAY AT A TIME, THEN?
ONE DAY AT A TIME.
BUT *FIRST...*
SQUEEENK
GEMS
TA-DAAA!
WHOA. THAT'S A *LOT* OF STOLEN STUFF!
WE GOTTA TAKE *EVERY SINGLE ITEM.*
Y'SURE THAT BUBBLE A' YERS CAN *HOLD* IT ALL?
I CAN EXPAND IT AS NEEDED.
OKAY, *ATOM MADAM,* LET'S LOAD 'ER UP!

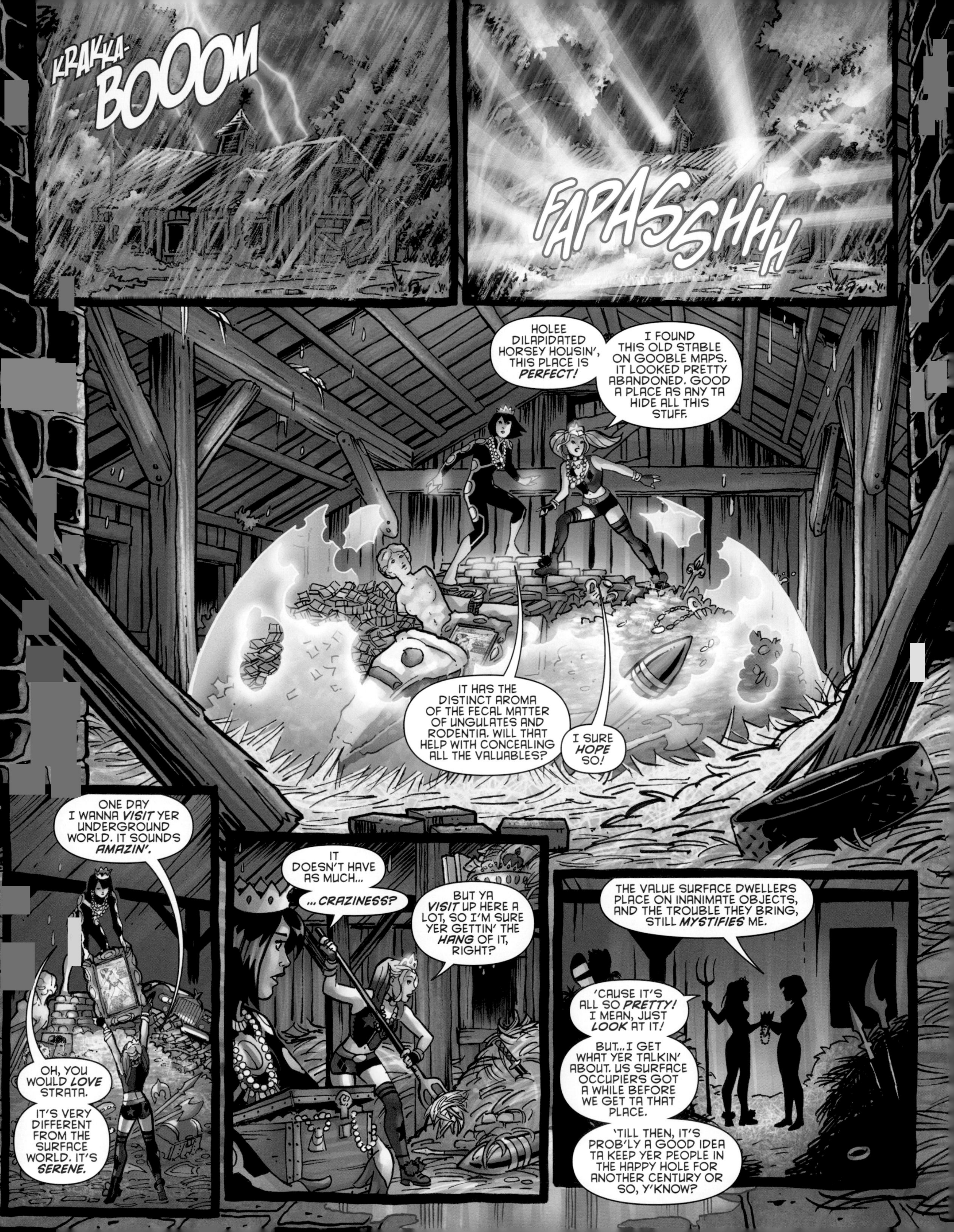
KRAKKA-BOOOOM
FAPASSHHH
HOLEE DILAPIDATED HORSEY HOUSIN', THIS PLACE IS *PERFECT!*
I FOUND THIS OLD STABLE ON GOOBLE MAPS. IT LOOKED PRETTY ABANDONED. GOOD A PLACE AS ANY TA HIDE ALL THIS STUFF.
IT HAS THE DISTINCT AROMA OF THE FECAL MATTER OF UNGULATES AND RODENTIA. WILL THAT HELP WITH CONCEALING ALL THE VALUABLES?
I SURE *HOPE* SO!
ONE DAY I WANNA *VISIT* YER UNDERGROUND WORLD. IT SOUNDS *AMAZIN'*.
OH, YOU WOULD *LOVE* STRATA.
IT'S VERY DIFFERENT FROM THE SURFACE WORLD. IT'S *SERENE.*
IT DOESN'T HAVE AS MUCH...
...CRAZINESS?
BUT YA *VISIT* UP HERE A LOT, SO I'M SURE YER GETTIN' THE *HANG* OF IT, RIGHT?
THE VALUE SURFACE DWELLERS PLACE ON INANIMATE OBJECTS, AND THE TROUBLE THEY BRING, STILL *MYSTIFIES* ME.
'CAUSE IT'S ALL SO *PRETTY!* I MEAN, JUST *LOOK* AT IT!
BUT... I GET WHAT YER TALKIN' ABOUT. US SURFACE OCCUPIERS GOT A WHILE BEFORE WE GET TA THAT PLACE.
'TILL THEN, IT'S PROB'LY A GOOD IDEA TA KEEP YER PEOPLE IN THE HAPPY HOLE FOR ANOTHER CENTURY OR SO, Y'KNOW?

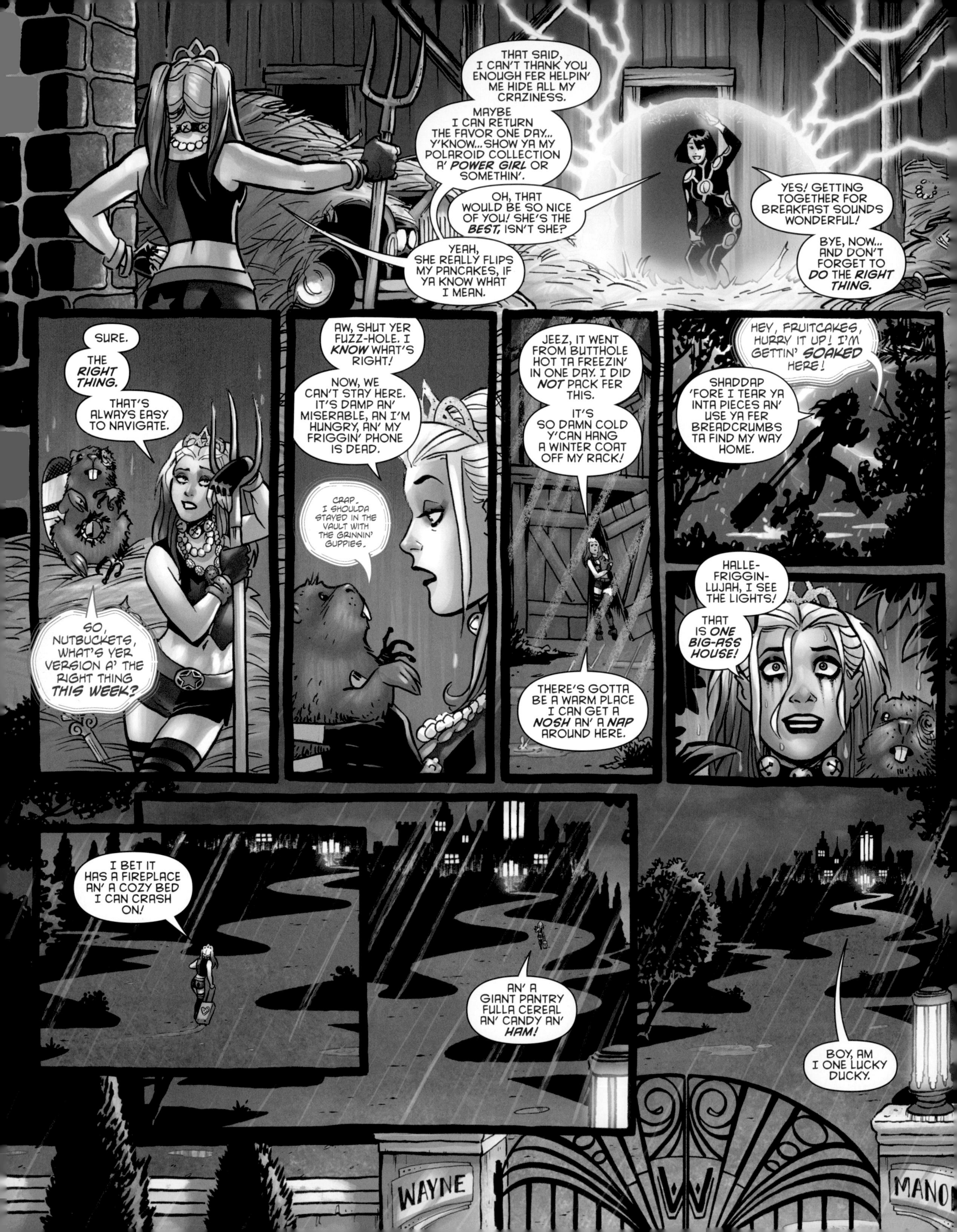
THAT SAID, I CAN'T THANK YOU ENOUGH FER HELPIN' ME HIDE ALL MY CRAZINESS.
MAYBE I CAN RETURN THE FAVOR ONE DAY... Y'KNOW... SHOW YA MY POLAROID COLLECTION A' POWER GIRL OR SOMETHIN'.
OH, THAT WOULD BE SO NICE OF YOU! SHE'S THE BEST, ISN'T SHE?
YEAH, SHE REALLY FLIPS MY PANCAKES, IF YA KNOW WHAT I MEAN.
YES! GETTING TOGETHER FOR BREAKFAST SOUNDS WONDERFUL!
BYE, NOW... AND DON'T FORGET TO DO THE RIGHT THING.
SURE.
THE RIGHT THING.
THAT'S ALWAYS EASY TO NAVIGATE.
SO, NUTBUCKETS, WHAT'S YER VERSION A' THE RIGHT THING THIS WEEK?
AW, SHUT YER FUZZ-HOLE. I KNOW WHAT'S RIGHT!
NOW, WE CAN'T STAY HERE. IT'S DAMP AN' MISERABLE, AN I'M HUNGRY, AN' MY FRIGGIN' PHONE IS DEAD.
CRAP. I SHOULDA STAYED IN THE VAULT WITH THE GRINNIN' GUPPIES.
JEEZ, IT WENT FROM BUTTHOLE HOT TA FREEZIN' IN ONE DAY. I DID NOT PACK FER THIS.
IT'S SO DAMN COLD Y'CAN HANG A WINTER COAT OFF MY RACK!
THERE'S GOTTA BE A WARM PLACE I CAN GET A NOSH AN' A NAP AROUND HERE.
HEY, FRUITCAKES, HURRY IT UP! I'M GETTIN' SOAKED HERE!
SHADDAP 'FORE I TEAR YA INTA PIECES AN' USE YA FER BREADCRUMBS TA FIND MY WAY HOME.
HALLE-FRIGGIN-LUJAH, I SEE THE LIGHTS!
THAT IS ONE BIG-ASS HOUSE!
I BET IT HAS A FIREPLACE AN' A COZY BED I CAN CRASH ON!
AN' A GIANT PANTRY FULLA CEREAL AN' CANDY AN' HAM!
BOY, AM I ONE LUCKY DUCKY.
WAYNE
MANO

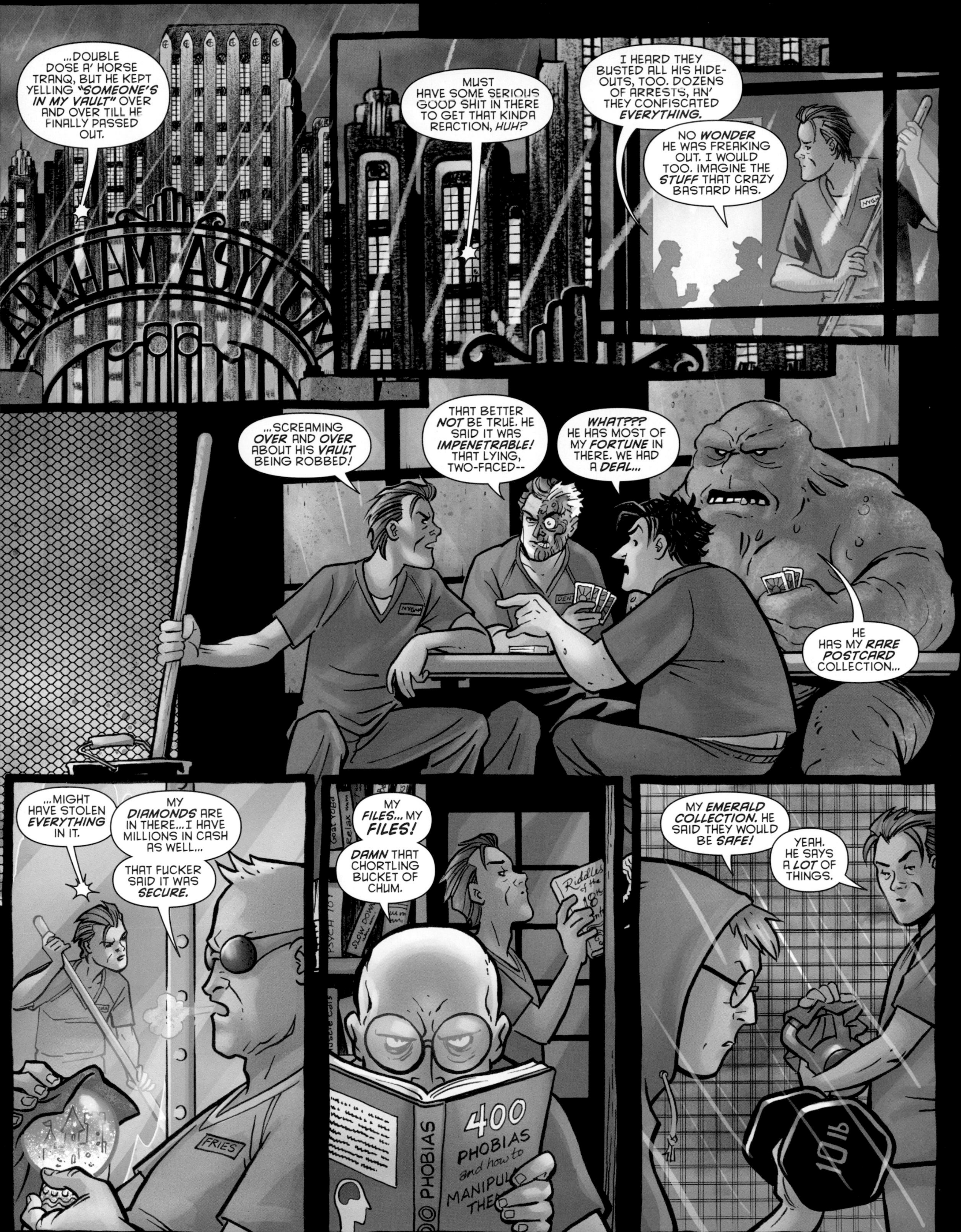

...DOUBLE DOSE A' HORSE TRANQ, BUT HE KEPT YELLING "SOMEONE'S IN MY VAULT" OVER AND OVER TILL HE FINALLY PASSED OUT.
ARKHAM ASYLUM
MUST HAVE SOME SERIOUS GOOD SHIT IN THERE TO GET THAT KINDA REACTION, HUH?
I HEARD THEY BUSTED ALL HIS HIDE-OUTS, TOO. DOZENS OF ARRESTS, AN' THEY CONFISCATED EVERYTHING.
NO WONDER HE WAS FREAKING OUT. I WOULD TOO. IMAGINE THE STUFF THAT CRAZY BASTARD HAS.
...SCREAMING OVER AND OVER ABOUT HIS VAULT BEING ROBBED!
THAT BETTER NOT BE TRUE. HE SAID IT WAS IMPENETRABLE! THAT LYING, TWO-FACED--
WHAT??? HE HAS MOST OF MY FORTUNE IN THERE. WE HAD A DEAL...
HE HAS MY RARE POSTCARD COLLECTION...
...MIGHT HAVE STOLEN EVERYTHING IN IT.
MY DIAMONDS ARE IN THERE...I HAVE MILLIONS IN CASH AS WELL...
THAT FUCKER SAID IT WAS SECURE.
FRIES
MY FILES... MY FILES!
DAMN THAT CHORTLING BUCKET OF CHUM.
400 PHOBIAS and how to MANIPULATE THEM
PHOBIAS
MY EMERALD COLLECTION. HE SAID THEY WOULD BE SAFE!
YEAH. HE SAYS A LOT OF THINGS.
10lb

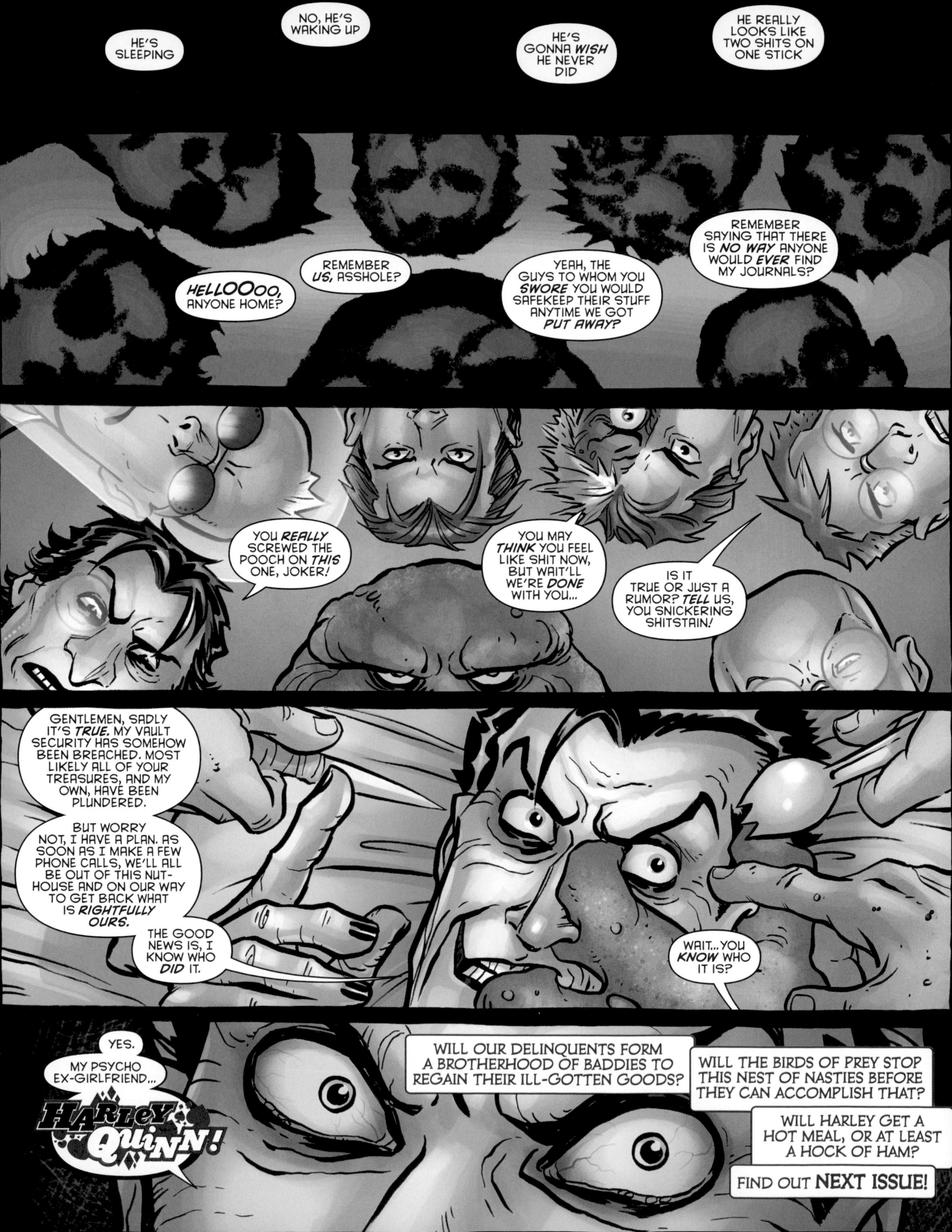
HE'S SLEEPING
NO, HE'S WAKING UP
HE'S GONNA WISH HE NEVER DID
HE REALLY LOOKS LIKE TWO SHITS ON ONE STICK
HELLOOoo, ANYONE HOME?
REMEMBER US, ASSHOLE?
YEAH, THE GUYS TO WHOM YOU SWORE YOU WOULD SAFEKEEP THEIR STUFF ANYTIME WE GOT PUT AWAY?
REMEMBER SAYING THAT THERE IS NO WAY ANYONE WOULD EVER FIND MY JOURNALS?
YOU REALLY SCREWED THE POOCH ON THIS ONE, JOKER!
YOU MAY THINK YOU FEEL LIKE SHIT NOW, BUT WAIT'LL WE'RE DONE WITH YOU...
IS IT TRUE OR JUST A RUMOR? TELL US, YOU SNICKERING SHITSTAIN!
GENTLEMEN, SADLY IT'S TRUE. MY VAULT SECURITY HAS SOMEHOW BEEN BREACHED. MOST LIKELY ALL OF YOUR TREASURES, AND MY OWN, HAVE BEEN PLUNDERED.
BUT WORRY NOT, I HAVE A PLAN. AS SOON AS I MAKE A FEW PHONE CALLS, WE'LL ALL BE OUT OF THIS NUT-HOUSE AND ON OUR WAY TO GET BACK WHAT IS RIGHTFULLY OURS.
THE GOOD NEWS IS, I KNOW WHO DID IT.
WAIT... YOU KNOW WHO IT IS?
YES.
MY PSYCHO EX-GIRLFRIEND...
HARLEY QUINN!
WILL OUR DELINQUENTS FORM A BROTHERHOOD OF BADDIES TO REGAIN THEIR ILL-GOTTEN GOODS?
WILL THE BIRDS OF PREY STOP THIS NEST OF NASTIES BEFORE THEY CAN ACCOMPLISH THAT?
WILL HARLEY GET A HOT MEAL, OR AT LEAST A HOCK OF HAM?
FIND OUT NEXT ISSUE!

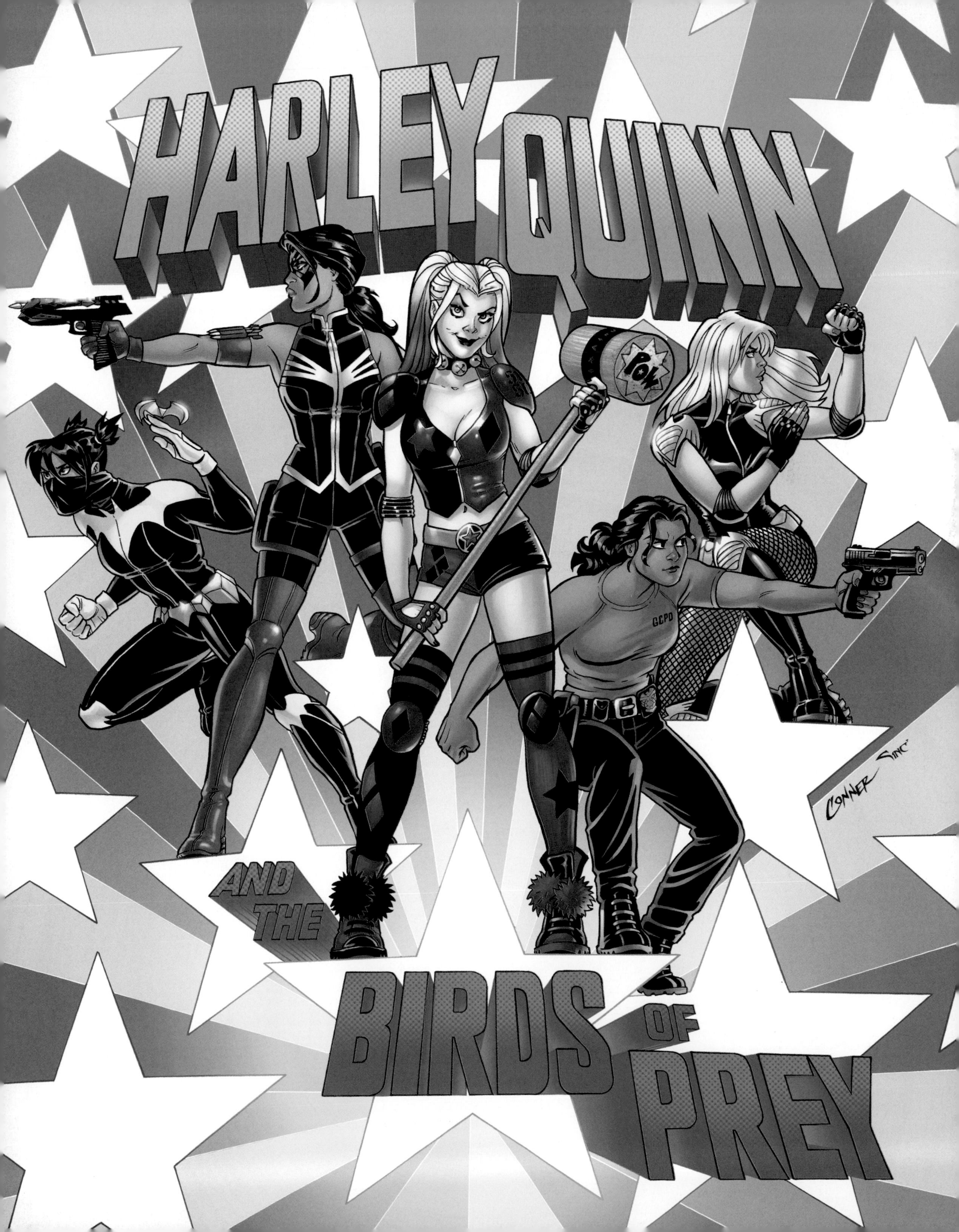
HARLEY QUINN
AND THE
BIRDS OF PREY
POW
GCPD
CONNER SINC

BOOK THREE
GOTHAM TOWN SMACKDOWN!

"I DO have a plan that maybe ya can help me with..."

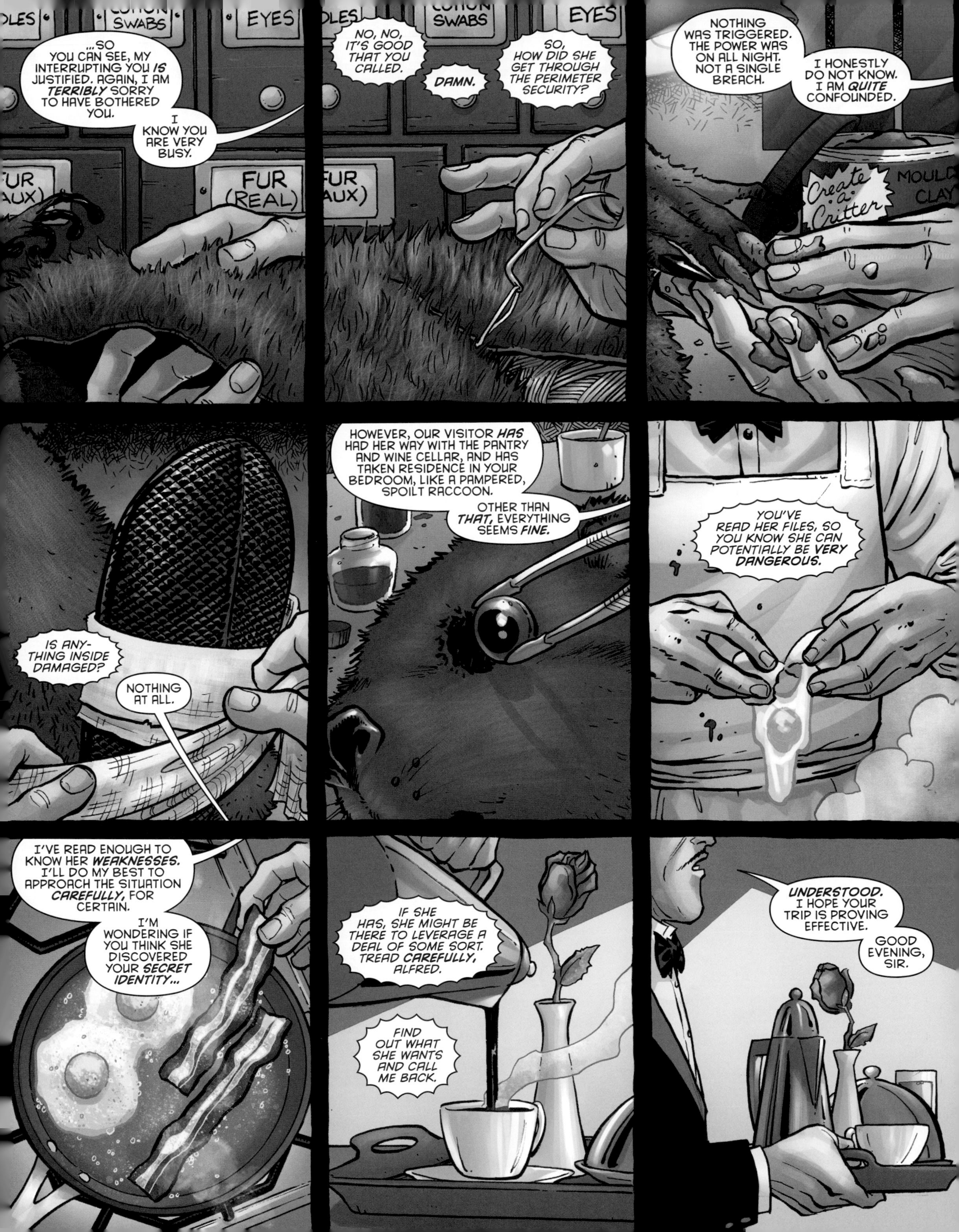

OLES
COTTON SWABS
EYES
...SO YOU CAN SEE, MY INTERRUPTING YOU *IS* JUSTIFIED. AGAIN, I AM *TERRIBLY* SORRY TO HAVE BOTHERED YOU.
I KNOW YOU ARE VERY BUSY.
FUR (FAUX)
FUR (REAL)
NO, NO, IT'S GOOD THAT YOU CALLED.
DAMN.
SO, HOW DID SHE GET THROUGH THE PERIMETER SECURITY?
FUR (FAUX)
NOTHING WAS TRIGGERED. THE POWER WAS ON ALL NIGHT. NOT A SINGLE BREACH.
I HONESTLY DO NOT KNOW. I AM *QUITE* CONFOUNDED.
Create a Critter
MOULD CLAY
IS ANYTHING INSIDE DAMAGED?
NOTHING AT ALL.
HOWEVER, OUR VISITOR *HAS* HAD HER WAY WITH THE PANTRY AND WINE CELLAR, AND HAS TAKEN RESIDENCE IN YOUR BEDROOM, LIKE A PAMPERED, SPOILT RACCOON.
OTHER THAN *THAT*, EVERYTHING SEEMS *FINE.*
YOU'VE READ HER FILES, SO YOU KNOW SHE CAN POTENTIALLY BE *VERY DANGEROUS.*
I'VE READ ENOUGH TO KNOW HER *WEAKNESSES.* I'LL DO MY BEST TO APPROACH THE SITUATION *CAREFULLY,* FOR CERTAIN.
I'M WONDERING IF YOU THINK SHE DISCOVERED YOUR *SECRET IDENTITY*...
IF SHE HAS, SHE MIGHT BE THERE TO LEVERAGE A DEAL OF SOME SORT. TREAD *CAREFULLY,* ALFRED.
FIND OUT WHAT SHE WANTS AND CALL ME BACK.
UNDERSTOOD. I HOPE YOUR TRIP IS PROVING EFFECTIVE.
GOOD EVENING, SIR.

GOTHAM TOWN SMACK DOWN

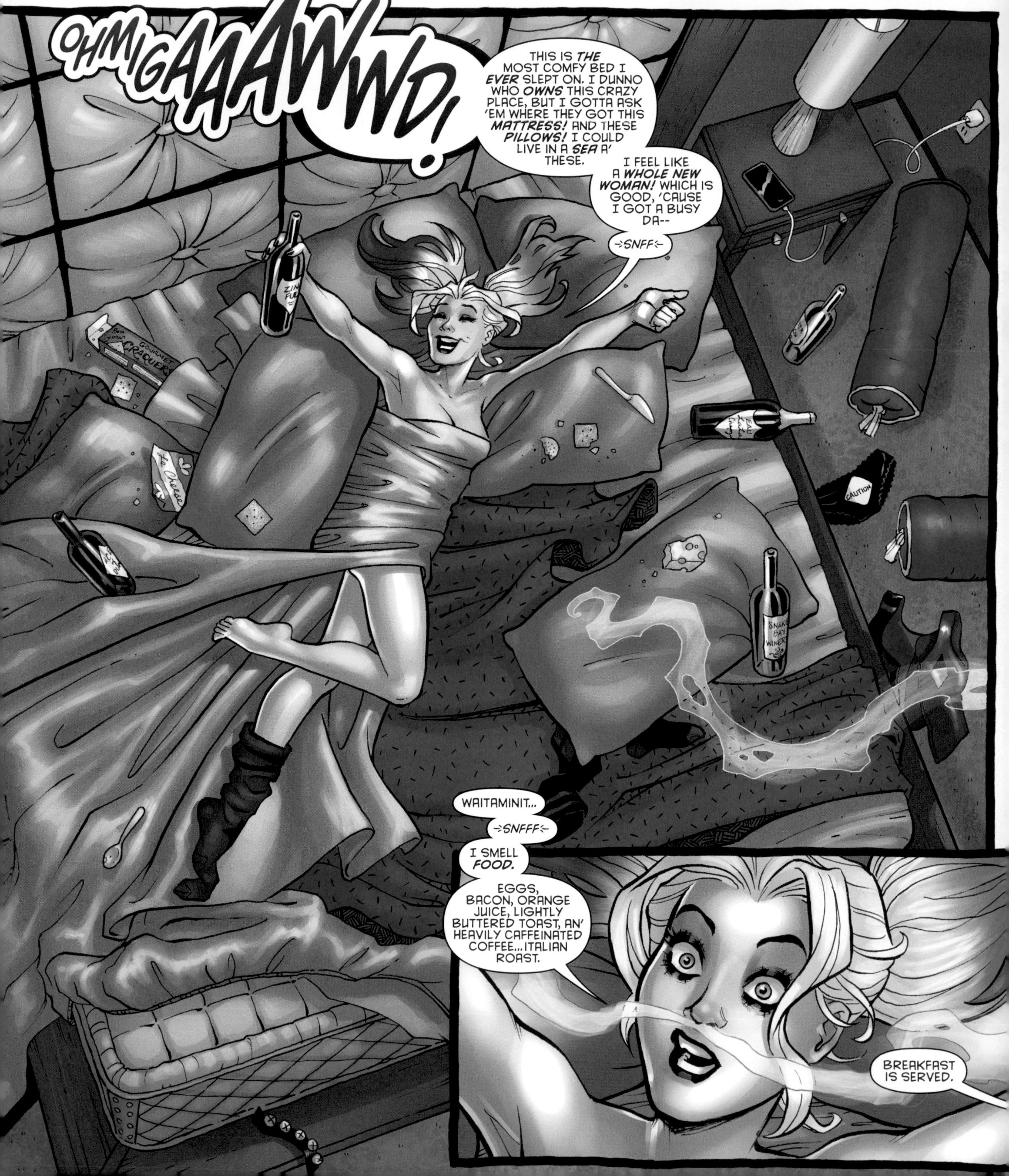
OHMIGAAAWWD!
THIS IS THE MOST COMFY BED I EVER SLEPT ON. I DUNNO WHO OWNS THIS CRAZY PLACE, BUT I GOTTA ASK 'EM WHERE THEY GOT THIS MATTRESS! AND THESE PILLOWS! I COULD LIVE IN A SEA A' THESE.
I FEEL LIKE A WHOLE NEW WOMAN! WHICH IS GOOD, 'CAUSE I GOT A BUSY DA--
SNFF
GOURMET CRAQUERS
Le Cheese
CAUTION
SNAKE BAY WINERY
WAITAMINIT...
SNFFF
I SMELL FOOD.
EGGS, BACON, ORANGE JUICE, LIGHTLY BUTTERED TOAST, AN' HEAVILY CAFFEINATED COFFEE... ITALIAN ROAST.
BREAKFAST IS SERVED.

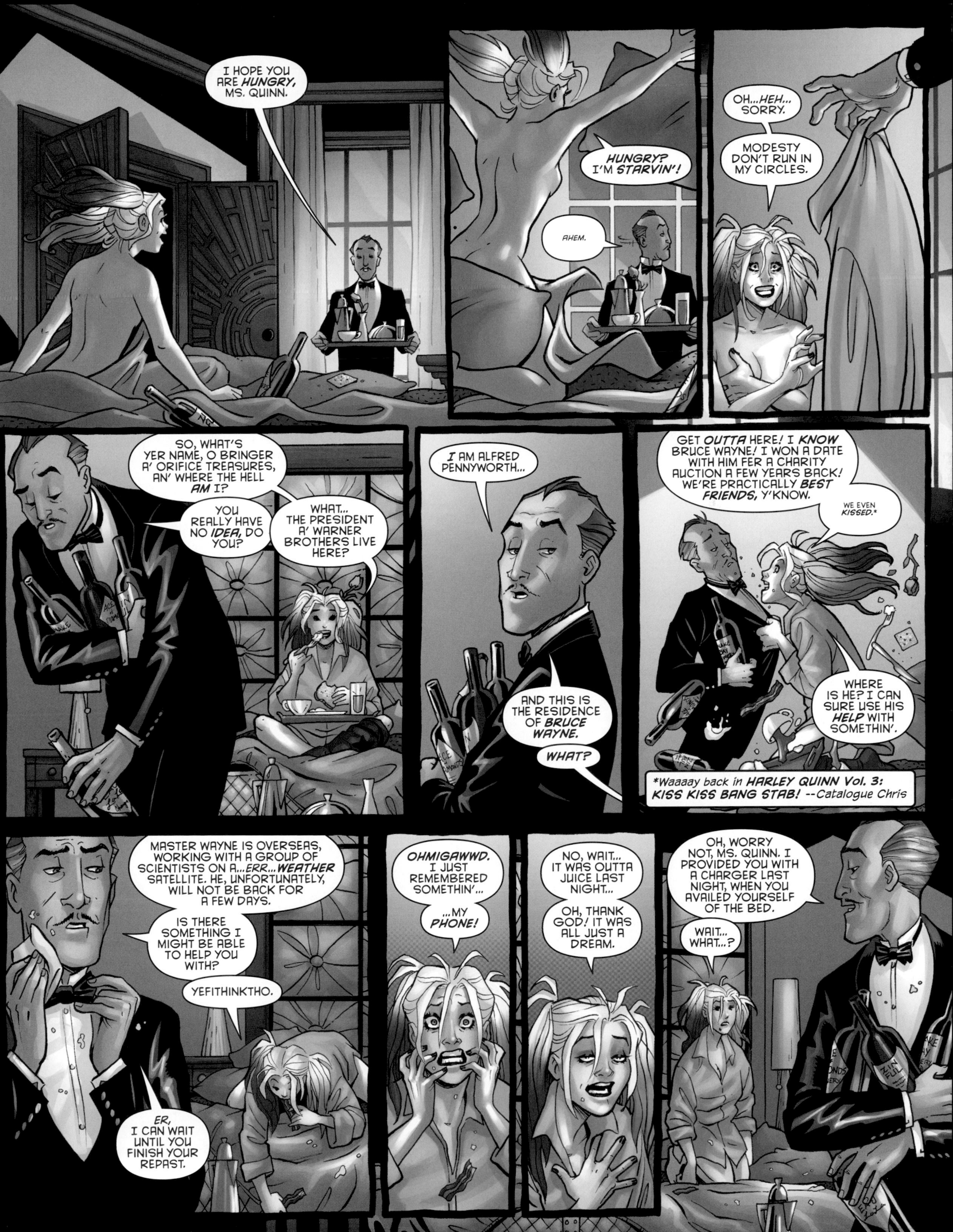

I HOPE YOU ARE HUNGRY, MS. QUINN.
HUNGRY? I'M STARVIN'!
AHEM.
OH...HEH... SORRY.
MODESTY DON'T RUN IN MY CIRCLES.
SO, WHAT'S YER NAME, O BRINGER A' ORIFICE TREASURES, AN' WHERE THE HELL AM I?
YOU REALLY HAVE NO IDEA, DO YOU?
WHAT... THE PRESIDENT A' WARNER BROTHERS LIVE HERE?
I AM ALFRED PENNYWORTH...
AND THIS IS THE RESIDENCE OF BRUCE WAYNE.
WHAT?
GET OUTTA HERE! I KNOW BRUCE WAYNE! I WON A DATE WITH HIM FER A CHARITY AUCTION A FEW YEARS BACK! WE'RE PRACTICALLY BEST FRIENDS, Y'KNOW.
WE EVEN KISSED.*
WHERE IS HE? I CAN SURE USE HIS HELP WITH SOMETHIN'.
*Waaaay back in HARLEY QUINN Vol. 3: KISS KISS BANG STAB! --Catalogue Chris
MASTER WAYNE IS OVERSEAS, WORKING WITH A GROUP OF SCIENTISTS ON A...ERR...WEATHER SATELLITE. HE, UNFORTUNATELY, WILL NOT BE BACK FOR A FEW DAYS.
IS THERE SOMETHING I MIGHT BE ABLE TO HELP YOU WITH?
YEFITHINKTHO.
ER, I CAN WAIT UNTIL YOU FINISH YOUR REPAST.
OHMIGAWWD. I JUST REMEMBERED SOMETHIN'...
...MY PHONE!
NO, WAIT... IT WAS OUTTA JUICE LAST NIGHT...
OH, THANK GOD! IT WAS ALL JUST A DREAM.
OH, WORRY NOT, MS. QUINN. I PROVIDED YOU WITH A CHARGER LAST NIGHT, WHEN YOU AVAILED YOURSELF OF THE BED.
WAIT... WHAT...?

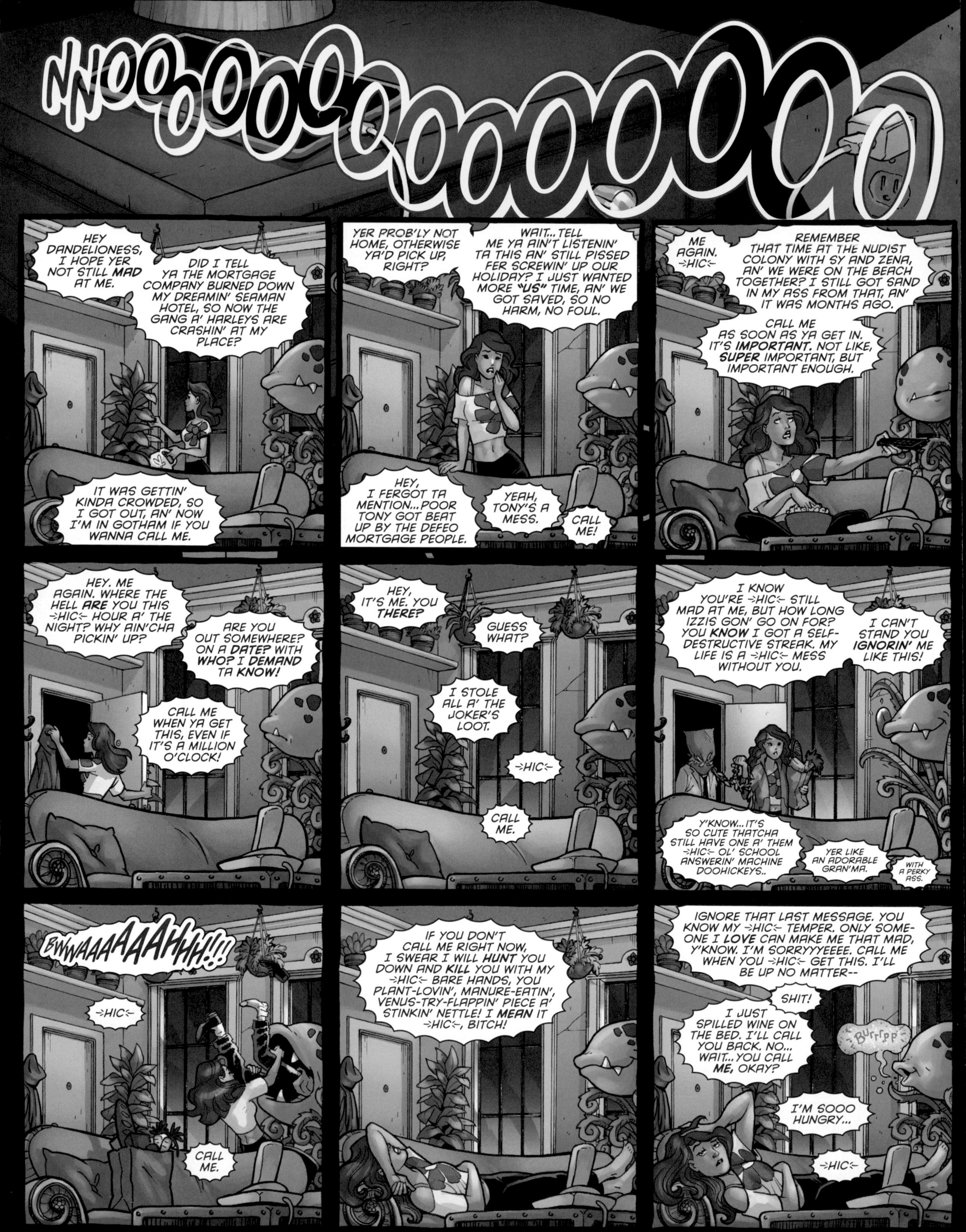
NNOOOOOOOOOOOOOOOO
HEY DANDELIONESS, I HOPE YER NOT STILL MAD AT ME.
DID I TELL YA THE MORTGAGE COMPANY BURNED DOWN MY DREAMIN' SEAMAN HOTEL, SO NOW THE GANG A' HARLEYS ARE CRASHIN' AT MY PLACE?
IT WAS GETTIN' KINDA CROWDED, SO I GOT OUT, AN' NOW I'M IN GOTHAM IF YOU WANNA CALL ME.
YER PROB'LY NOT HOME, OTHERWISE YA'D PICK UP, RIGHT?
WAIT... TELL ME YA AIN'T LISTENIN' TA THIS AN' STILL PISSED FER SCREWIN' UP OUR HOLIDAY? I JUST WANTED MORE "US" TIME, AN' WE GOT SAVED, SO NO HARM, NO FOUL.
HEY, I FERGOT TA MENTION... POOR TONY GOT BEAT UP BY THE DEFEO MORTGAGE PEOPLE.
YEAH, TONY'S A MESS.
CALL ME!
ME AGAIN. ~HIC~
REMEMBER THAT TIME AT THE NUDIST COLONY WITH SY AND ZENA, AN' WE WERE ON THE BEACH TOGETHER? I STILL GOT SAND IN MY ASS FROM THAT, AN' IT WAS MONTHS AGO.
CALL ME AS SOON AS YA GET IN. IT'S IMPORTANT. NOT LIKE, SUPER IMPORTANT, BUT IMPORTANT ENOUGH.
HEY. ME AGAIN. WHERE THE HELL ARE YOU THIS ~HIC~ HOUR A' THE NIGHT? WHY AIN'CHA PICKIN' UP?
ARE YOU OUT SOMEWHERE? ON A DATE? WITH WHO? I DEMAND TA KNOW!
CALL ME WHEN YA GET THIS, EVEN IF IT'S A MILLION O'CLOCK!
HEY, IT'S ME. YOU THERE?
GUESS WHAT?
I STOLE ALL A' THE JOKER'S LOOT.
~HIC~
CALL ME.
I KNOW YOU'RE ~HIC~ STILL MAD AT ME, BUT HOW LONG IZZIS GON' GO ON FOR? YOU KNOW I GOT A SELF-DESTRUCTIVE STREAK. MY LIFE IS A ~HIC~ MESS WITHOUT YOU.
I CAN'T STAND YOU IGNORIN' ME LIKE THIS!
Y'KNOW... IT'S SO CUTE THATCHA STILL HAVE ONE A' THEM ~HIC~ OL' SCHOOL ANSWERIN' MACHINE DOOHICKEYS..
YER LIKE AN ADORABLE GRAN'MA.
WITH A PERKY ASS.
BWWAAAAAAAHHH!!!
~HIC~
CALL ME.
IF YOU DON'T CALL ME RIGHT NOW, I SWEAR I WILL HUNT YOU DOWN AND KILL YOU WITH MY ~HIC~ BARE HANDS, YOU PLANT-LOVIN', MANURE-EATIN', VENUS-TRY-FLAPPIN' PIECE A' STINKIN' NETTLE! I MEAN IT ~HIC~, BITCH!
IGNORE THAT LAST MESSAGE. YOU KNOW MY ~HIC~ TEMPER. ONLY SOME-ONE I LOVE CAN MAKE ME THAT MAD, Y'KNOW. I'M SORRYYYEEEE. CALL ME WHEN YOU ~HIC~ GET THIS. I'LL BE UP NO MATTER--
SHIT!
I JUST SPILLED WINE ON THE BED. I'LL CALL YOU BACK. NO... WAIT... YOU CALL ME, OKAY?
BURRRPP
I'M SOOO HUNGRY...
~HIC~

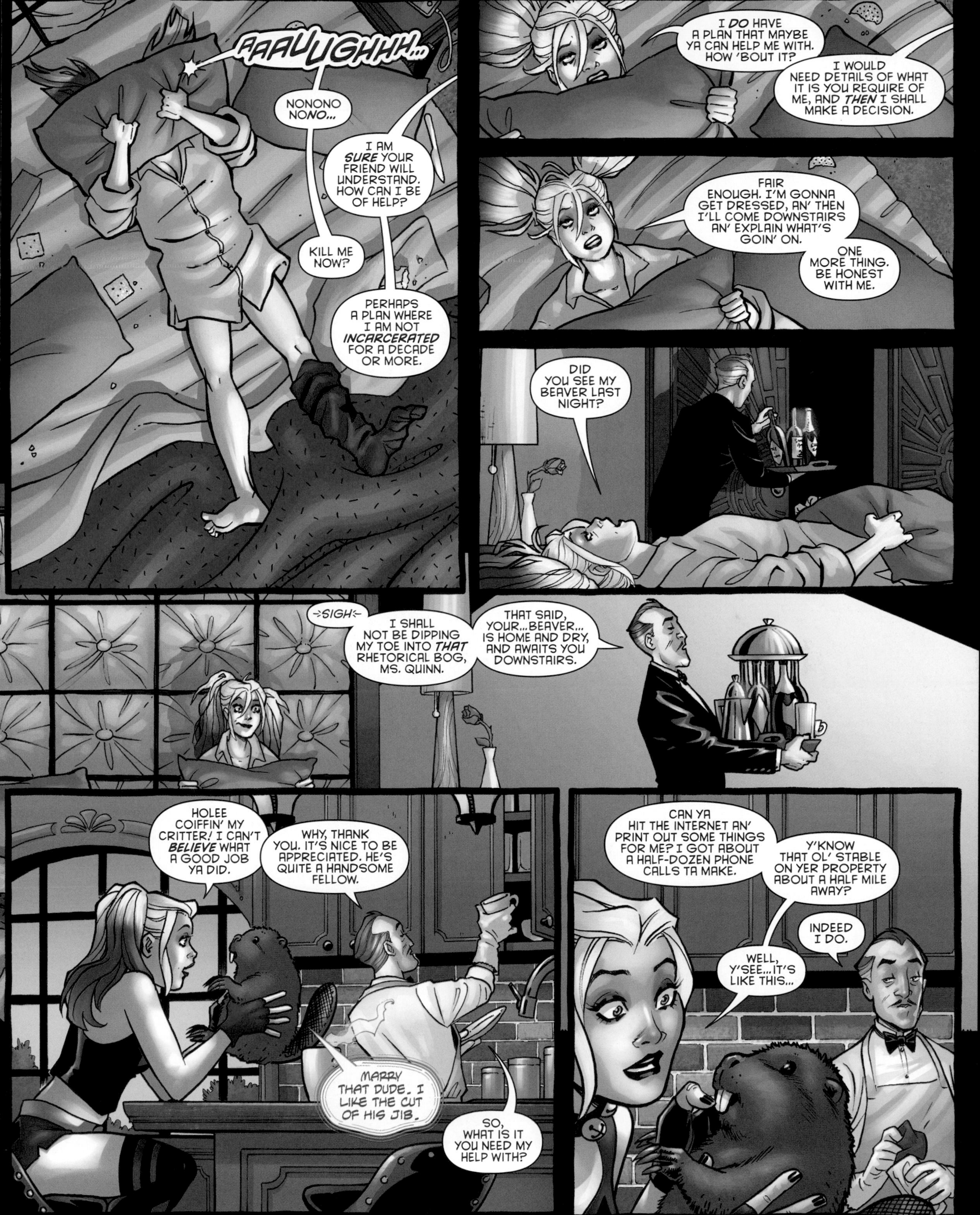
AAAUUGHHH...
NONONO NONO...
I AM SURE YOUR FRIEND WILL UNDERSTAND. HOW CAN I BE OF HELP?
KILL ME NOW?
PERHAPS A PLAN WHERE I AM NOT INCARCERATED FOR A DECADE OR MORE.
I DO HAVE A PLAN THAT MAYBE YA CAN HELP ME WITH. HOW 'BOUT IT?
I WOULD NEED DETAILS OF WHAT IT IS YOU REQUIRE OF ME, AND THEN I SHALL MAKE A DECISION.
FAIR ENOUGH. I'M GONNA GET DRESSED, AN' THEN I'LL COME DOWNSTAIRS AN' EXPLAIN WHAT'S GOIN' ON.
ONE MORE THING. BE HONEST WITH ME.
DID YOU SEE MY BEAVER LAST NIGHT?
SIGH
I SHALL NOT BE DIPPING MY TOE INTO THAT RHETORICAL BOG, MS. QUINN.
THAT SAID, YOUR...BEAVER... IS HOME AND DRY, AND AWAITS YOU DOWNSTAIRS.
HOLEE COIFFIN' MY CRITTER! I CAN'T BELIEVE WHAT A GOOD JOB YA DID.
WHY, THANK YOU. IT'S NICE TO BE APPRECIATED. HE'S QUITE A HANDSOME FELLOW.
MARRY THAT DUDE. I LIKE THE CUT OF HIS JIB.
SO, WHAT IS IT YOU NEED MY HELP WITH?
CAN YA HIT THE INTERNET AN' PRINT OUT SOME THINGS FOR ME? I GOT ABOUT A HALF-DOZEN PHONE CALLS TA MAKE.
Y'KNOW THAT OL' STABLE ON YER PROPERTY ABOUT A HALF MILE AWAY?
INDEED I DO.
WELL, Y'SEE...IT'S LIKE THIS...

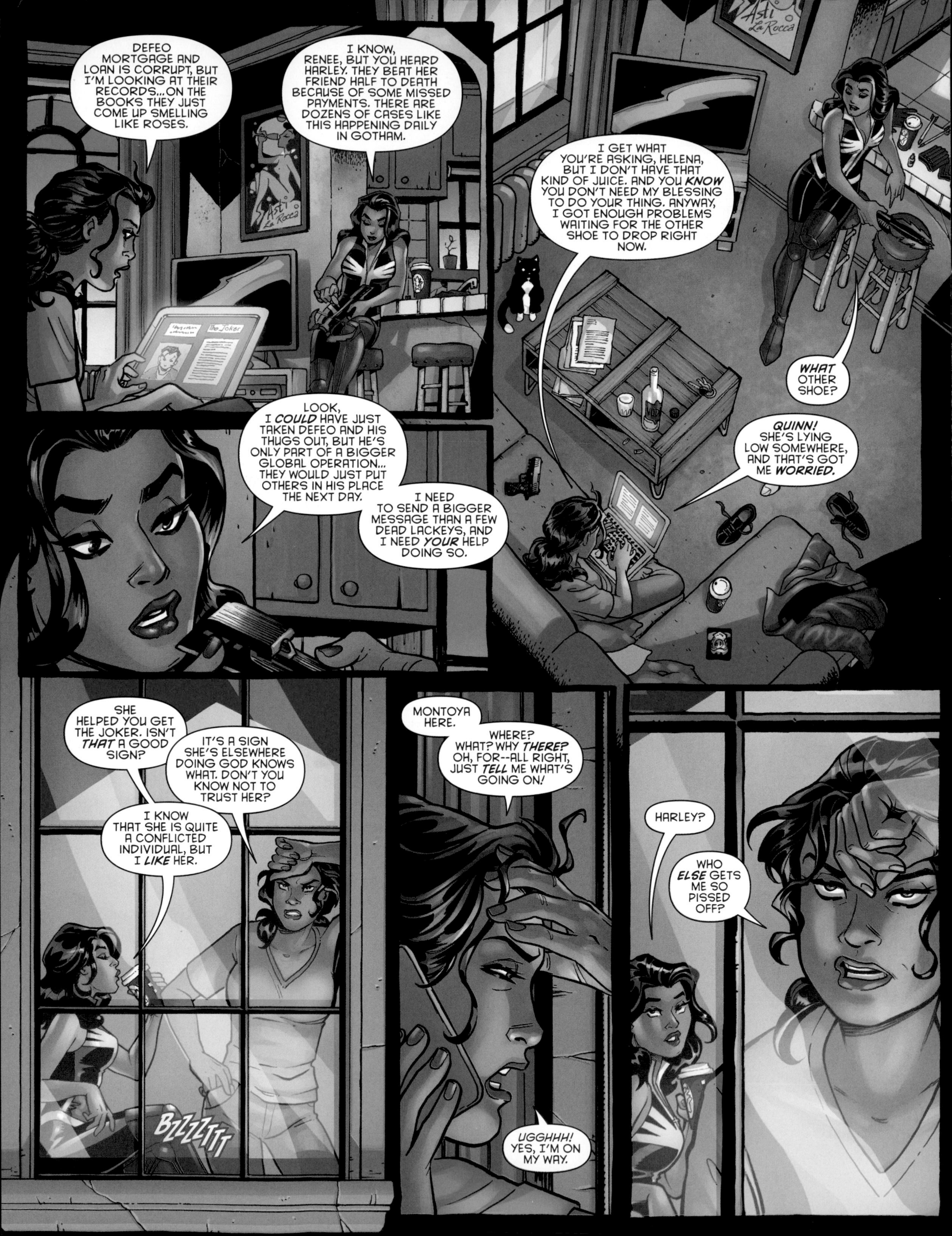
DEFEO MORTGAGE AND LOAN IS CORRUPT, BUT I'M LOOKING AT THEIR RECORDS...ON THE BOOKS THEY JUST COME UP SMELLING LIKE ROSES.
I KNOW, RENEE, BUT YOU HEARD HARLEY. THEY BEAT HER FRIEND HALF TO DEATH BECAUSE OF SOME MISSED PAYMENTS. THERE ARE DOZENS OF CASES LIKE THIS HAPPENING DAILY IN GOTHAM.
Asti La Rocca
The Joker
LOOK, I COULD HAVE JUST TAKEN DEFEO AND HIS THUGS OUT, BUT HE'S ONLY PART OF A BIGGER GLOBAL OPERATION... THEY WOULD JUST PUT OTHERS IN HIS PLACE THE NEXT DAY.
I NEED TO SEND A BIGGER MESSAGE THAN A FEW DEAD LACKEYS, AND I NEED YOUR HELP DOING SO.
I GET WHAT YOU'RE ASKING, HELENA, BUT I DON'T HAVE THAT KIND OF JUICE. AND YOU KNOW YOU DON'T NEED MY BLESSING TO DO YOUR THING. ANYWAY, I GOT ENOUGH PROBLEMS WAITING FOR THE OTHER SHOE TO DROP RIGHT NOW.
WHAT OTHER SHOE?
QUINN! SHE'S LYING LOW SOMEWHERE, AND THAT'S GOT ME WORRIED.
SHE HELPED YOU GET THE JOKER. ISN'T THAT A GOOD SIGN?
IT'S A SIGN SHE'S ELSEWHERE DOING GOD KNOWS WHAT. DON'T YOU KNOW NOT TO TRUST HER?
I KNOW THAT SHE IS QUITE A CONFLICTED INDIVIDUAL, BUT I LIKE HER.
BZZZZTTT
MONTOYA HERE.
WHERE? WHAT? WHY THERE? OH, FOR--ALL RIGHT, JUST TELL ME WHAT'S GOING ON!
UGGHHH! YES, I'M ON MY WAY.
HARLEY?
WHO ELSE GETS ME SO PISSED OFF?

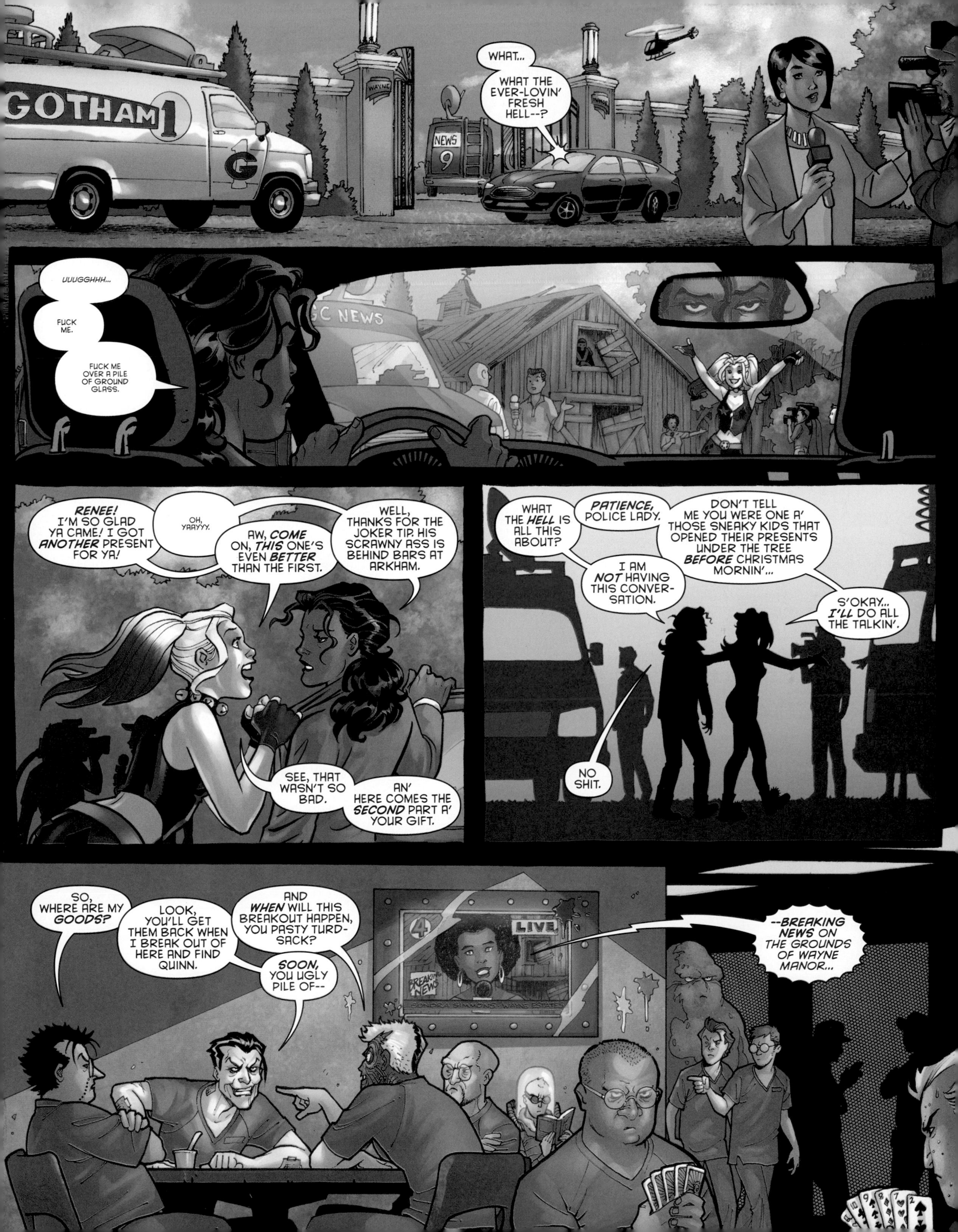
GOTHAM 1
NEWS 9
WHAT...
WHAT THE EVER-LOVIN' FRESH HELL--?
UUUGGHHH...
FUCK ME.
FUCK ME OVER A PILE OF GROUND GLASS.
GC NEWS
RENEE! I'M SO GLAD YA CAME! I GOT ANOTHER PRESENT FOR YA!
OH, YAAYYY.
AW, COME ON, THIS ONE'S EVEN BETTER THAN THE FIRST.
WELL, THANKS FOR THE JOKER TIP. HIS SCRAWNY ASS IS BEHIND BARS AT ARKHAM.
SEE, THAT WASN'T SO BAD.
AN' HERE COMES THE SECOND PART A' YOUR GIFT.
WHAT THE HELL IS ALL THIS ABOUT?
PATIENCE, POLICE LADY.
DON'T TELL ME YOU WERE ONE A' THOSE SNEAKY KIDS THAT OPENED THEIR PRESENTS UNDER THE TREE BEFORE CHRISTMAS MORNIN'...
I AM NOT HAVING THIS CONVERSATION.
S'OKAY... I'LL DO ALL THE TALKIN'.
NO SHIT.
SO, WHERE ARE MY GOODS?
LOOK, YOU'LL GET THEM BACK WHEN I BREAK OUT OF HERE AND FIND QUINN.
AND WHEN WILL THIS BREAKOUT HAPPEN, YOU PASTY TURD-SACK?
SOON, YOU UGLY PILE OF--
LIVE
BREAKING NEWS
--BREAKING NEWS ON THE GROUNDS OF WAYNE MANOR...

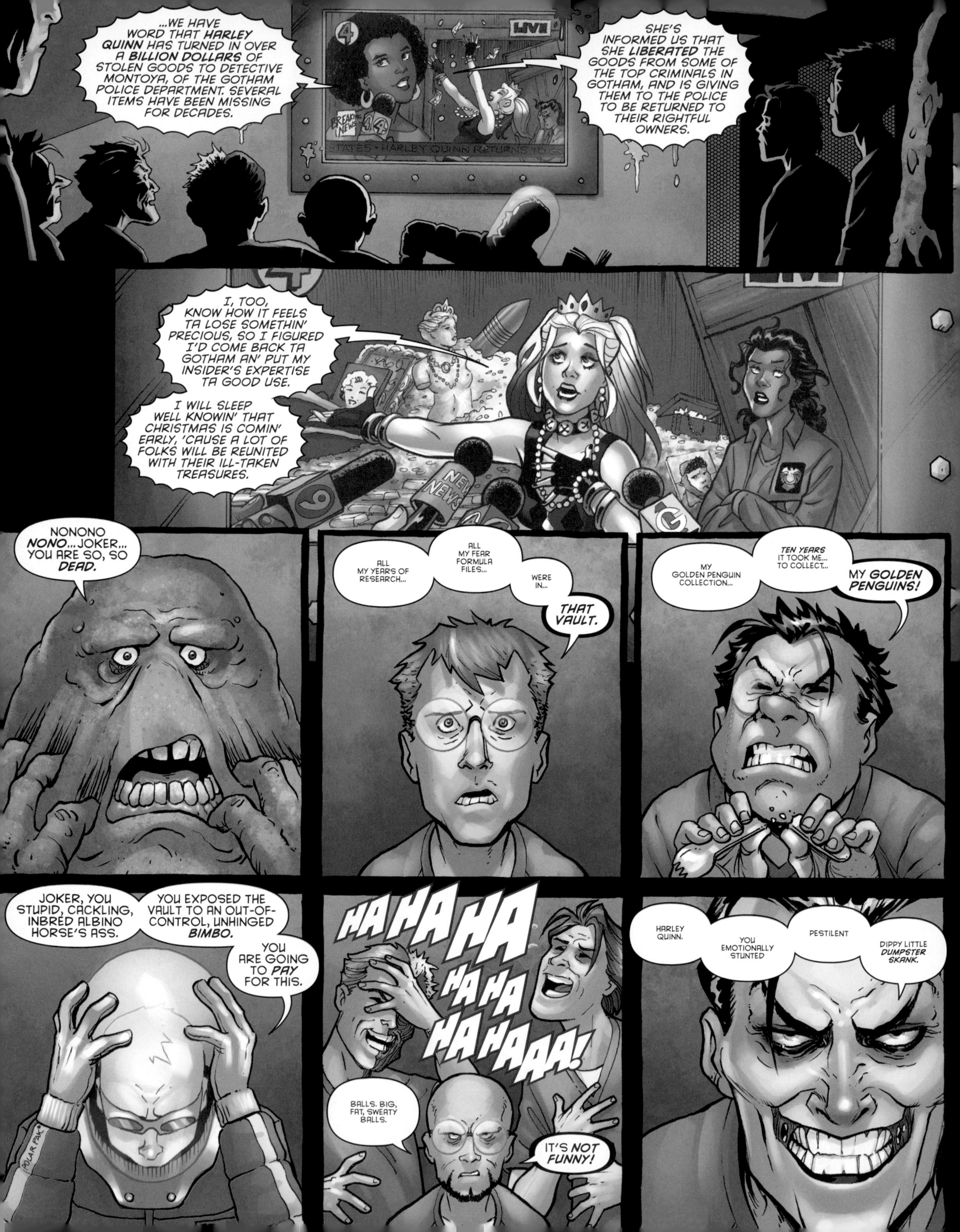
...WE HAVE WORD THAT HARLEY QUINN HAS TURNED IN OVER A BILLION DOLLARS OF STOLEN GOODS TO DETECTIVE MONTOYA, OF THE GOTHAM POLICE DEPARTMENT. SEVERAL ITEMS HAVE BEEN MISSING FOR DECADES.
LIVE
BREAKING NEWS
STATES • HARLEY QUINN RETURNS TO G
SHE'S INFORMED US THAT SHE LIBERATED THE GOODS FROM SOME OF THE TOP CRIMINALS IN GOTHAM, AND IS GIVING THEM TO THE POLICE TO BE RETURNED TO THEIR RIGHTFUL OWNERS.
I, TOO, KNOW HOW IT FEELS TA LOSE SOMETHIN' PRECIOUS, SO I FIGURED I'D COME BACK TA GOTHAM AN' PUT MY INSIDER'S EXPERTISE TA GOOD USE.
I WILL SLEEP WELL KNOWIN' THAT CHRISTMAS IS COMIN' EARLY, 'CAUSE A LOT OF FOLKS WILL BE REUNITED WITH THEIR ILL-TAKEN TREASURES.
NONONO NONO...JOKER... YOU ARE SO, SO DEAD.
ALL MY YEARS OF RESEARCH...
ALL MY FEAR FORMULA FILES...
WERE IN...
THAT VAULT.
MY GOLDEN PENGUIN COLLECTION...
TEN YEARS IT TOOK ME... TO COLLECT...
MY GOLDEN PENGUINS!
JOKER, YOU STUPID, CACKLING, INBRED ALBINO HORSE'S ASS.
YOU EXPOSED THE VAULT TO AN OUT-OF-CONTROL, UNHINGED BIMBO.
YOU ARE GOING TO PAY FOR THIS.
HA HA HA HA HA HA HA HA HAAA!
BALLS. BIG, FAT, SWEATY BALLS.
IT'S NOT FUNNY!
HARLEY QUINN.
YOU EMOTIONALLY STUNTED
PESTILENT
DIPPY LITTLE DUMPSTER SKANK.

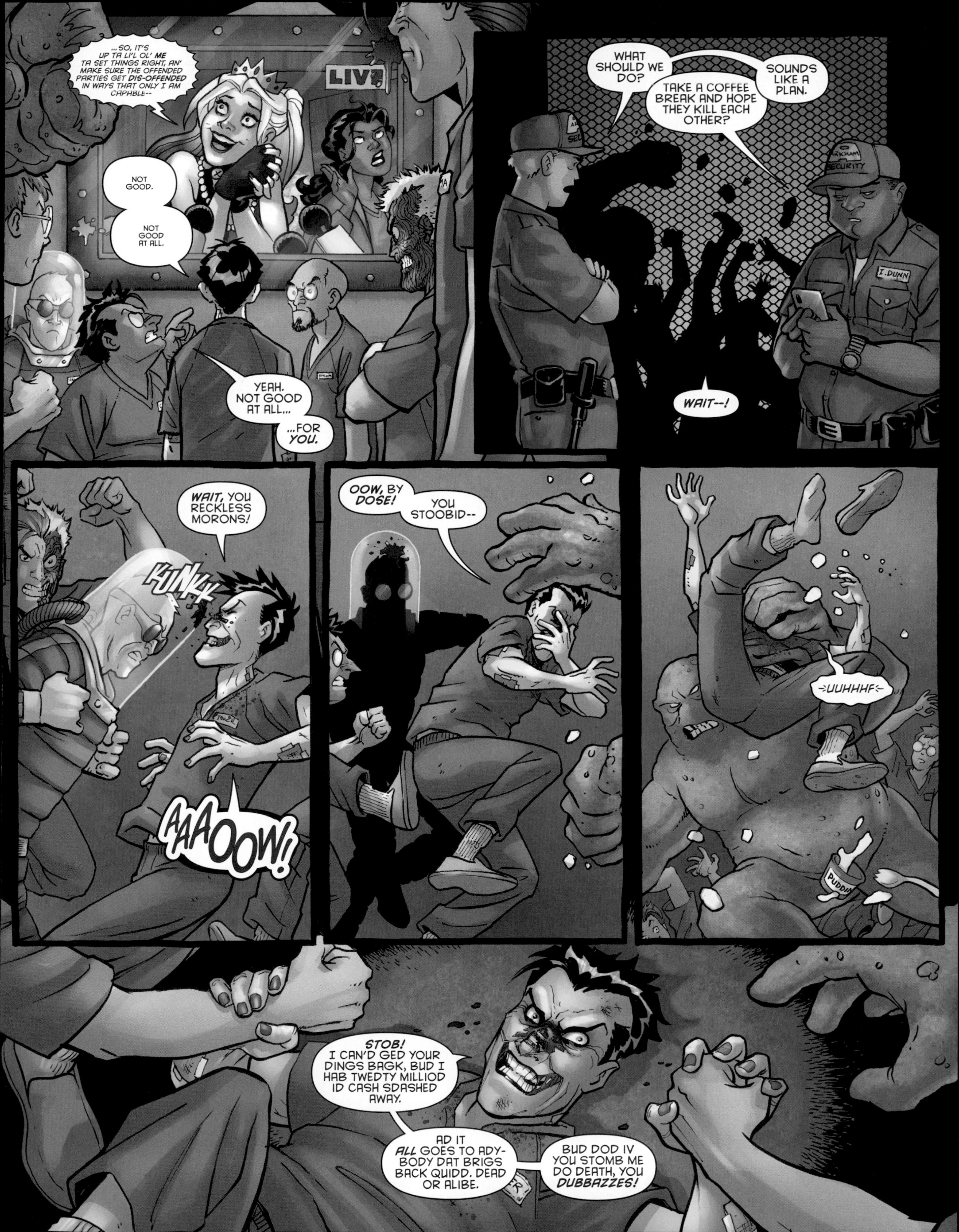
...SO, IT'S UP TA LI'L OL' *ME* TA SET THINGS RIGHT, AN' MAKE SURE THE OFFENDED PARTIES GET *DIS-OFFENDED* IN WAYS THAT ONLY I AM CAPABLE--
LIVE
NOT GOOD.
NOT GOOD AT ALL.
YEAH. NOT GOOD AT ALL...
...FOR *YOU.*
WHAT SHOULD WE DO?
TAKE A COFFEE BREAK AND HOPE THEY KILL EACH OTHER?
SOUNDS LIKE A PLAN.
ARKHAM SECURITY
I. DUNN
WAIT--!
WAIT, YOU RECKLESS MORONS!
KUNKK
AAAOOW!
OOW, BY DOSE!
YOU STOOBID--
-UUHHHF-
STOB! I CAN'D GED YOUR DINGS BAGK, BUD I HAB TWEDTY MILLIOD ID CASH SDASHED AWAY.
AD IT *ALL* GOES TO ADY-BODY DAT BRIGS BACK QUIDD. DEAD OR ALIBE.
BUD DOD IV YOU STOMB ME DO DEATH, YOU *DUBBAZZES!*

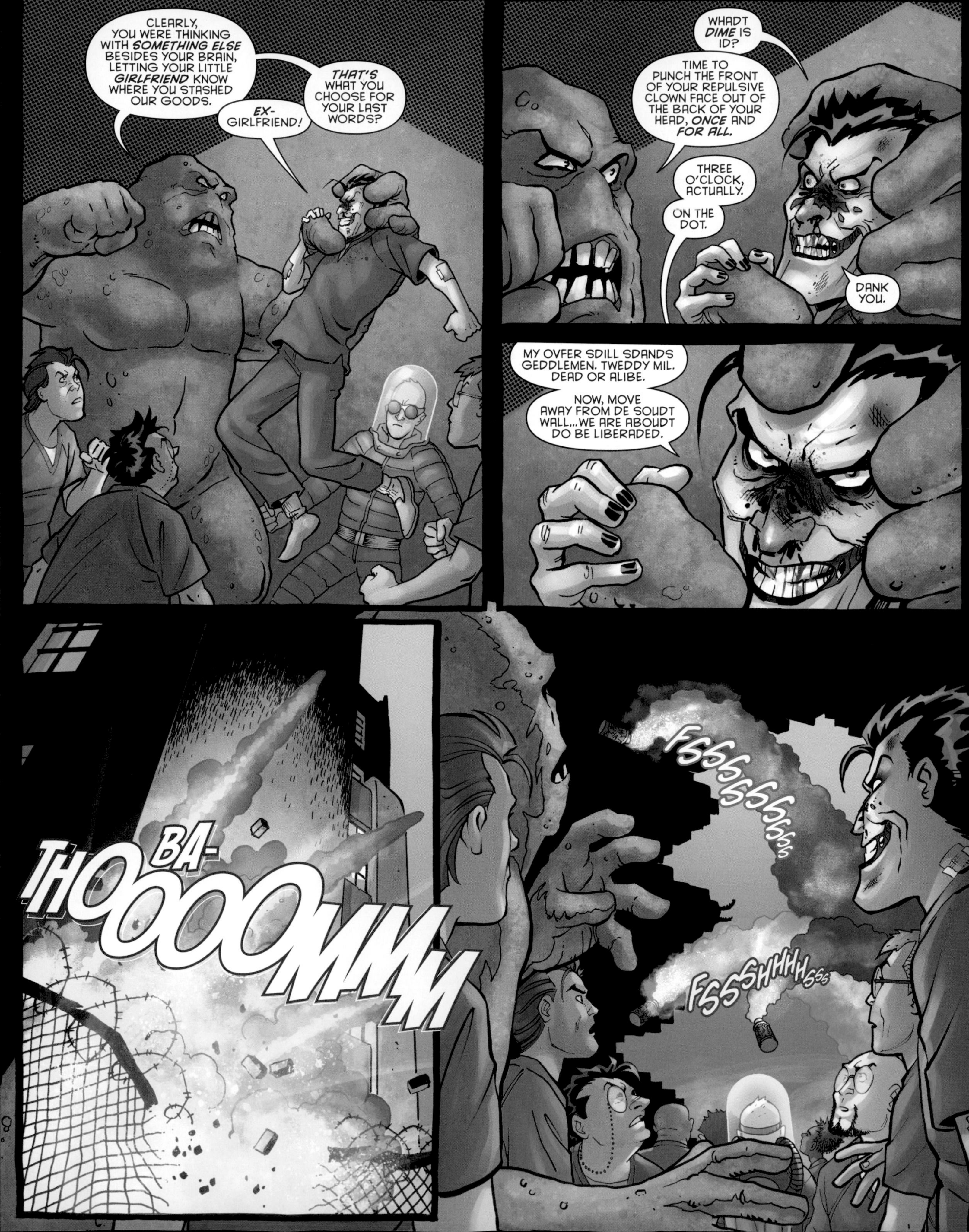
CLEARLY, YOU WERE THINKING WITH SOMETHING ELSE BESIDES YOUR BRAIN, LETTING YOUR LITTLE GIRLFRIEND KNOW WHERE YOU STASHED OUR GOODS.
EX-GIRLFRIEND!
THAT'S WHAT YOU CHOOSE FOR YOUR LAST WORDS?
WHADT DIME IS ID?
TIME TO PUNCH THE FRONT OF YOUR REPULSIVE CLOWN FACE OUT OF THE BACK OF YOUR HEAD, ONCE AND FOR ALL.
THREE O'CLOCK, ACTUALLY.
ON THE DOT.
DANK YOU.
MY OVFER SDILL SDANDS GEDDLEMEN. TWEDDY MIL. DEAD OR ALIBE.
NOW, MOVE AWAY FROM DE SOUDT WALL...WE ARE ABOUDT DO BE LIBERADED.
BA-THOOOOOMMMM
FSSSSSSSSSSS
FSSSHHHHSSS

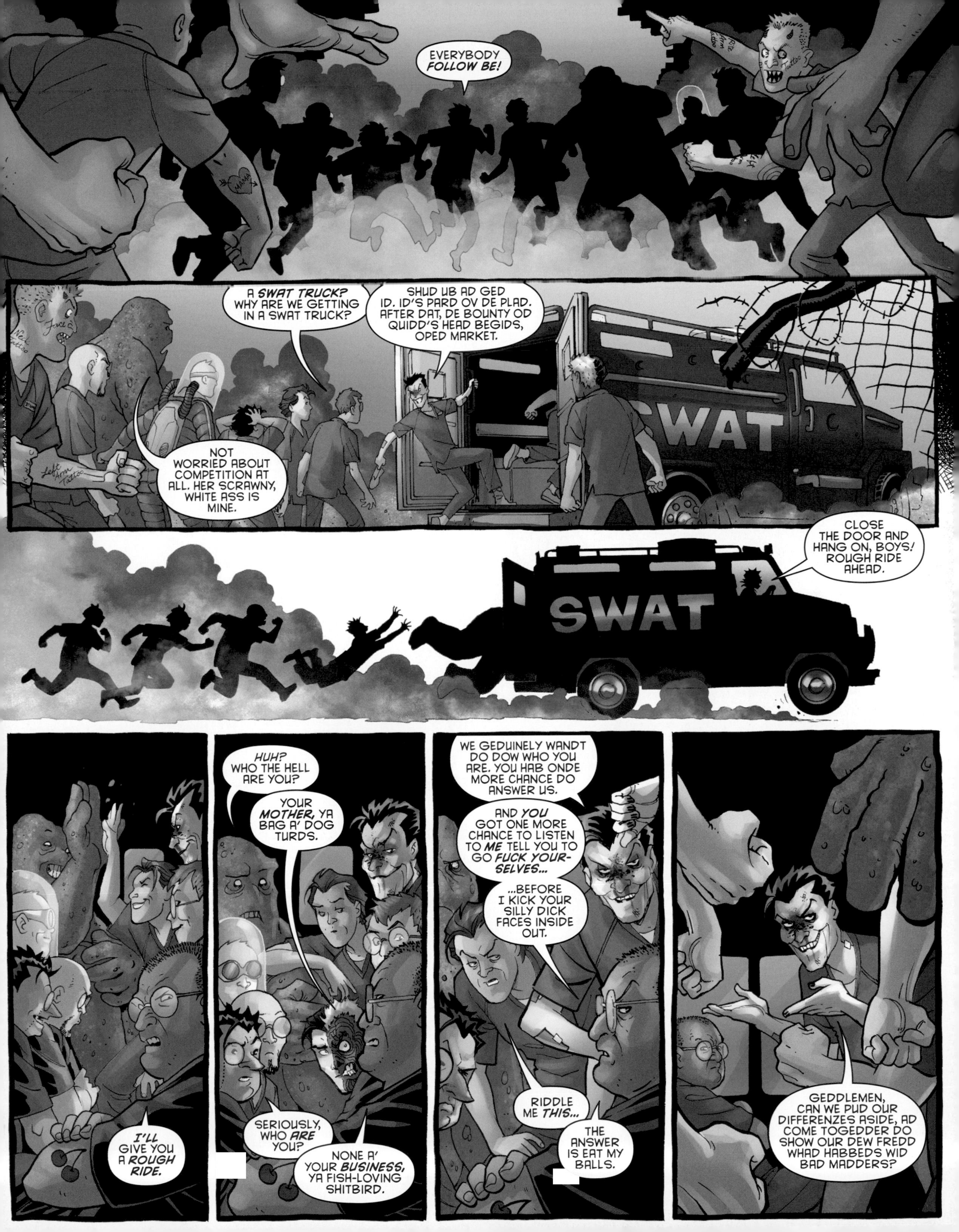
EVERYBODY *FOLLOW BE!*
A *SWAT TRUCK?* WHY ARE WE GETTING IN A SWAT TRUCK?
SHUD UB AD GED ID. ID'S PARD OV DE PLAD. AFTER DAT, DE BOUNTY OD QUIDD'S HEAD BEGIDS, OPED MARKET.
NOT WORRIED ABOUT COMPETITION AT ALL. HER SCRAWNY, WHITE ASS IS MINE.
SWAT
SWAT
CLOSE THE DOOR AND HANG ON, BOYS! ROUGH RIDE AHEAD.
I'LL GIVE YOU A *ROUGH RIDE.*
HUH? WHO THE HELL ARE YOU?
YOUR *MOTHER,* YA BAG A' DOG TURDS.
SERIOUSLY, WHO *ARE* YOU?
NONE A' YOUR *BUSINESS,* YA FISH-LOVING SHITBIRD.
WE GEDUINELY WANDT DO DOW WHO YOU ARE. YOU HAB ONDE MORE CHANCE DO ANSWER US.
AND *YOU* GOT ONE MORE CHANCE TO LISTEN TO *ME* TELL YOU TO GO *FUCK YOUR-SELVES...*
...BEFORE I KICK YOUR SILLY DICK FACES INSIDE OUT.
RIDDLE ME *THIS...*
THE ANSWER IS EAT MY BALLS.
GEDDLEMEN, CAN WE PUD OUR DIFFERENZES ASIDE, AD COME TOGEDDER DO SHOW OUR DEW FREDD WHAD HABBEDS WID BAD MADDERS?

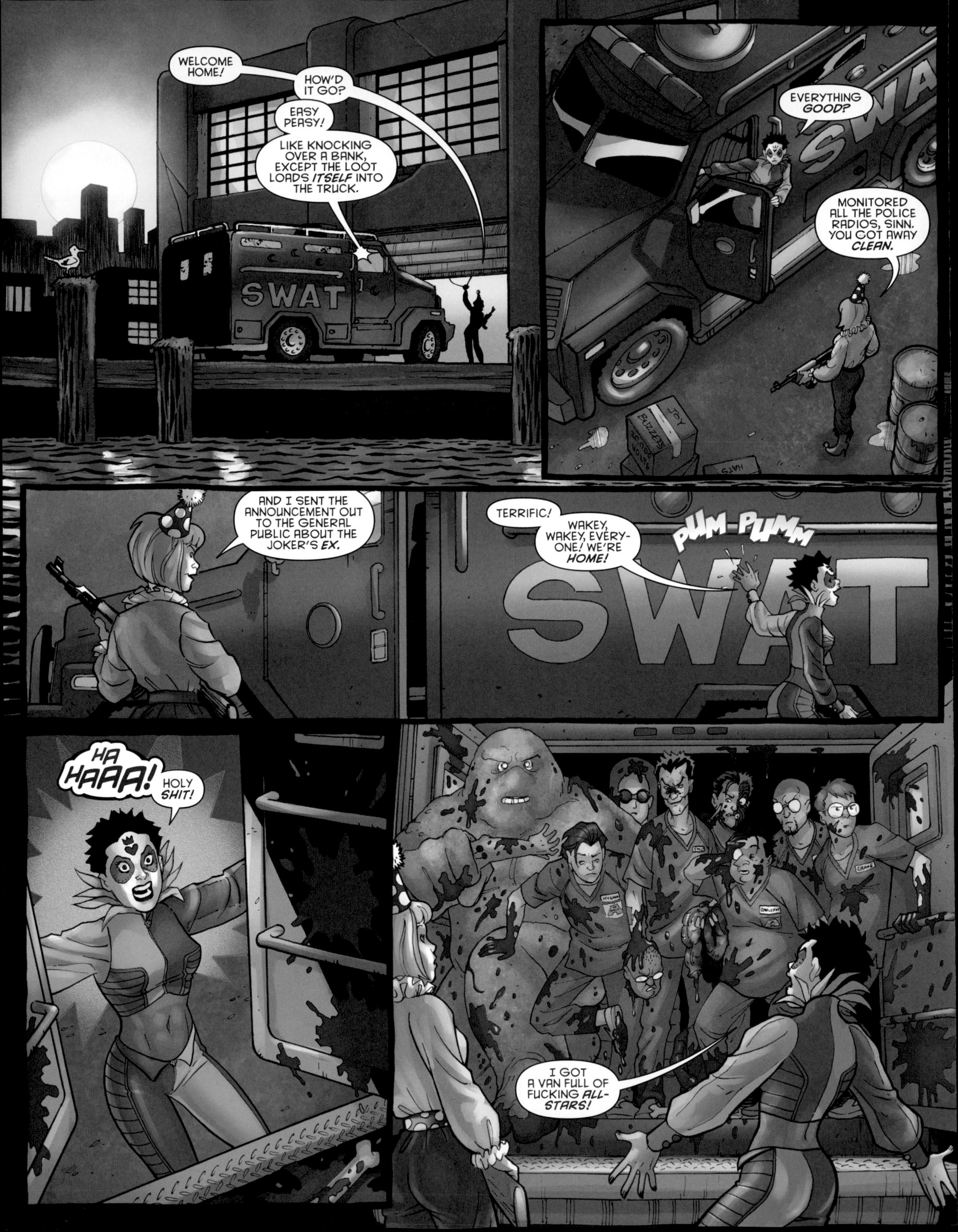
WELCOME HOME!
HOW'D IT GO?
EASY PEASY!
LIKE KNOCKING OVER A BANK, EXCEPT THE LOOT LOADS ITSELF INTO THE TRUCK.
SWAT
EVERYTHING GOOD?
MONITORED ALL THE POLICE RADIOS, SINN. YOU GOT AWAY CLEAN.
AND I SENT THE ANNOUNCEMENT OUT TO THE GENERAL PUBLIC ABOUT THE JOKER'S EX.
TERRIFIC!
WAKEY, WAKEY, EVERYONE! WE'RE HOME!
PUM-PUMM
SWAT
HA HAAA!
HOLY SHIT!
I GOT A VAN FULL OF FUCKING ALL-STARS!

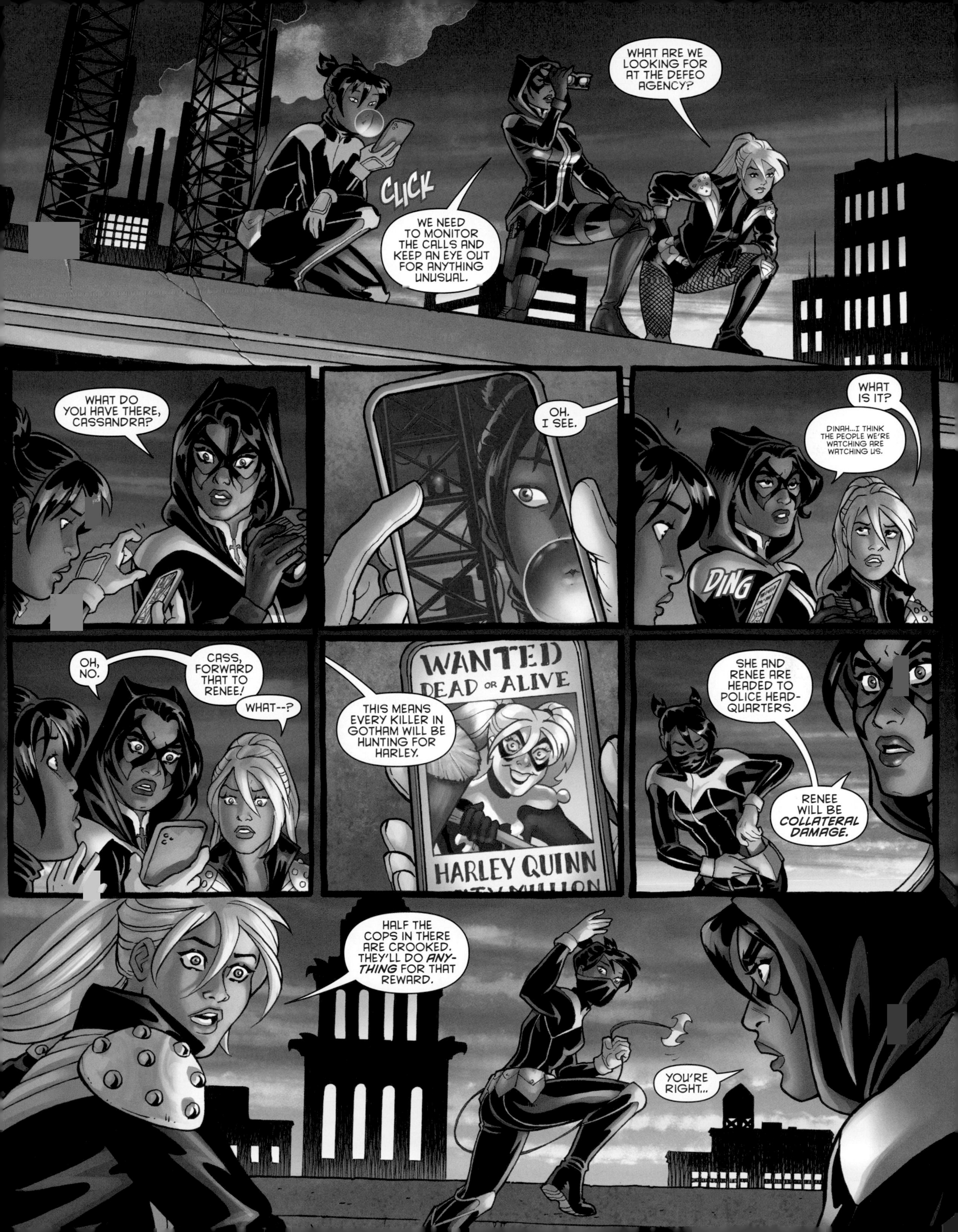
WHAT ARE WE LOOKING FOR AT THE DEFEO AGENCY?
CLICK
WE NEED TO MONITOR THE CALLS AND KEEP AN EYE OUT FOR ANYTHING UNUSUAL.
WHAT DO YOU HAVE THERE, CASSANDRA?
OH. I SEE.
WHAT IS IT?
DINAH...I THINK THE PEOPLE WE'RE WATCHING ARE WATCHING US.
DING
OH, NO.
CASS, FORWARD THAT TO RENEE!
WHAT--?
WANTED
DEAD OR ALIVE
HARLEY QUINN
THIS MEANS EVERY KILLER IN GOTHAM WILL BE HUNTING FOR HARLEY.
SHE AND RENEE ARE HEADED TO POLICE HEAD-QUARTERS.
RENEE WILL BE *COLLATERAL DAMAGE.*
HALF THE COPS IN THERE ARE CROOKED. THEY'LL DO *ANY-THING* FOR THAT REWARD.
YOU'RE RIGHT...

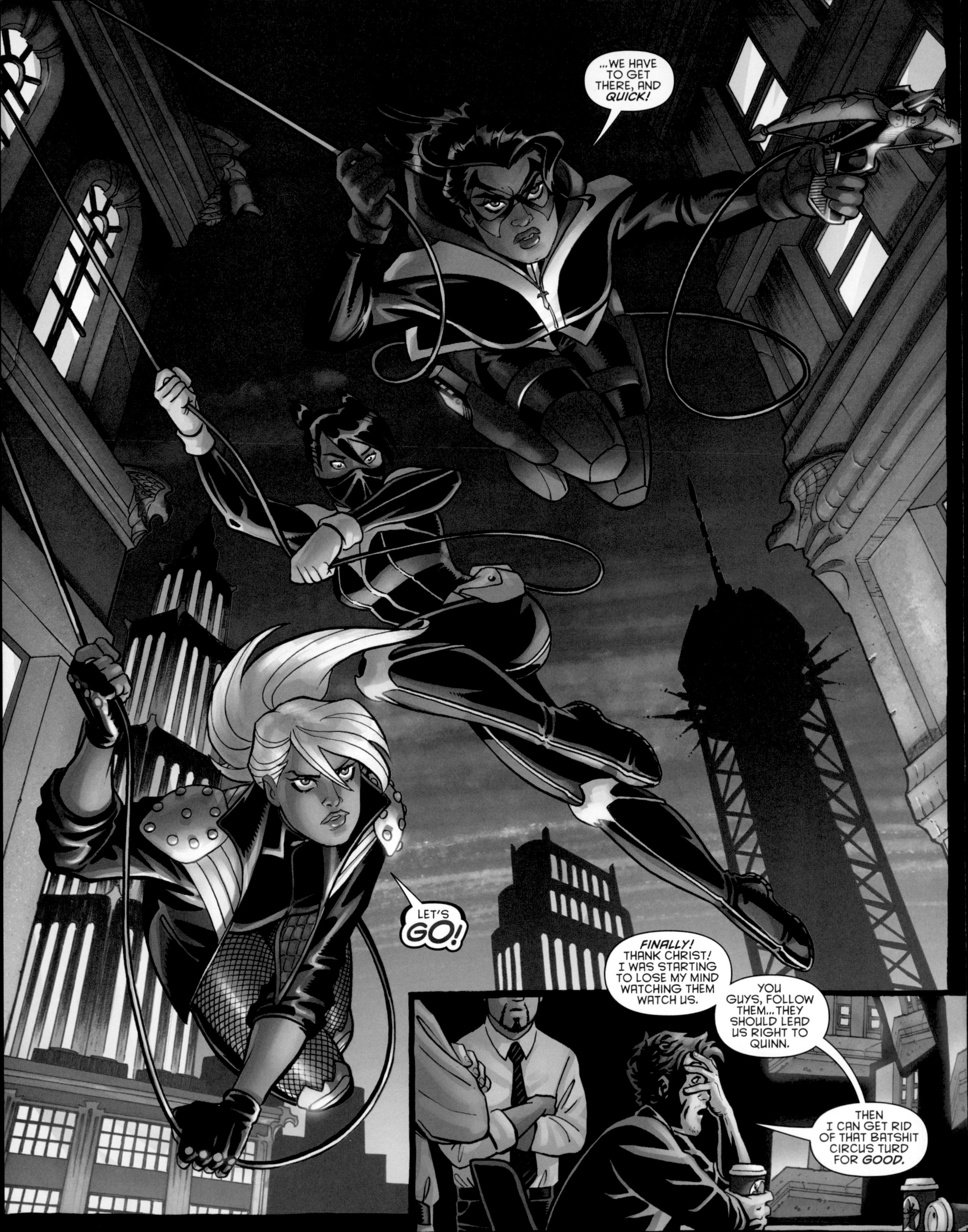
...WE HAVE TO GET THERE, AND QUICK!
LET'S GO!
FINALLY! THANK CHRIST! I WAS STARTING TO LOSE MY MIND WATCHING THEM WATCH US.
YOU GUYS, FOLLOW THEM... THEY SHOULD LEAD US RIGHT TO QUINN.
THEN I CAN GET RID OF THAT BATSHIT CIRCUS TURD FOR GOOD.

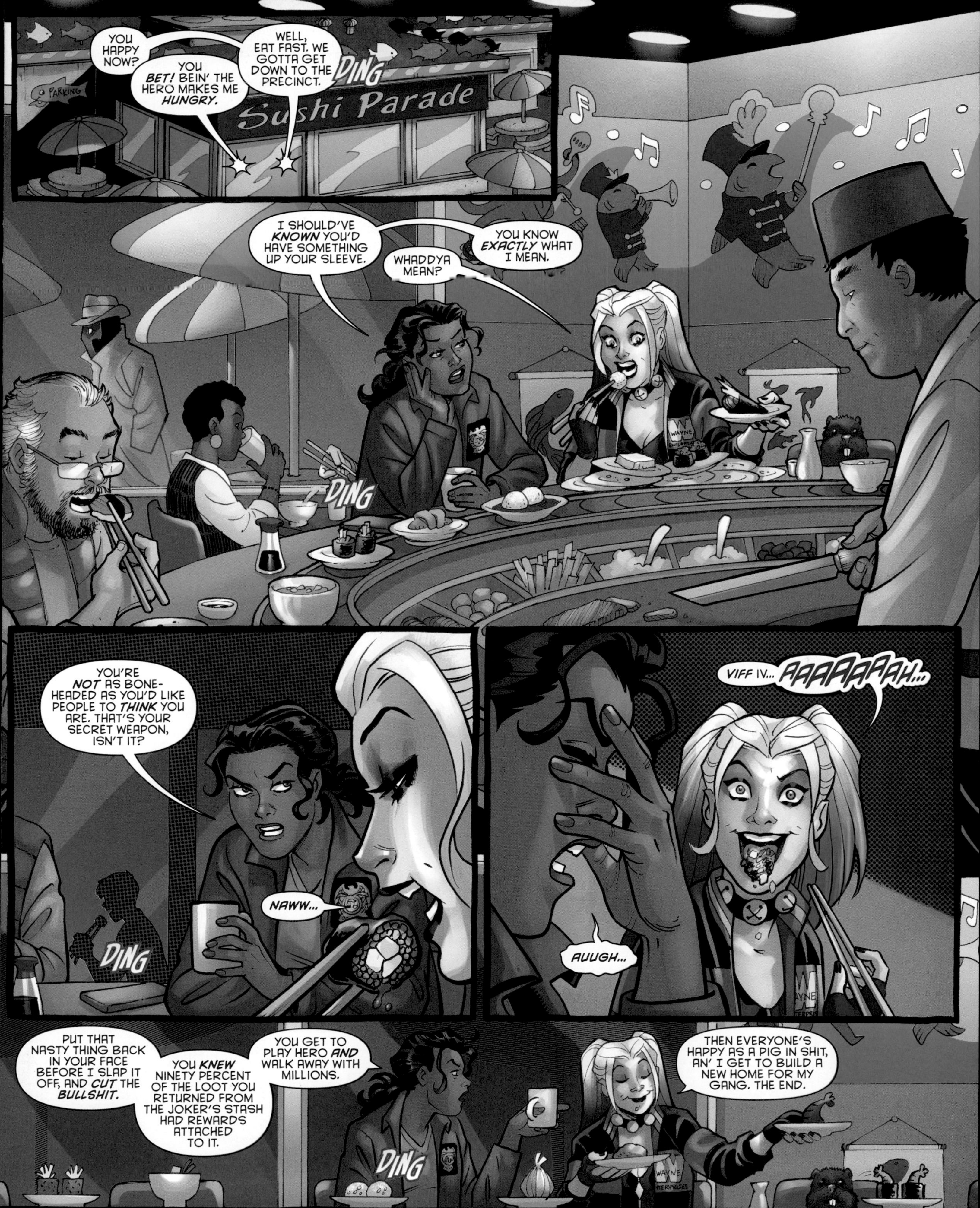
YOU HAPPY NOW?
YOU BET! BEIN' THE HERO MAKES ME HUNGRY.
WELL, EAT FAST. WE GOTTA GET DOWN TO THE PRECINCT.
DING
PARKING
Sushi Parade
I SHOULD'VE KNOWN YOU'D HAVE SOMETHING UP YOUR SLEEVE.
WHADDYA MEAN?
YOU KNOW EXACTLY WHAT I MEAN.
DING
YOU'RE NOT AS BONE-HEADED AS YOU'D LIKE PEOPLE TO THINK YOU ARE. THAT'S YOUR SECRET WEAPON, ISN'T IT?
NAWW...
DING
VIFF IV... AAAAAAAH...
AUUGH...
PUT THAT NASTY THING BACK IN YOUR FACE BEFORE I SLAP IT OFF, AND CUT THE BULLSHIT.
YOU KNEW NINETY PERCENT OF THE LOOT YOU RETURNED FROM THE JOKER'S STASH HAD REWARDS ATTACHED TO IT.
YOU GET TO PLAY HERO AND WALK AWAY WITH MILLIONS.
THEN EVERYONE'S HAPPY AS A PIG IN SHIT, AN' I GET TO BUILD A NEW HOME FOR MY GANG. THE END.
DING

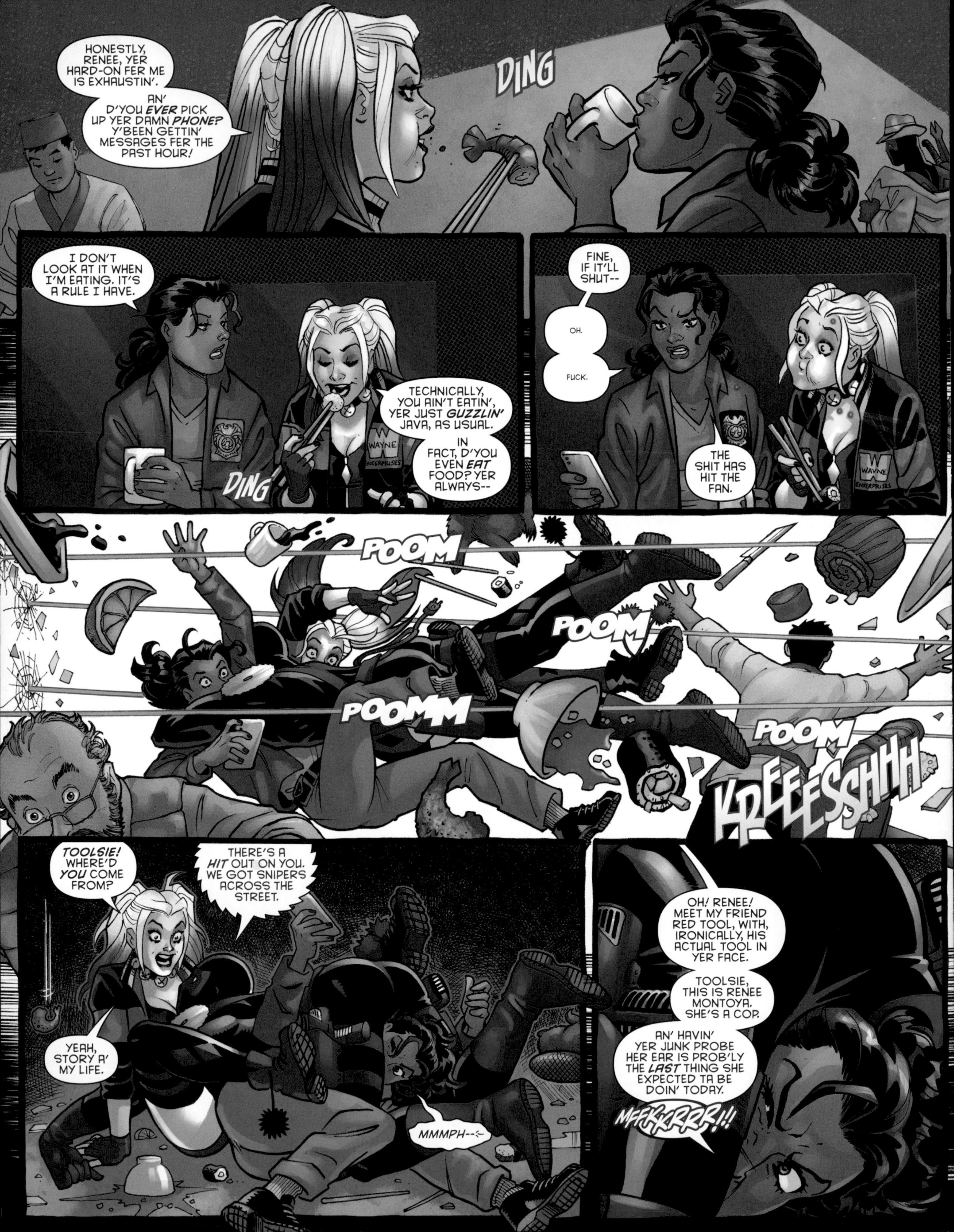
HONESTLY, RENEE, YER HARD-ON FER ME IS EXHAUSTIN'.
AN' D'YOU EVER PICK UP YER DAMN PHONE? Y'BEEN GETTIN' MESSAGES FER THE PAST HOUR!
DING
I DON'T LOOK AT IT WHEN I'M EATING. IT'S A RULE I HAVE.
TECHNICALLY, YOU AIN'T EATIN', YER JUST GUZZLIN' JAVA, AS USUAL.
IN FACT, D'YOU EVEN EAT FOOD? YER ALWAYS--
DING
FINE, IF IT'LL SHUT--
OH.
FUCK.
THE SHIT HAS HIT THE FAN.
POOM
POOM
POOMM
POOM
KREEESSHHH
TOOLSIE! WHERE'D YOU COME FROM?
THERE'S A HIT OUT ON YOU. WE GOT SNIPERS ACROSS THE STREET.
YEAH, STORY A' MY LIFE.
MMMPH--
OH! RENEE! MEET MY FRIEND RED TOOL, WITH, IRONICALLY, HIS ACTUAL TOOL IN YER FACE.
TOOLSIE, THIS IS RENEE MONTOYA. SHE'S A COP.
AN' HAVIN' YER JUNK PROBE HER EAR IS PROB'LY THE LAST THING SHE EXPECTED TA BE DOIN' TODAY.
MFFKKRRR!!!

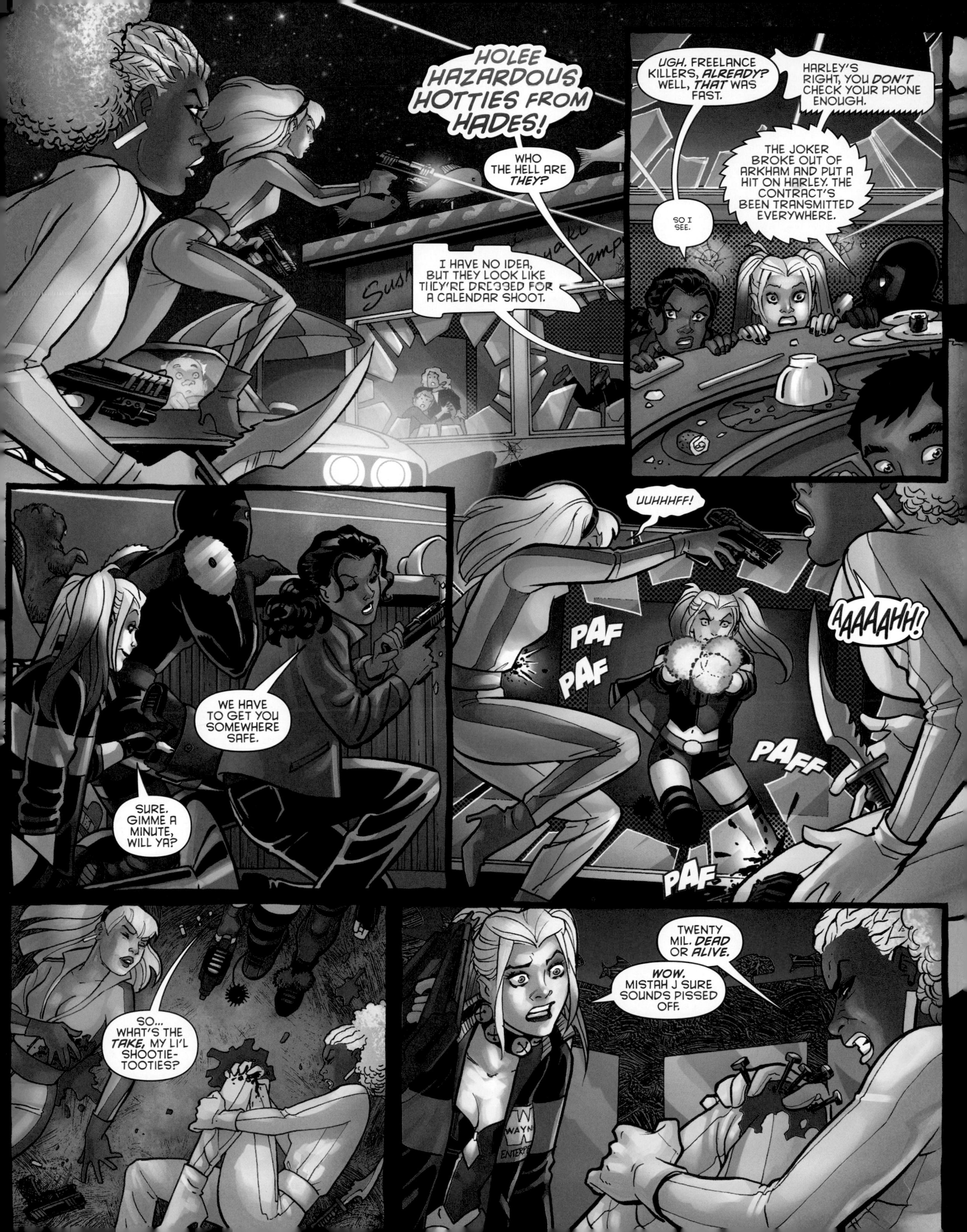
HOLEE HAZARDOUS HOTTIES FROM HADES!
WHO THE HELL ARE THEY?
I HAVE NO IDEA, BUT THEY LOOK LIKE THEY'RE DRESSED FOR A CALENDAR SHOOT.
UGH. FREELANCE KILLERS, ALREADY? WELL, THAT WAS FAST.
HARLEY'S RIGHT, YOU DON'T CHECK YOUR PHONE ENOUGH.
THE JOKER BROKE OUT OF ARKHAM AND PUT A HIT ON HARLEY. THE CONTRACT'S BEEN TRANSMITTED EVERYWHERE.
SO I SEE.
WE HAVE TO GET YOU SOMEWHERE SAFE.
SURE. GIMME A MINUTE, WILL YA?
UUHHHFF!
PAF
PAF
AAAAAHH!
PAFF
PAF
SO... WHAT'S THE TAKE, MY LI'L SHOOTIE-TOOTIES?
TWENTY MIL. DEAD OR ALIVE.
WOW. MISTAH J SURE SOUNDS PISSED OFF.

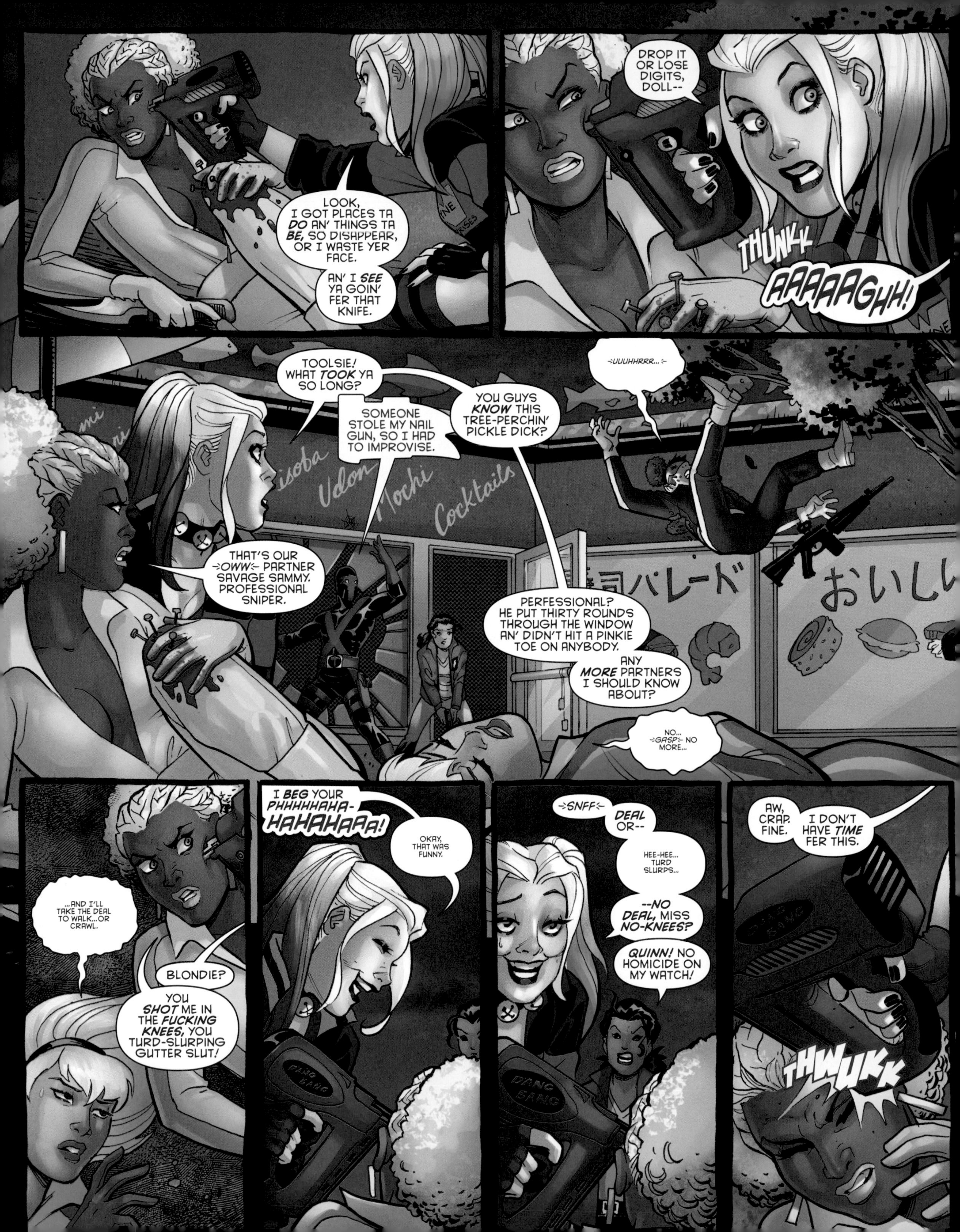

LOOK, I GOT PLACES TA DO AN' THINGS TA BE, SO DISAPPEAR, OR I WASTE YER FACE.
AN' I SEE YA GOIN' FER THAT KNIFE.
DROP IT OR LOSE DIGITS, DOLL--
THUNKK
AAAAAGHH!
TOOLSIE! WHAT TOOK YA SO LONG?
SOMEONE STOLE MY NAIL GUN, SO I HAD TO IMPROVISE.
YOU GUYS KNOW THIS TREE-PERCHIN' PICKLE DICK?
UUUHHRRR...
Udon
Mochi
Cocktails
THAT'S OUR OWW PARTNER SAVAGE SAMMY. PROFESSIONAL SNIPER.
PERFESSIONAL? HE PUT THIRTY ROUNDS THROUGH THE WINDOW AN' DIDN'T HIT A PINKIE TOE ON ANYBODY.
ANY MORE PARTNERS I SHOULD KNOW ABOUT?
NO... GASP NO MORE...
...AND I'LL TAKE THE DEAL TO WALK...OR CRAWL.
BLONDIE?
YOU SHOT ME IN THE FUCKING KNEES, YOU TURD-SLURPING GUTTER SLUT!
I BEG YOUR PHHHHHAHA-HAHAHAHAAA!
OKAY, THAT WAS FUNNY.
SNFF
DEAL OR--
HEE-HEE... TURD SLURPS...
--NO DEAL, MISS NO-KNEES?
QUINN! NO HOMICIDE ON MY WATCH!
AW, CRAP. FINE.
I DON'T HAVE TIME FER THIS.
THWUKK

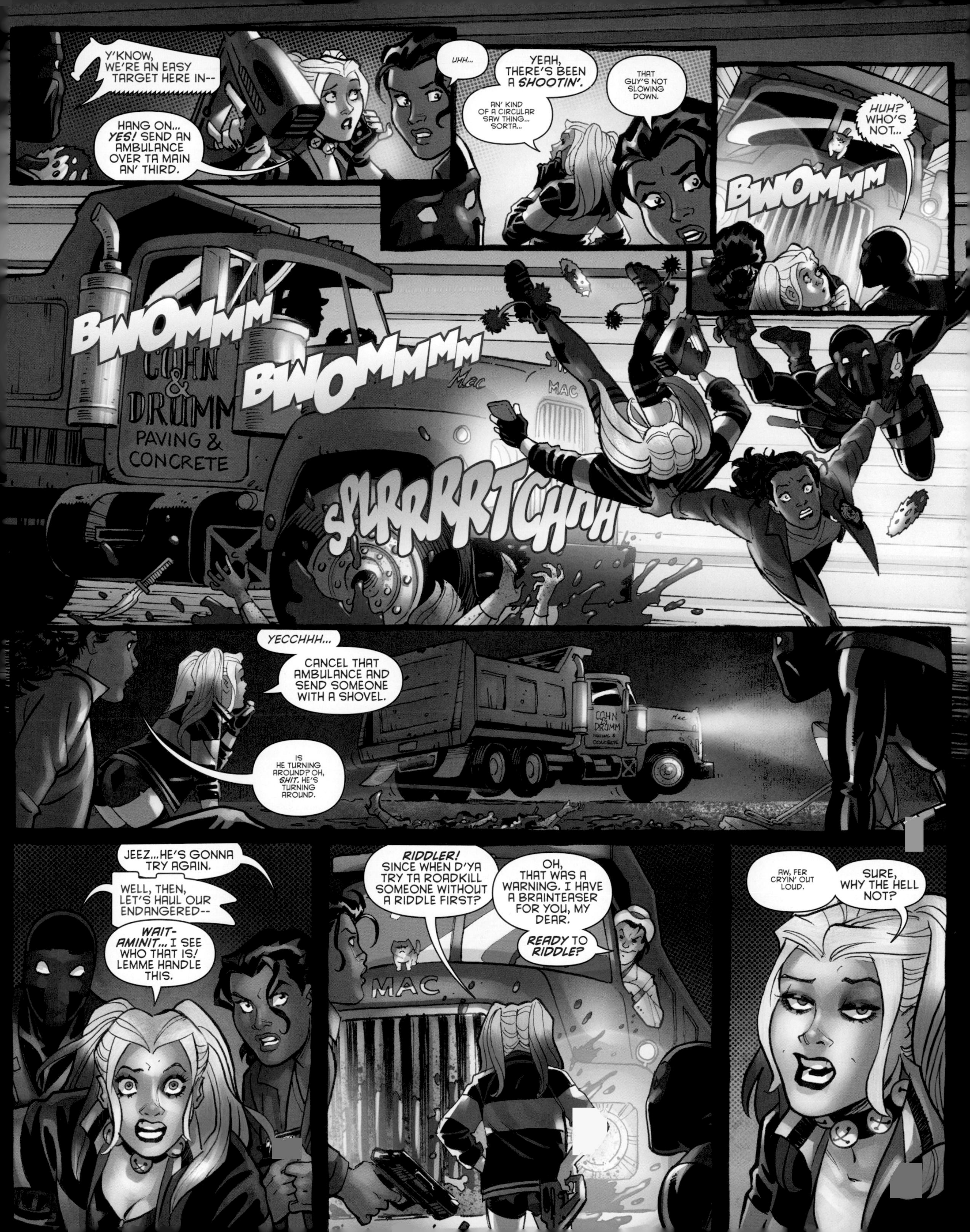
Y'KNOW, WE'RE AN EASY TARGET HERE IN--
HANG ON... YES! SEND AN AMBULANCE OVER TA MAIN AN' THIRD.
UHH...
YEAH, THERE'S BEEN A SHOOTIN'.
AN' KIND OF A CIRCULAR SAW THING... SORTA...
THAT GUY'S NOT SLOWING DOWN.
HUH? WHO'S NOT...
BWOMMM
BWOMMM
BWOMMMM
COHN & DRUMM PAVING & CONCRETE
MAC
SPLRRRRTCHHH
YECCHHH...
CANCEL THAT AMBULANCE AND SEND SOMEONE WITH A SHOVEL.
IS HE TURNING AROUND? OH, SHIT. HE'S TURNING AROUND.
JEEZ...HE'S GONNA TRY AGAIN.
WELL, THEN, LET'S HAUL OUR ENDANGERED--
WAIT-AMINIT... I SEE WHO THAT IS! LEMME HANDLE THIS.
RIDDLER! SINCE WHEN D'YA TRY TA ROADKILL SOMEONE WITHOUT A RIDDLE FIRST?
OH, THAT WAS A WARNING. I HAVE A BRAINTEASER FOR YOU, MY DEAR.
READY TO RIDDLE?
MAC
AW, FER CRYIN' OUT LOUD.
SURE, WHY THE HELL NOT?

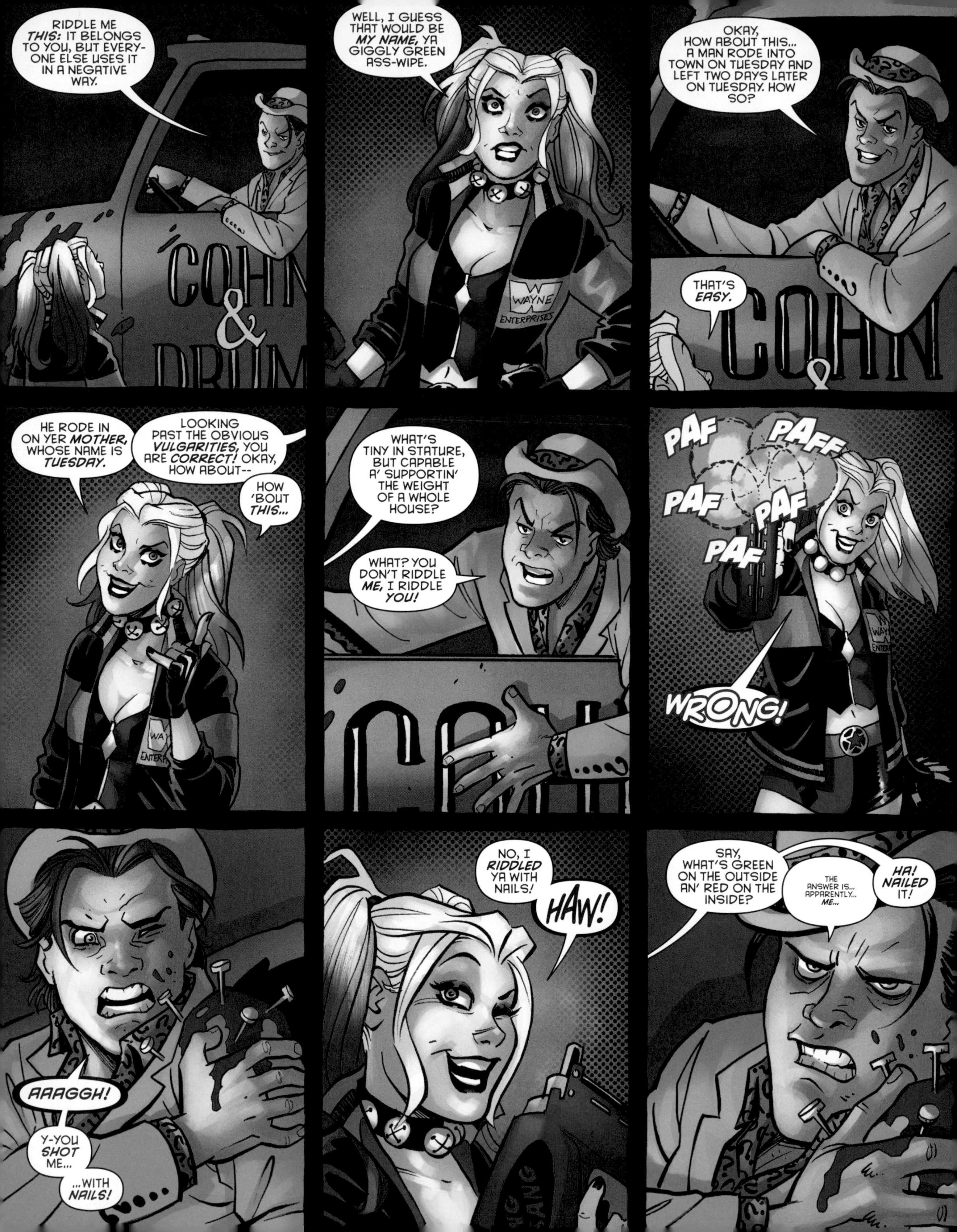
RIDDLE ME THIS: IT BELONGS TO YOU, BUT EVERY-ONE ELSE USES IT IN A NEGATIVE WAY.
COHN & DRUM
WELL, I GUESS THAT WOULD BE MY NAME, YA GIGGLY GREEN ASS-WIPE.
WAYNE ENTERPRISES
OKAY, HOW ABOUT THIS... A MAN RODE INTO TOWN ON TUESDAY AND LEFT TWO DAYS LATER ON TUESDAY. HOW SO?
THAT'S EASY.
COHN
HE RODE IN ON YER MOTHER, WHOSE NAME IS TUESDAY.
LOOKING PAST THE OBVIOUS VULGARITIES, YOU ARE CORRECT! OKAY, HOW ABOUT--
HOW 'BOUT THIS...
WHAT'S TINY IN STATURE, BUT CAPABLE A' SUPPORTIN' THE WEIGHT OF A WHOLE HOUSE?
WHAT? YOU DON'T RIDDLE ME, I RIDDLE YOU!
PAF
PAFF
PAF
PAF
PAF
WRONG!
AAAGGH!
Y-YOU SHOT ME...
...WITH NAILS!
NO, I RIDDLED YA WITH NAILS!
HAW!
SAY, WHAT'S GREEN ON THE OUTSIDE AN' RED ON THE INSIDE?
THE ANSWER IS... APPARENTLY... ME...
HA! NAILED IT!

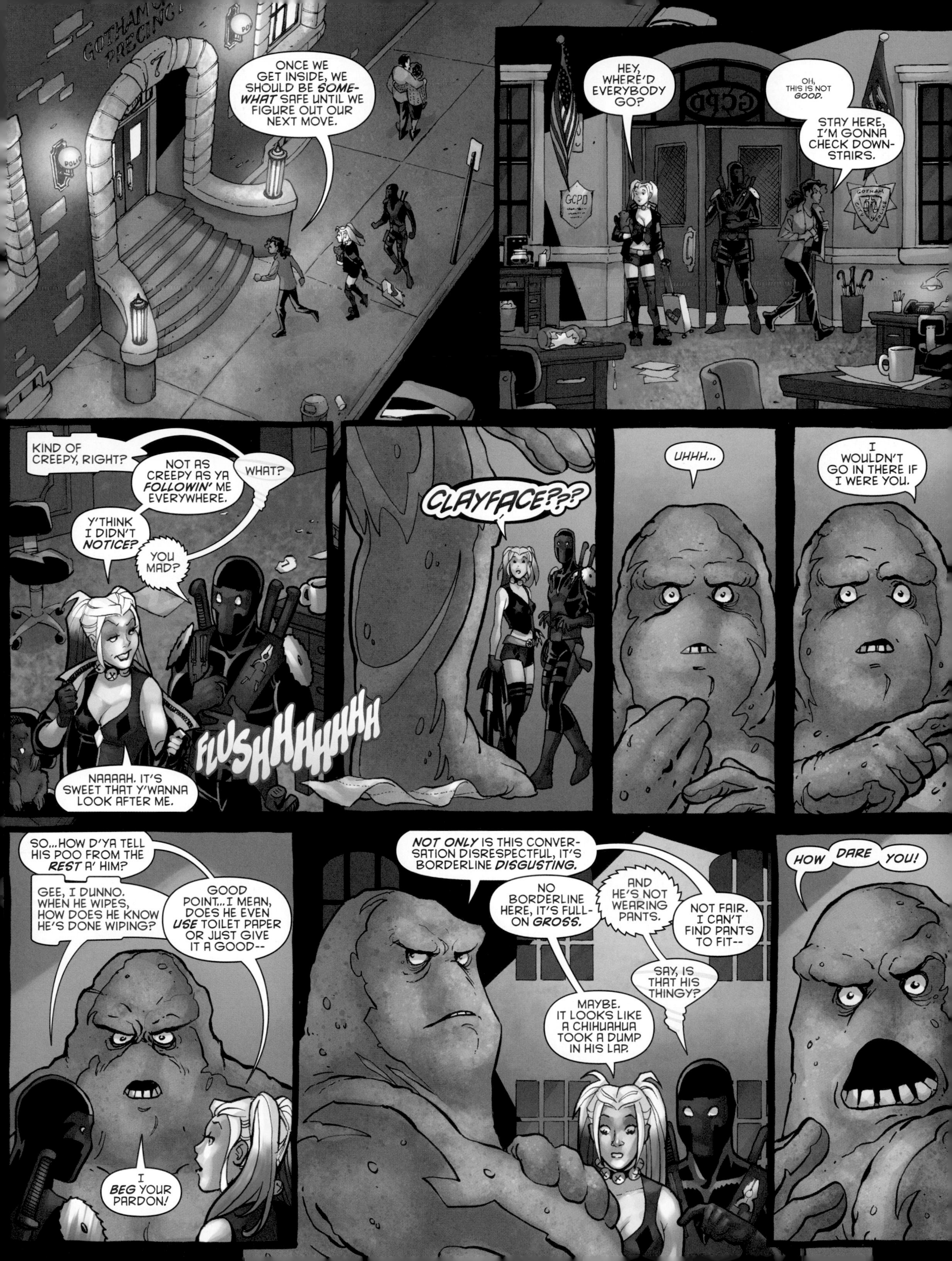
GOTHAM CITY PRECINCT
7
ONCE WE GET INSIDE, WE SHOULD BE SOME-WHAT SAFE UNTIL WE FIGURE OUT OUR NEXT MOVE.
GCPD
HEY, WHERE'D EVERYBODY GO?
OH, THIS IS NOT GOOD.
STAY HERE, I'M GONNA CHECK DOWN-STAIRS.
KIND OF CREEPY, RIGHT?
NOT AS CREEPY AS YA FOLLOWIN' ME EVERYWHERE.
WHAT?
Y'THINK I DIDN'T NOTICE?
YOU MAD?
NAAAAH. IT'S SWEET THAT Y'WANNA LOOK AFTER ME.
FLUSHHHHHHH
CLAYFACE???
UHHH...
I WOULDN'T GO IN THERE IF I WERE YOU.
SO...HOW D'YA TELL HIS POO FROM THE REST A' HIM?
GEE, I DUNNO. WHEN HE WIPES, HOW DOES HE KNOW HE'S DONE WIPING?
GOOD POINT...I MEAN, DOES HE EVEN USE TOILET PAPER OR JUST GIVE IT A GOOD--
I BEG YOUR PARDON!
NOT ONLY IS THIS CONVERSATION DISRESPECTFUL, IT'S BORDERLINE DISGUSTING.
NO BORDERLINE HERE, IT'S FULL-ON GROSS.
AND HE'S NOT WEARING PANTS.
NOT FAIR. I CAN'T FIND PANTS TO FIT--
SAY, IS THAT HIS THINGY?
MAYBE. IT LOOKS LIKE A CHIHUAHUA TOOK A DUMP IN HIS LAP.
HOW DARE YOU!

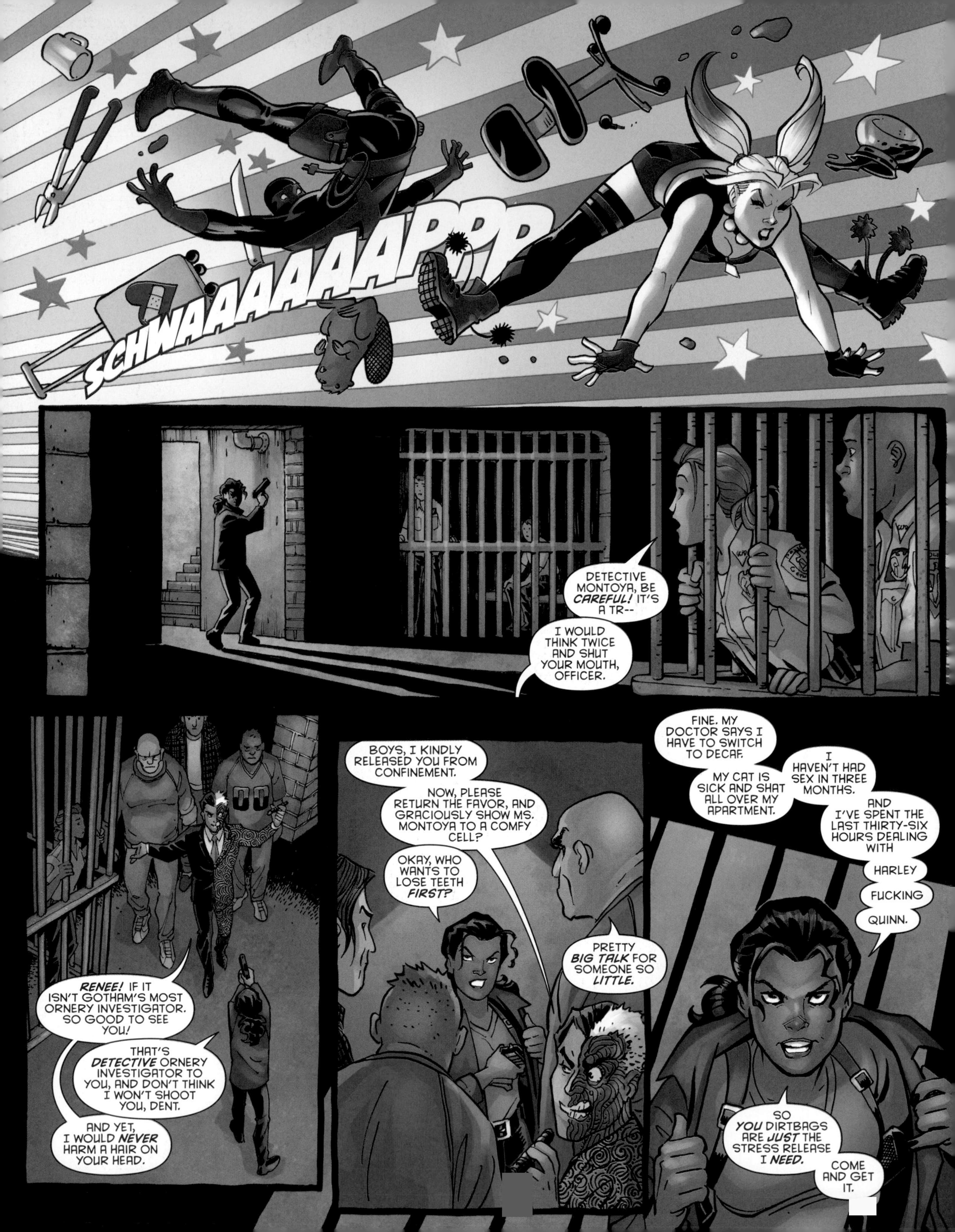
SCHWAAAAAAAPPP
DETECTIVE MONTOYA, BE *CAREFUL!* IT'S A TR--
I WOULD THINK TWICE AND SHUT YOUR MOUTH, OFFICER.
RENEE! IF IT ISN'T GOTHAM'S MOST ORNERY INVESTIGATOR. SO GOOD TO SEE YOU!
THAT'S *DETECTIVE* ORNERY INVESTIGATOR TO YOU, AND DON'T THINK I WON'T SHOOT YOU, DENT.
AND YET, I WOULD *NEVER* HARM A HAIR ON YOUR HEAD.
BOYS, I KINDLY RELEASED YOU FROM CONFINEMENT.
NOW, PLEASE RETURN THE FAVOR, AND GRACIOUSLY SHOW MS. MONTOYA TO A COMFY CELL?
OKAY, WHO WANTS TO LOSE TEETH *FIRST?*
PRETTY *BIG TALK* FOR SOMEONE SO *LITTLE.*
FINE. MY DOCTOR SAYS I HAVE TO SWITCH TO DECAF.
MY CAT IS SICK AND SHAT ALL OVER MY APARTMENT.
I HAVEN'T HAD SEX IN THREE MONTHS.
AND I'VE SPENT THE LAST THIRTY-SIX HOURS DEALING WITH
HARLEY
FUCKING
QUINN.
SO *YOU* DIRTBAGS ARE *JUST* THE STRESS RELEASE I *NEED.*
COME AND GET IT.

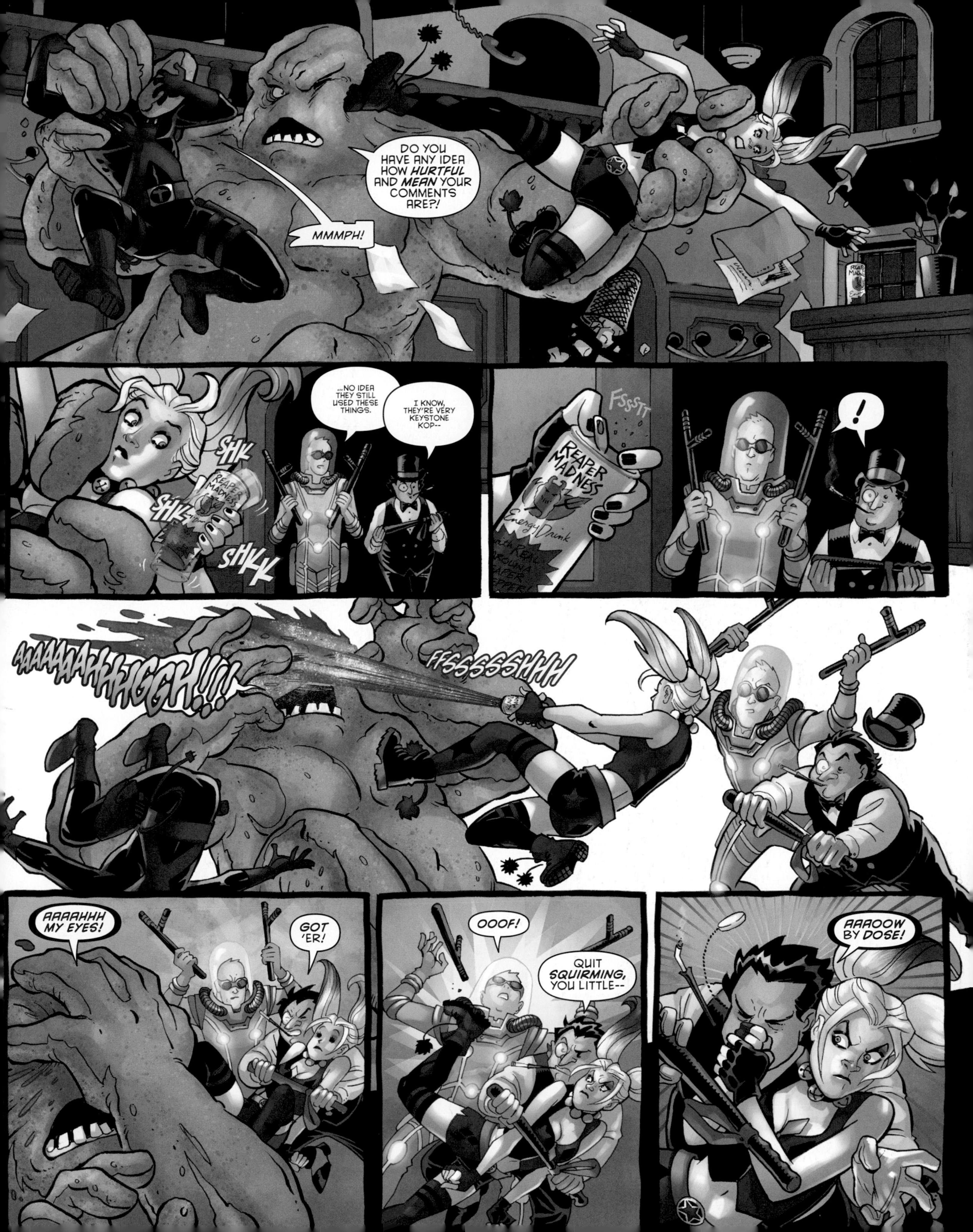
DO YOU HAVE ANY IDEA HOW HURTFUL AND MEAN YOUR COMMENTS ARE?!
MMMPH!
SHK
SHK
SHKK
...NO IDEA THEY STILL USED THESE THINGS.
I KNOW, THEY'RE VERY KEYSTONE KOP--
FSSSTT
REAPER MADNESS
Energy Drink
!
AAAAAAHHHGGH!!!!
FFSSSSSSHHH
AAAAHHH MY EYES!
GOT 'ER!
OOOF!
QUIT SQUIRMING, YOU LITTLE--
AAAOOW BY DOSE!

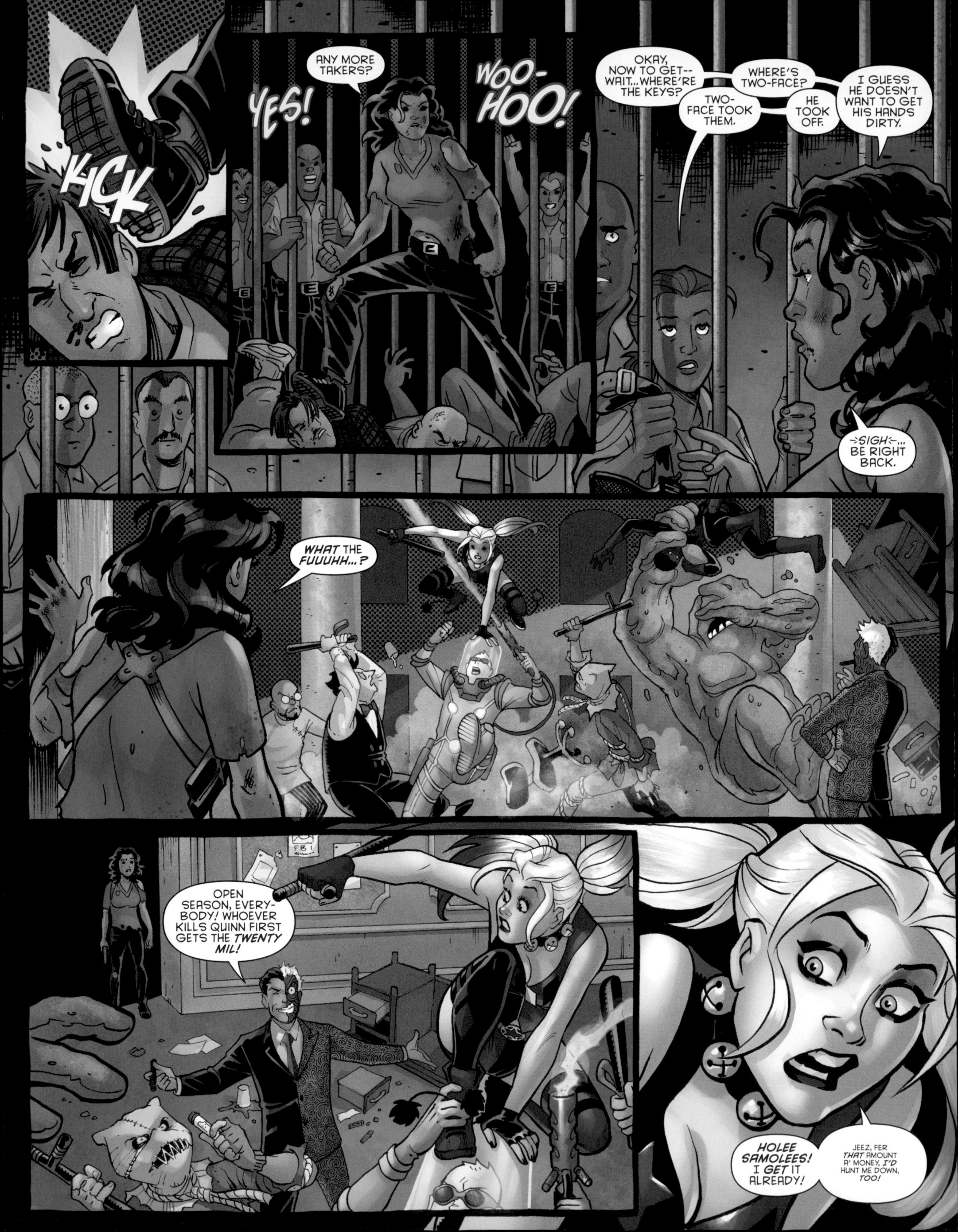
KICK
ANY MORE TAKERS?
YES!
WOO-HOO!
OKAY, NOW TO GET-- WAIT...WHERE'RE THE KEYS?
TWO-FACE TOOK THEM.
WHERE'S TWO-FACE?
HE TOOK OFF.
I GUESS HE DOESN'T WANT TO GET HIS HANDS DIRTY.
-SIGH-... BE RIGHT BACK.
WHAT THE FUUUHH...?
OPEN SEASON, EVERY-BODY! WHOEVER KILLS QUINN FIRST GETS THE TWENTY MIL!
HOLEE SAMOLEES! I GET IT ALREADY!
JEEZ, FER THAT AMOUNT A' MONEY, I'D HUNT ME DOWN, TOO!

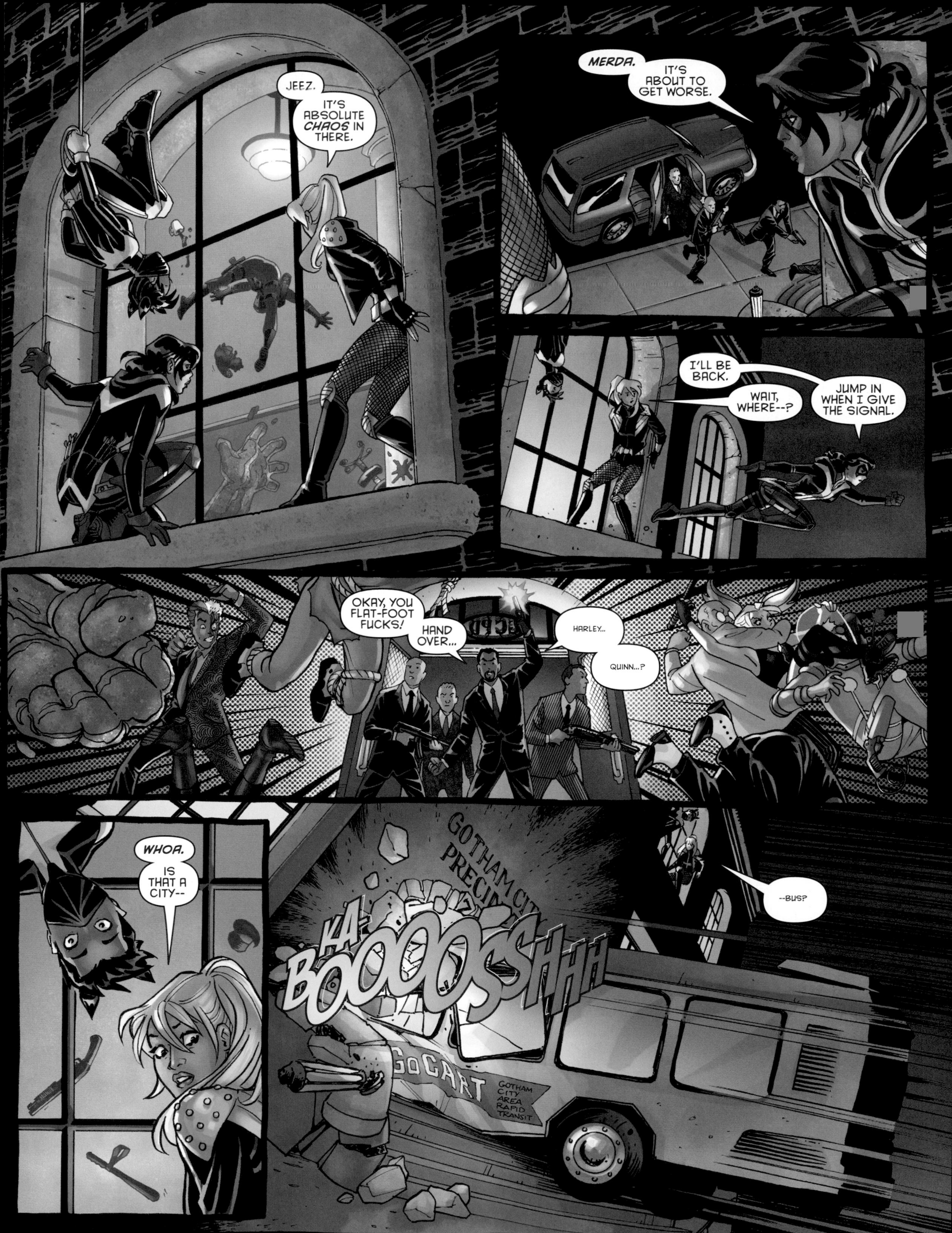
JEEZ.
IT'S ABSOLUTE CHAOS IN THERE.
MERDA.
IT'S ABOUT TO GET WORSE.
I'LL BE BACK.
WAIT, WHERE--?
JUMP IN WHEN I GIVE THE SIGNAL.
OKAY, YOU FLAT-FOOT FUCKS!
HAND OVER...
HARLEY...
QUINN...?
WHOA.
IS THAT A CITY--
--BUS?
GOTHAM CITY PRECI
KA-BOOOOSHHH
GO CART
GOTHAM CITY AREA RAPID TRANSIT

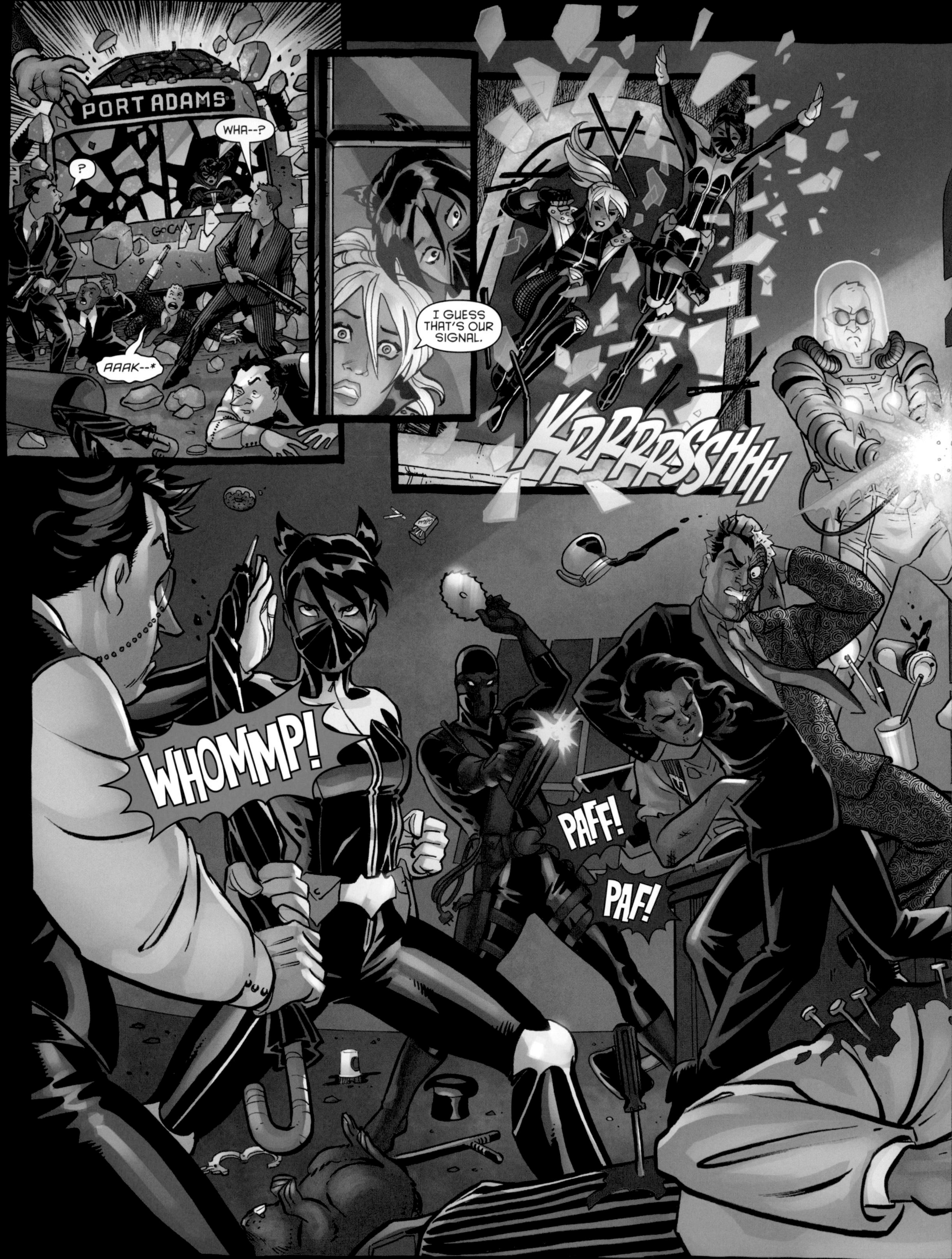
PORT ADAMS
WHA--?
?
AAAK--*
I GUESS THAT'S OUR SIGNAL.
KRRRRRSSHHH
WHOMMP!
PAFF!
PAF!

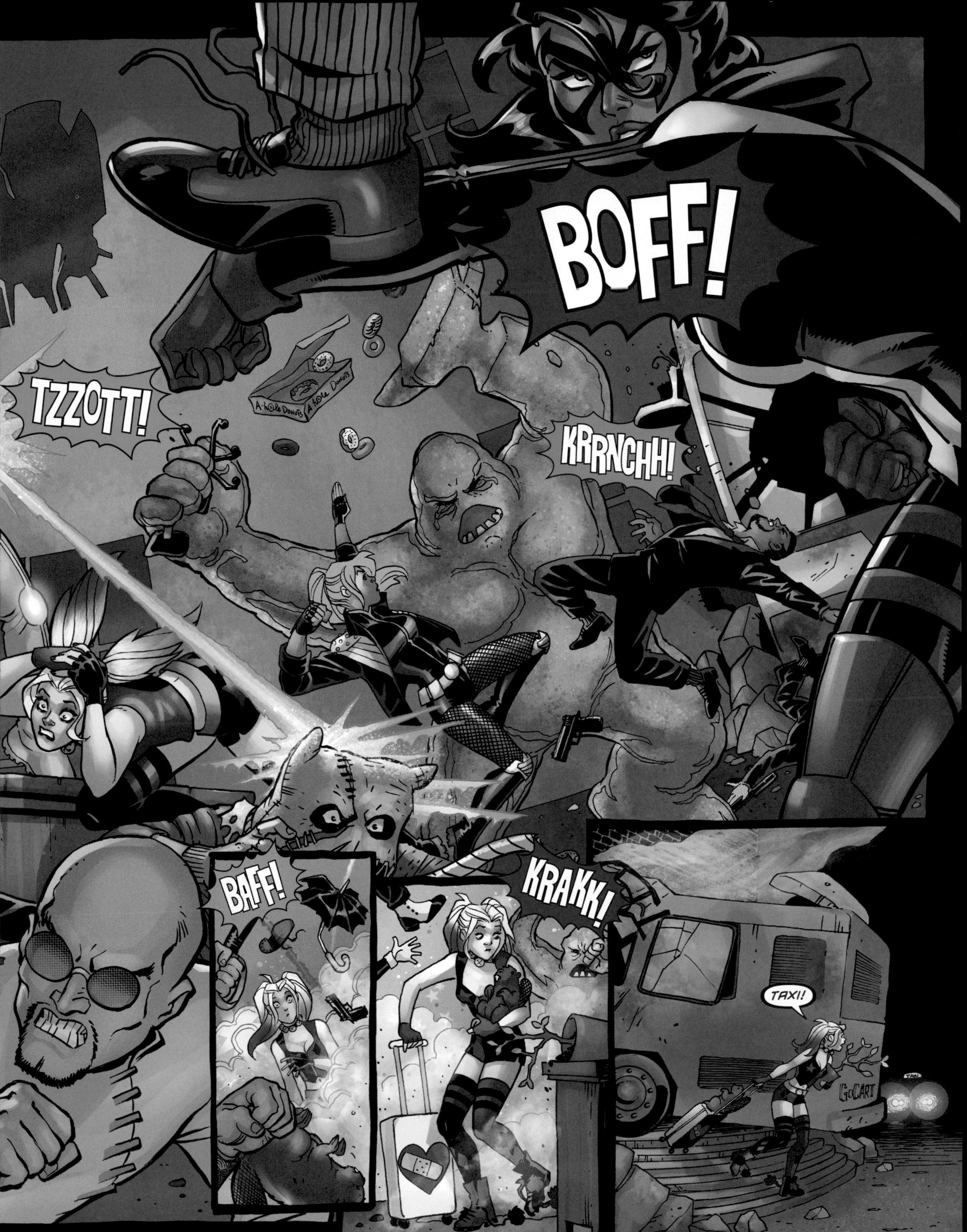
BOFF!
TZZOTT!
A-hole Donuts
A-hole Donuts
KRRNCHH!
BAFF!
KRAKK!
TAXI!
GoCART

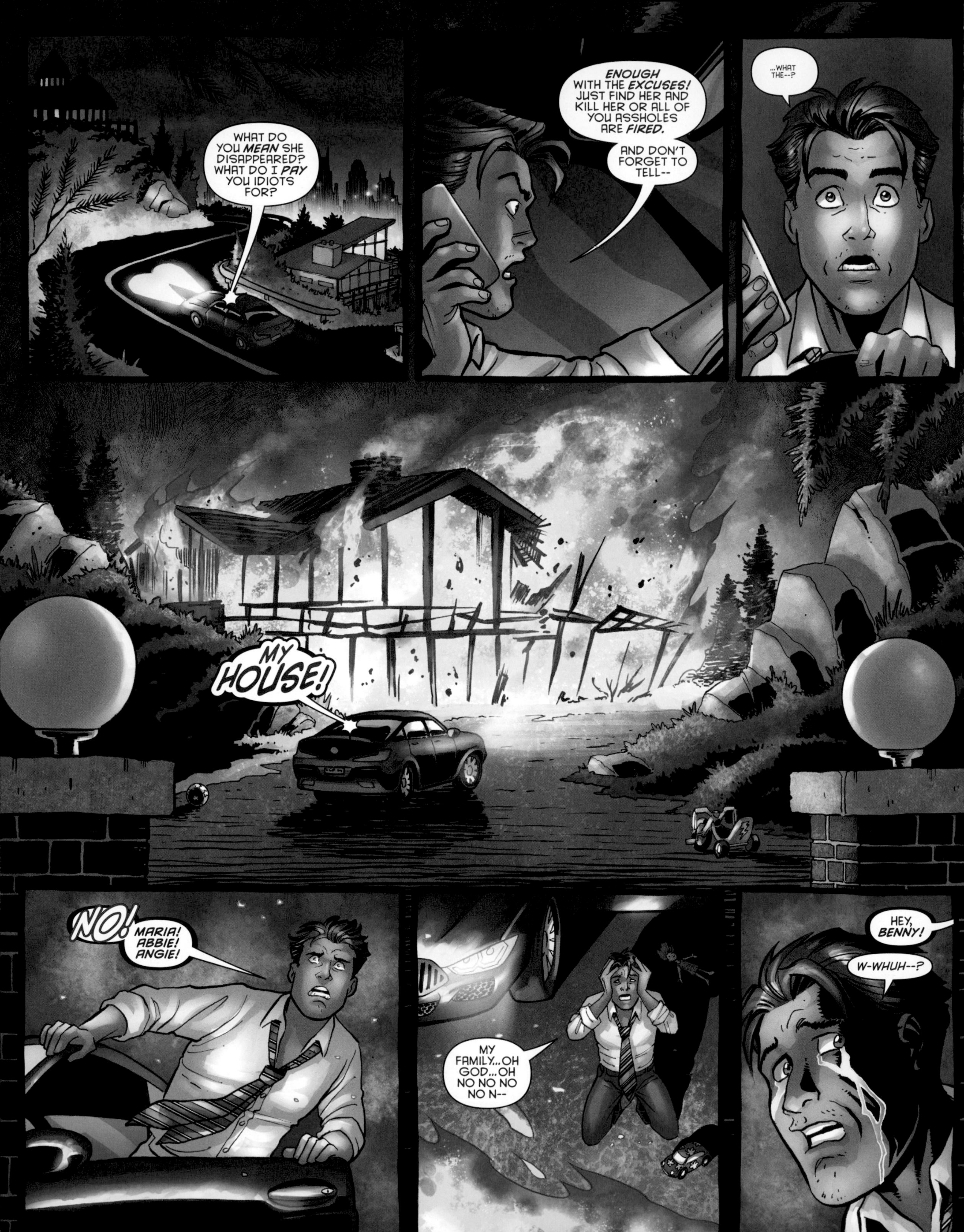
WHAT DO YOU MEAN SHE DISAPPEARED? WHAT DO I PAY YOU IDIOTS FOR?
ENOUGH WITH THE EXCUSES! JUST FIND HER AND KILL HER OR ALL OF YOU ASSHOLES ARE FIRED.
AND DON'T FORGET TO TELL--
...WHAT THE--?
MY HOUSE!
NO!
MARIA! ABBIE! ANGIE!
MY FAMILY...OH GOD...OH NO NO NO NO N--
HEY, BENNY!
W-WHUH--?

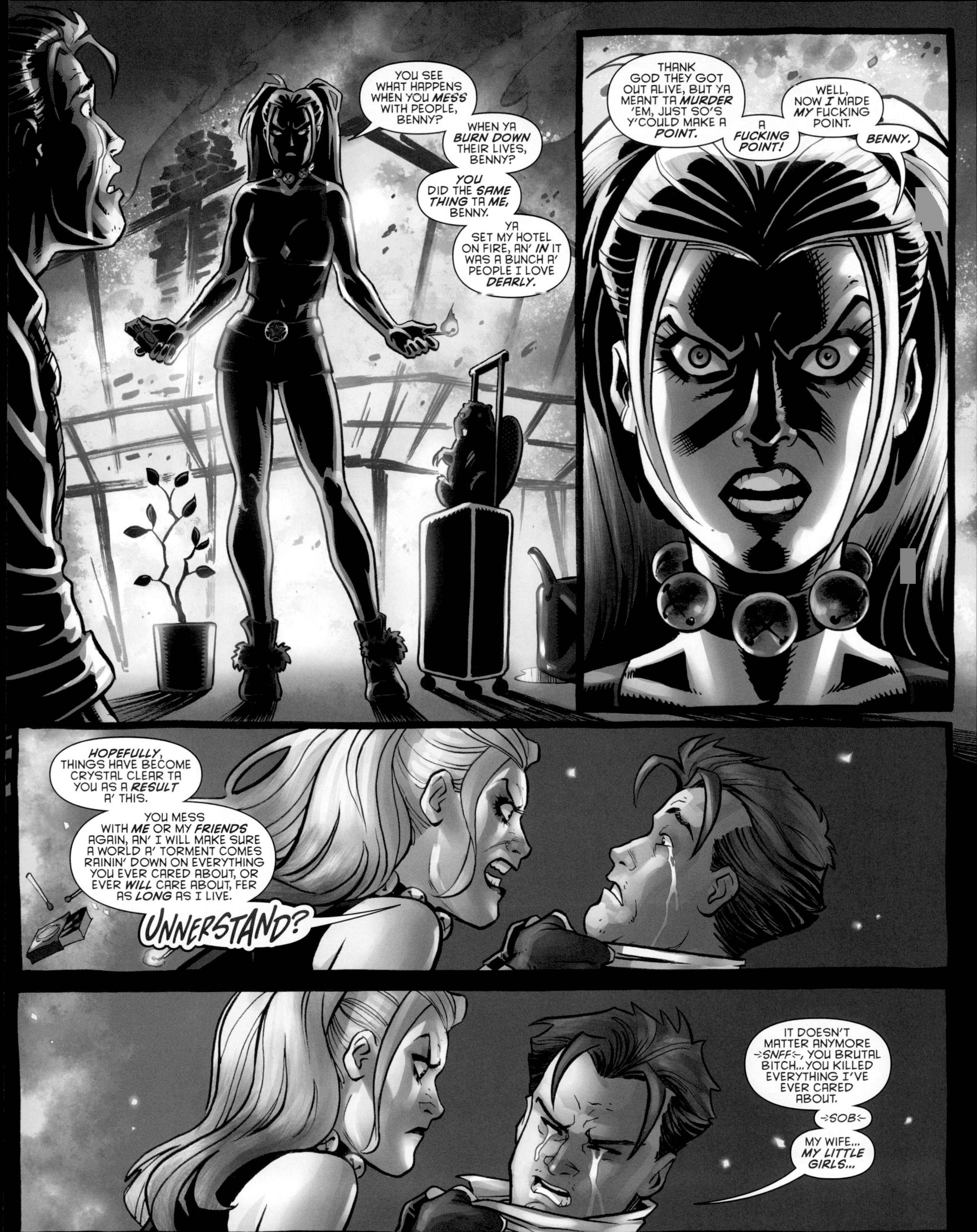
YOU SEE WHAT HAPPENS WHEN YOU MESS WITH PEOPLE, BENNY?
WHEN YA BURN DOWN THEIR LIVES, BENNY?
YOU DID THE SAME THING TA ME, BENNY.
YA SET MY HOTEL ON FIRE, AN' IN IT WAS A BUNCH A' PEOPLE I LOVE DEARLY.
THANK GOD THEY GOT OUT ALIVE, BUT YA MEANT TA MURDER 'EM, JUST SO'S Y'COULD MAKE A POINT.
A FUCKING POINT!
WELL, NOW I MADE MY FUCKING POINT.
BENNY.
HOPEFULLY, THINGS HAVE BECOME CRYSTAL CLEAR TA YOU AS A RESULT A' THIS.
YOU MESS WITH ME OR MY FRIENDS AGAIN, AN' I WILL MAKE SURE A WORLD A' TORMENT COMES RAININ' DOWN ON EVERYTHING YOU EVER CARED ABOUT, OR EVER WILL CARE ABOUT, FER AS LONG AS I LIVE.
UNNERSTAND?
IT DOESN'T MATTER ANYMORE ->SNFF<-, YOU BRUTAL BITCH...YOU KILLED EVERYTHING I'VE EVER CARED ABOUT.
->SOB<-
MY WIFE... MY LITTLE GIRLS...

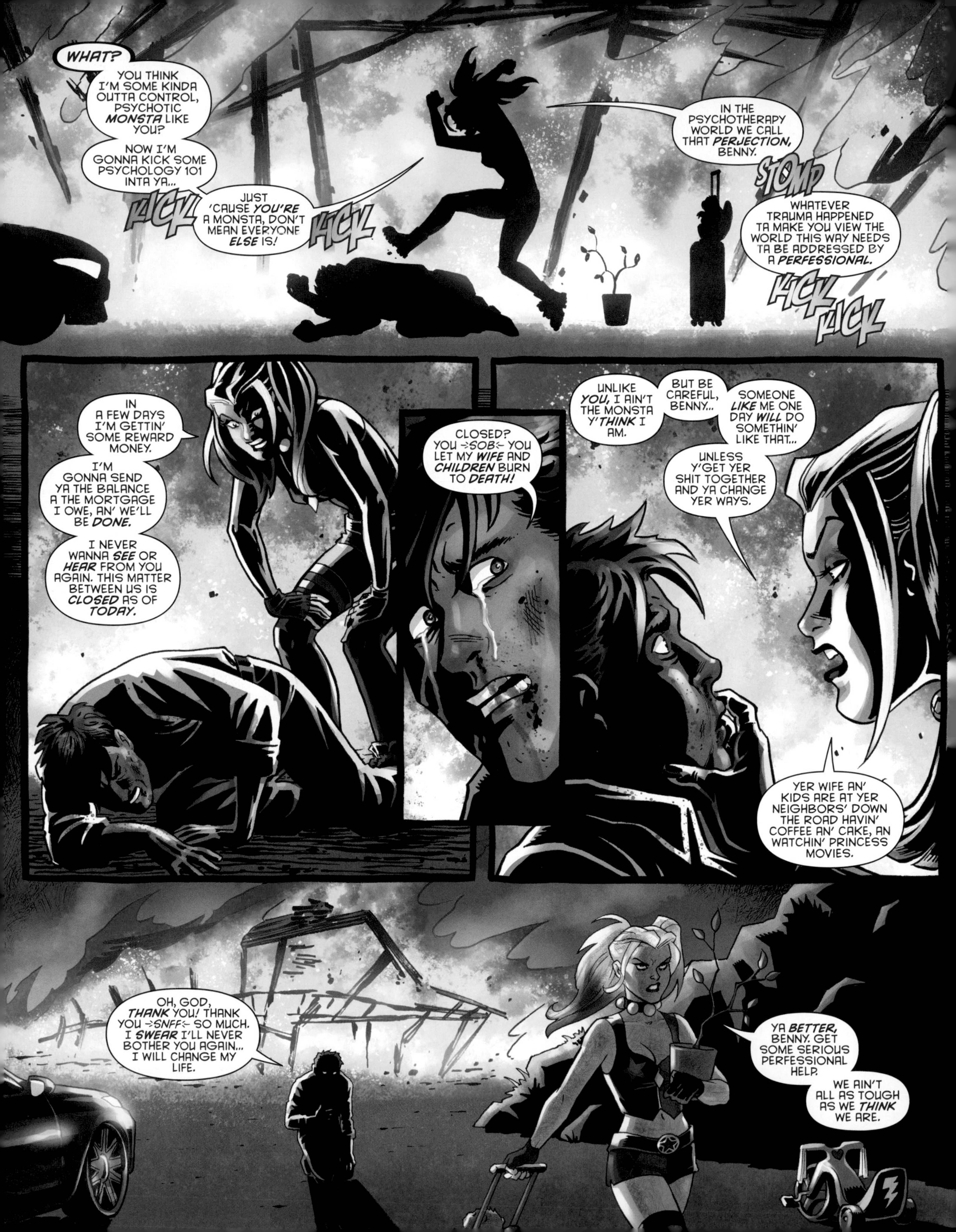
WHAT?
YOU THINK I'M SOME KINDA OUTTA CONTROL, PSYCHOTIC MONSTA LIKE YOU?
NOW I'M GONNA KICK SOME PSYCHOLOGY 101 INTA YA...
KICK
JUST 'CAUSE YOU'RE A MONSTA, DON'T MEAN EVERYONE ELSE IS!
KICK
IN THE PSYCHOTHERAPY WORLD WE CALL THAT PERJECTION, BENNY.
STOMP
WHATEVER TRAUMA HAPPENED TA MAKE YOU VIEW THE WORLD THIS WAY NEEDS TA BE ADDRESSED BY A PERFESSIONAL.
KICK
KICK
IN A FEW DAYS I'M GETTIN' SOME REWARD MONEY.
I'M GONNA SEND YA THE BALANCE A THE MORTGAGE I OWE, AN' WE'LL BE DONE.
I NEVER WANNA SEE OR HEAR FROM YOU AGAIN. THIS MATTER BETWEEN US IS CLOSED AS OF TODAY.
CLOSED? YOU ⇒SOB⇐ YOU LET MY WIFE AND CHILDREN BURN TO DEATH!
UNLIKE YOU, I AIN'T THE MONSTA Y'THINK I AM.
BUT BE CAREFUL, BENNY...
SOMEONE LIKE ME ONE DAY WILL DO SOMETHIN' LIKE THAT...
UNLESS Y'GET YER SHIT TOGETHER AND YA CHANGE YER WAYS.
YER WIFE AN' KIDS ARE AT YER NEIGHBORS' DOWN THE ROAD HAVIN' COFFEE AN' CAKE, AN WATCHIN' PRINCESS MOVIES.
OH, GOD, THANK YOU! THANK YOU ⇒SNFF⇐ SO MUCH. I SWEAR I'LL NEVER BOTHER YOU AGAIN... I WILL CHANGE MY LIFE.
YA BETTER, BENNY. GET SOME SERIOUS PERFESSIONAL HELP.
WE AIN'T ALL AS TOUGH AS WE THINK WE ARE.

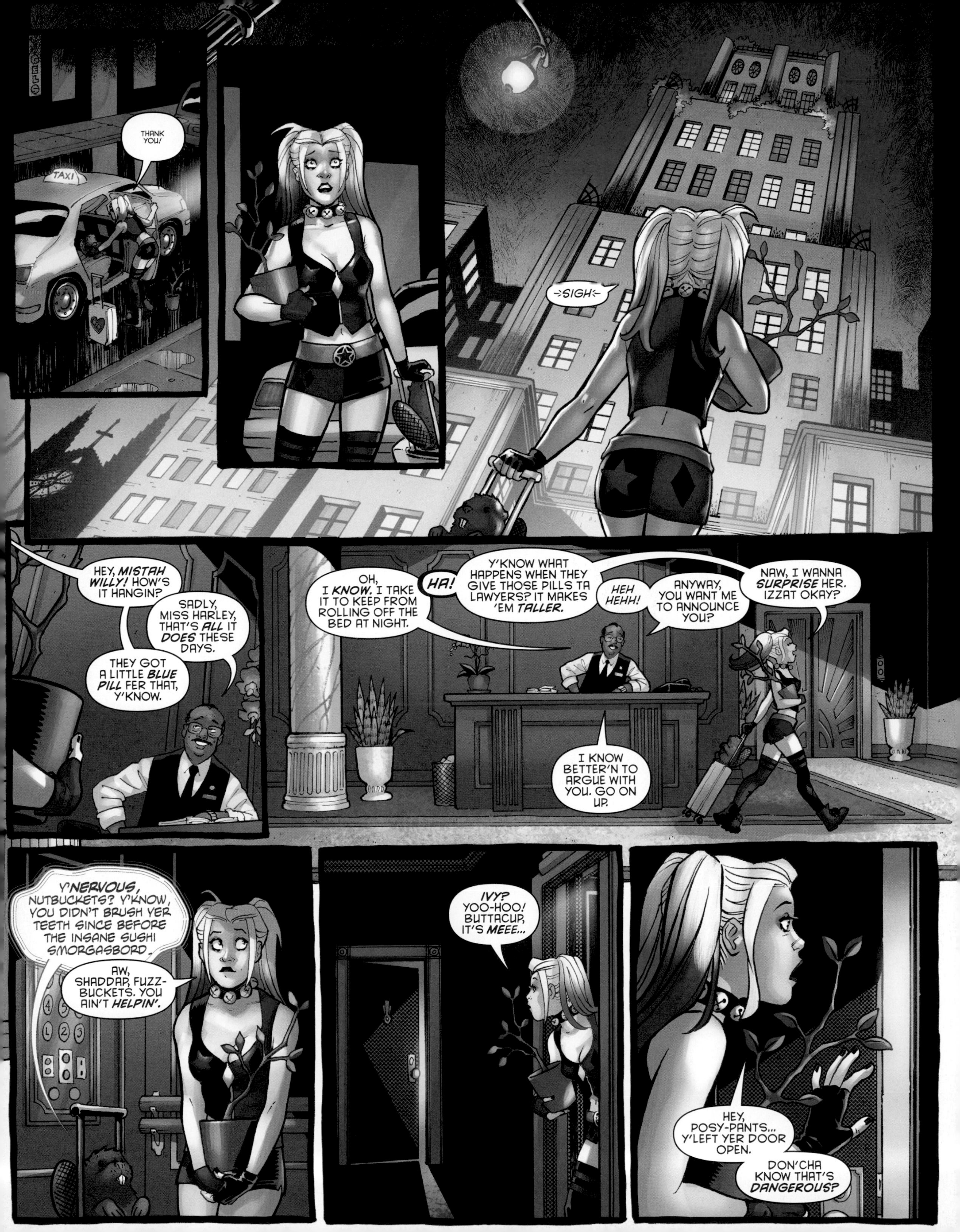
THANK YOU!
TAXI
-SIGH-
HEY, MISTAH WILLY! HOW'S IT HANGIN?
SADLY, MISS HARLEY, THAT'S ALL IT DOES THESE DAYS.
THEY GOT A LITTLE BLUE PILL FER THAT, Y'KNOW.
OH, I KNOW. I TAKE IT TO KEEP FROM ROLLING OFF THE BED AT NIGHT.
HA!
Y'KNOW WHAT HAPPENS WHEN THEY GIVE THOSE PILLS TA LAWYERS? IT MAKES 'EM TALLER.
HEH HEHH!
ANYWAY, YOU WANT ME TO ANNOUNCE YOU?
NAW, I WANNA SURPRISE HER. IZZAT OKAY?
I KNOW BETTER'N TO ARGUE WITH YOU. GO ON UP.
Y'NERVOUS, NUTBUCKETS? Y'KNOW, YOU DIDN'T BRUSH YER TEETH SINCE BEFORE THE INSANE SUSHI SMORGASBORD.
AW, SHADDAP, FUZZ-BUCKETS. YOU AIN'T HELPIN'.
IVY? YOO-HOO! BUTTACUP, IT'S MEEE...
HEY, POSY-PANTS... Y'LEFT YER DOOR OPEN.
DON'CHA KNOW THAT'S DANGEROUS?

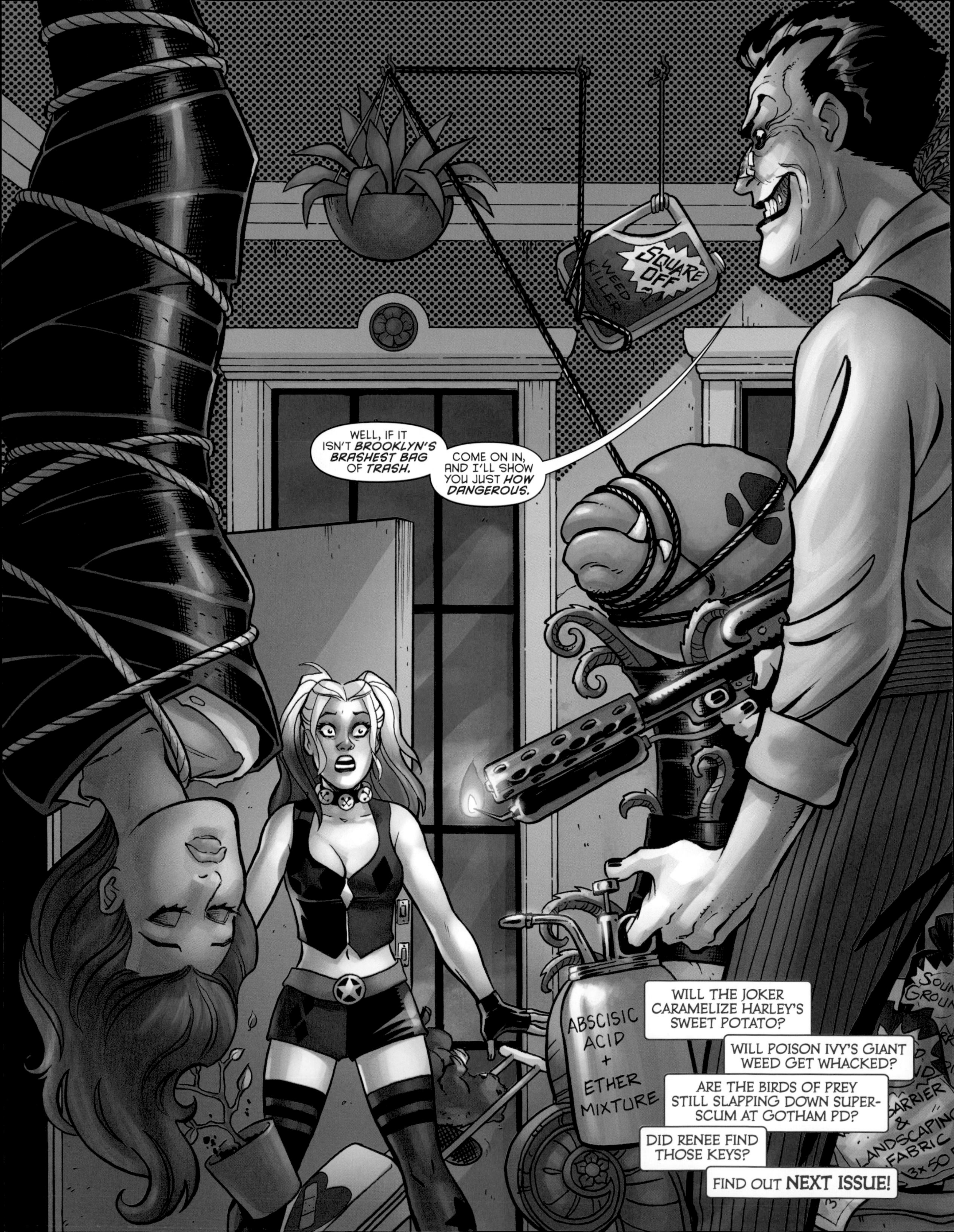
SQUARE OFF
WEED KILLER
WELL, IF IT ISN'T BROOKLYN'S BRASHEST BAG OF TRASH.
COME ON IN, AND I'LL SHOW YOU JUST HOW DANGEROUS.
ABSCISIC ACID + ETHER MIXTURE
WILL THE JOKER CARAMELIZE HARLEY'S SWEET POTATO?
WILL POISON IVY'S GIANT WEED GET WHACKED?
ARE THE BIRDS OF PREY STILL SLAPPING DOWN SUPER-SCUM AT GOTHAM PD?
DID RENEE FIND THOSE KEYS?
FIND OUT NEXT ISSUE!
BARRIER & LANDSCAPING FABRIC

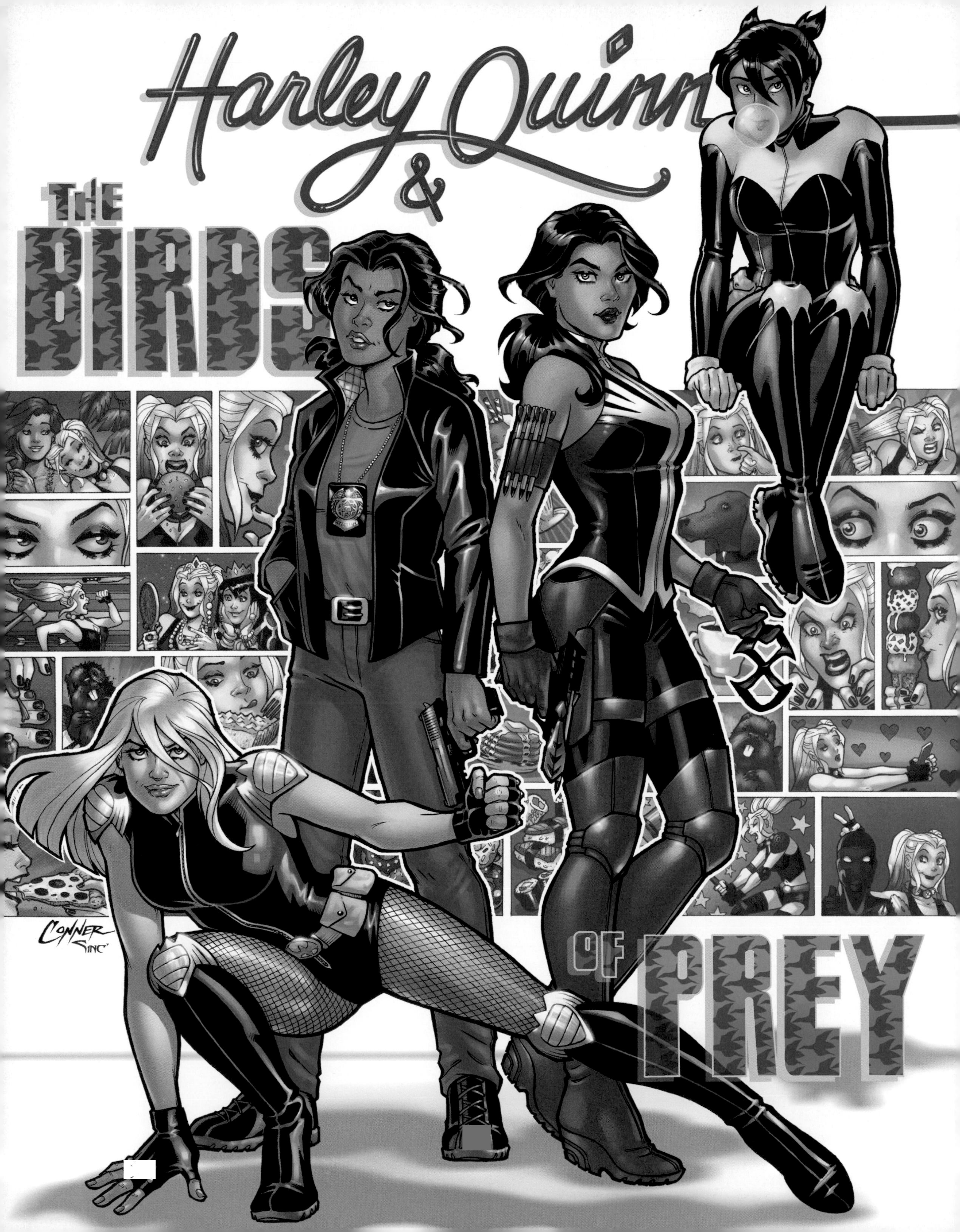
Harley Quinn
&
THE BIRDS OF PREY
CONNER SINC'

BOOK FOUR
FLOWERING INFERNO

"It's MY turn now."

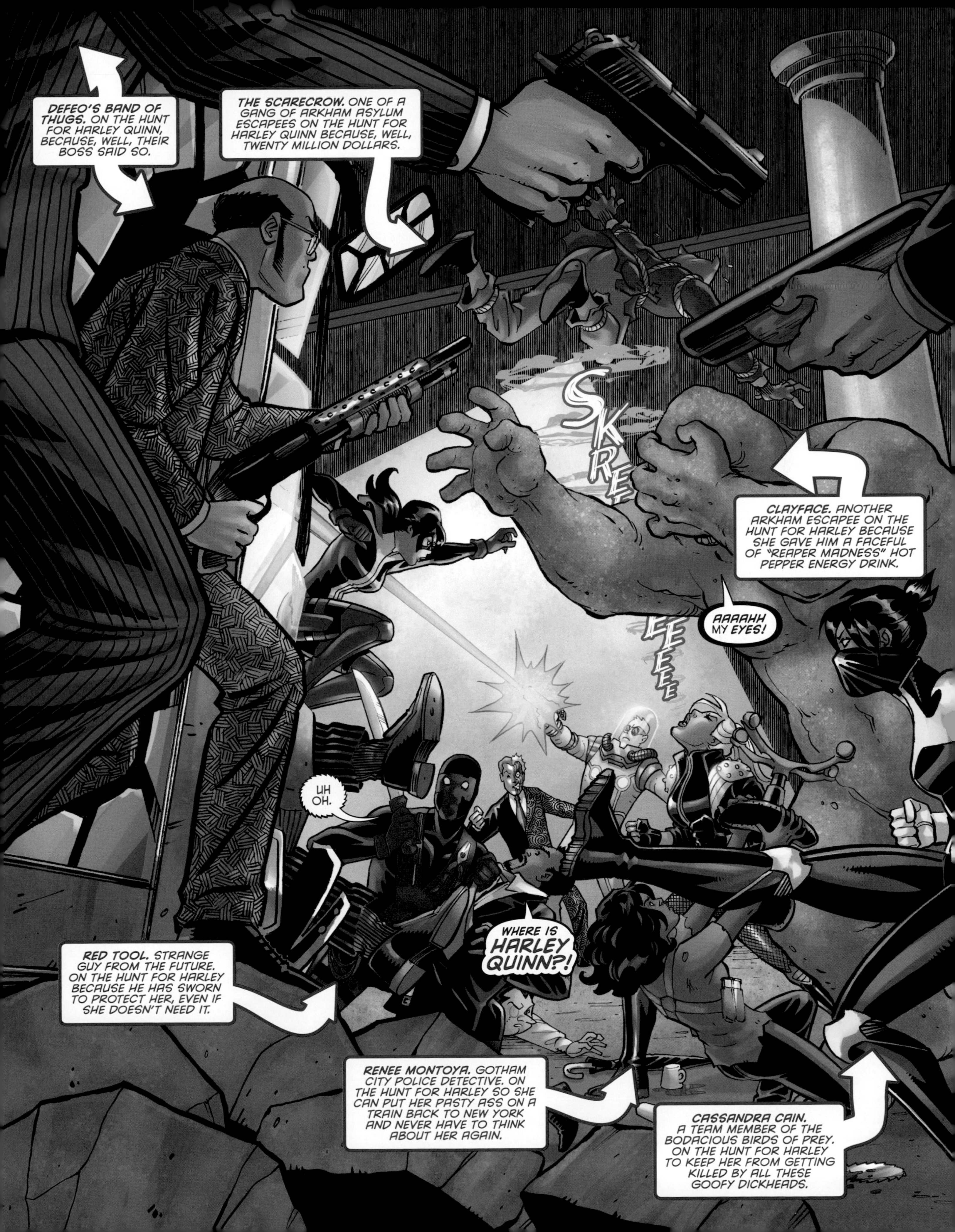
DEFEO'S BAND OF THUGS. ON THE HUNT FOR HARLEY QUINN, BECAUSE, WELL, THEIR BOSS SAID SO.
THE SCARECROW. ONE OF A GANG OF ARKHAM ASYLUM ESCAPEES ON THE HUNT FOR HARLEY QUINN BECAUSE, WELL, TWENTY MILLION DOLLARS.
SKREEEEEE
CLAYFACE. ANOTHER ARKHAM ESCAPEE ON THE HUNT FOR HARLEY BECAUSE SHE GAVE HIM A FACEFUL OF "REAPER MADNESS" HOT PEPPER ENERGY DRINK.
AAAAHH MY EYES!
UH OH.
WHERE IS HARLEY QUINN?!
RED TOOL. STRANGE GUY FROM THE FUTURE. ON THE HUNT FOR HARLEY BECAUSE HE HAS SWORN TO PROTECT HER, EVEN IF SHE DOESN'T NEED IT.
RENEE MONTOYA. GOTHAM CITY POLICE DETECTIVE. ON THE HUNT FOR HARLEY SO SHE CAN PUT HER PASTY ASS ON A TRAIN BACK TO NEW YORK AND NEVER HAVE TO THINK ABOUT HER AGAIN.
CASSANDRA CAIN. A TEAM MEMBER OF THE BODACIOUS BIRDS OF PREY. ON THE HUNT FOR HARLEY TO KEEP HER FROM GETTING KILLED BY ALL THESE GOOFY DICKHEADS.

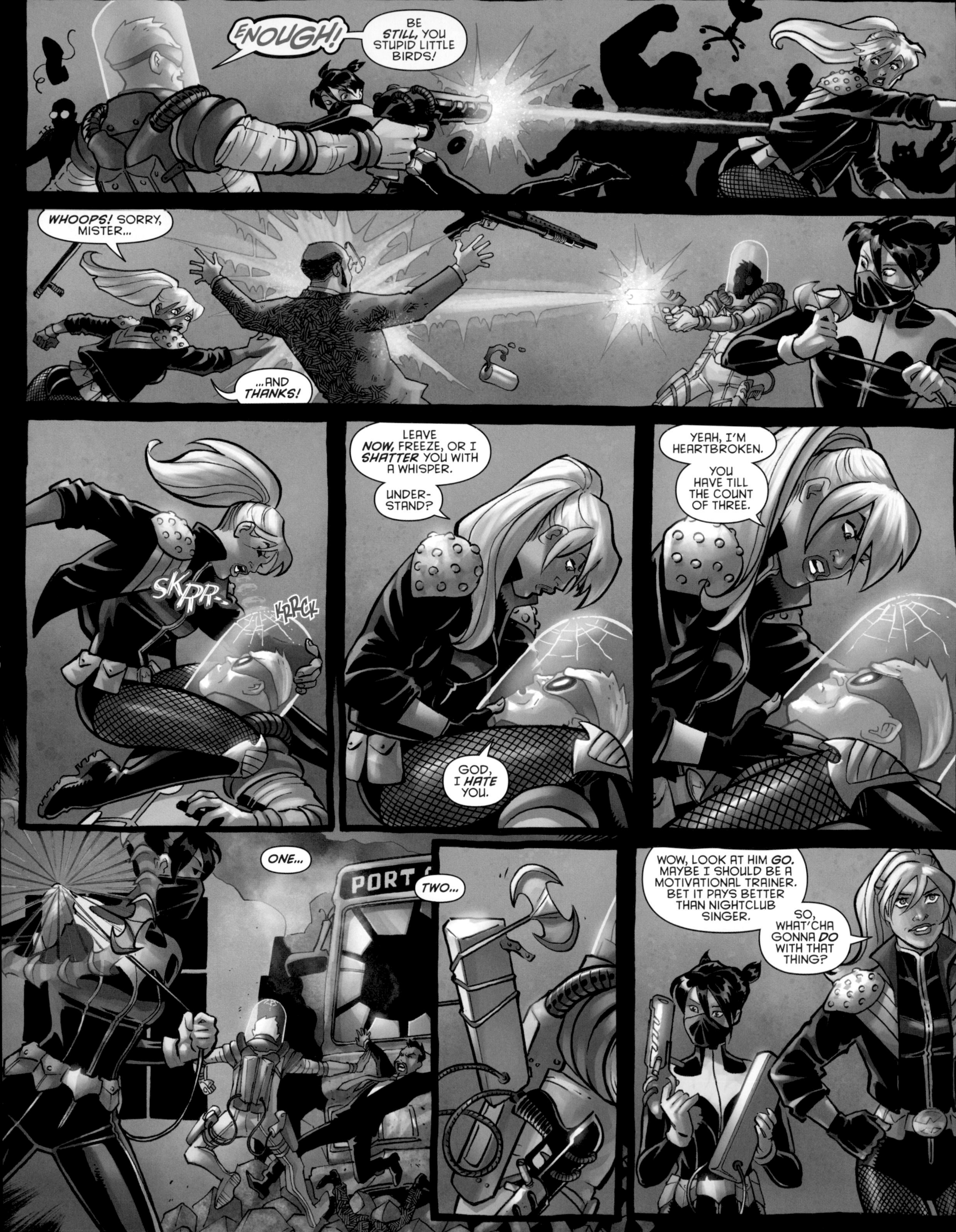
ENOUGH!
BE STILL, YOU STUPID LITTLE BIRDS!
WHOOPS! SORRY, MISTER...
...AND THANKS!
SKRR-
KRRCK
LEAVE NOW, FREEZE, OR I SHATTER YOU WITH A WHISPER.
UNDER-STAND?
GOD, I HATE YOU.
YEAH, I'M HEARTBROKEN.
YOU HAVE TILL THE COUNT OF THREE.
ONE...
PORT
TWO...
WOW, LOOK AT HIM GO. MAYBE I SHOULD BE A MOTIVATIONAL TRAINER. BET IT PAYS BETTER THAN NIGHTCLUB SINGER.
SO, WHAT'CHA GONNA DO WITH THAT THING?

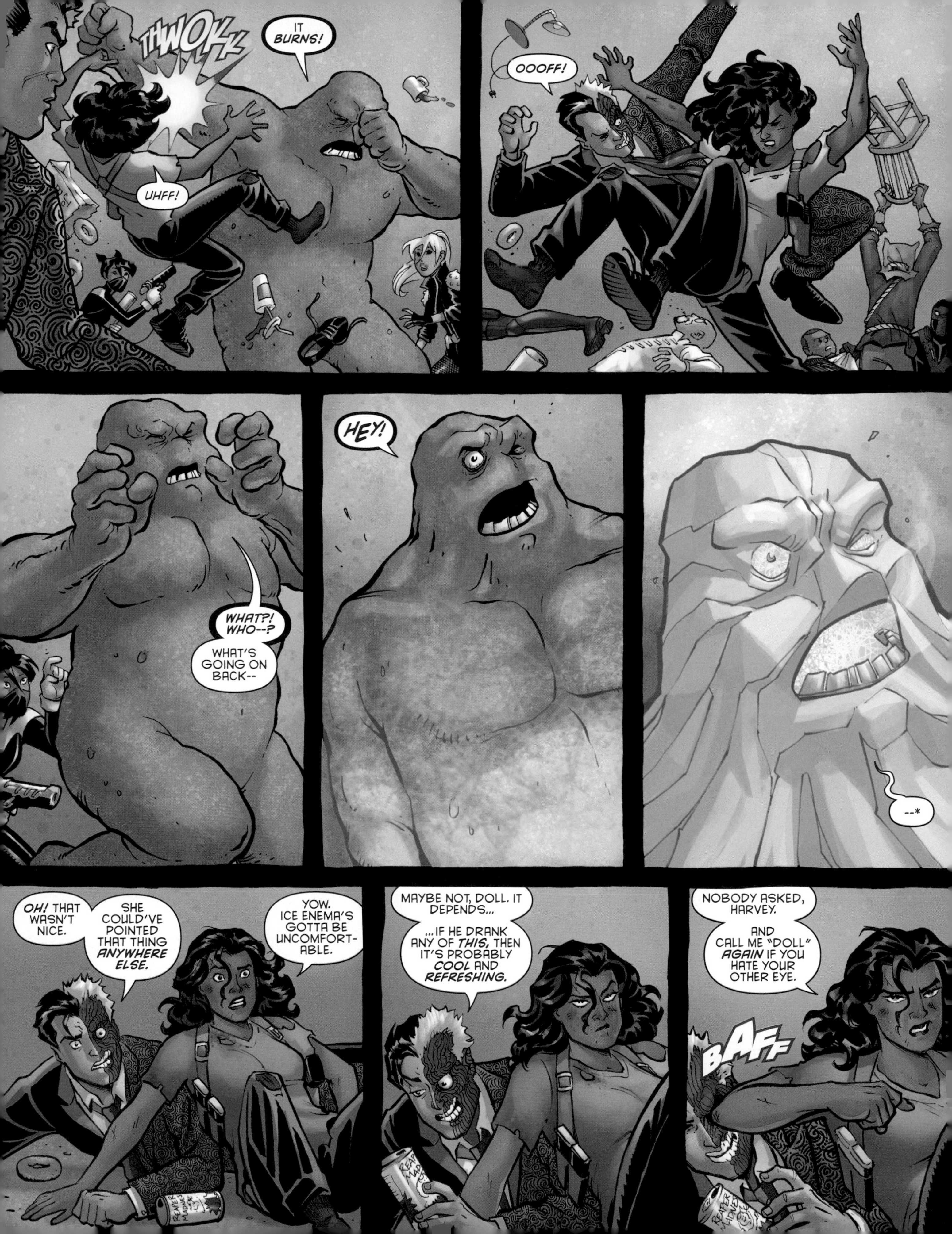
THWOKK
IT BURNS!
UHFF!
OOOFF!
WHAT?! WHO--?
WHAT'S GOING ON BACK--
HEY!
--*
OH! THAT WASN'T NICE.
SHE COULD'VE POINTED THAT THING ANYWHERE ELSE.
YOW. ICE ENEMA'S GOTTA BE UNCOMFORT-ABLE.
MAYBE NOT, DOLL. IT DEPENDS...
...IF HE DRANK ANY OF THIS, THEN IT'S PROBABLY COOL AND REFRESHING.
NOBODY ASKED, HARVEY.
AND CALL ME "DOLL" AGAIN IF YOU HATE YOUR OTHER EYE.
BAFF

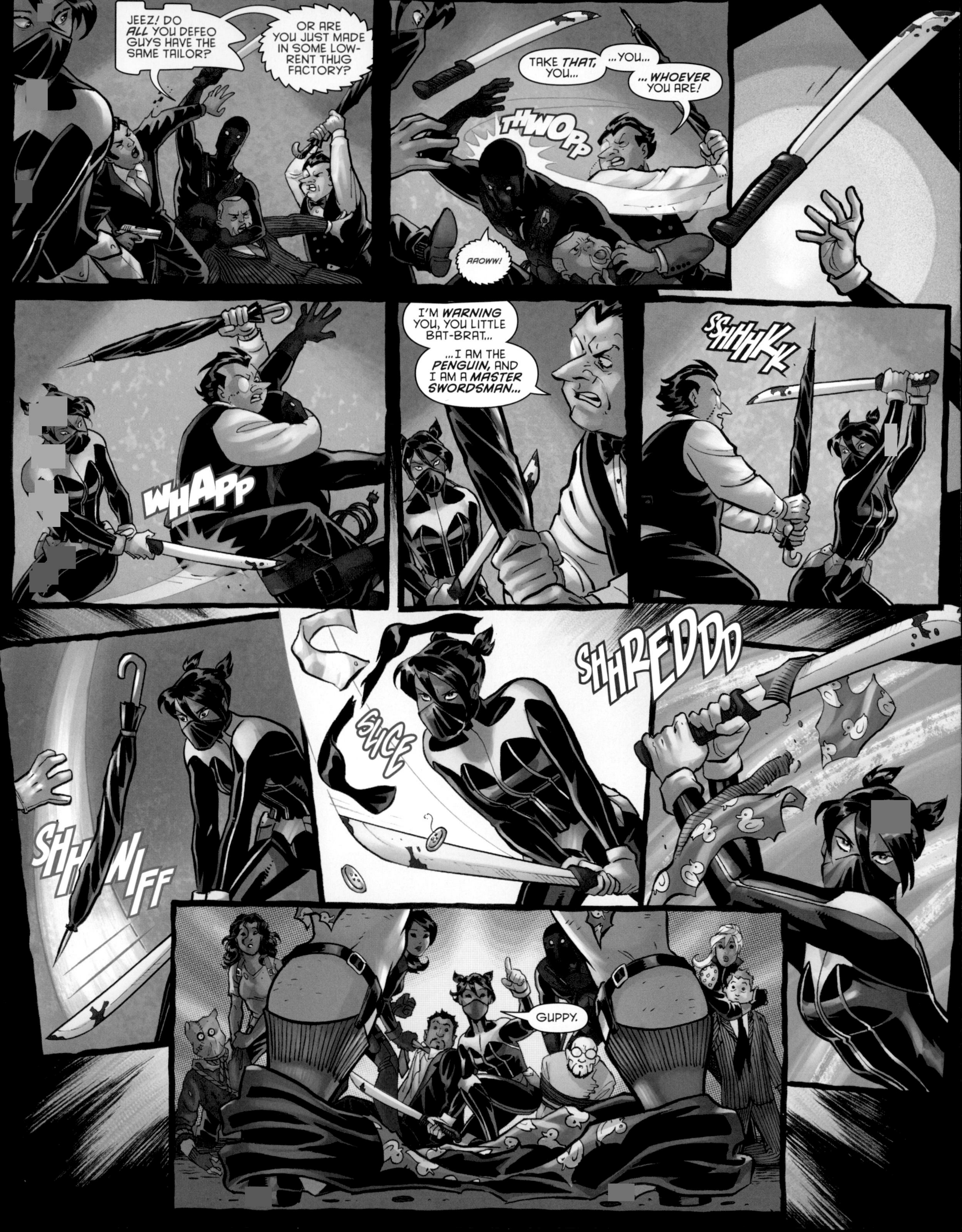
JEEZ! DO ALL YOU DEFEO GUYS HAVE THE SAME TAILOR?
OR ARE YOU JUST MADE IN SOME LOW-RENT THUG FACTORY?
TAKE THAT, YOU...
...YOU...
...WHOEVER YOU ARE!
THWOPP
ARoWW!
WHAPP
I'M WARNING YOU, YOU LITTLE BAT-BRAT...
...I AM THE PENGUIN, AND I AM A MASTER SWORDSMAN...
SSHHKKK
SHHNIFF
SLICE
SHHREDDD
GUPPY.

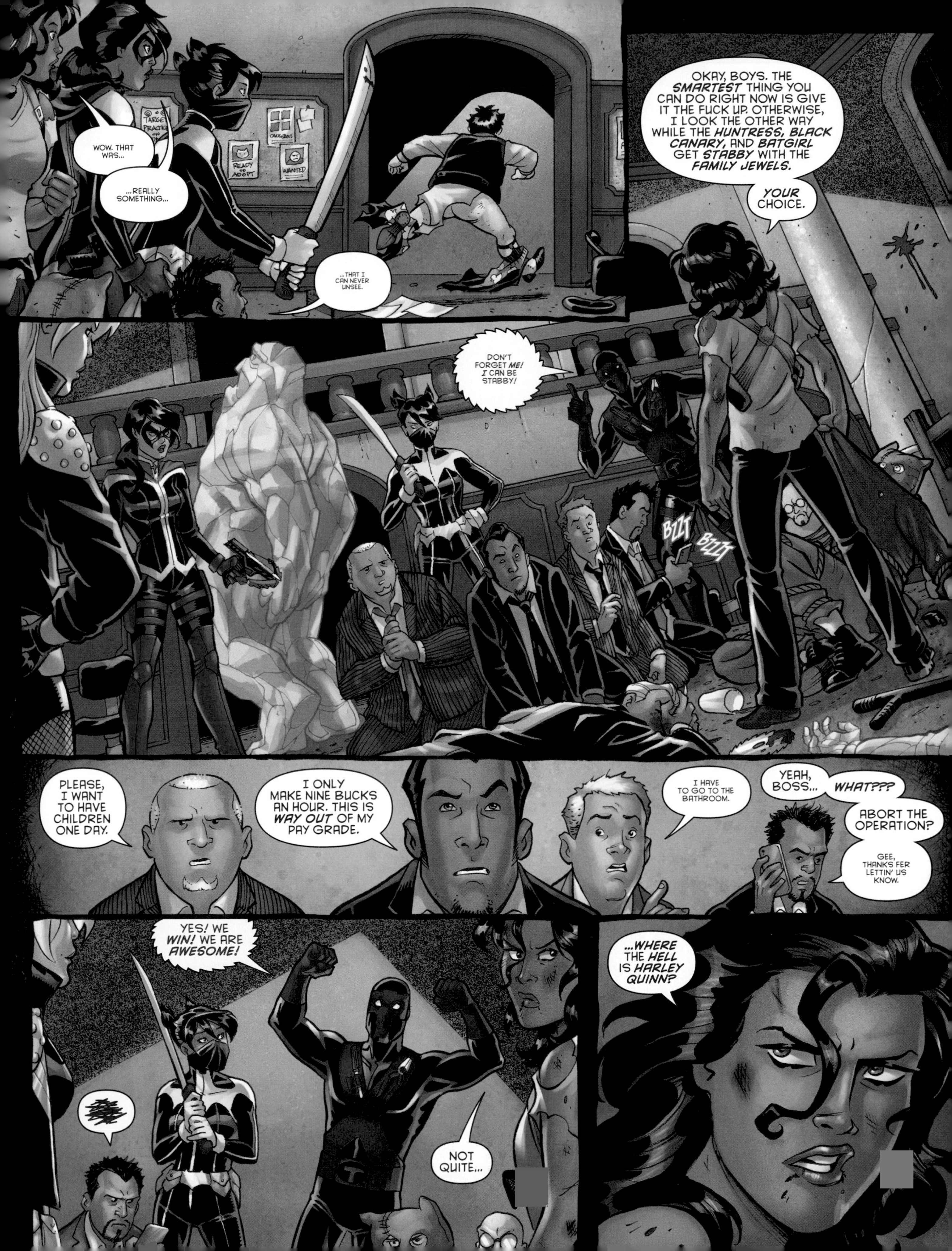

WOW. THAT WAS...
...REALLY SOMETHING...
...THAT I CAN NEVER UNSEE.
OKAY, BOYS. THE SMARTEST THING YOU CAN DO RIGHT NOW IS GIVE IT THE FUCK UP. OTHERWISE, I LOOK THE OTHER WAY WHILE THE HUNTRESS, BLACK CANARY, AND BATGIRL GET STABBY WITH THE FAMILY JEWELS.
YOUR CHOICE.
DON'T FORGET ME! I CAN BE STABBY!
BZZT
BZZZT
PLEASE, I WANT TO HAVE CHILDREN ONE DAY.
I ONLY MAKE NINE BUCKS AN HOUR. THIS IS WAY OUT OF MY PAY GRADE.
I HAVE TO GO TO THE BATHROOM.
YEAH, BOSS... WHAT???
ABORT THE OPERATION?
GEE, THANKS FER LETTIN' US KNOW.
YES! WE WIN! WE ARE AWESOME!
NOT QUITE...
...WHERE THE HELL IS HARLEY QUINN?

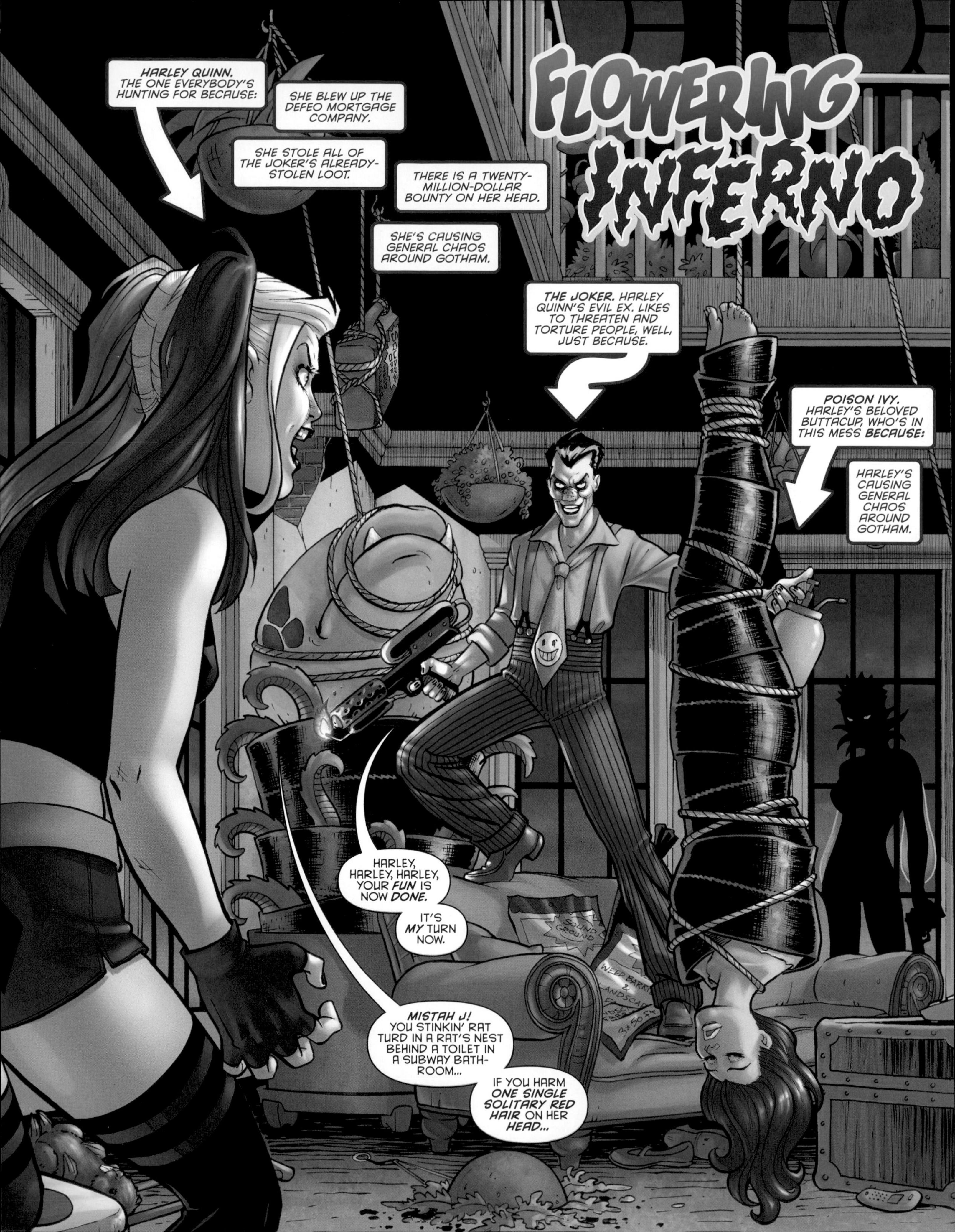

FLOWERING INFERNO
HARLEY QUINN. THE ONE EVERYBODY'S HUNTING FOR BECAUSE:
SHE BLEW UP THE DEFEO MORTGAGE COMPANY.
SHE STOLE ALL OF THE JOKER'S ALREADY-STOLEN LOOT.
THERE IS A TWENTY-MILLION-DOLLAR BOUNTY ON HER HEAD.
SHE'S CAUSING GENERAL CHAOS AROUND GOTHAM.
THE JOKER. HARLEY QUINN'S EVIL EX. LIKES TO THREATEN AND TORTURE PEOPLE, WELL, JUST BECAUSE.
POISON IVY. HARLEY'S BELOVED BUTTACUP, WHO'S IN THIS MESS BECAUSE:
HARLEY'S CAUSING GENERAL CHAOS AROUND GOTHAM.
HARLEY, HARLEY, HARLEY, YOUR FUN IS NOW DONE.
IT'S MY TURN NOW.
MISTAH J! YOU STINKIN' RAT TURD IN A RAT'S NEST BEHIND A TOILET IN A SUBWAY BATH-ROOM...
IF YOU HARM ONE SINGLE SOLITARY RED HAIR ON HER HEAD...

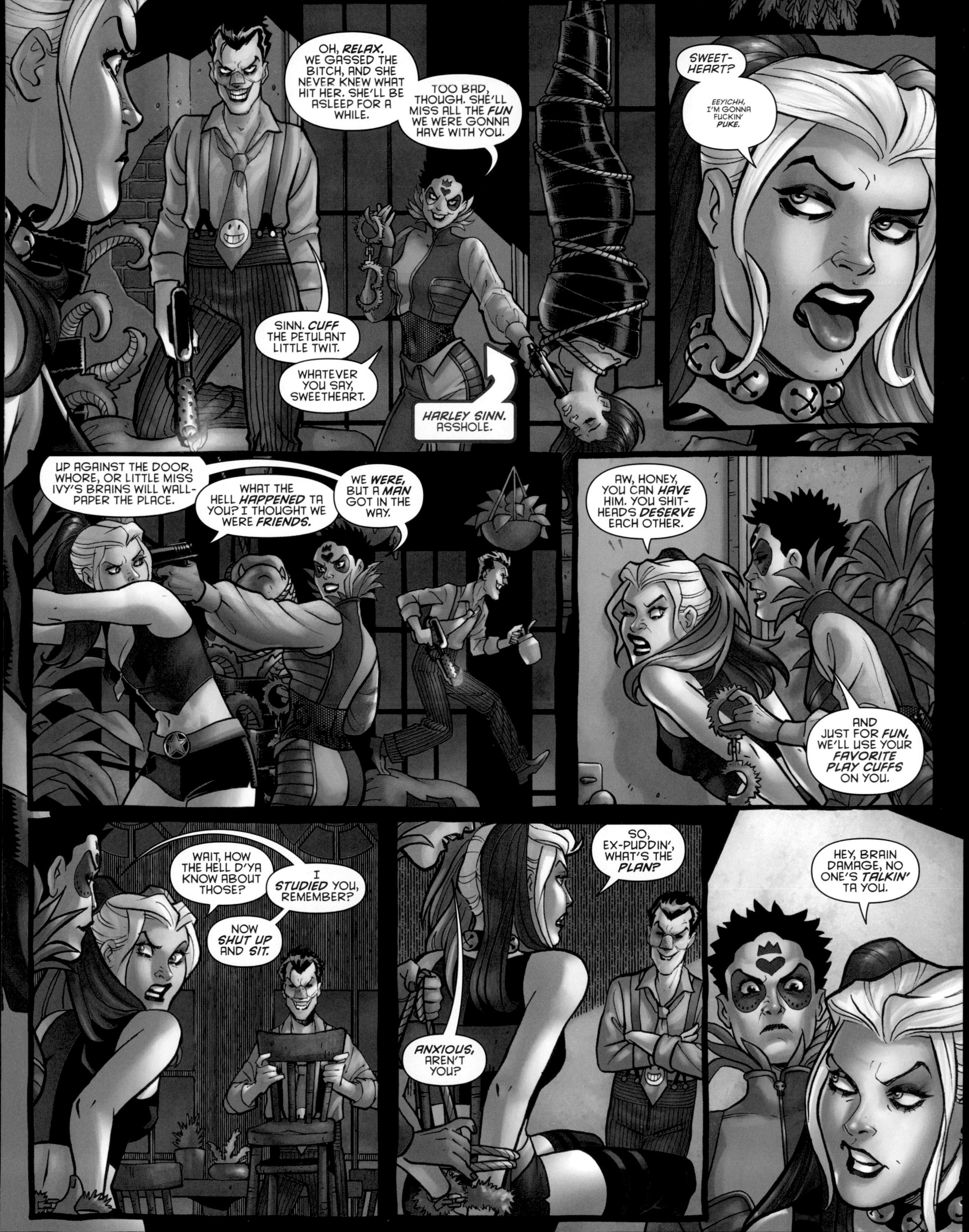
OH, RELAX. WE GASSED THE BITCH, AND SHE NEVER KNEW WHAT HIT HER. SHE'LL BE ASLEEP FOR A WHILE.
TOO BAD, THOUGH. SHE'LL MISS ALL THE FUN WE WERE GONNA HAVE WITH YOU.
SINN. CUFF THE PETULANT LITTLE TWIT.
WHATEVER YOU SAY, SWEETHEART.
HARLEY SINN. ASSHOLE.
SWEET-HEART?
EEYICHH, I'M GONNA FUCKIN' PUKE.
UP AGAINST THE DOOR, WHORE, OR LITTLE MISS IVY'S BRAINS WILL WALL-PAPER THE PLACE.
WHAT THE HELL HAPPENED TA YOU? I THOUGHT WE WERE FRIENDS.
WE WERE, BUT A MAN GOT IN THE WAY.
AW, HONEY, YOU CAN HAVE HIM. YOU SHIT-HEADS DESERVE EACH OTHER.
AND JUST FOR FUN, WE'LL USE YOUR FAVORITE PLAY CUFFS ON YOU.
WAIT, HOW THE HELL D'YA KNOW ABOUT THOSE?
I STUDIED YOU, REMEMBER?
NOW SHUT UP AND SIT.
SO, EX-PUDDIN', WHAT'S THE PLAN?
ANXIOUS, AREN'T YOU?
HEY, BRAIN DAMAGE, NO ONE'S TALKIN' TA YOU.

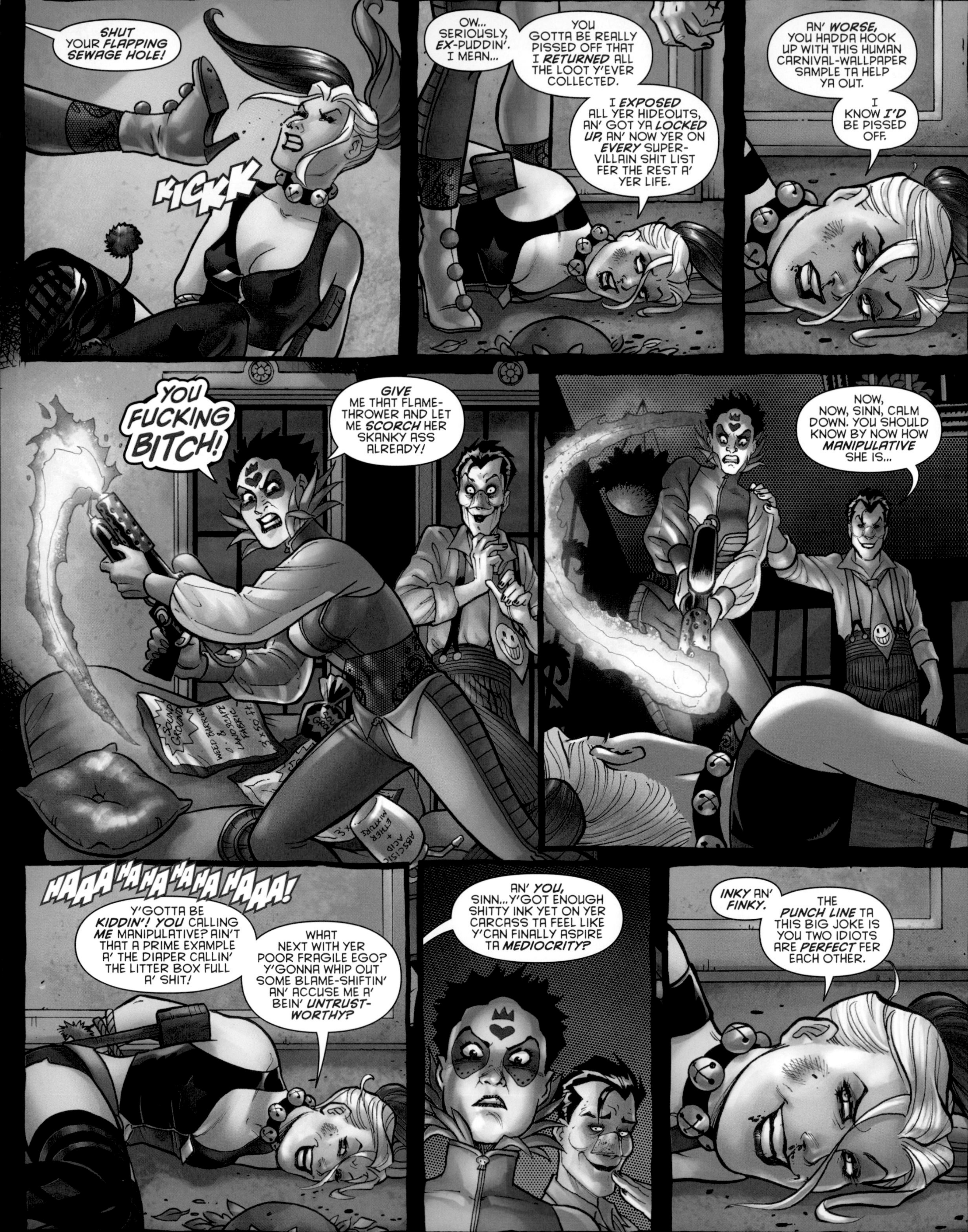
SHUT YOUR FLAPPING SEWAGE HOLE!
KICKK
OW... SERIOUSLY, EX-PUDDIN'. I MEAN...
YOU GOTTA BE REALLY PISSED OFF THAT I RETURNED ALL THE LOOT Y'EVER COLLECTED.
I EXPOSED ALL YER HIDEOUTS, AN' GOT YA LOCKED UP, AN' NOW YER ON EVERY SUPER-VILLAIN SHIT LIST FER THE REST A' YER LIFE.
AN' WORSE, YOU HADDA HOOK UP WITH THIS HUMAN CARNIVAL-WALLPAPER SAMPLE TA HELP YA OUT.
I KNOW I'D BE PISSED OFF.
YOU FUCKING BITCH!
GIVE ME THAT FLAME-THROWER AND LET ME SCORCH HER SKANKY ASS ALREADY!
NOW, NOW, SINN, CALM DOWN. YOU SHOULD KNOW BY NOW HOW MANIPULATIVE SHE IS...
HAAA HA HA HA HA HAAA!
Y'GOTTA BE KIDDIN'! YOU CALLING ME MANIPULATIVE? AIN'T THAT A PRIME EXAMPLE A' THE DIAPER CALLIN' THE LITTER BOX FULL A' SHIT!
WHAT NEXT WITH YER POOR FRAGILE EGO? Y'GONNA WHIP OUT SOME BLAME-SHIFTIN' AN' ACCUSE ME A' BEIN' UNTRUST-WORTHY?
AN' YOU, SINN...Y'GOT ENOUGH SHITTY INK YET ON YER CARCASS TA FEEL LIKE Y'CAN FINALLY ASPIRE TA MEDIOCRITY?
INKY AN' FINKY.
THE PUNCH LINE TA THIS BIG JOKE IS YOU TWO IDIOTS ARE PERFECT FER EACH OTHER.

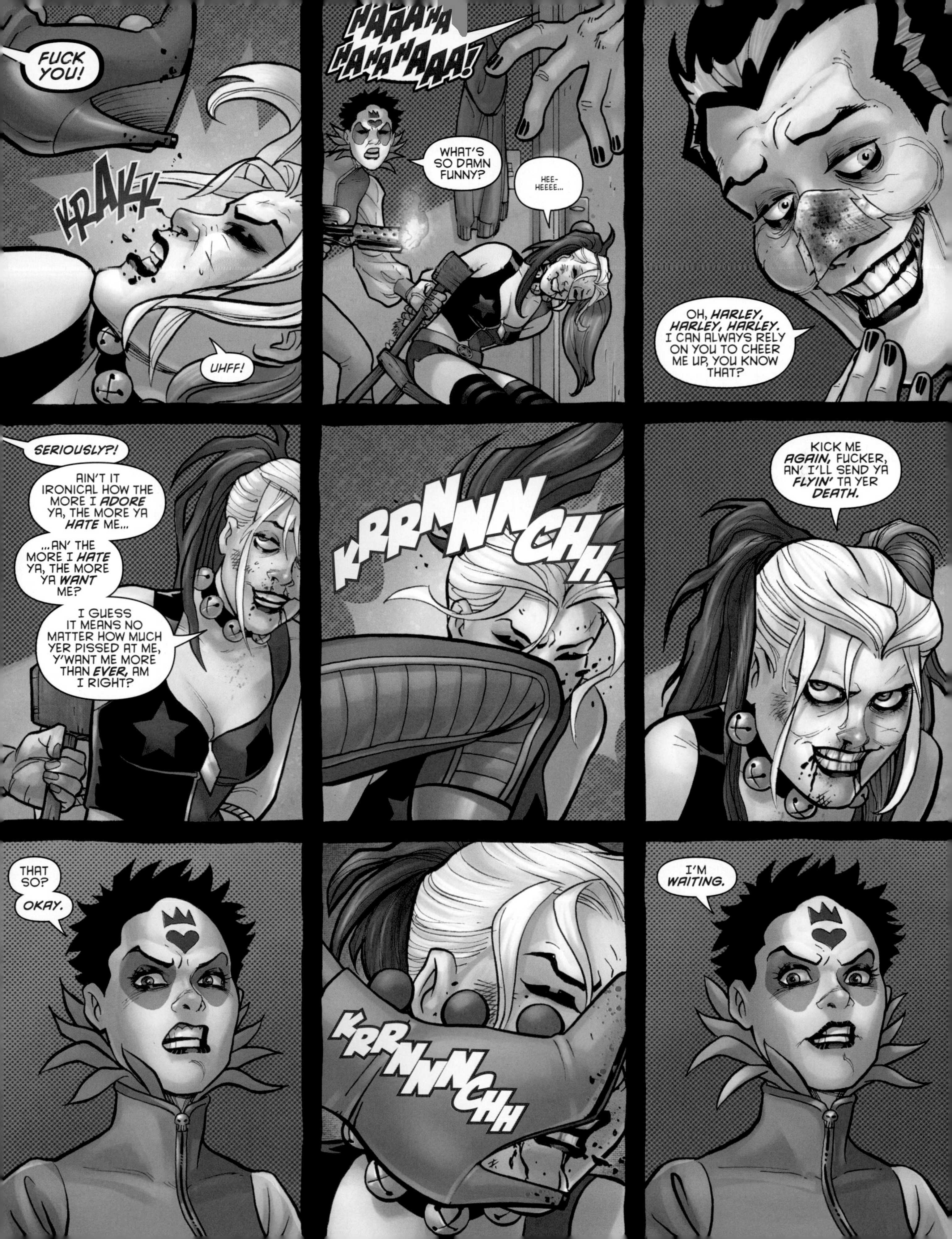
FUCK YOU!
KRAKKK
UHFF!
HAAAHA HAHAHAAA!
WHAT'S SO DAMN FUNNY?
HEE-HEEEE...
OH, HARLEY, HARLEY, HARLEY. I CAN ALWAYS RELY ON YOU TO CHEER ME UP, YOU KNOW THAT?
SERIOUSLY?!
AIN'T IT IRONICAL HOW THE MORE I ADORE YA, THE MORE YA HATE ME...
...AN' THE MORE I HATE YA, THE MORE YA WANT ME?
I GUESS IT MEANS NO MATTER HOW MUCH YER PISSED AT ME, Y'WANT ME MORE THAN EVER, AM I RIGHT?
KRRNNNNCHH
KICK ME AGAIN, FUCKER, AN' I'LL SEND YA FLYIN' TA YER DEATH.
THAT SO?
OKAY.
KRRNNNCHH
I'M WAITING.

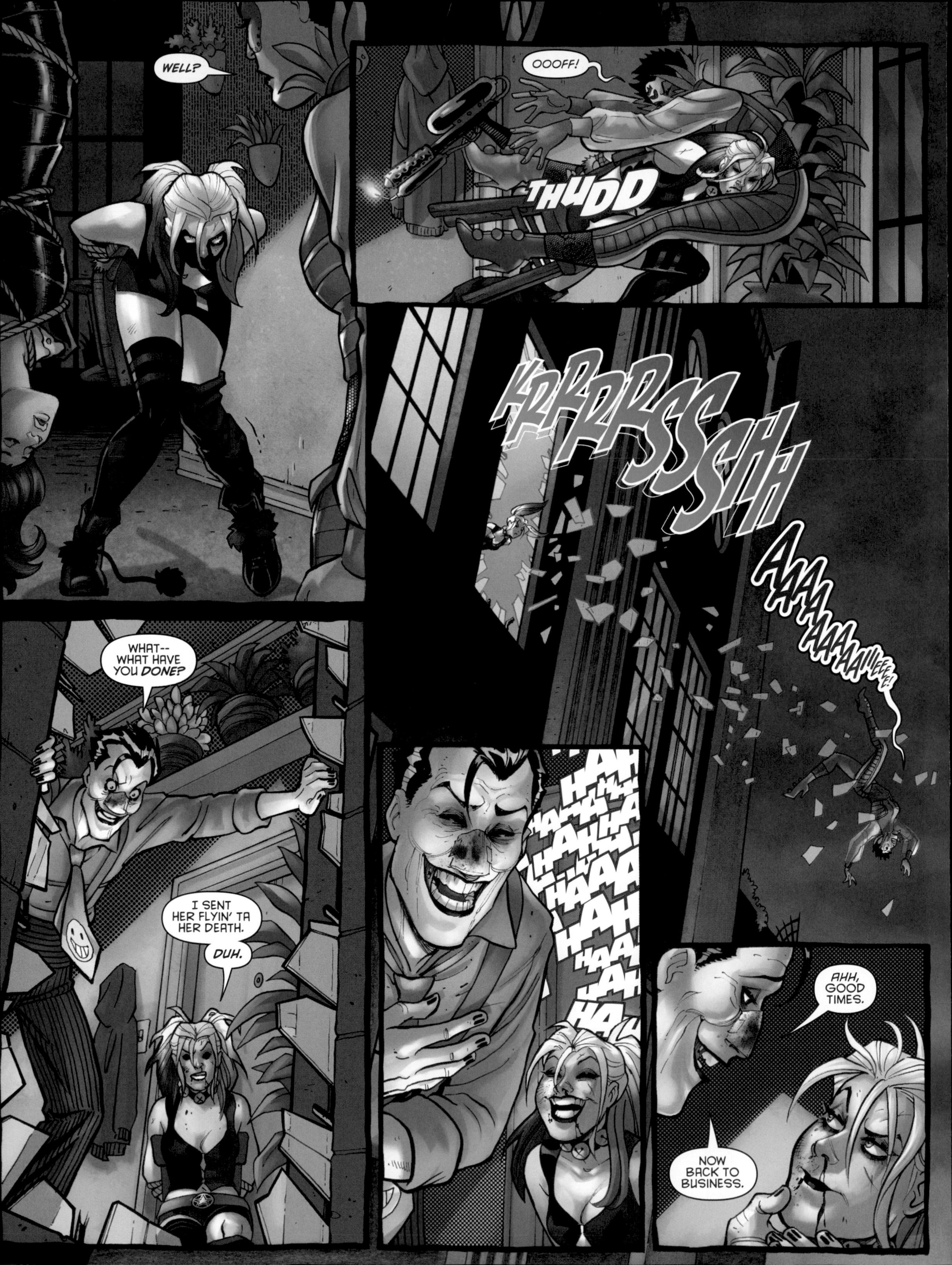
WELL?
OOOFF!
THUDD
KRRRRSSSHH
AAAAAAAAAIIEEEE
WHAT--
WHAT HAVE YOU DONE?
I SENT HER FLYIN' TA HER DEATH.
DUH.
HAHAHAHAHAHAHAHAHAHAHA
AHH, GOOD TIMES.
NOW BACK TO BUSINESS.

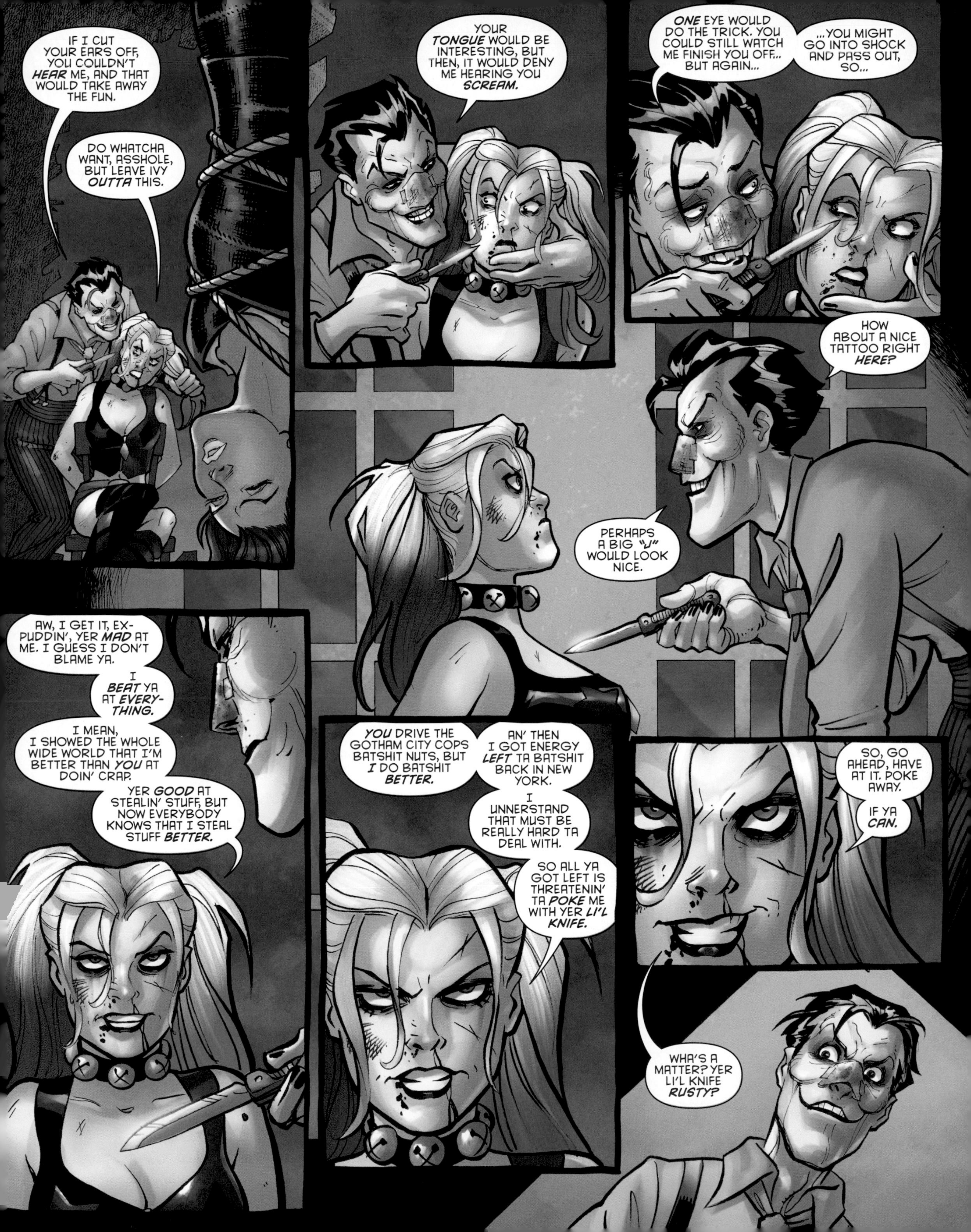
IF I CUT YOUR EARS OFF, YOU COULDN'T HEAR ME, AND THAT WOULD TAKE AWAY THE FUN.
DO WHATCHA WANT, ASSHOLE, BUT LEAVE IVY OUTTA THIS.
YOUR TONGUE WOULD BE INTERESTING, BUT THEN, IT WOULD DENY ME HEARING YOU SCREAM.
ONE EYE WOULD DO THE TRICK. YOU COULD STILL WATCH ME FINISH YOU OFF... BUT AGAIN...
...YOU MIGHT GO INTO SHOCK AND PASS OUT, SO...
HOW ABOUT A NICE TATTOO RIGHT HERE?
PERHAPS A BIG "J" WOULD LOOK NICE.
AW, I GET IT, EX-PUDDIN', YER MAD AT ME. I GUESS I DON'T BLAME YA.
I BEAT YA AT EVERY-THING.
I MEAN, I SHOWED THE WHOLE WIDE WORLD THAT I'M BETTER THAN YOU AT DOIN' CRAP.
YER GOOD AT STEALIN' STUFF, BUT NOW EVERYBODY KNOWS THAT I STEAL STUFF BETTER.
YOU DRIVE THE GOTHAM CITY COPS BATSHIT NUTS, BUT I DO BATSHIT BETTER.
AN' THEN I GOT ENERGY LEFT TA BATSHIT BACK IN NEW YORK.
I UNNERSTAND THAT MUST BE REALLY HARD TA DEAL WITH.
SO ALL YA GOT LEFT IS THREATENIN' TA POKE ME WITH YER LI'L KNIFE.
SO, GO AHEAD, HAVE AT IT. POKE AWAY.
IF YA CAN.
WHA'S A MATTER? YER LI'L KNIFE RUSTY?

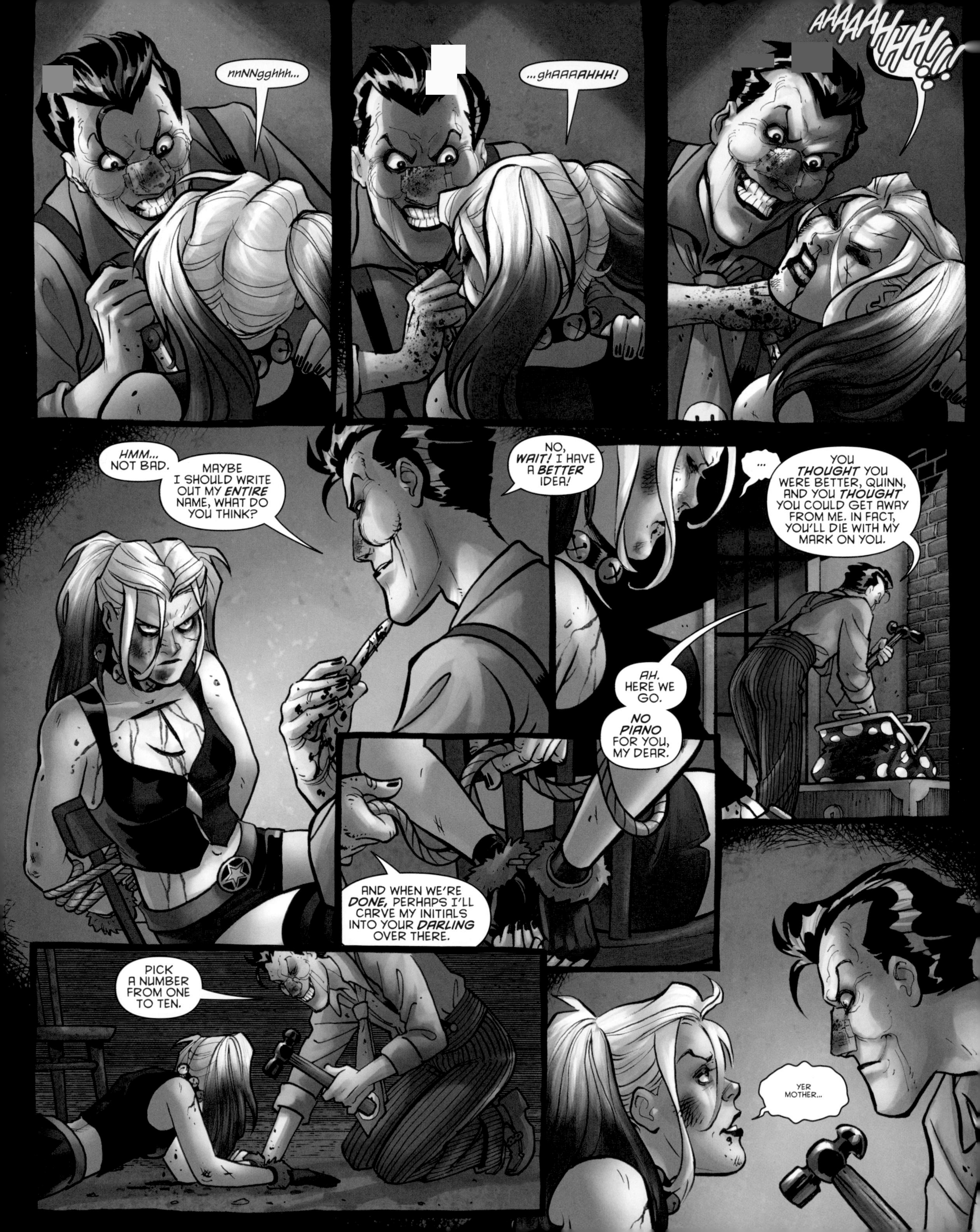
nnNNgghhh...
...ghAAAAHHH!
AAAAAHHHH!!!
HMM... NOT BAD.
MAYBE I SHOULD WRITE OUT MY ENTIRE NAME, WHAT DO YOU THINK?
NO, WAIT! I HAVE A BETTER IDEA!
...
YOU THOUGHT YOU WERE BETTER, QUINN, AND YOU THOUGHT YOU COULD GET AWAY FROM ME. IN FACT, YOU'LL DIE WITH MY MARK ON YOU.
AH. HERE WE GO.
NO PIANO FOR YOU, MY DEAR.
AND WHEN WE'RE DONE, PERHAPS I'LL CARVE MY INITIALS INTO YOUR DARLING OVER THERE.
PICK A NUMBER FROM ONE TO TEN.
YER MOTHER...

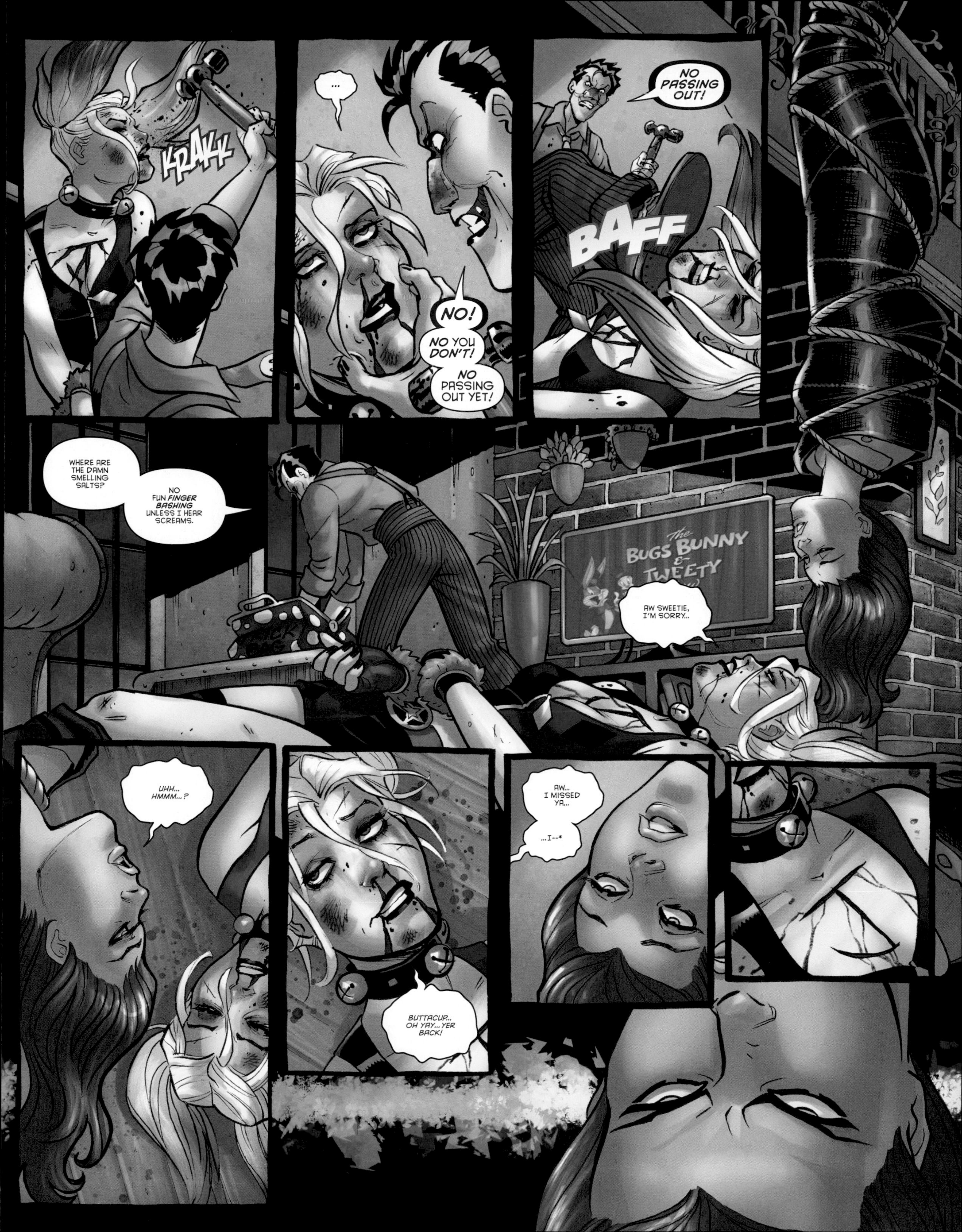
KRAKK
...
NO!
NO YOU DON'T!
NO PASSING OUT YET!
NO PASSING OUT!
BAFF
WHERE ARE THE DAMN SMELLING SALTS?
NO FUN FINGER BASHING UNLESS I HEAR SCREAMS.
The BUGS BUNNY & TWEETY
AW SWEETIE, I'M SORRY...
UHH... HMMM...?
BUTTACUP... OH YAY... YER BACK!
AW... I MISSED YA...
...I--*

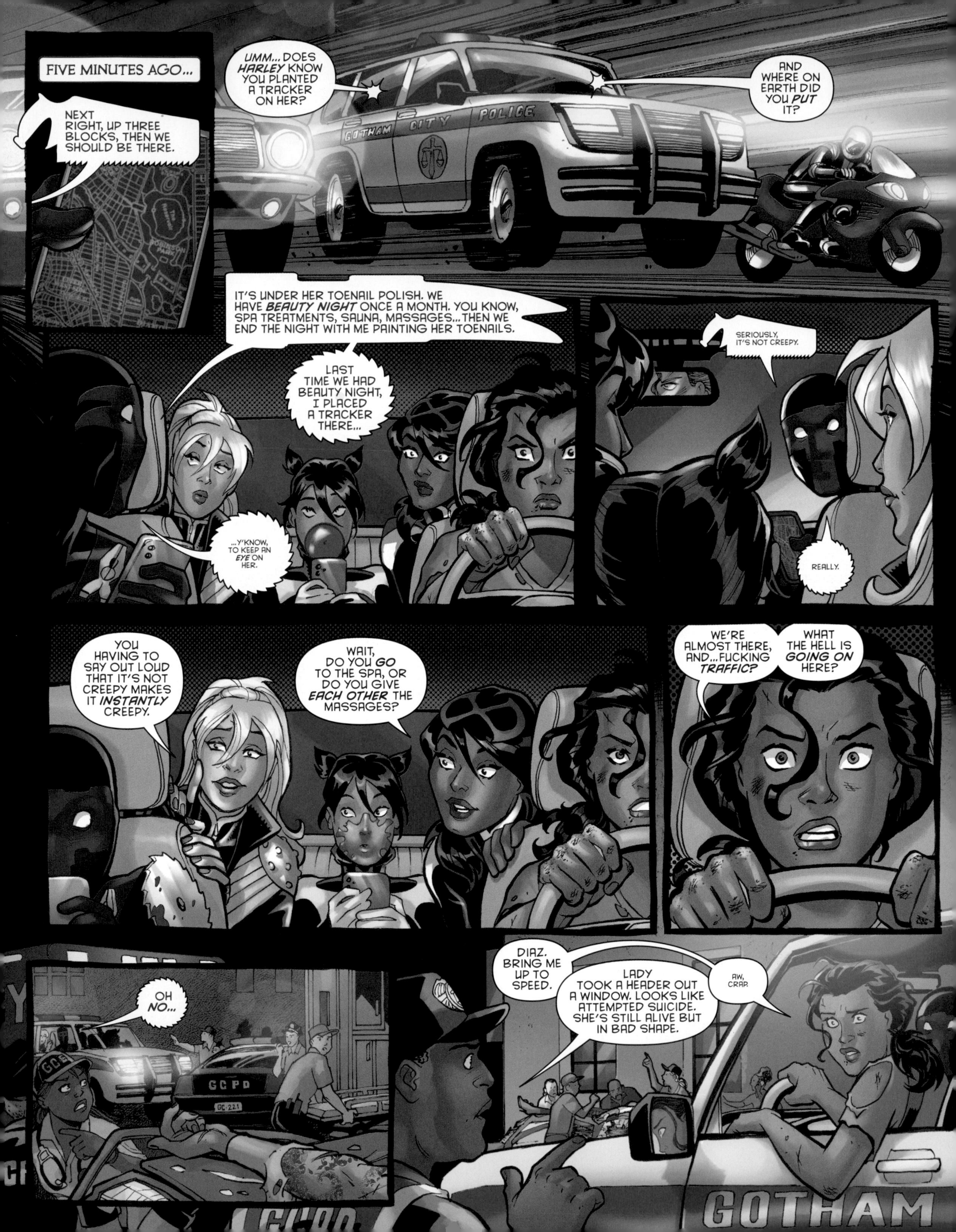
FIVE MINUTES AGO...
NEXT RIGHT, UP THREE BLOCKS, THEN WE SHOULD BE THERE.
UMM... DOES HARLEY KNOW YOU PLANTED A TRACKER ON HER?
AND WHERE ON EARTH DID YOU PUT IT?
GOTHAM CITY POLICE
IT'S UNDER HER TOENAIL POLISH. WE HAVE BEAUTY NIGHT ONCE A MONTH. YOU KNOW, SPA TREATMENTS, SAUNA, MASSAGES... THEN WE END THE NIGHT WITH ME PAINTING HER TOENAILS.
LAST TIME WE HAD BEAUTY NIGHT, I PLACED A TRACKER THERE...
...Y'KNOW, TO KEEP AN EYE ON HER.
SERIOUSLY, IT'S NOT CREEPY.
REALLY.
YOU HAVING TO SAY OUT LOUD THAT IT'S NOT CREEPY MAKES IT INSTANTLY CREEPY.
WAIT, DO YOU GO TO THE SPA, OR DO YOU GIVE EACH OTHER THE MASSAGES?
WE'RE ALMOST THERE, AND... FUCKING TRAFFIC?
WHAT THE HELL IS GOING ON HERE?
OH NO...
GCPD
DIAZ. BRING ME UP TO SPEED.
LADY TOOK A HEADER OUT A WINDOW. LOOKS LIKE ATTEMPTED SUICIDE. SHE'S STILL ALIVE BUT IN BAD SHAPE.
AW, CRAP.
GOTHAM

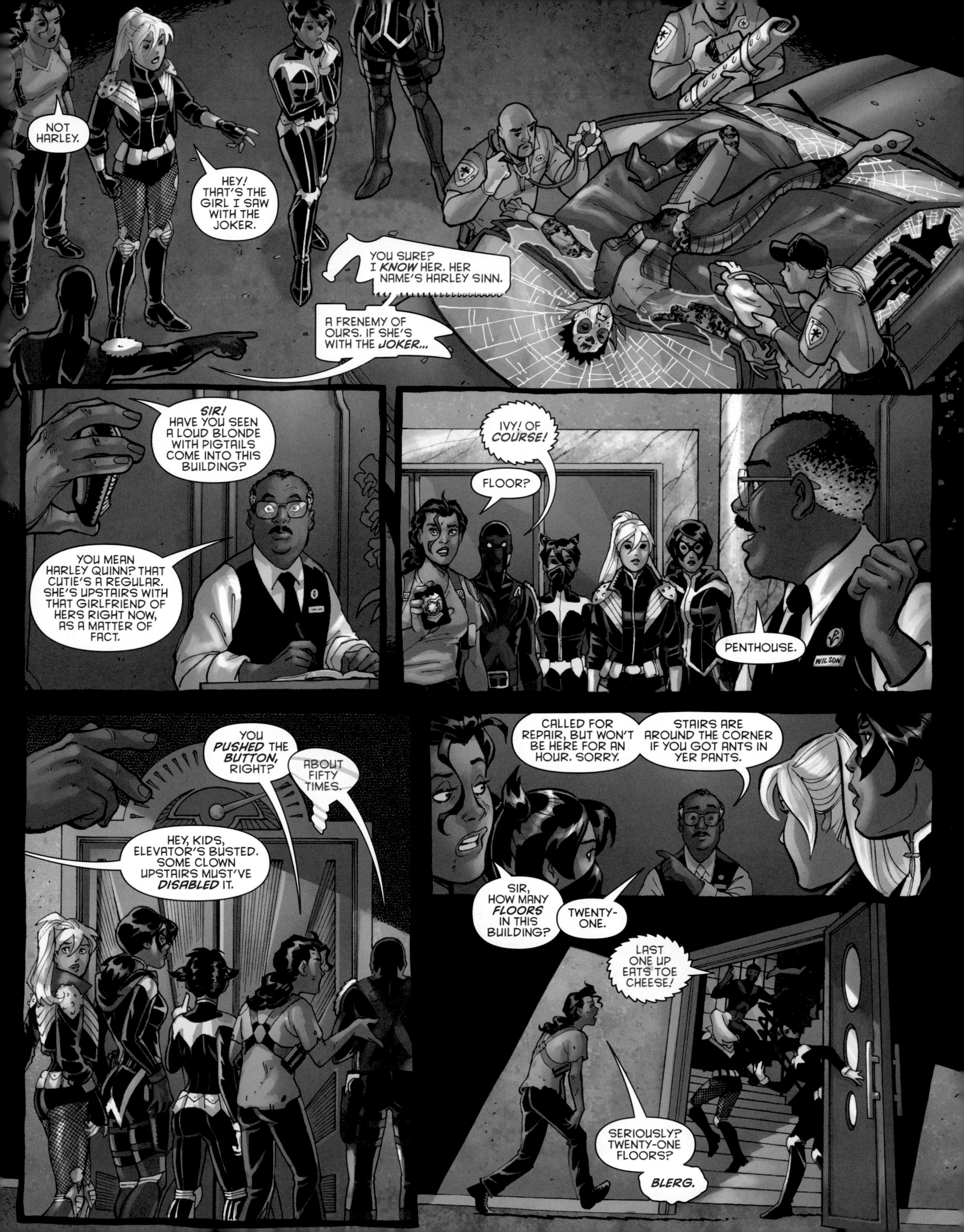
NOT HARLEY.
HEY! THAT'S THE GIRL I SAW WITH THE JOKER.
YOU SURE? I KNOW HER. HER NAME'S HARLEY SINN.
A FRENEMY OF OURS. IF SHE'S WITH THE JOKER...
SIR! HAVE YOU SEEN A LOUD BLONDE WITH PIGTAILS COME INTO THIS BUILDING?
YOU MEAN HARLEY QUINN? THAT CUTIE'S A REGULAR. SHE'S UPSTAIRS WITH THAT GIRLFRIEND OF HERS RIGHT NOW, AS A MATTER OF FACT.
IVY! OF COURSE!
FLOOR?
PENTHOUSE.
WILSON
YOU PUSHED THE BUTTON, RIGHT?
ABOUT FIFTY TIMES.
HEY, KIDS, ELEVATOR'S BUSTED. SOME CLOWN UPSTAIRS MUST'VE DISABLED IT.
CALLED FOR REPAIR, BUT WON'T BE HERE FOR AN HOUR. SORRY.
STAIRS ARE AROUND THE CORNER IF YOU GOT ANTS IN YER PANTS.
SIR, HOW MANY FLOORS IN THIS BUILDING?
TWENTY-ONE.
LAST ONE UP EATS TOE CHEESE!
SERIOUSLY? TWENTY-ONE FLOORS?
BLERG.

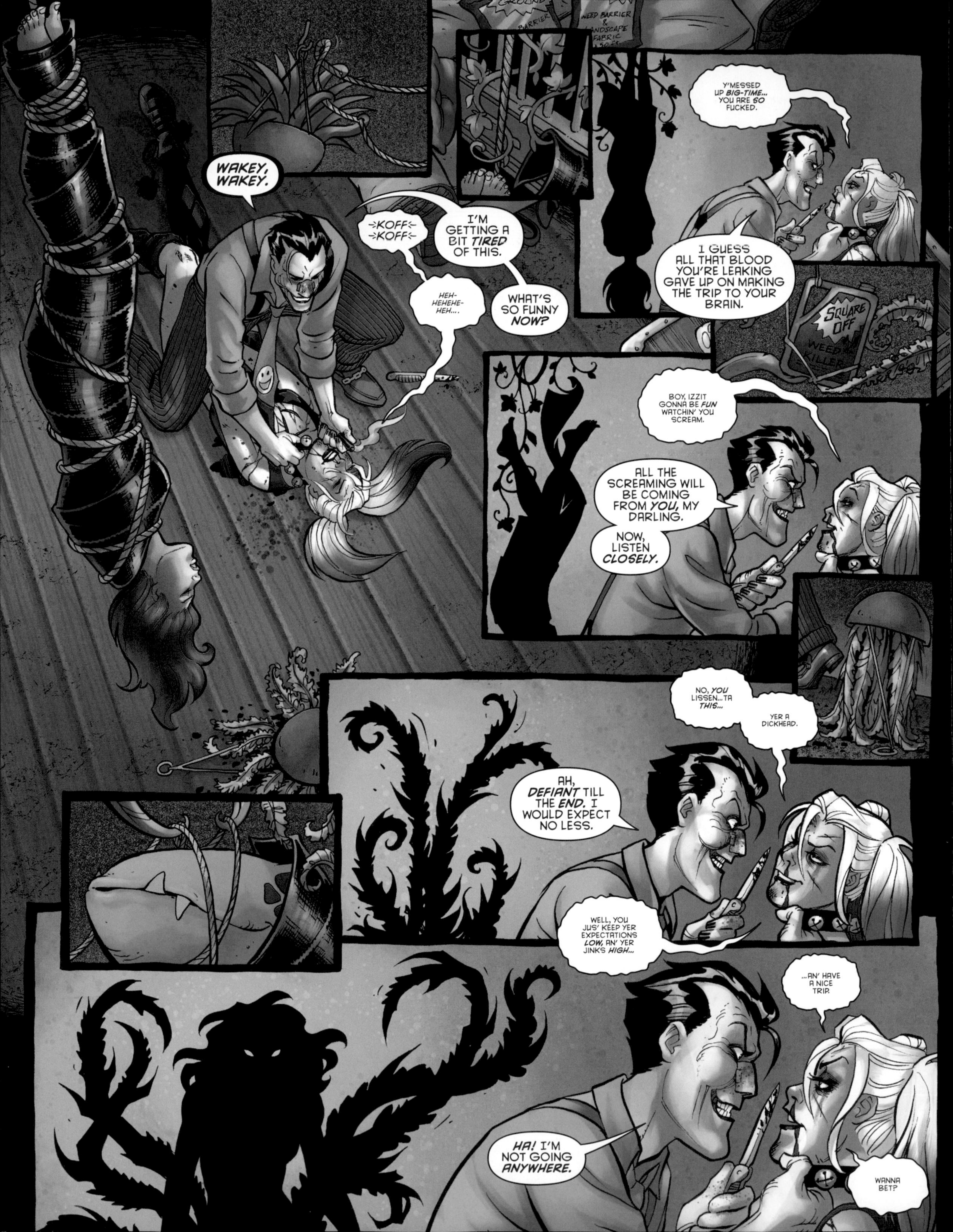
WEED BARRIER & LANDSCAPE FABRIC
WAKEY, WAKEY.
-KOFF- -KOFF-
HEH-HEHEHE-HEH....
I'M GETTING A BIT TIRED OF THIS.
WHAT'S SO FUNNY NOW?
Y'MESSED UP BIG-TIME... YOU ARE SO FUCKED.
I GUESS ALL THAT BLOOD YOU'RE LEAKING GAVE UP ON MAKING THE TRIP TO YOUR BRAIN.
SQUARE OFF WEED KILLER
BOY, IZZIT GONNA BE FUN WATCHIN' YOU SCREAM.
ALL THE SCREAMING WILL BE COMING FROM YOU, MY DARLING.
NOW, LISTEN CLOSELY.
NO, YOU LISSEN...TA THIS...
YER A DICKHEAD.
AH, DEFIANT TILL THE END. I WOULD EXPECT NO LESS.
WELL, YOU JUS' KEEP YER EXPECTATIONS LOW, AN' YER JINKS HIGH...
...AN' HAVE A NICE TRIP.
HA! I'M NOT GOING ANYWHERE.
WANNA BET?

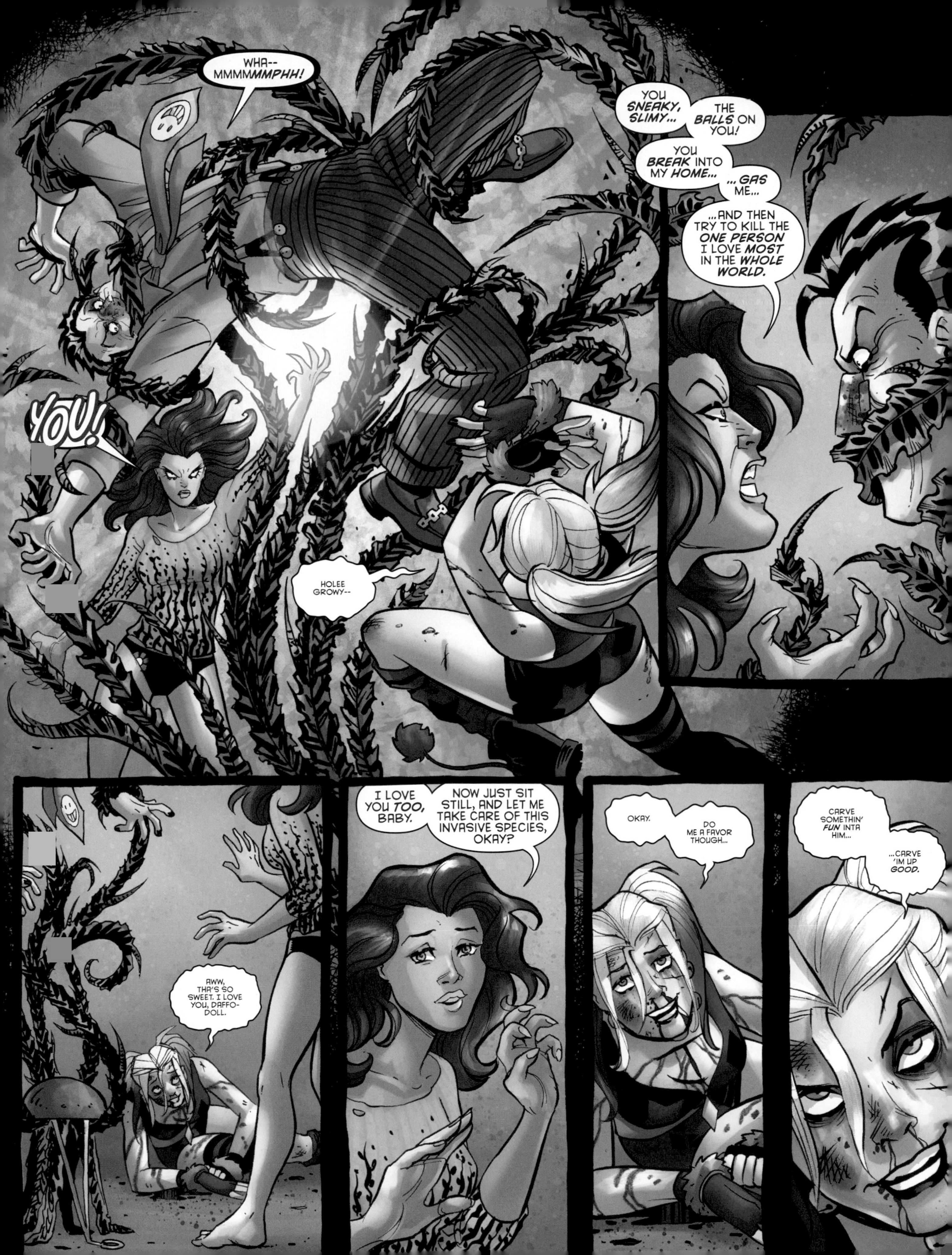

WHA-- MMMMMMMPHH!
YOU!
HOLEE GROWY--
YOU SNEAKY, SLIMY...
THE BALLS ON YOU!
YOU BREAK INTO MY HOME...
...GAS ME...
...AND THEN TRY TO KILL THE ONE PERSON I LOVE MOST IN THE WHOLE WORLD.
AWW, THA'S SO SWEET. I LOVE YOU, DAFFO-DOLL.
I LOVE YOU TOO, BABY.
NOW JUST SIT STILL, AND LET ME TAKE CARE OF THIS INVASIVE SPECIES, OKAY?
OKAY.
DO ME A FAVOR THOUGH...
CARVE SOMETHIN' FUN INTA HIM...
...CARVE 'IM UP GOOD.

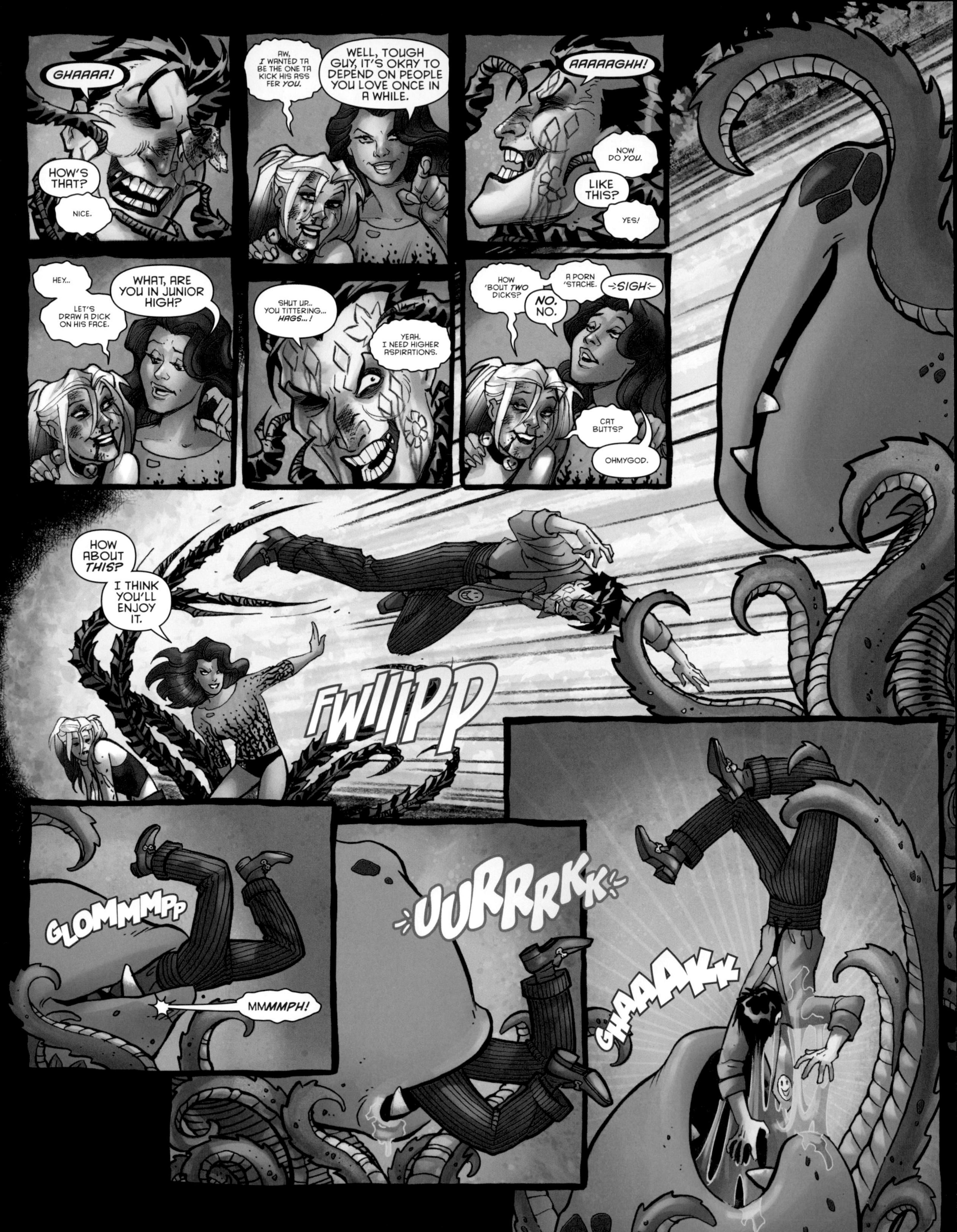
GHAAAA!
HOW'S THAT?
NICE.
AW, I WANTED TA BE THE ONE TA KICK HIS ASS FER YOU.
WELL, TOUGH GUY, IT'S OKAY TO DEPEND ON PEOPLE YOU LOVE ONCE IN A WHILE.
AAAAAGHH!
NOW DO YOU.
LIKE THIS?
YES!
HEY...
LET'S DRAW A DICK ON HIS FACE.
WHAT, ARE YOU IN JUNIOR HIGH?
SHUT UP... YOU TITTERING... HAGS...!
YEAH. I NEED HIGHER ASPIRATIONS.
HOW 'BOUT TWO DICKS?
NO. NO.
A PORN 'STACHE.
SIGH
CAT BUTTS?
OHMYGOD.
HOW ABOUT THIS?
I THINK YOU'LL ENJOY IT.
FWIIIPP
GLOMMMPP
MMMMPH!
UURRRKK
GHAAAKK

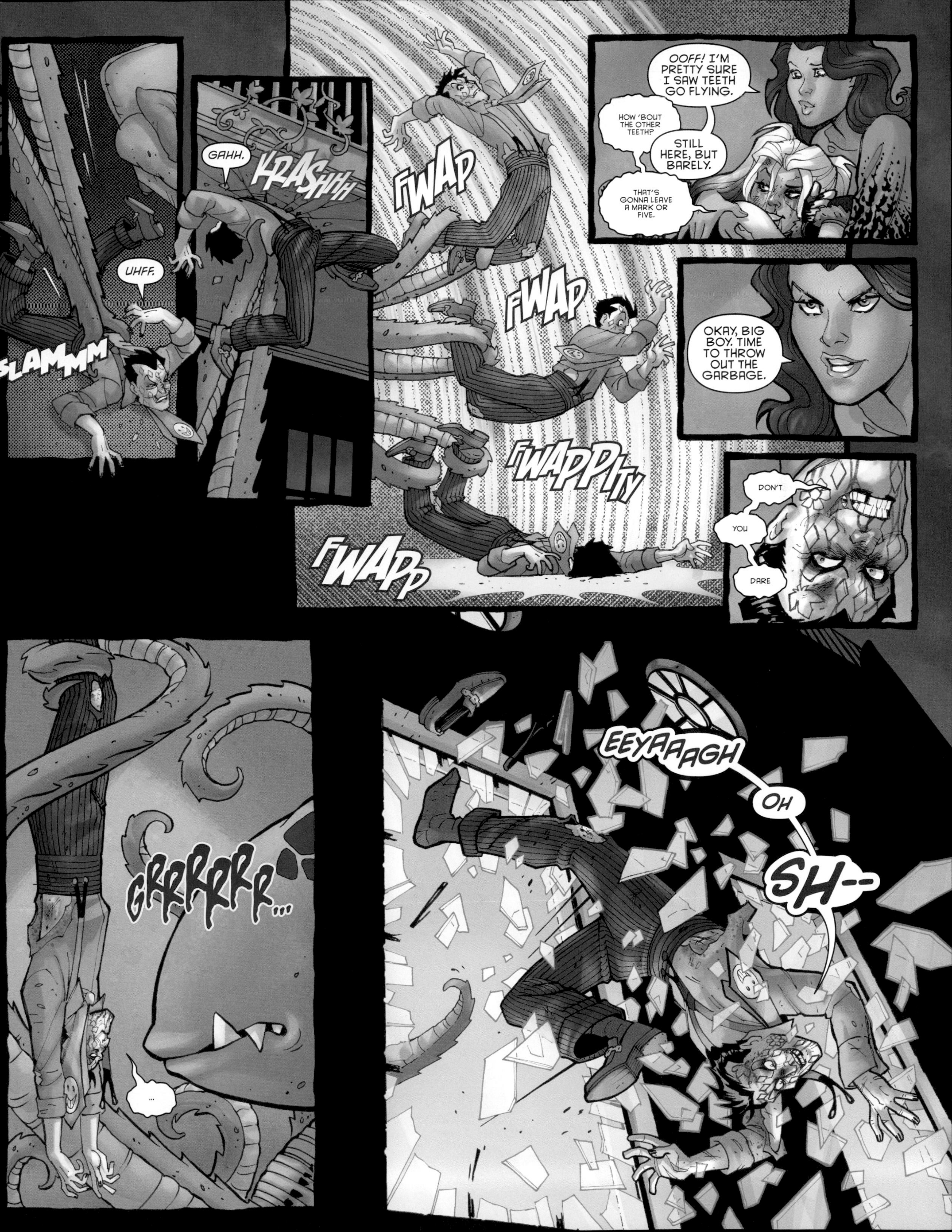

UHFF.
SLAMMMM
GAHH.
KRASHHH
FWAP
FWAP
FWAPPITY
FWAPP
OOFF! I'M PRETTY SURE I SAW TEETH GO FLYING.
HOW 'BOUT THE OTHER TEETH?
STILL HERE, BUT BARELY.
THAT'S GONNA LEAVE A MARK OR FIVE.
OKAY, BIG BOY. TIME TO THROW OUT THE GARBAGE.
DON'T
YOU
DARE
GRRRRRR...
...
EEYAAAAGH
OH
SH--

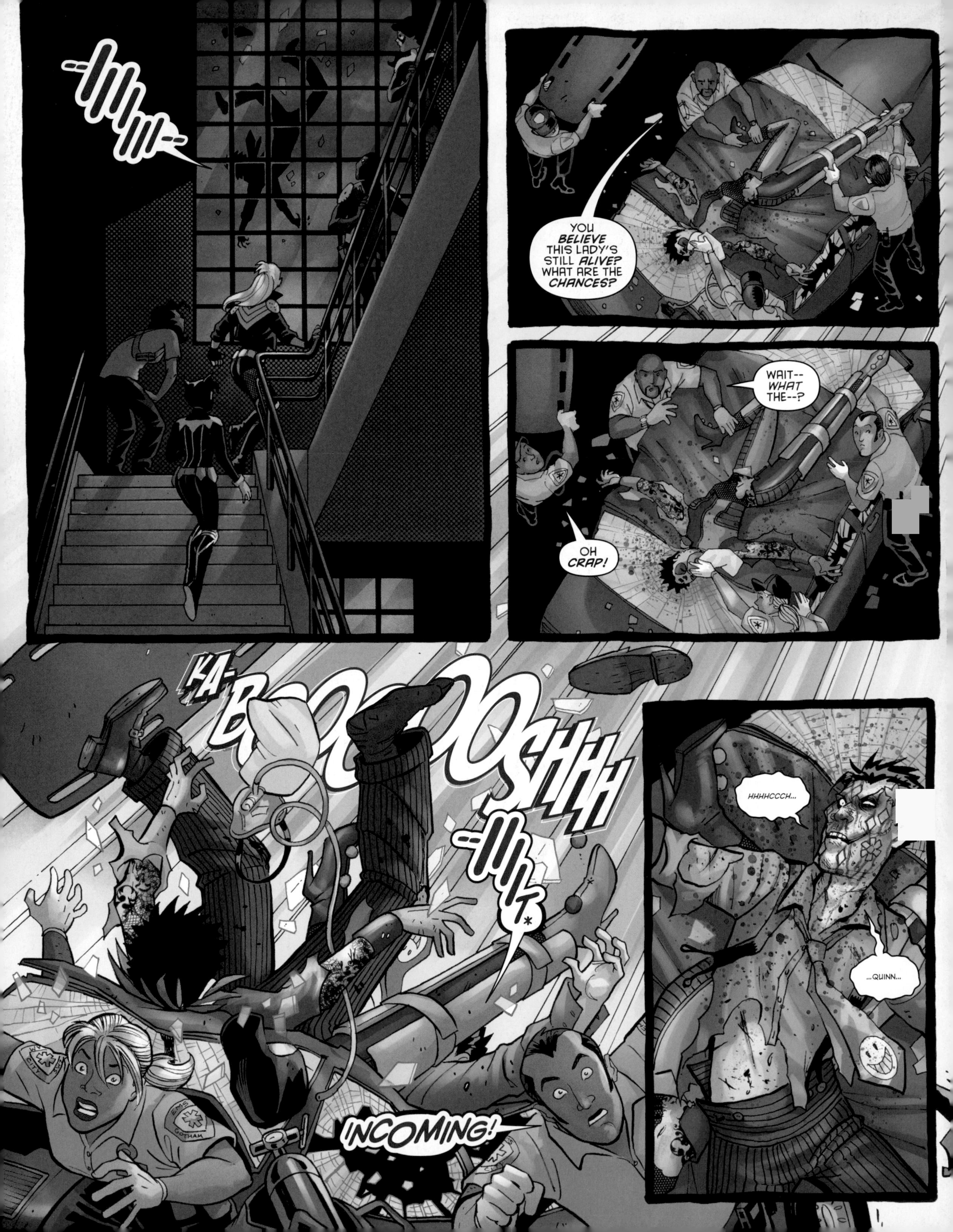
YOU BELIEVE THIS LADY'S STILL ALIVE? WHAT ARE THE CHANCES?
WAIT-- WHAT THE--?
OH CRAP!
KA-BOOOOOSHHH
INCOMING!
HHHHCCCH...
...QUINN...

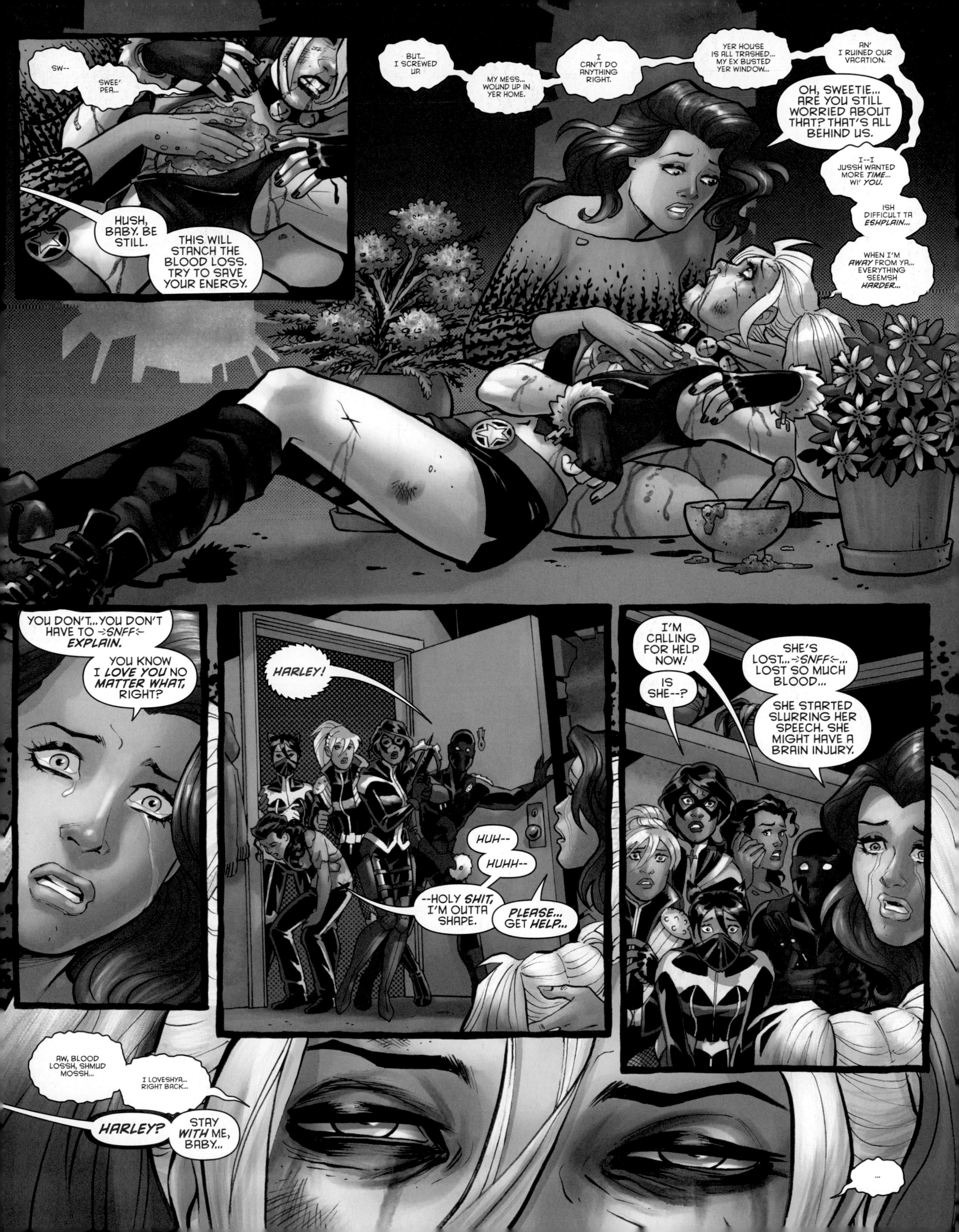
SW--
SWEE' PEA...
HUSH, BABY. BE STILL.
THIS WILL STANCH THE BLOOD LOSS. TRY TO SAVE YOUR ENERGY.
BUT... I SCREWED UP.
MY MESS... WOUND UP IN YER HOME.
I CAN'T DO ANYTHING RIGHT.
YER HOUSE IS ALL TRASHED... MY EX BUSTED YER WINDOW...
AN' I RUINED OUR VACATION.
OH, SWEETIE... ARE YOU STILL WORRIED ABOUT THAT? THAT'S ALL BEHIND US.
I--I JUSSH WANTED MORE TIME... WI' YOU.
ISH DIFFICULT TA ESHPLAIN...
WHEN I'M AWAY FROM YA... EVERYTHING SEEMSH HARDER...
YOU DON'T... YOU DON'T HAVE TO →SNFF← EXPLAIN.
YOU KNOW I LOVE YOU NO MATTER WHAT, RIGHT?
HARLEY!
HUH--
HUHH--
--HOLY SHIT, I'M OUTTA SHAPE.
PLEASE... GET HELP...
I'M CALLING FOR HELP NOW!
IS SHE--?
SHE'S LOST... →SNFF←... LOST SO MUCH BLOOD...
SHE STARTED SLURRING HER SPEECH. SHE MIGHT HAVE A BRAIN INJURY.
AW, BLOOD LOSSH, SHMUD MOSSH...
I LOVESHYA... RIGHT BACK...
HARLEY?
STAY WITH ME, BABY...
...

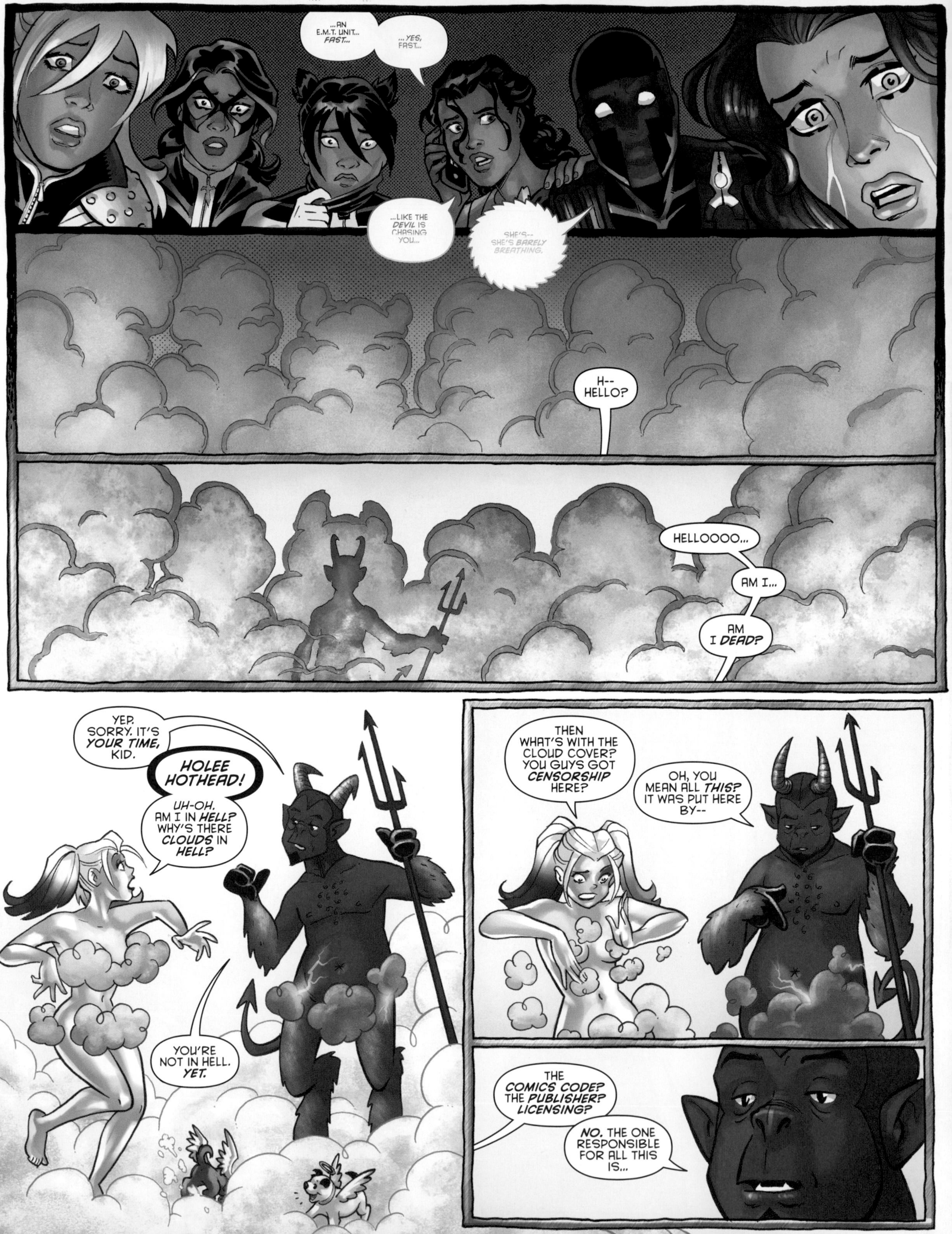

...AN E.M.T. UNIT... FAST...
...YES, FAST...
...LIKE THE DEVIL IS CHASING YOU...
SHE'S-- SHE'S BARELY BREATHING.
H-- HELLO?
HELLOOOO...
AM I...
AM I DEAD?
YEP. SORRY. IT'S YOUR TIME, KID.
HOLEE HOTHEAD!
UH-OH. AM I IN HELL? WHY'S THERE CLOUDS IN HELL?
YOU'RE NOT IN HELL. YET.
THEN WHAT'S WITH THE CLOUD COVER? YOU GUYS GOT CENSORSHIP HERE?
OH, YOU MEAN ALL THIS? IT WAS PUT HERE BY--
THE COMICS CODE? THE PUBLISHER? LICENSING?
NO. THE ONE RESPONSIBLE FOR ALL THIS IS...

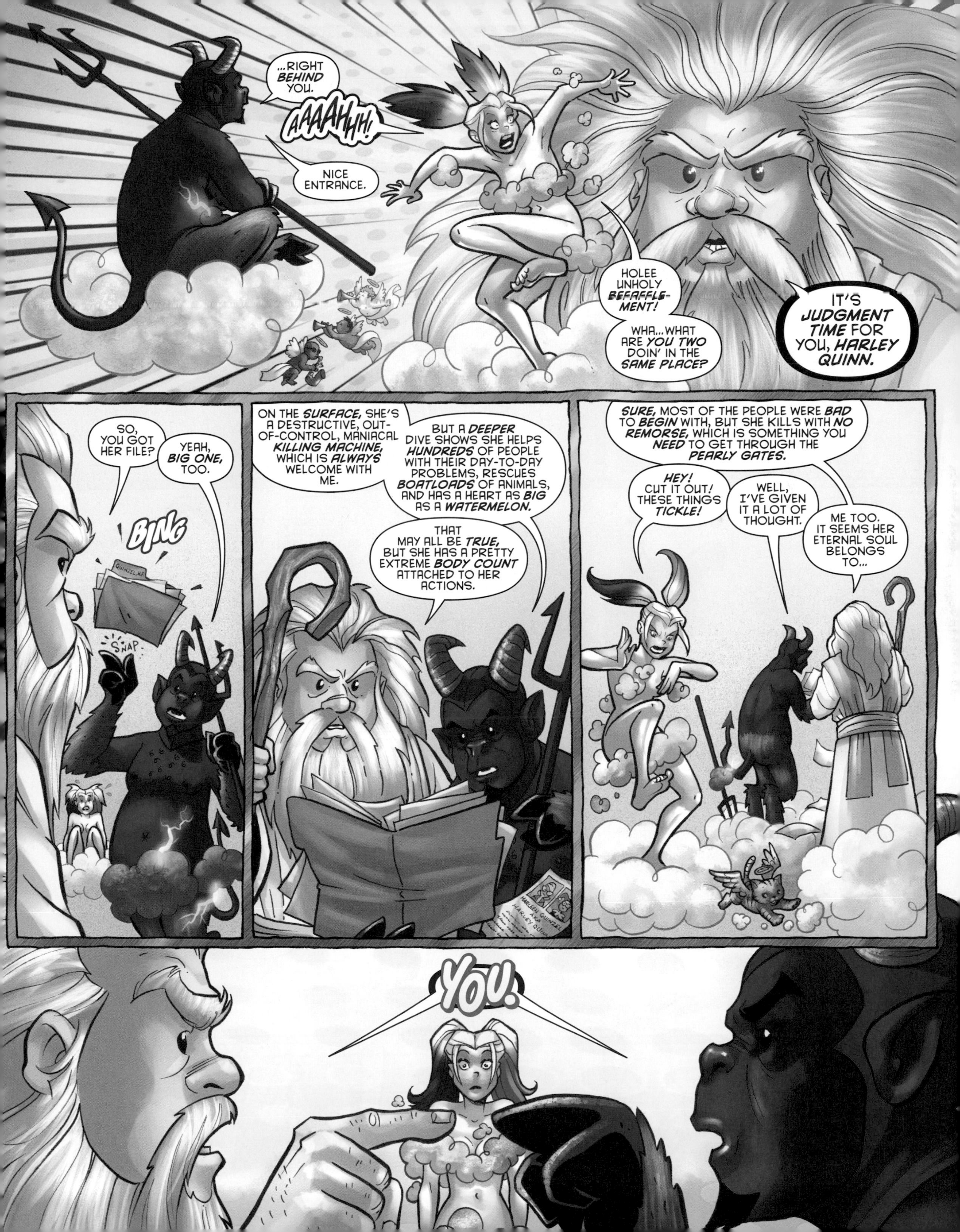
...RIGHT BEHIND YOU.
AAAAHHH!
NICE ENTRANCE.
HOLEE UNHOLY BEFAFFLE-MENT!
WHA...WHAT ARE YOU TWO DOIN' IN THE SAME PLACE?
IT'S JUDGMENT TIME FOR YOU, HARLEY QUINN.
SO, YOU GOT HER FILE?
YEAH, BIG ONE, TOO.
BING
SNAP
ON THE SURFACE, SHE'S A DESTRUCTIVE, OUT-OF-CONTROL, MANIACAL KILLING MACHINE, WHICH IS ALWAYS WELCOME WITH ME.
BUT A DEEPER DIVE SHOWS SHE HELPS HUNDREDS OF PEOPLE WITH THEIR DAY-TO-DAY PROBLEMS, RESCUES BOATLOADS OF ANIMALS, AND HAS A HEART AS BIG AS A WATERMELON.
THAT MAY ALL BE TRUE, BUT SHE HAS A PRETTY EXTREME BODY COUNT ATTACHED TO HER ACTIONS.
SURE, MOST OF THE PEOPLE WERE BAD TO BEGIN WITH, BUT SHE KILLS WITH NO REMORSE, WHICH IS SOMETHING YOU NEED TO GET THROUGH THE PEARLY GATES.
HEY! CUT IT OUT! THESE THINGS TICKLE!
WELL, I'VE GIVEN IT A LOT OF THOUGHT.
ME TOO. IT SEEMS HER ETERNAL SOUL BELONGS TO...
YOU.

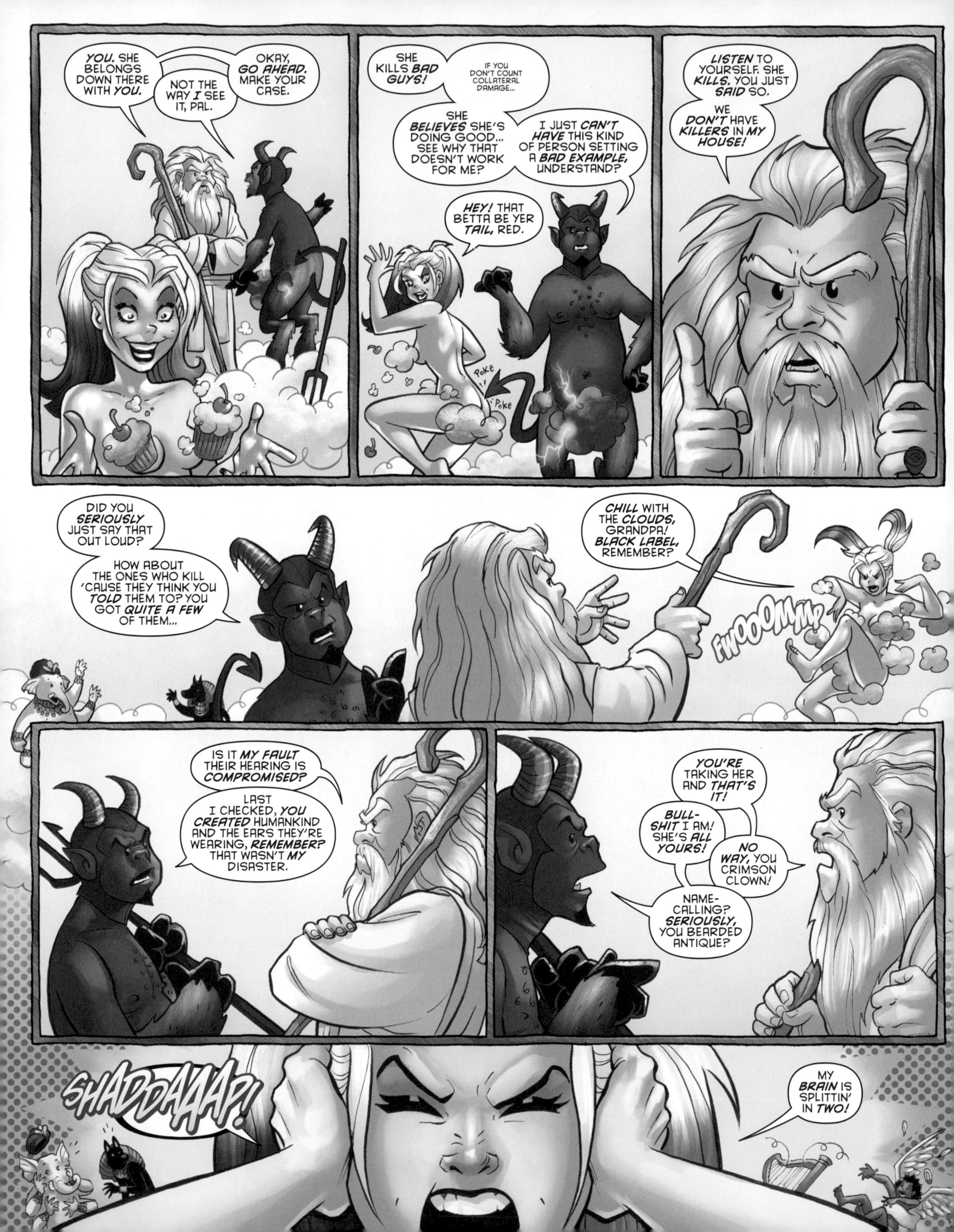

YOU. SHE BELONGS DOWN THERE WITH YOU.
OKAY, GO AHEAD. MAKE YOUR CASE.
NOT THE WAY I SEE IT, PAL.
SHE KILLS BAD GUYS!
IF YOU DON'T COUNT COLLATERAL DAMAGE...
SHE BELIEVES SHE'S DOING GOOD... SEE WHY THAT DOESN'T WORK FOR ME?
I JUST CAN'T HAVE THIS KIND OF PERSON SETTING A BAD EXAMPLE, UNDERSTAND?
HEY! THAT BETTA BE YER TAIL, RED.
POKE
POKE
LISTEN TO YOURSELF. SHE KILLS. YOU JUST SAID SO.
WE DON'T HAVE KILLERS IN MY HOUSE!
DID YOU SERIOUSLY JUST SAY THAT OUT LOUD?
HOW ABOUT THE ONES WHO KILL 'CAUSE THEY THINK YOU TOLD THEM TO? YOU GOT QUITE A FEW OF THEM...
CHILL WITH THE CLOUDS, GRANDPA! BLACK LABEL, REMEMBER?
FWOOOMMP
IS IT MY FAULT THEIR HEARING IS COMPROMISED?
LAST I CHECKED, YOU CREATED HUMANKIND AND THE EARS THEY'RE WEARING, REMEMBER? THAT WASN'T MY DISASTER.
YOU'RE TAKING HER AND THAT'S IT!
BULL-SHIT I AM! SHE'S ALL YOURS!
NO WAY, YOU CRIMSON CLOWN!
NAME-CALLING? SERIOUSLY, YOU BEARDED ANTIQUE?
SHADDAAAAP!
MY BRAIN IS SPLITTIN' IN TWO!

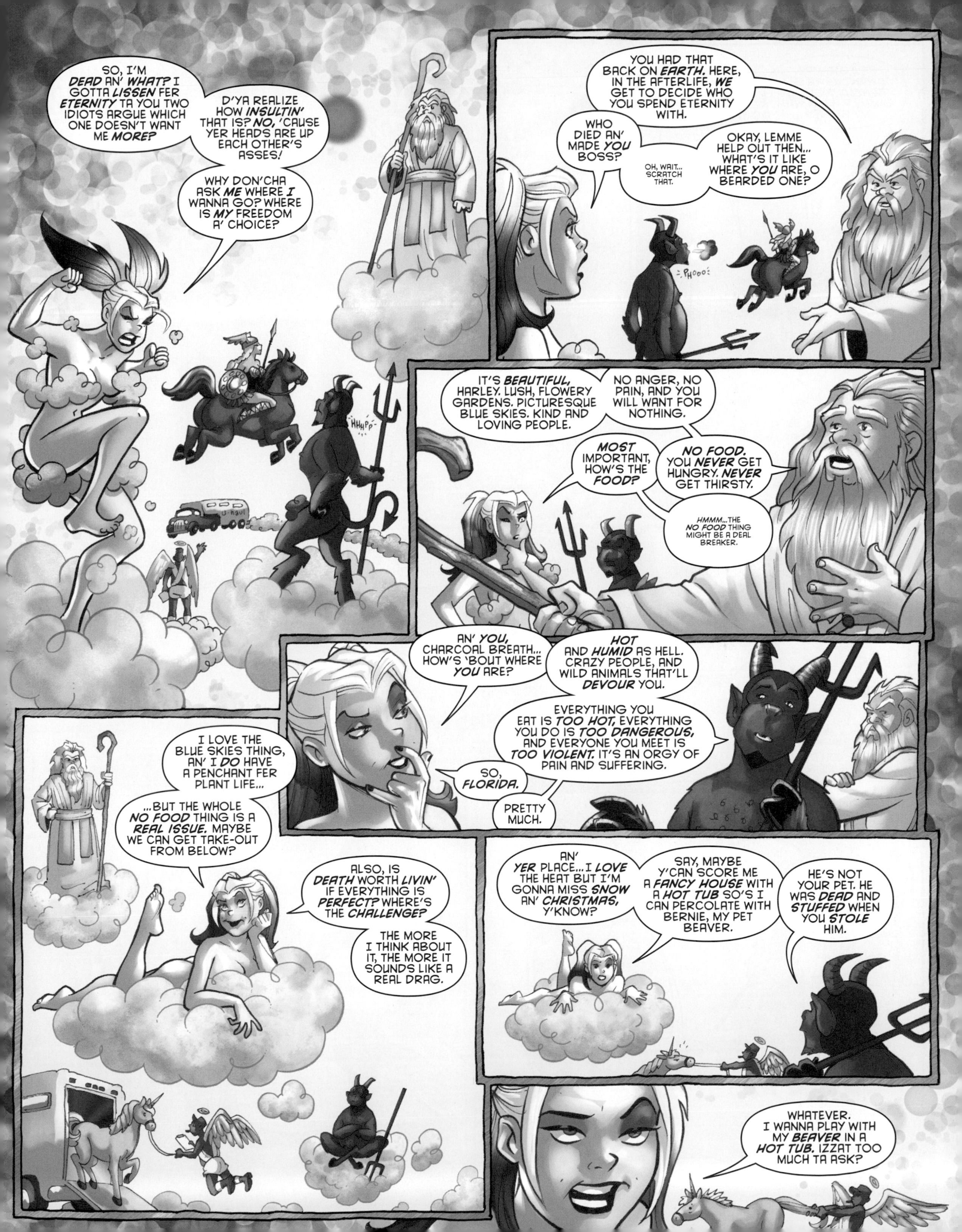
SO, I'M DEAD AN' WHAT? I GOTTA LISSEN FER ETERNITY TA YOU TWO IDIOTS ARGUE WHICH ONE DOESN'T WANT ME MORE?
D'YA REALIZE HOW INSULTIN' THAT IS? NO, 'CAUSE YER HEADS ARE UP EACH OTHER'S ASSES!
WHY DON'CHA ASK ME WHERE I WANNA GO? WHERE IS MY FREEDOM A' CHOICE?
HHHPP
U-HAUL
YOU HAD THAT BACK ON EARTH. HERE, IN THE AFTERLIFE, WE GET TO DECIDE WHO YOU SPEND ETERNITY WITH.
WHO DIED AN' MADE YOU BOSS?
OH, WAIT... SCRATCH THAT.
OKAY, LEMME HELP OUT THEN... WHAT'S IT LIKE WHERE YOU ARE, O BEARDED ONE?
PHOOO
IT'S BEAUTIFUL, HARLEY. LUSH, FLOWERY GARDENS. PICTURESQUE BLUE SKIES. KIND AND LOVING PEOPLE.
NO ANGER, NO PAIN, AND YOU WILL WANT FOR NOTHING.
MOST IMPORTANT, HOW'S THE FOOD?
NO FOOD. YOU NEVER GET HUNGRY. NEVER GET THIRSTY.
HMMM...THE NO FOOD THING MIGHT BE A DEAL BREAKER.
AN' YOU, CHARCOAL BREATH... HOW'S 'BOUT WHERE YOU ARE?
HOT AND HUMID AS HELL. CRAZY PEOPLE, AND WILD ANIMALS THAT'LL DEVOUR YOU.
EVERYTHING YOU EAT IS TOO HOT, EVERYTHING YOU DO IS TOO DANGEROUS, AND EVERYONE YOU MEET IS TOO VIOLENT. IT'S AN ORGY OF PAIN AND SUFFERING.
SO, FLORIDA.
PRETTY MUCH.
I LOVE THE BLUE SKIES THING, AN' I DO HAVE A PENCHANT FER PLANT LIFE...
...BUT THE WHOLE NO FOOD THING IS A REAL ISSUE. MAYBE WE CAN GET TAKE-OUT FROM BELOW?
ALSO, IS DEATH WORTH LIVIN' IF EVERYTHING IS PERFECT? WHERE'S THE CHALLENGE?
THE MORE I THINK ABOUT IT, THE MORE IT SOUNDS LIKE A REAL DRAG.
AN' YER PLACE... I LOVE THE HEAT BUT I'M GONNA MISS SNOW AN' CHRISTMAS, Y'KNOW?
SAY, MAYBE Y'CAN SCORE ME A FANCY HOUSE WITH A HOT TUB SO'S I CAN PERCOLATE WITH BERNIE, MY PET BEAVER.
HE'S NOT YOUR PET. HE WAS DEAD AND STUFFED WHEN YOU STOLE HIM.
WHATEVER. I WANNA PLAY WITH MY BEAVER IN A HOT TUB. IZZAT TOO MUCH TA ASK?

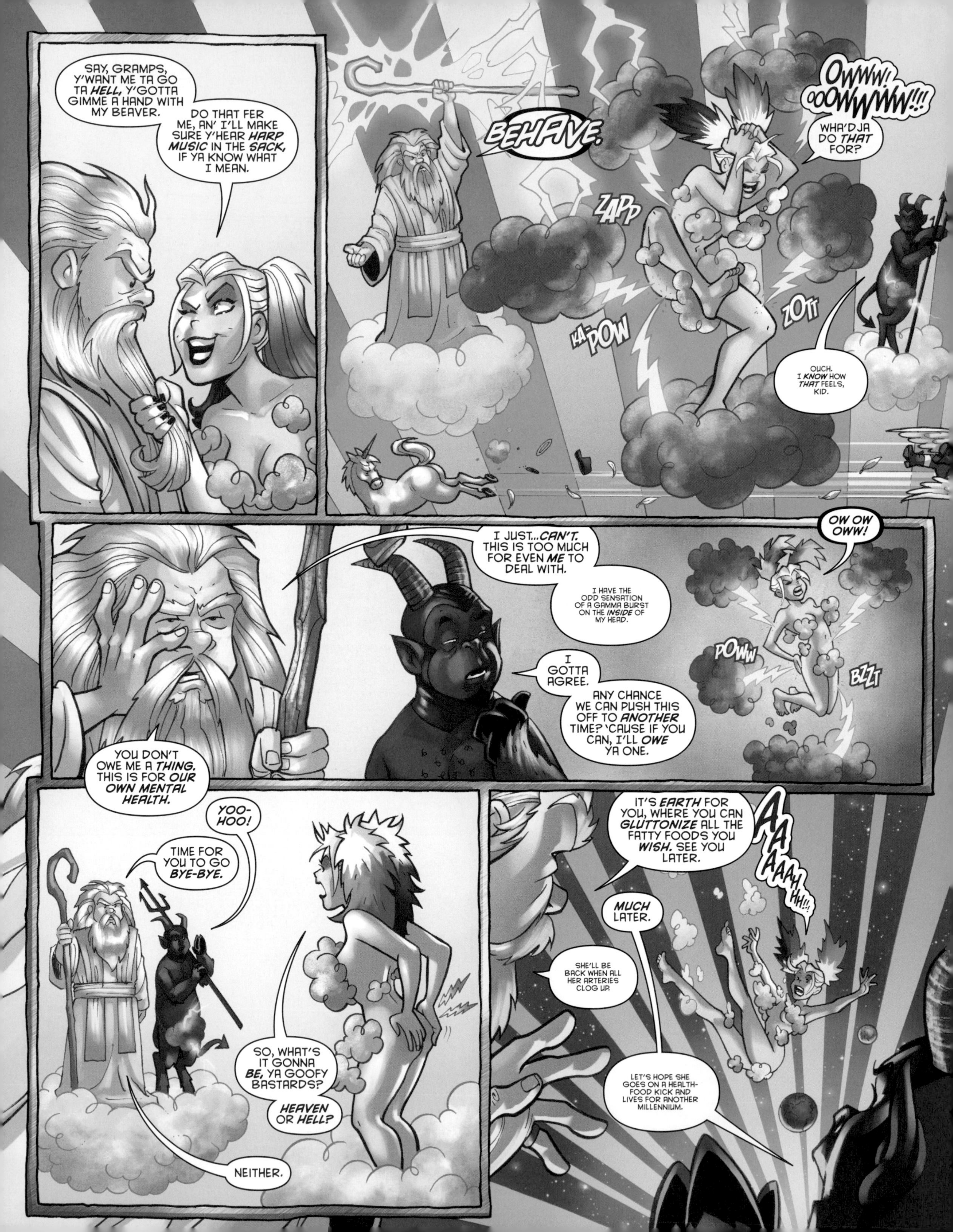
SAY, GRAMPS, Y'WANT ME TA GO TA HELL, Y'GOTTA GIMME A HAND WITH MY BEAVER.
DO THAT FER ME, AN' I'LL MAKE SURE Y'HEAR HARP MUSIC IN THE SACK, IF YA KNOW WHAT I MEAN.
BEHAVE.
OWWW! OOOWWWW!!!
WHA'DJA DO THAT FOR?
ZAPP
KA-POW
ZOTT
OUCH. I KNOW HOW THAT FEELS, KID.
I JUST...CAN'T. THIS IS TOO MUCH FOR EVEN ME TO DEAL WITH.
I HAVE THE ODD SENSATION OF A GAMMA BURST ON THE INSIDE OF MY HEAD.
OW OW OWW!
I GOTTA AGREE.
ANY CHANCE WE CAN PUSH THIS OFF TO ANOTHER TIME? 'CAUSE IF YOU CAN, I'LL OWE YA ONE.
POWW
BZZT
YOU DON'T OWE ME A THING. THIS IS FOR OUR OWN MENTAL HEALTH.
YOO-HOO!
TIME FOR YOU TO GO BYE-BYE.
SO, WHAT'S IT GONNA BE, YA GOOFY BASTARDS?
HEAVEN OR HELL?
NEITHER.
IT'S EARTH FOR YOU, WHERE YOU CAN GLUTTONIZE ALL THE FATTY FOODS YOU WISH. SEE YOU LATER.
AAAAAHHH!!!
MUCH LATER.
SHE'LL BE BACK WHEN ALL HER ARTERIES CLOG UP.
LET'S HOPE SHE GOES ON A HEALTH-FOOD KICK AND LIVES FOR ANOTHER MILLENNIUM.

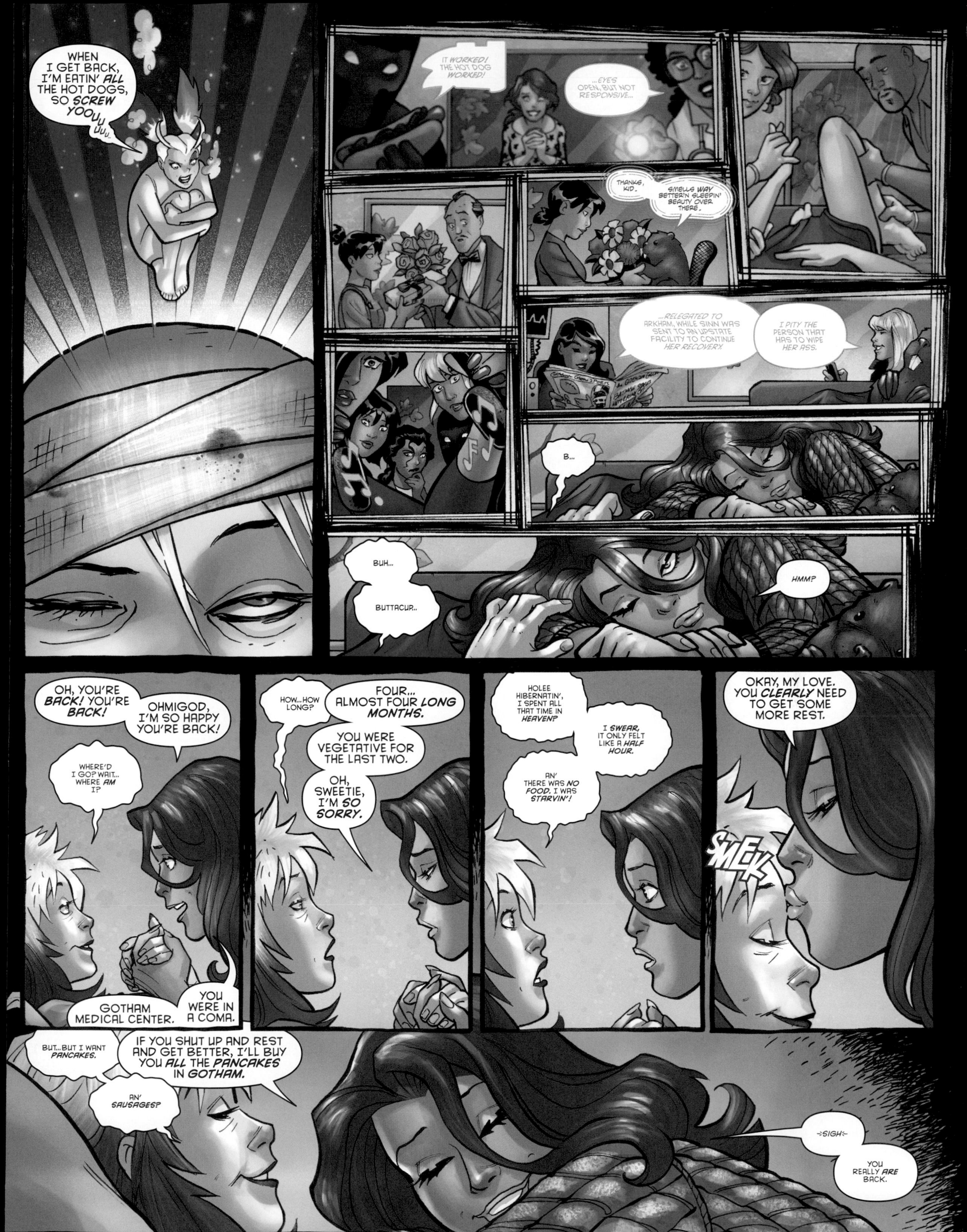
WHEN I GET BACK, I'M EATIN' ALL THE HOT DOGS, SO SCREW YOOUUUUU...
IT WORKED! THE HOT DOG WORKED!
...EYES OPEN, BUT NOT RESPONSIVE...
THANKS, KID.
SMELLS WAY BETTER'N SLEEPIN' BEAUTY OVER THERE.
...RELEGATED TO ARKHAM, WHILE SINN WAS SENT TO AN UPSTATE FACILITY TO CONTINUE HER RECOVERY.
I PITY THE PERSON THAT HAS TO WIPE HER ASS.
B...
BUH...
BUTTACUP...
HMM?
OH, YOU'RE BACK! YOU'RE BACK!
OHMIGOD, I'M SO HAPPY YOU'RE BACK!
WHERE'D I GO? WAIT... WHERE AM I?
GOTHAM MEDICAL CENTER.
YOU WERE IN A COMA.
HOW...HOW LONG?
FOUR... ALMOST FOUR LONG MONTHS.
YOU WERE VEGETATIVE FOR THE LAST TWO.
OH, SWEETIE, I'M SO SORRY.
HOLEE HIBERNATIN', I SPENT ALL THAT TIME IN HEAVEN?
I SWEAR, IT ONLY FELT LIKE A HALF HOUR.
AN' THERE WAS NO FOOD. I WAS STARVIN'!
OKAY, MY LOVE. YOU CLEARLY NEED TO GET SOME MORE REST.
SMEK
BUT...BUT I WANT PANCAKES.
IF YOU SHUT UP AND REST AND GET BETTER, I'LL BUY YOU ALL THE PANCAKES IN GOTHAM.
AN' SAUSAGES?
SIGH
YOU REALLY ARE BACK.

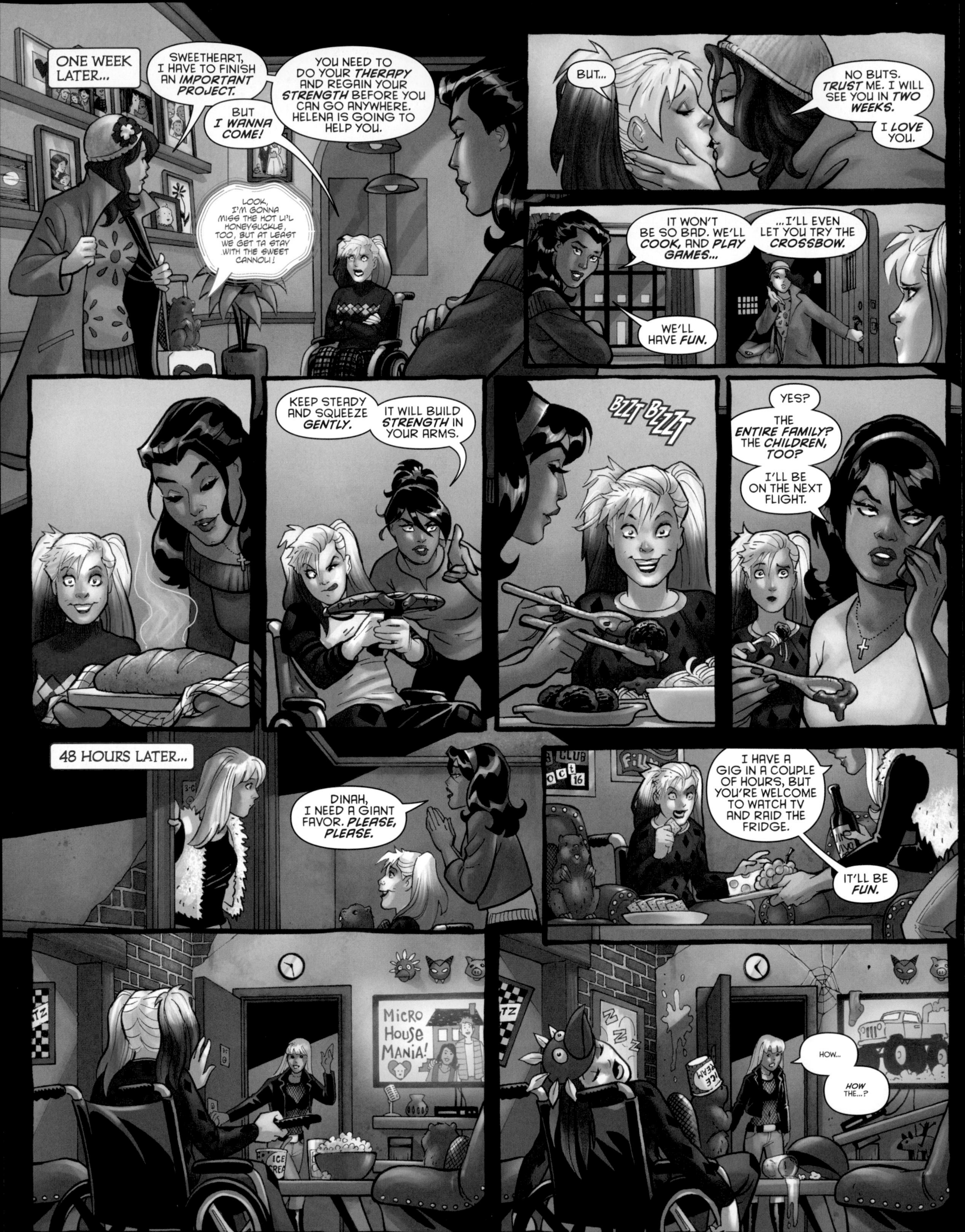

ONE WEEK LATER...
SWEETHEART, I HAVE TO FINISH AN IMPORTANT PROJECT.
BUT I WANNA COME!
YOU NEED TO DO YOUR THERAPY AND REGAIN YOUR STRENGTH BEFORE YOU CAN GO ANYWHERE. HELENA IS GOING TO HELP YOU.
LOOK, I'M GONNA MISS THE HOT LI'L HONEYSUCKLE, TOO, BUT AT LEAST WE GET TA STAY WITH THE SWEET CANNOLI!
BUT...
NO BUTS. TRUST ME. I WILL SEE YOU IN TWO WEEKS.
I LOVE YOU.
IT WON'T BE SO BAD. WE'LL COOK, AND PLAY GAMES...
...I'LL EVEN LET YOU TRY THE CROSSBOW.
WE'LL HAVE FUN.
KEEP STEADY AND SQUEEZE GENTLY.
IT WILL BUILD STRENGTH IN YOUR ARMS.
BZZT BZZZT
YES?
THE ENTIRE FAMILY? THE CHILDREN, TOO?
I'LL BE ON THE NEXT FLIGHT.
48 HOURS LATER...
DINAH, I NEED A GIANT FAVOR. PLEASE, PLEASE.
I HAVE A GIG IN A COUPLE OF HOURS, BUT YOU'RE WELCOME TO WATCH TV AND RAID THE FRIDGE.
IT'LL BE FUN.
MICRO HOUSE MANIA!
HOW...
HOW THE...?

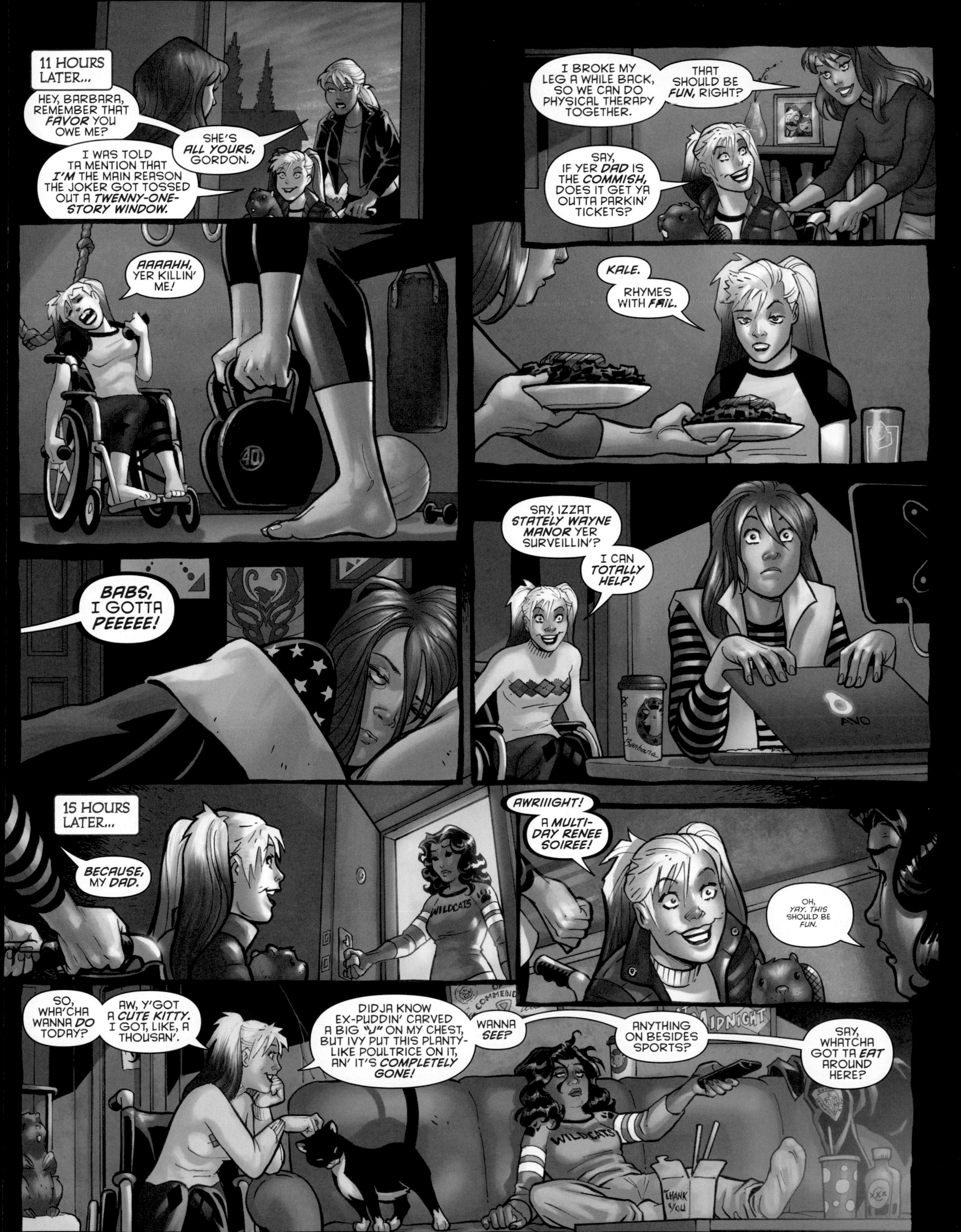
11 HOURS LATER...
HEY, BARBARA, REMEMBER THAT *FAVOR* YOU OWE ME?
SHE'S *ALL YOURS,* GORDON.
I WAS TOLD TA MENTION THAT *I'M* THE MAIN REASON THE JOKER GOT TOSSED OUT A *TWENNY-ONE-STORY WINDOW.*
I BROKE MY LEG A WHILE BACK, SO WE CAN DO PHYSICAL THERAPY TOGETHER.
THAT SHOULD BE *FUN,* RIGHT?
SAY, IF YER *DAD* IS THE *COMMISH,* DOES IT GET YA OUTTA PARKIN' TICKETS?
AAAAHH, YER KILLIN' ME!
40
KALE.
RHYMES WITH *FAIL.*
BABS, I GOTTA PEEEEE!
SAY, IZZAT *STATELY WAYNE MANOR* YER SURVEILLIN'?
I CAN *TOTALLY HELP!*
Barbara
AVO
15 HOURS LATER...
BECAUSE, MY *DAD.*
WILDCATS
AWRIIIGHT!
A *MULTI-DAY RENEE SOIREE!*
OH, *YAY.* THIS SHOULD BE *FUN.*
SO, WHA'CHA WANNA *DO* TODAY?
AW, Y'GOT A *CUTE KITTY.* I GOT, LIKE, A THOUSAN'.
DIDJA KNOW EX-PUDDIN' CARVED A BIG *"J"* ON MY CHEST, BUT IVY PUT THIS PLANTY-LIKE POULTRICE ON IT, AN' IT'S *COMPLETELY GONE!*
WANNA *SEE?*
ANYTHING ON BESIDES SPORTS?
SAY, WHATCHA GOT TA *EAT* AROUND HERE?
WILDCATS
THANK YOU

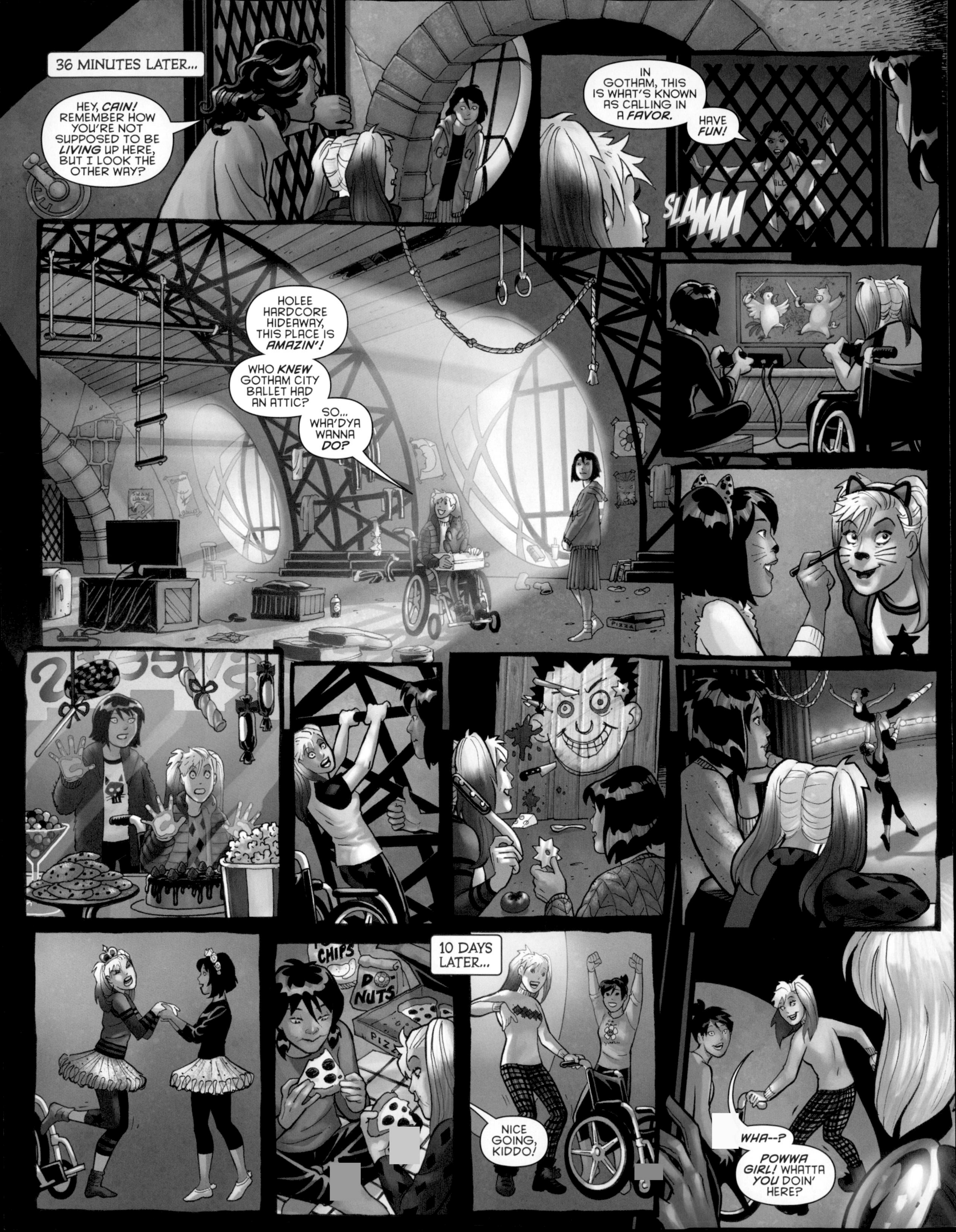
36 MINUTES LATER...
HEY, CAIN! REMEMBER HOW YOU'RE NOT SUPPOSED TO BE LIVING UP HERE, BUT I LOOK THE OTHER WAY?
IN GOTHAM, THIS IS WHAT'S KNOWN AS CALLING IN A FAVOR.
HAVE FUN!
SLAMM
HOLEE HARDCORE HIDEAWAY, THIS PLACE IS AMAZIN'!
WHO KNEW GOTHAM CITY BALLET HAD AN ATTIC?
SO... WHA'DYA WANNA DO?
PIZZA
CHIPS
DO-NUTS
10 DAYS LATER...
NICE GOING, KIDDO!
WHA--?
POWWA GIRL! WHATTA YOU DOIN' HERE?

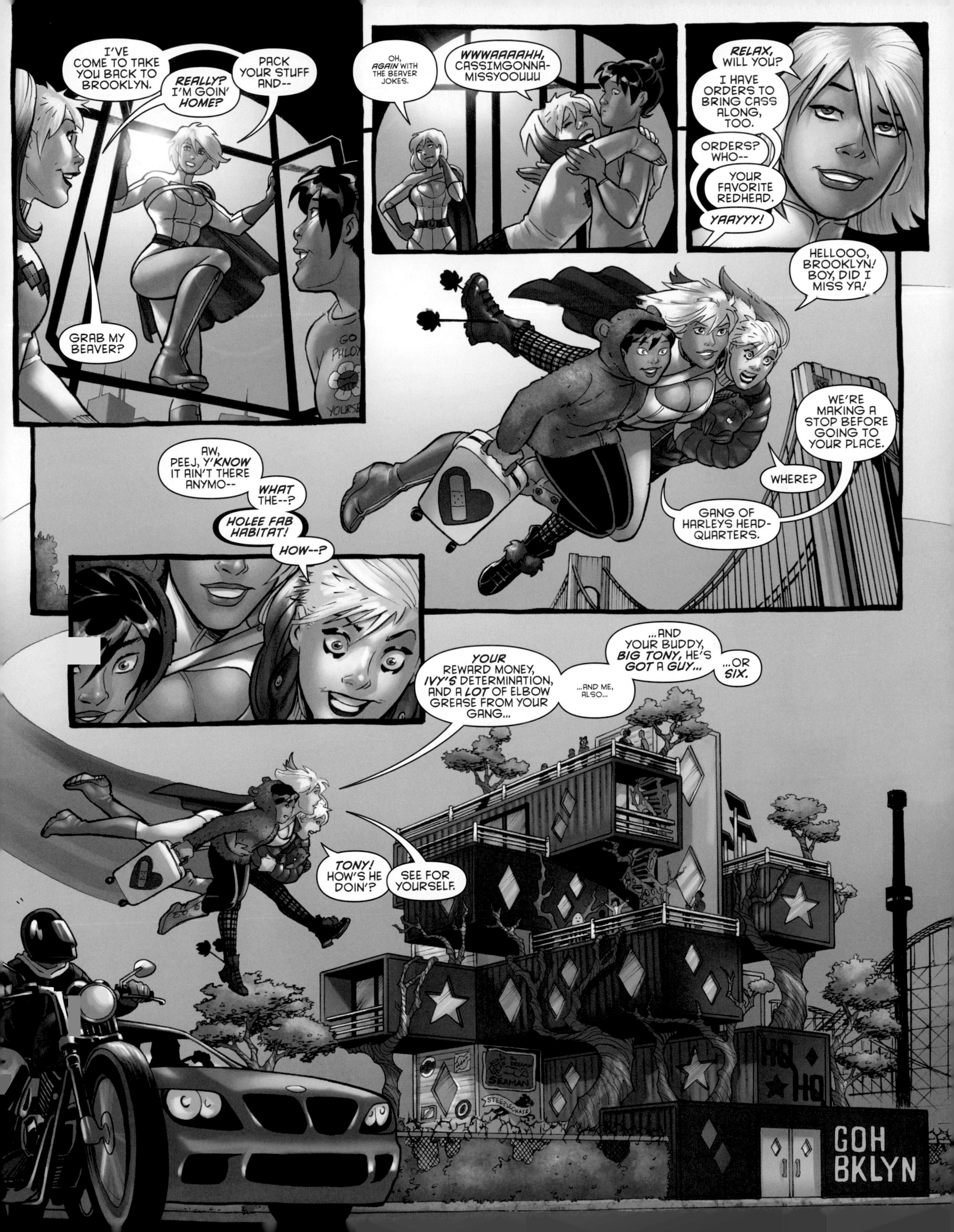

I'VE COME TO TAKE YOU BACK TO BROOKLYN.
REALLY? I'M GOIN' HOME?
PACK YOUR STUFF AND--
GRAB MY BEAVER?
OH, AGAIN WITH THE BEAVER JOKES.
WWWAAAAHH, CASSIMGONNA-MISSYOOUUU
RELAX, WILL YOU?
I HAVE ORDERS TO BRING CASS ALONG, TOO.
ORDERS? WHO--
YOUR FAVORITE REDHEAD.
YAAYYY!
HELLOOO, BROOKLYN! BOY, DID I MISS YA!
WE'RE MAKING A STOP BEFORE GOING TO YOUR PLACE.
WHERE?
GANG OF HARLEYS HEAD-QUARTERS.
AW, PEEJ, Y'KNOW IT AIN'T THERE ANYMO--
WHAT THE--?
HOLEE FAB HABITAT!
HOW--?
YOUR REWARD MONEY, IVY'S DETERMINATION, AND A LOT OF ELBOW GREASE FROM YOUR GANG...
...AND ME, ALSO...
...AND YOUR BUDDY, BIG TONY, HE'S GOT A GUY...
...OR SIX.
TONY! HOW'S HE DOIN'?
SEE FOR YOURSELF.
HQ
GOH BKLYN

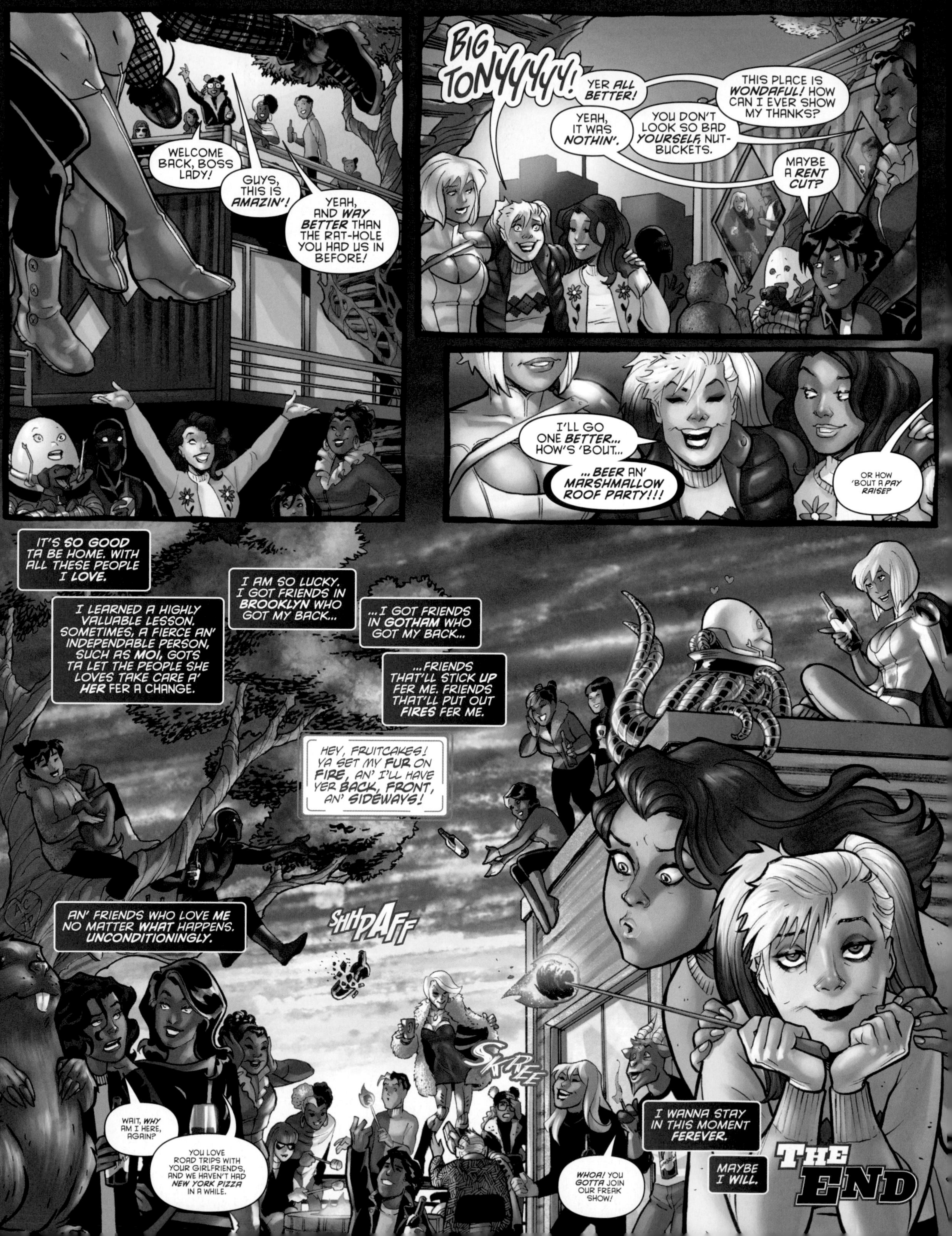
WELCOME BACK, BOSS LADY!
GUYS, THIS IS AMAZIN'!
YEAH, AND WAY BETTER THAN THE RAT-HOLE YOU HAD US IN BEFORE!
BIG TONYYYYY!
YER ALL BETTER!
YEAH, IT WAS NOTHIN'.
THIS PLACE IS WONDAFUL! HOW CAN I EVER SHOW MY THANKS?
YOU DON'T LOOK SO BAD YOURSELF, NUT-BUCKETS.
MAYBE A RENT CUT?
I'LL GO ONE BETTER... HOW'S 'BOUT...
...BEER AN' MARSHMALLOW ROOF PARTY!!!
OR HOW 'BOUT A PAY RAISE?
IT'S SO GOOD TA BE HOME. WITH ALL THESE PEOPLE I LOVE.
I LEARNED A HIGHLY VALUABLE LESSON. SOMETIMES, A FIERCE AN' INDEPENDABLE PERSON, SUCH AS MOI, GOTS TA LET THE PEOPLE SHE LOVES TAKE CARE A' HER FER A CHANGE.
I AM SO LUCKY. I GOT FRIENDS IN BROOKLYN WHO GOT MY BACK...
...I GOT FRIENDS IN GOTHAM WHO GOT MY BACK...
...FRIENDS THAT'LL STICK UP FER ME. FRIENDS THAT'LL PUT OUT FIRES FER ME.
HEY, FRUITCAKES! YA SET MY FUR ON FIRE, AN' I'LL HAVE YER BACK, FRONT, AN' SIDEWAYS!
AN' FRIENDS WHO LOVE ME NO MATTER WHAT HAPPENS. UNCONDITIONINGLY.
SHHPAFF
SKREE
WAIT, WHY AM I HERE, AGAIN?
YOU LOVE ROAD TRIPS WITH YOUR GIRLFRIENDS, AND WE HAVEN'T HAD NEW YORK PIZZA IN A WHILE.
WHOA! YOU GOTTA JOIN OUR FREAK SHOW!
I WANNA STAY IN THIS MOMENT FOREVER.
MAYBE I WILL.
THE END

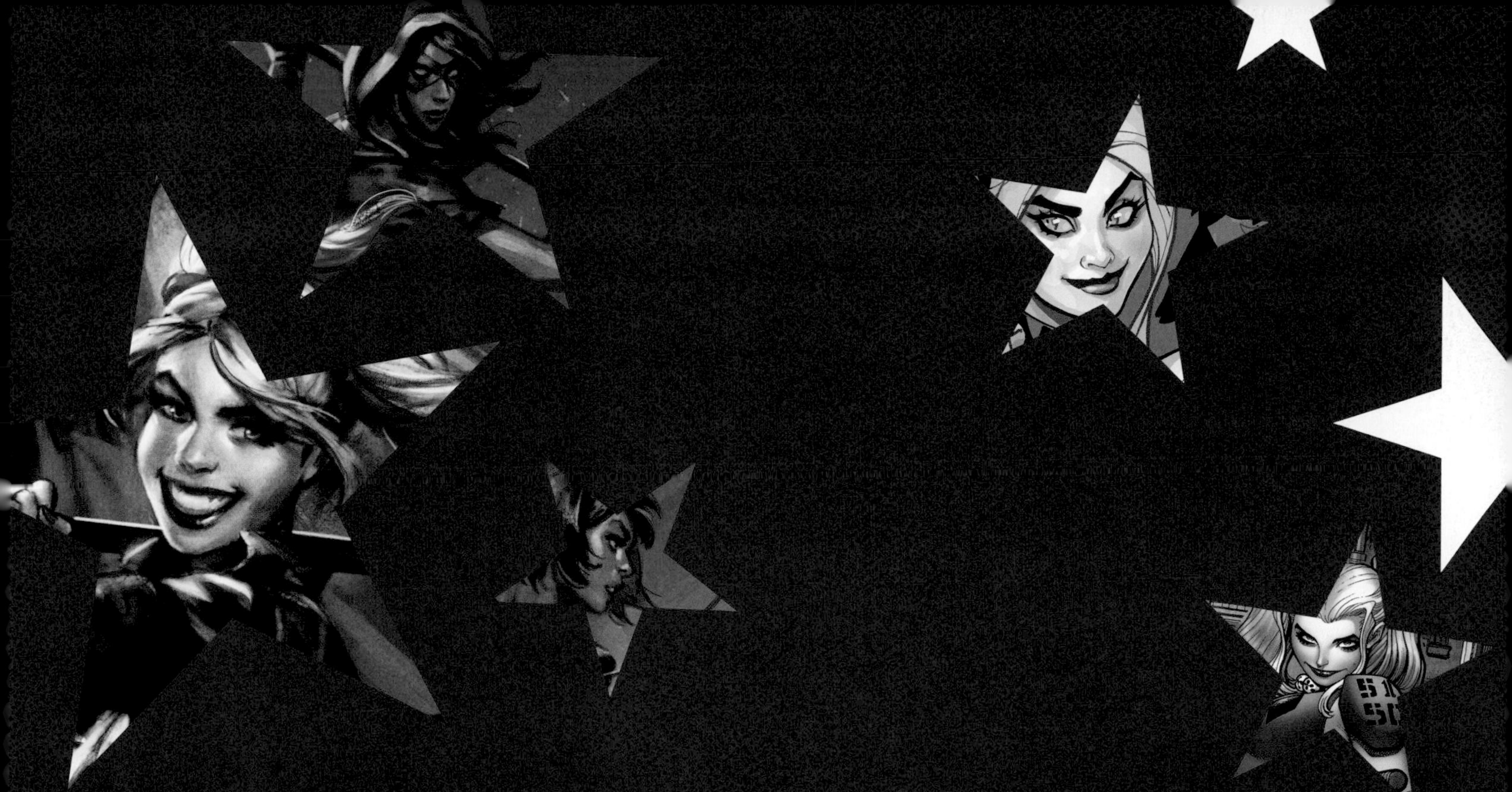

HARLEY QUINN
and the BIRDS OF PREY

VARIANT COVER GALLERY

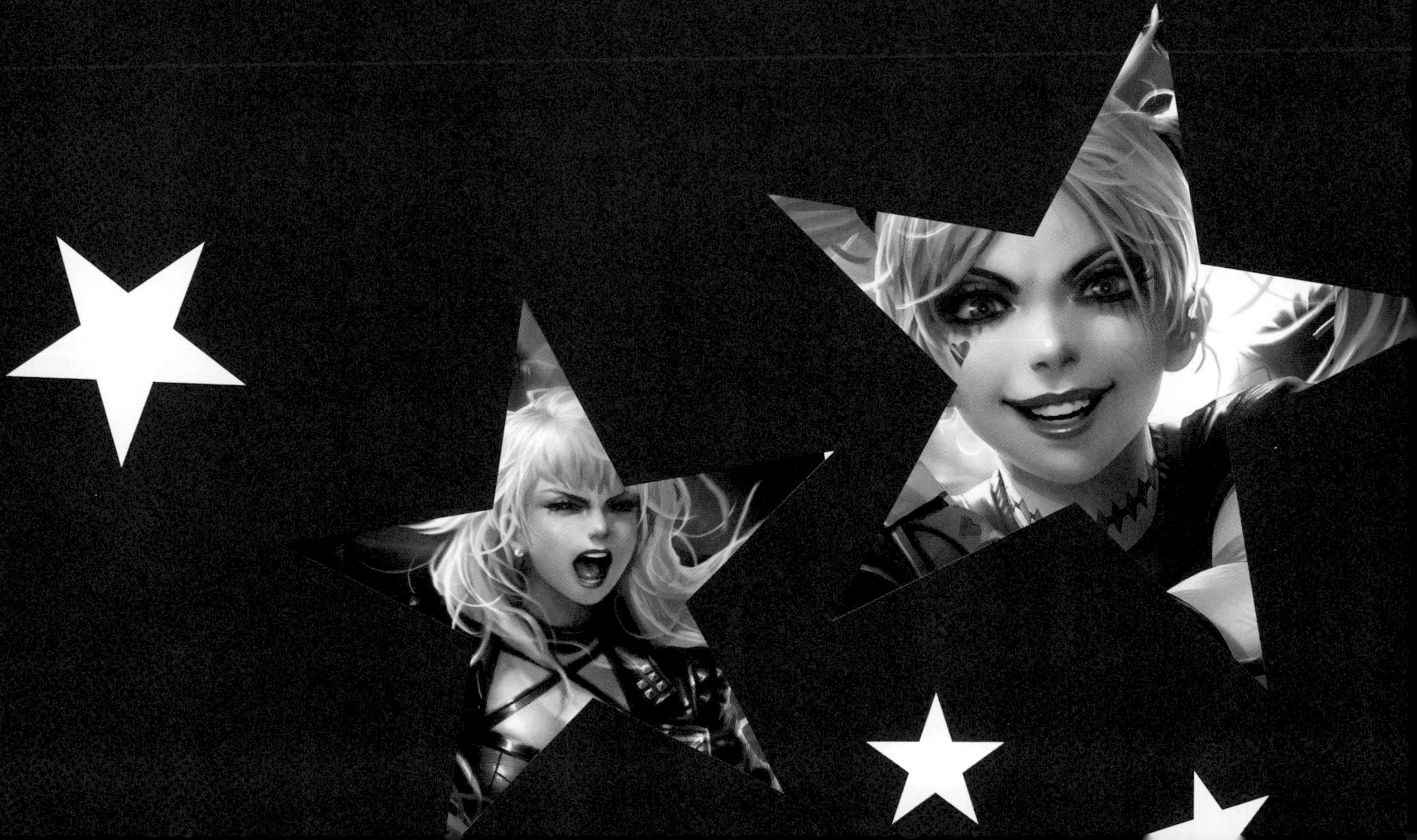

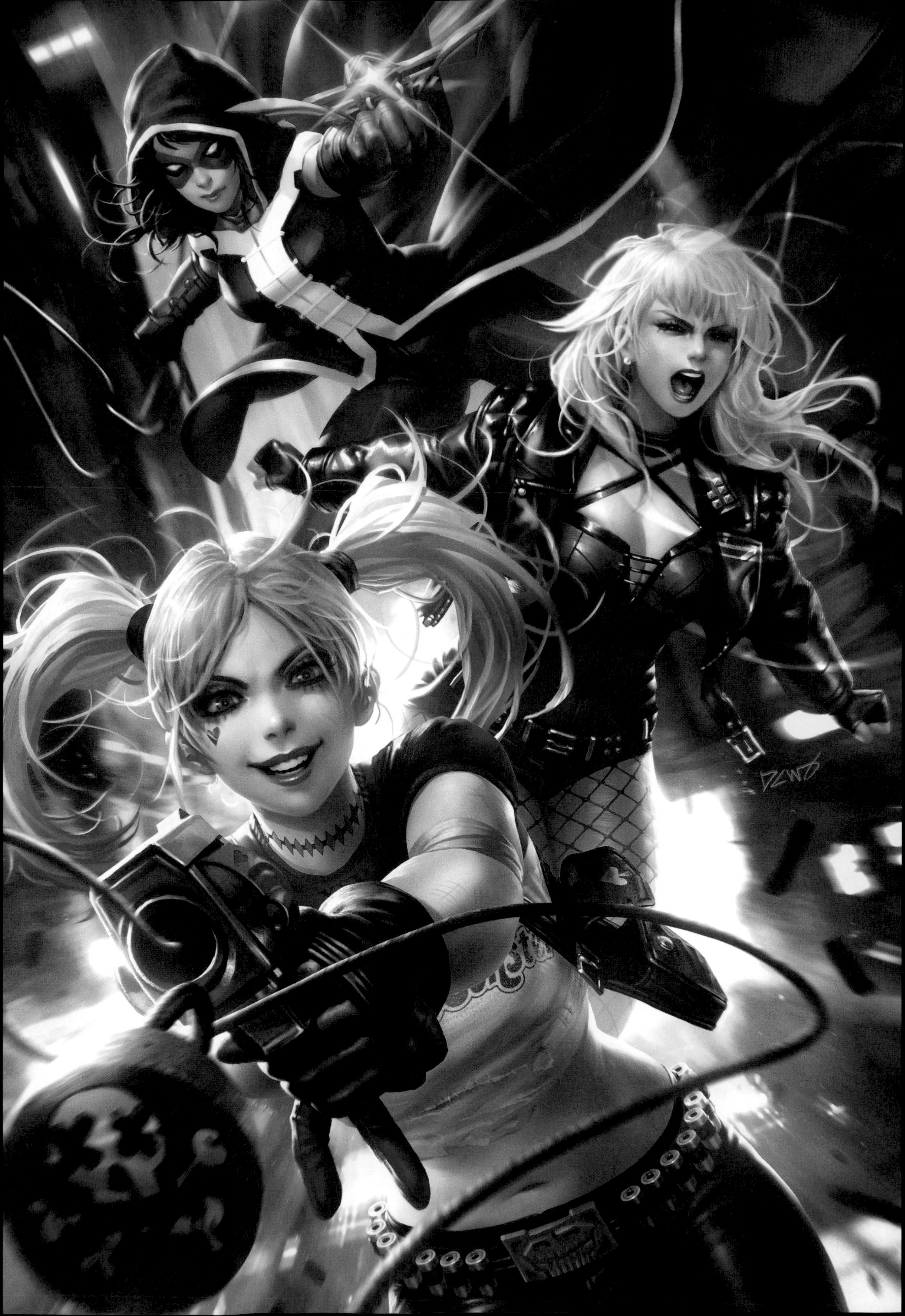

Issue #1 variant cover art by DERRICK CHEW

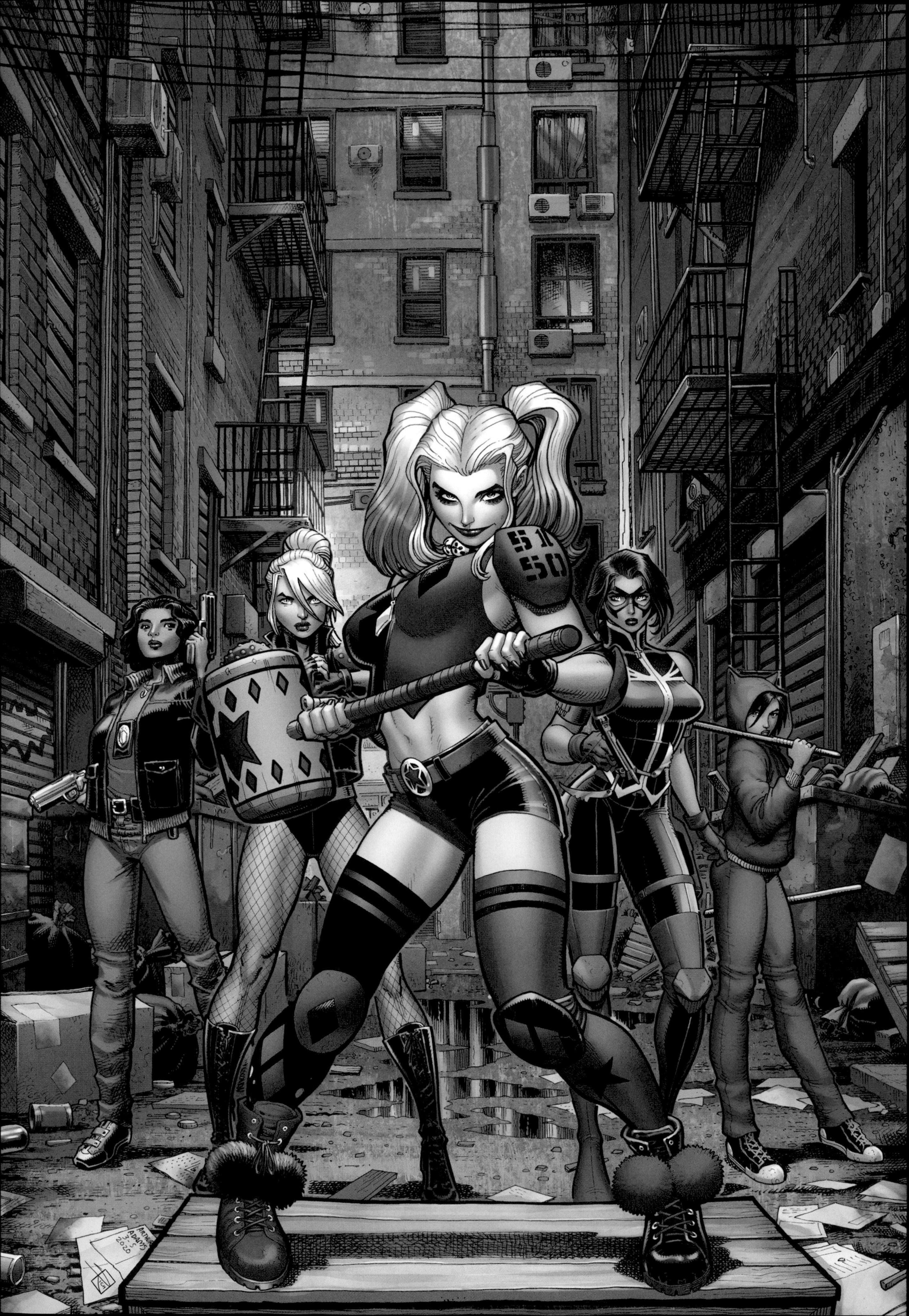
51
50
Issue #2 variant cover art by ARTHUR ADAMS & SABINE RICH

Issue #3 variant cover art by IAN MacDONALD

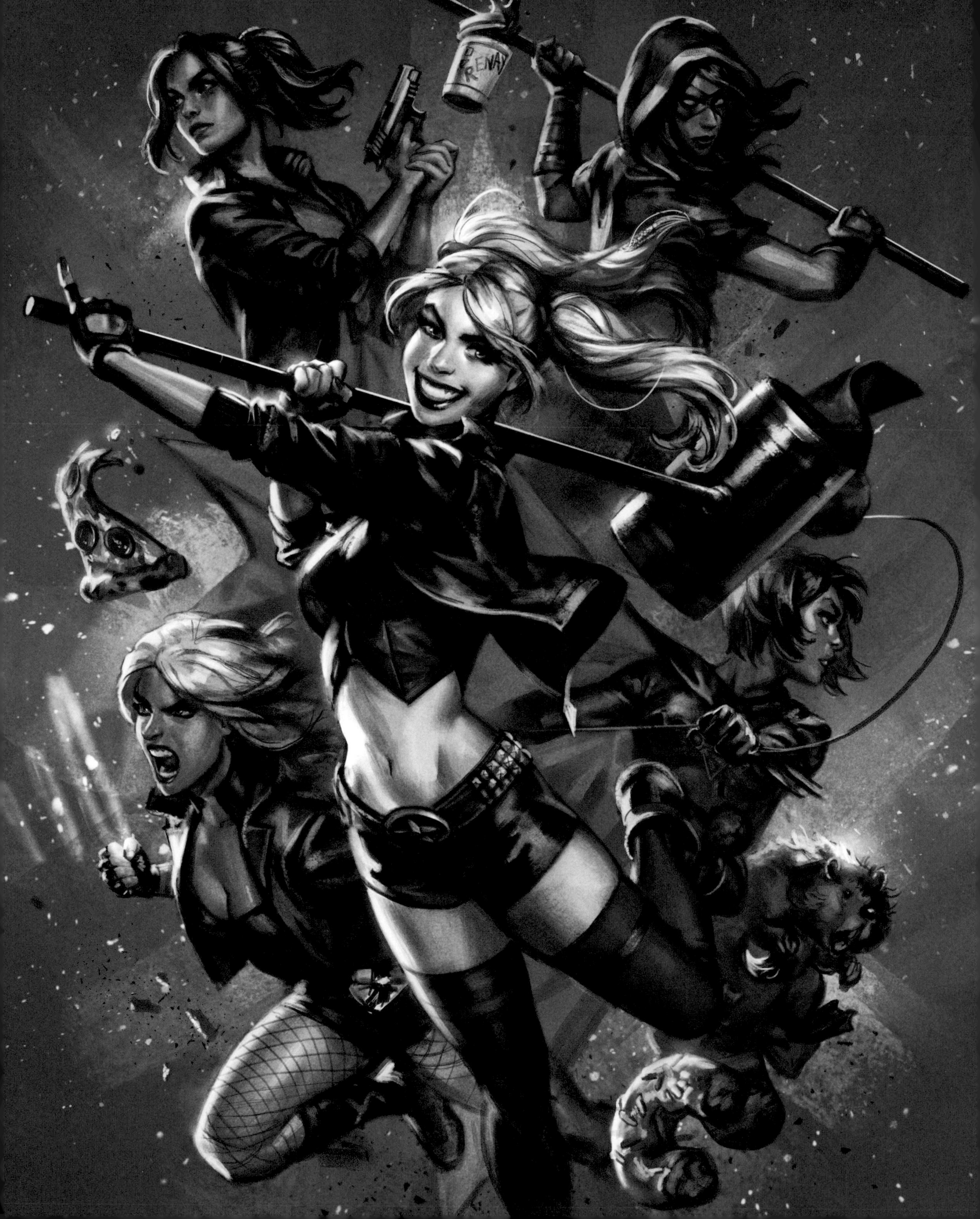

Issue #4 variant cover art by TERRY DODSON & RACHEL DODSON

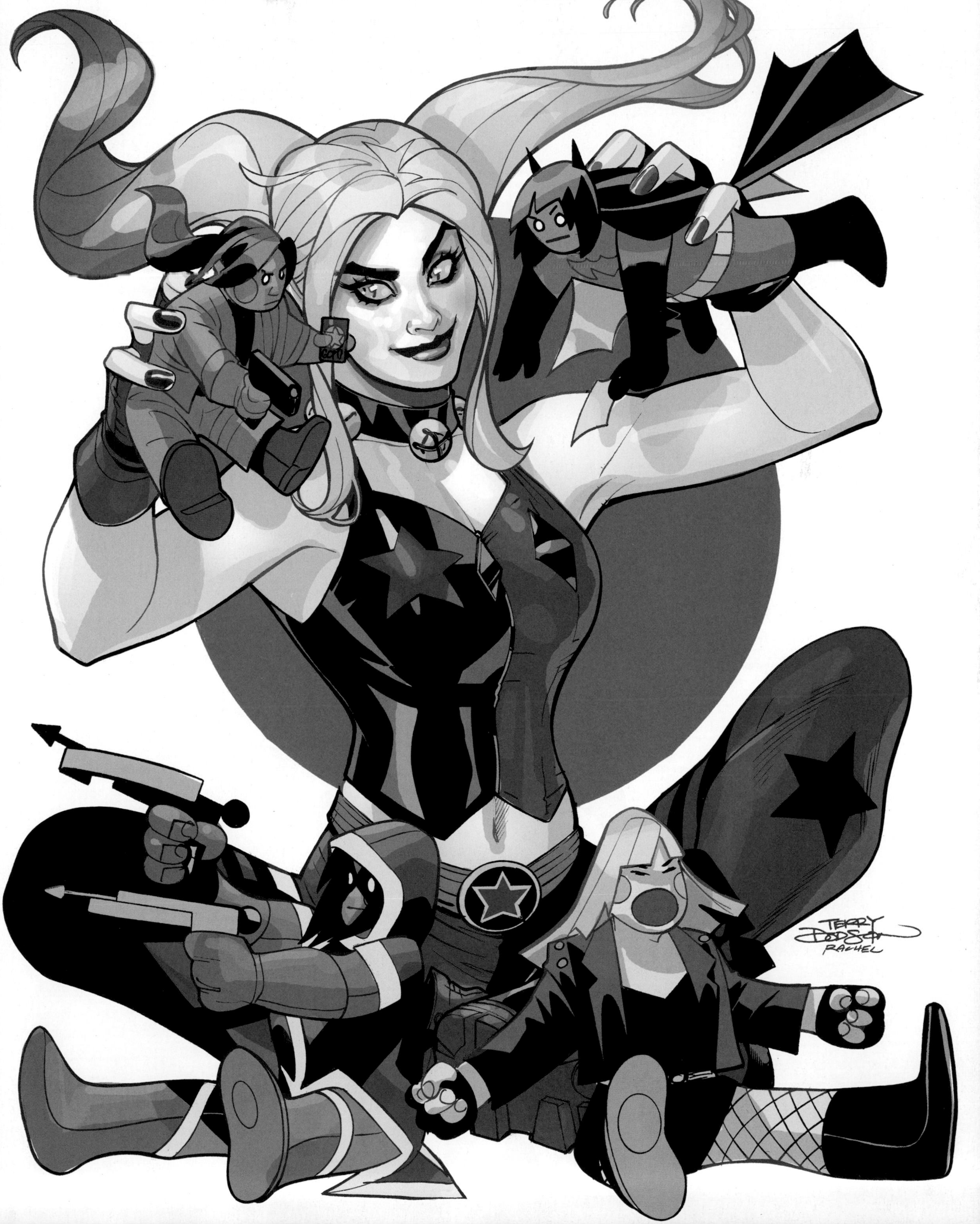
TERRY
DODSON
RACHEL

HARLEY QUINN
BLACK and WHITE
RED

CHAPTER
TWELVE

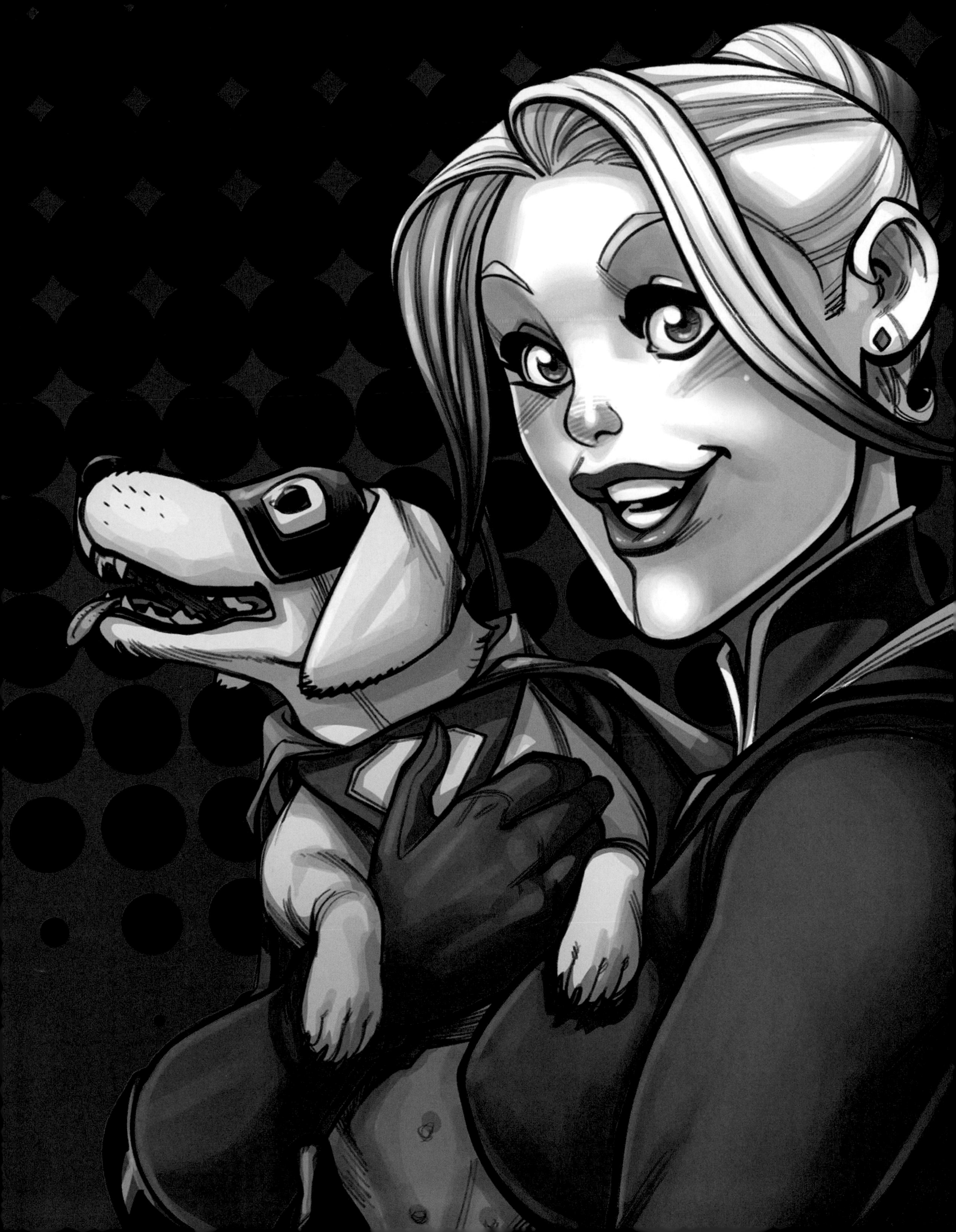

BLACK + WHITE + RED

"HARLEY QUINN & THE ANNIHILATORS"

STORY
JIMMY PALMIOTTI
& AMANDA CONNER

ART
CHAD HARDIN

COLORS
ENRICA EREN ANGIOLINI

LETTERING
DAVE SHARPE

ASSOCIATE EDITOR
AMEDEO TURTURRO

EDITOR
CHRIS CONROY

HARLEY QUINN CREATED BY
PAUL DINI & BRUCE TIMM

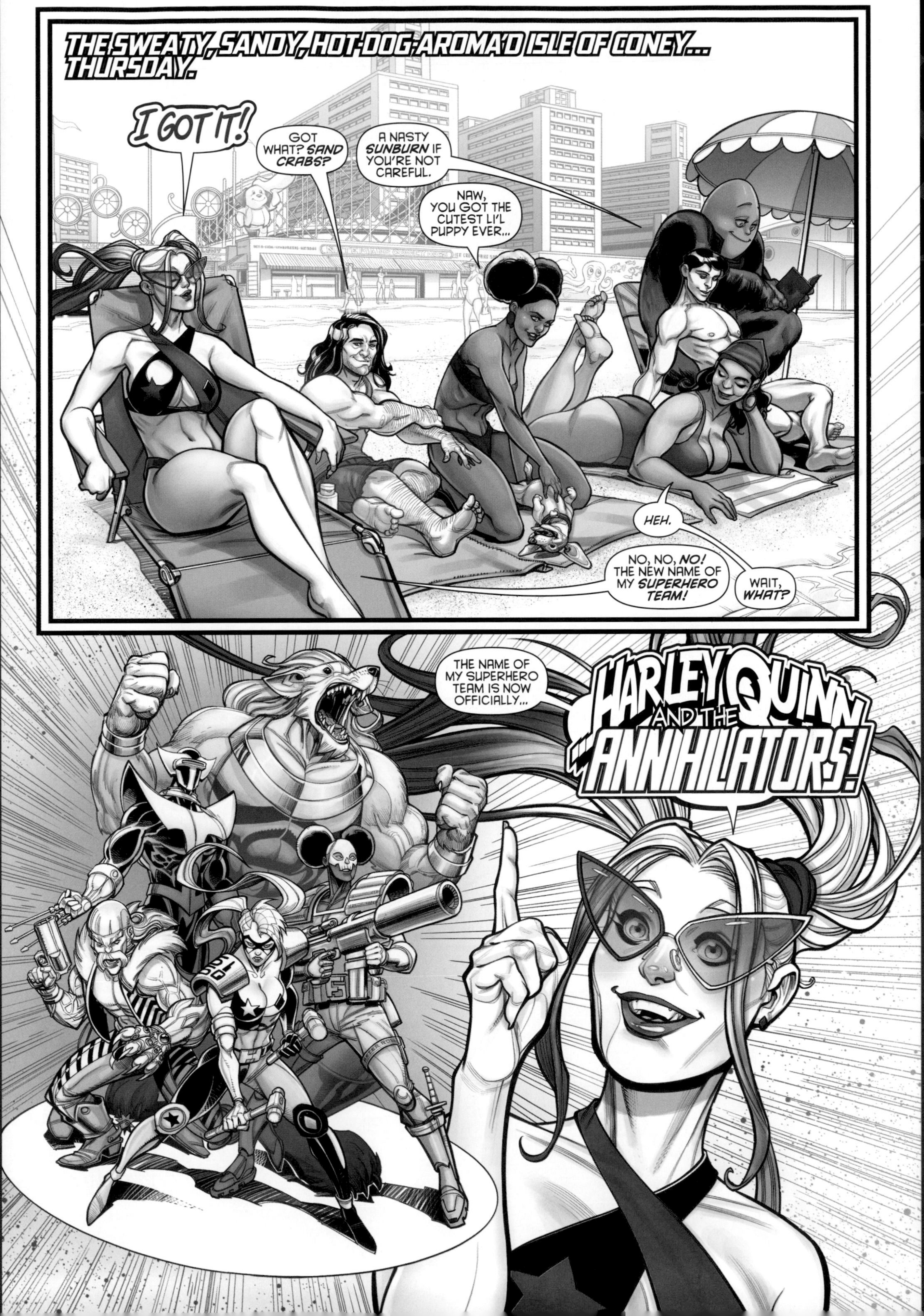
THE SWEATY, SANDY, HOT-DOG-AROMA'D ISLE OF CONEY... THURSDAY.
I GOT IT!
GOT WHAT? SAND CRABS?
A NASTY SUNBURN IF YOU'RE NOT CAREFUL.
NAW, YOU GOT THE CUTEST LI'L PUPPY EVER...
HEH.
NO, NO, NO! THE NEW NAME OF MY SUPERHERO TEAM!
WAIT, WHAT?
THE NAME OF MY SUPERHERO TEAM IS NOW OFFICIALLY...
HARLEY QUINN AND THE ANNIHILATORS!

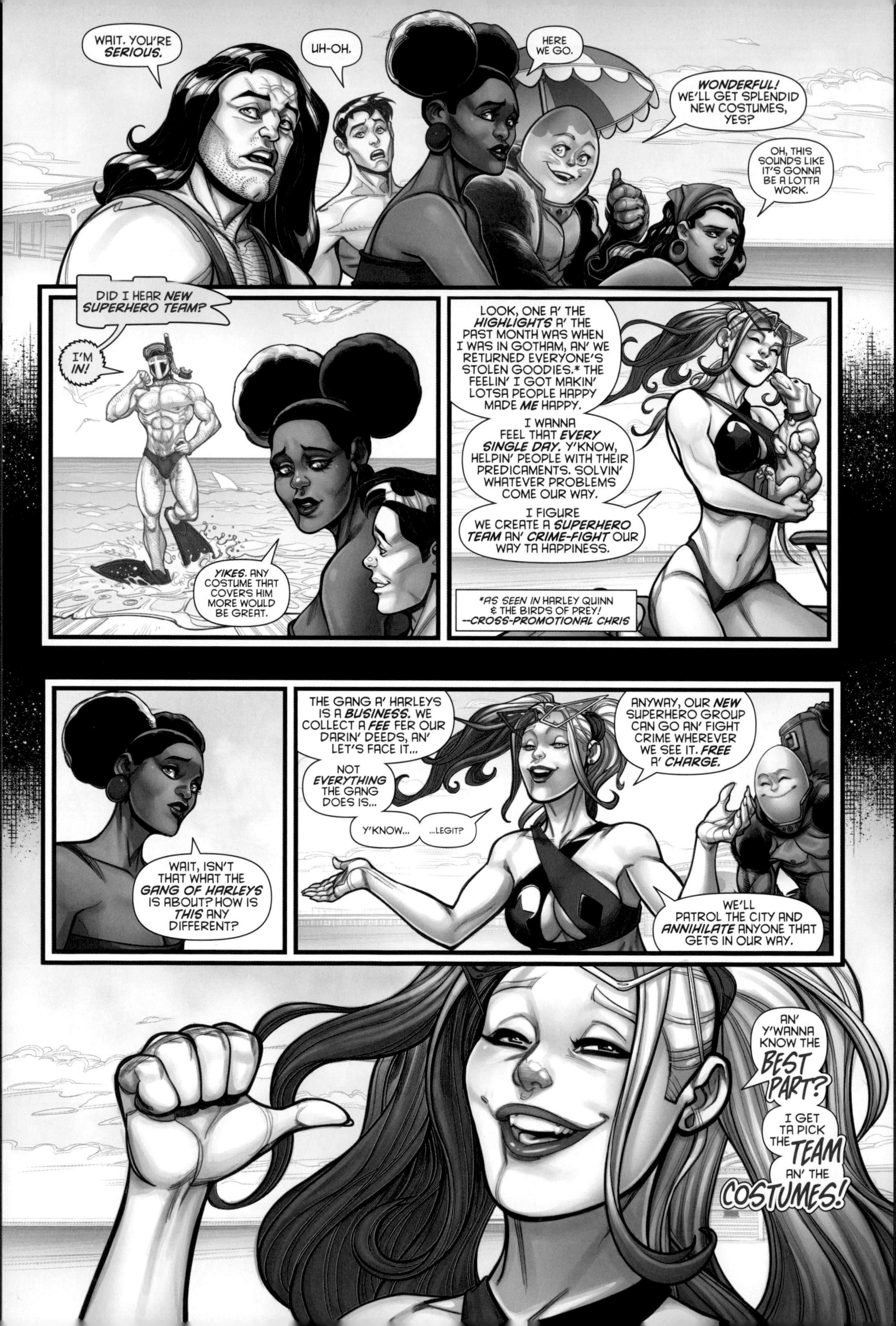
WAIT. YOU'RE SERIOUS.
UH-OH.
HERE WE GO.
WONDERFUL! WE'LL GET SPLENDID NEW COSTUMES, YES?
OH, THIS SOUND'S LIKE IT'S GONNA BE A LOTTA WORK.
DID I HEAR NEW SUPERHERO TEAM?
I'M IN!
YIKES. ANY COSTUME THAT COVERS HIM MORE WOULD BE GREAT.
LOOK, ONE A' THE HIGHLIGHTS A' THE PAST MONTH WAS WHEN I WAS IN GOTHAM, AN' WE RETURNED EVERYONE'S STOLEN GOODIES.* THE FEELIN' I GOT MAKIN' LOTSA PEOPLE HAPPY MADE ME HAPPY.
I WANNA FEEL THAT EVERY SINGLE DAY. Y'KNOW, HELPIN' PEOPLE WITH THEIR PREDICAMENTS. SOLVIN' WHATEVER PROBLEMS COME OUR WAY.
I FIGURE WE CREATE A SUPERHERO TEAM AN' CRIME-FIGHT OUR WAY TA HAPPINESS.
*AS SEEN IN HARLEY QUINN & THE BIRDS OF PREY! --CROSS-PROMOTIONAL CHRIS
WAIT, ISN'T THAT WHAT THE GANG OF HARLEYS IS ABOUT? HOW IS THIS ANY DIFFERENT?
THE GANG A' HARLEYS IS A BUSINESS. WE COLLECT A FEE FER OUR DARIN' DEEDS, AN' LET'S FACE IT...
NOT EVERYTHING THE GANG DOES IS...
Y'KNOW...
...LEGIT?
ANYWAY, OUR NEW SUPERHERO GROUP CAN GO AN' FIGHT CRIME WHEREVER WE SEE IT. FREE A' CHARGE.
WE'LL PATROL THE CITY AND ANNIHILATE ANYONE THAT GETS IN OUR WAY.
AN' Y'WANNA KNOW THE BEST PART?
I GET TA PICK THE TEAM AN' THE COSTUMES!

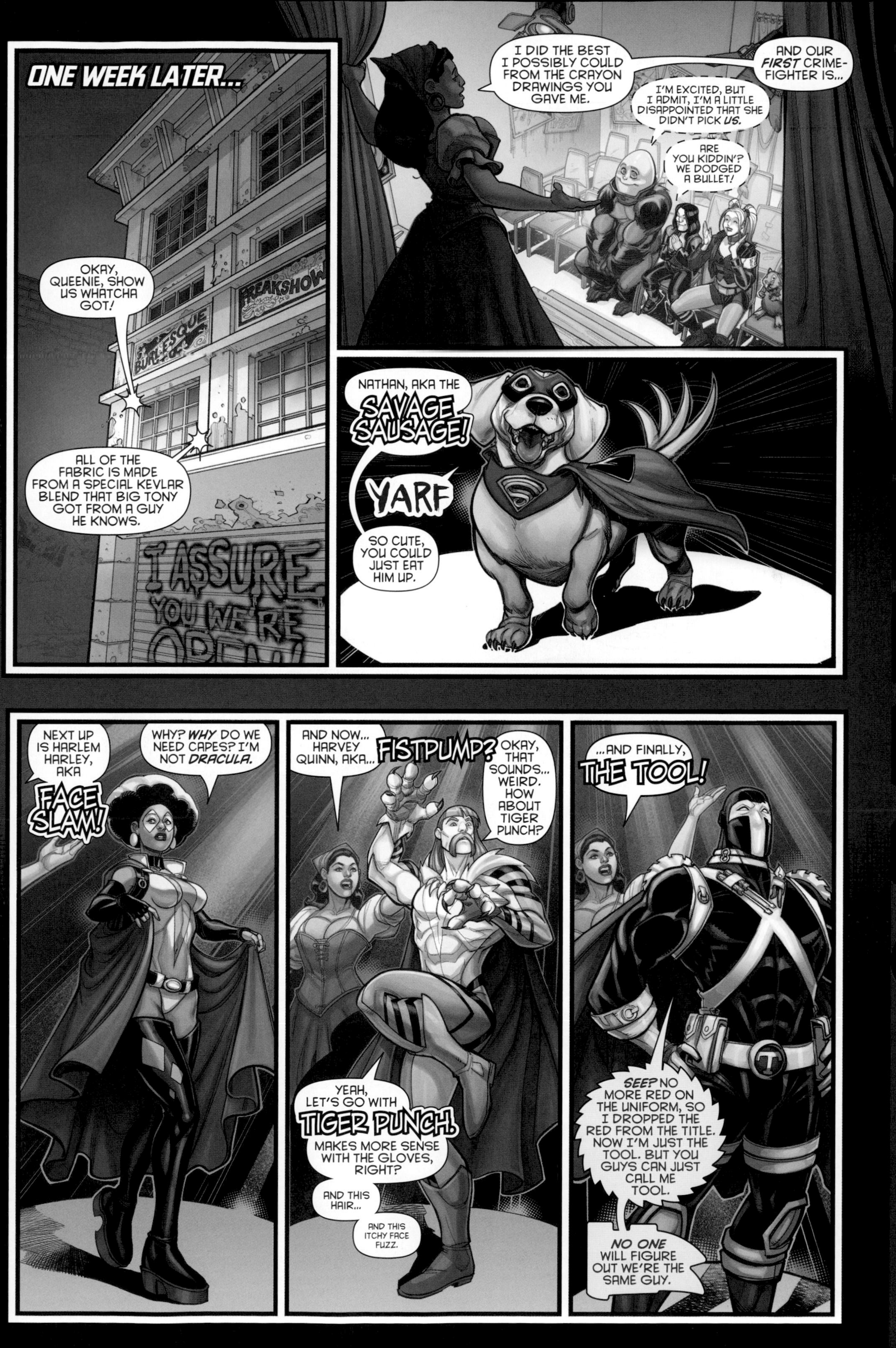
ONE WEEK LATER...
FREAKSHOW
BURLESQUE
OKAY, QUEENIE, SHOW US WHATCHA GOT!
ALL OF THE FABRIC IS MADE FROM A SPECIAL KEVLAR BLEND THAT BIG TONY GOT FROM A GUY HE KNOWS.
I ASSURE YOU WE'RE OPEN!
I DID THE BEST I POSSIBLY COULD FROM THE CRAYON DRAWINGS YOU GAVE ME.
AND OUR FIRST CRIME-FIGHTER IS...
I'M EXCITED, BUT I ADMIT, I'M A LITTLE DISAPPOINTED THAT SHE DIDN'T PICK US.
ARE YOU KIDDIN'? WE DODGED A BULLET!
NATHAN, AKA THE SAVAGE SAUSAGE!
YARF
SO CUTE, YOU COULD JUST EAT HIM UP.
NEXT UP IS HARLEM HARLEY, AKA FACE SLAM!
WHY? WHY DO WE NEED CAPES? I'M NOT DRACULA.
AND NOW... HARVEY QUINN, AKA... FISTPUMP?
OKAY, THAT SOUNDS... WEIRD. HOW ABOUT TIGER PUNCH?
YEAH, LET'S GO WITH TIGER PUNCH. MAKES MORE SENSE WITH THE GLOVES, RIGHT?
AND THIS HAIR...
AND THIS ITCHY FACE FUZZ.
...AND FINALLY, THE TOOL!
SEE? NO MORE RED ON THE UNIFORM, SO I DROPPED THE RED FROM THE TITLE. NOW I'M JUST THE TOOL. BUT YOU GUYS CAN JUST CALL ME TOOL.
NO ONE WILL FIGURE OUT WE'RE THE SAME GUY.

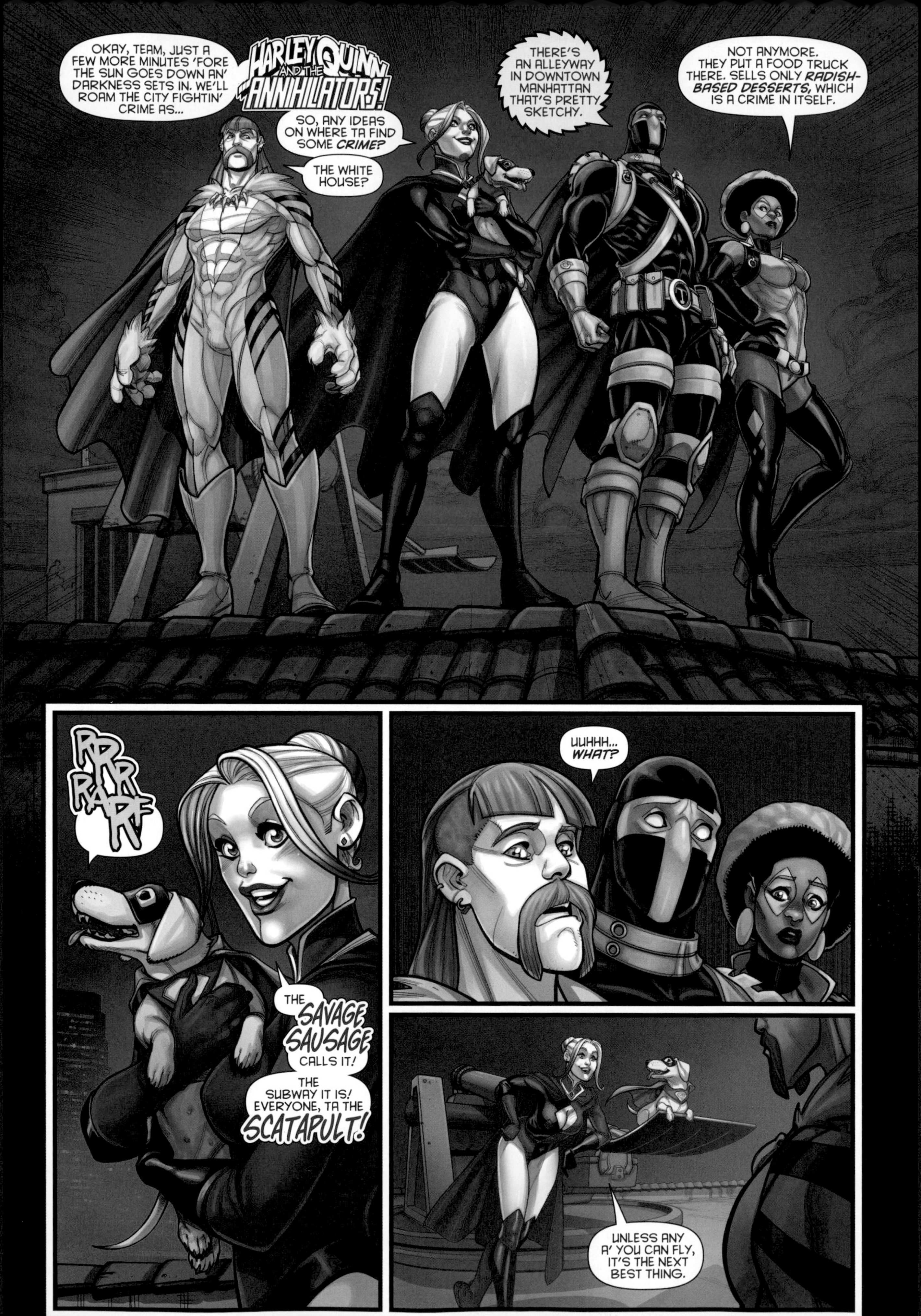
OKAY, TEAM, JUST A FEW MORE MINUTES 'FORE THE SUN GOES DOWN AN' DARKNESS SETS IN. WE'LL ROAM THE CITY FIGHTIN' CRIME AS...
HARLEY QUINN AND THE ANNIHILATORS!
SO, ANY IDEAS ON WHERE TA FIND SOME CRIME?
THE WHITE HOUSE?
THERE'S AN ALLEYWAY IN DOWNTOWN MANHATTAN THAT'S PRETTY SKETCHY.
NOT ANYMORE. THEY PUT A FOOD TRUCK THERE. SELLS ONLY RADISH-BASED DESSERTS, WHICH IS A CRIME IN ITSELF.
RRRRARF
THE SAVAGE SAUSAGE CALLS IT!
THE SUBWAY IT IS! EVERYONE, TA THE SCATAPULT!
UUHHH... WHAT?
UNLESS ANY A' YOU CAN FLY, IT'S THE NEXT BEST THING.

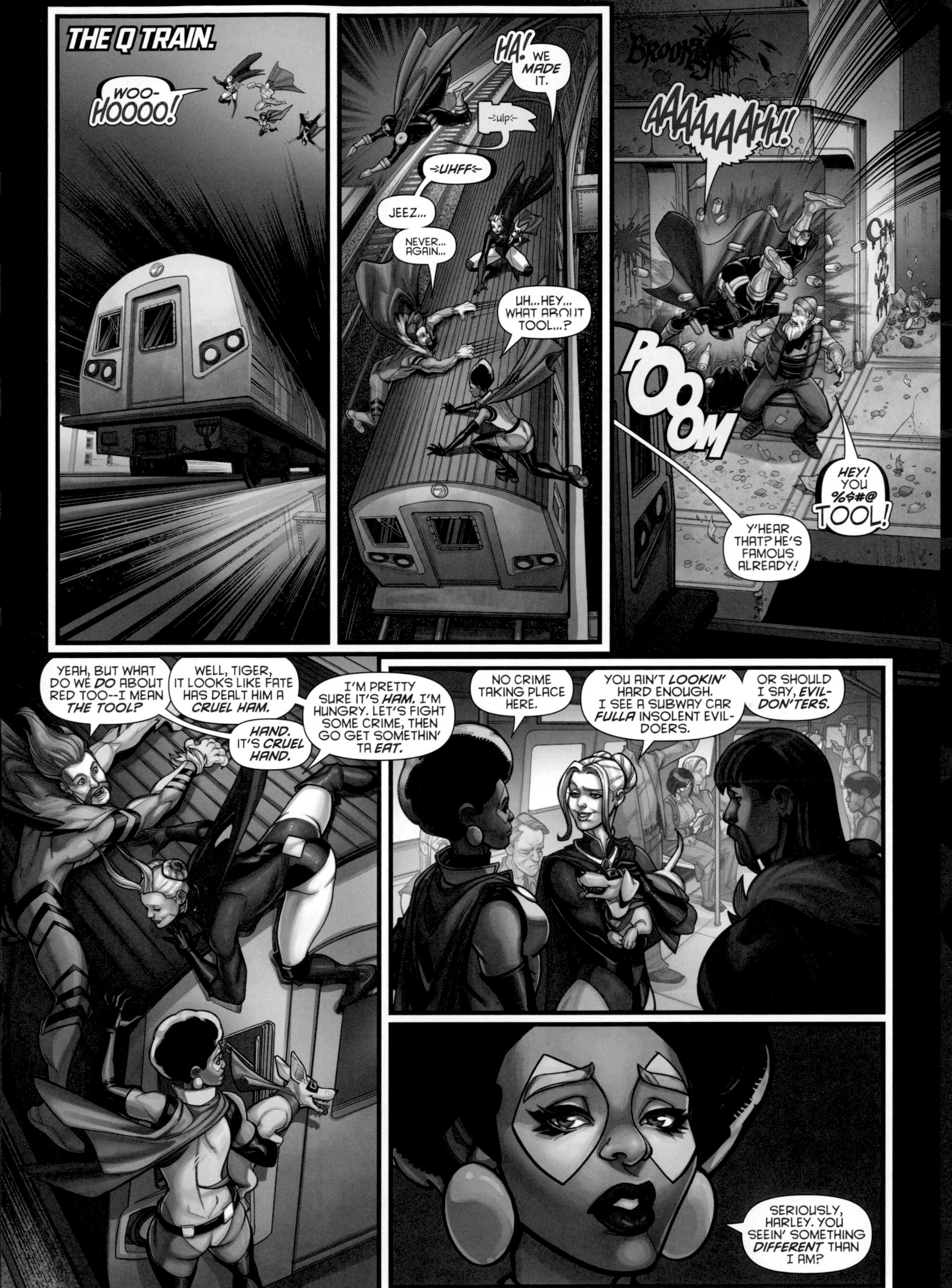
THE Q TRAIN.
WOO-HOOOO!
HA!
WE MADE IT.
ulp
UHFF
JEEZ...
NEVER... AGAIN...
UH...HEY... WHAT ABOUT TOOL...?
AAAAAAAHH!
BOOOOM
HEY! YOU %$#@ TOOL!
Y'HEAR THAT? HE'S FAMOUS ALREADY!
YEAH, BUT WHAT DO WE DO ABOUT RED TOO--I MEAN THE TOOL?
WELL, TIGER, IT LOOKS LIKE FATE HAS DEALT HIM A CRUEL HAM.
HAND. IT'S CRUEL HAND.
I'M PRETTY SURE IT'S HAM. I'M HUNGRY. LET'S FIGHT SOME CRIME, THEN GO GET SOMETHIN' TA EAT.
NO CRIME TAKING PLACE HERE.
YOU AIN'T LOOKIN' HARD ENOUGH. I SEE A SUBWAY CAR FULLA INSOLENT EVIL-DOERS.
OR SHOULD I SAY, EVIL-DON'TERS.
SERIOUSLY, HARLEY. YOU SEEIN' SOMETHING DIFFERENT THAN I AM?

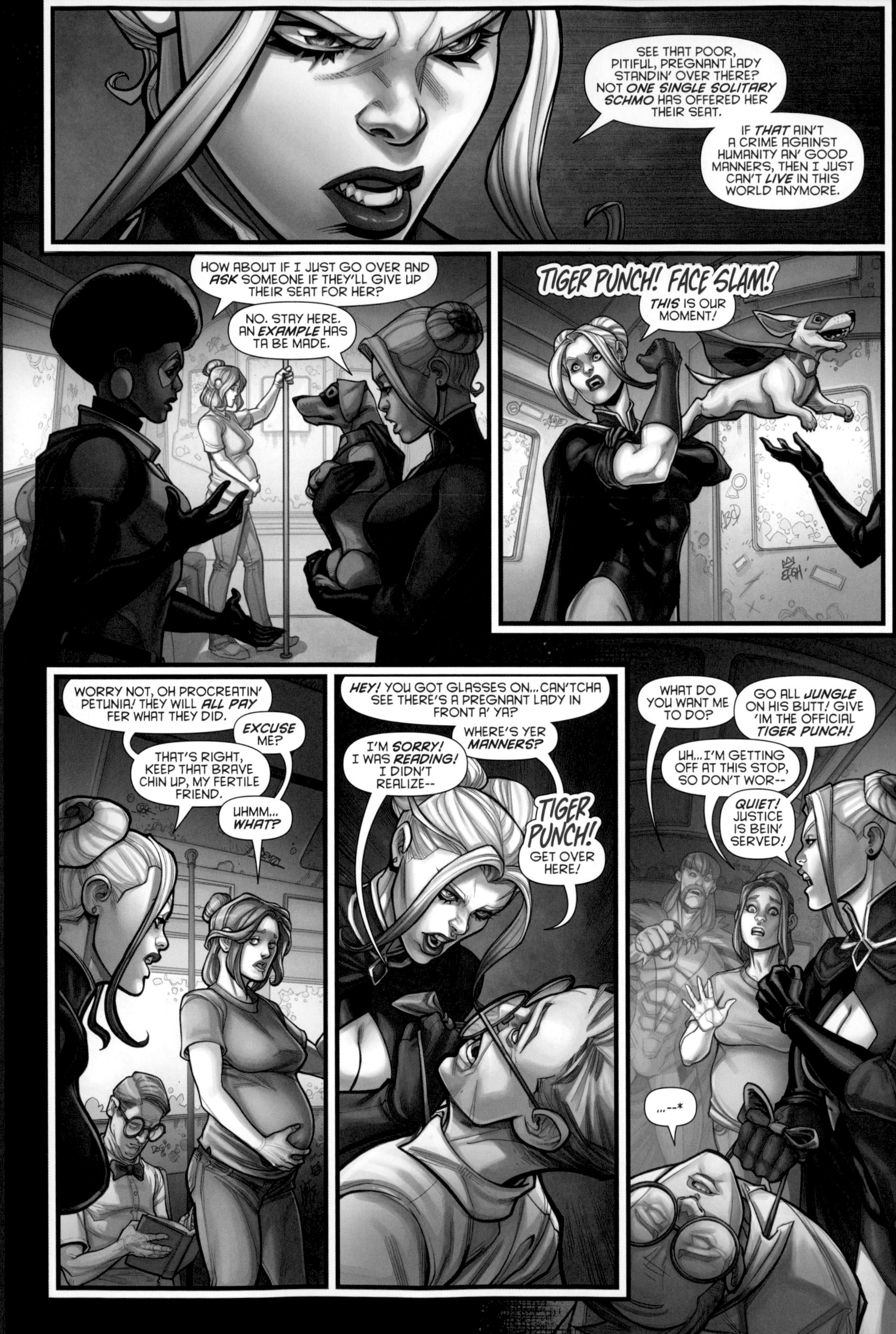

SEE THAT POOR, PITIFUL, PREGNANT LADY STANDIN' OVER THERE? NOT ONE SINGLE SOLITARY SCHMO HAS OFFERED HER THEIR SEAT.
IF THAT AIN'T A CRIME AGAINST HUMANITY AN' GOOD MANNERS, THEN I JUST CAN'T LIVE IN THIS WORLD ANYMORE.
HOW ABOUT IF I JUST GO OVER AND ASK SOMEONE IF THEY'LL GIVE UP THEIR SEAT FOR HER?
NO. STAY HERE. AN EXAMPLE HAS TA BE MADE.
TIGER PUNCH! FACE SLAM!
THIS IS OUR MOMENT!
WORRY NOT, OH PROCREATIN' PETUNIA! THEY WILL ALL PAY FER WHAT THEY DID.
EXCUSE ME?
THAT'S RIGHT, KEEP THAT BRAVE CHIN UP, MY FERTILE FRIEND.
UHMM... WHAT?
HEY! YOU GOT GLASSES ON...CAN'TCHA SEE THERE'S A PREGNANT LADY IN FRONT A' YA?
WHERE'S YER MANNERS?
I'M SORRY! I WAS READING! I DIDN'T REALIZE--
TIGER PUNCH! GET OVER HERE!
WHAT DO YOU WANT ME TO DO?
GO ALL JUNGLE ON HIS BUTT! GIVE 'IM THE OFFICIAL TIGER PUNCH!
UH...I'M GETTING OFF AT THIS STOP, SO DON'T WOR--
QUIET! JUSTICE IS BEIN' SERVED!
...--*

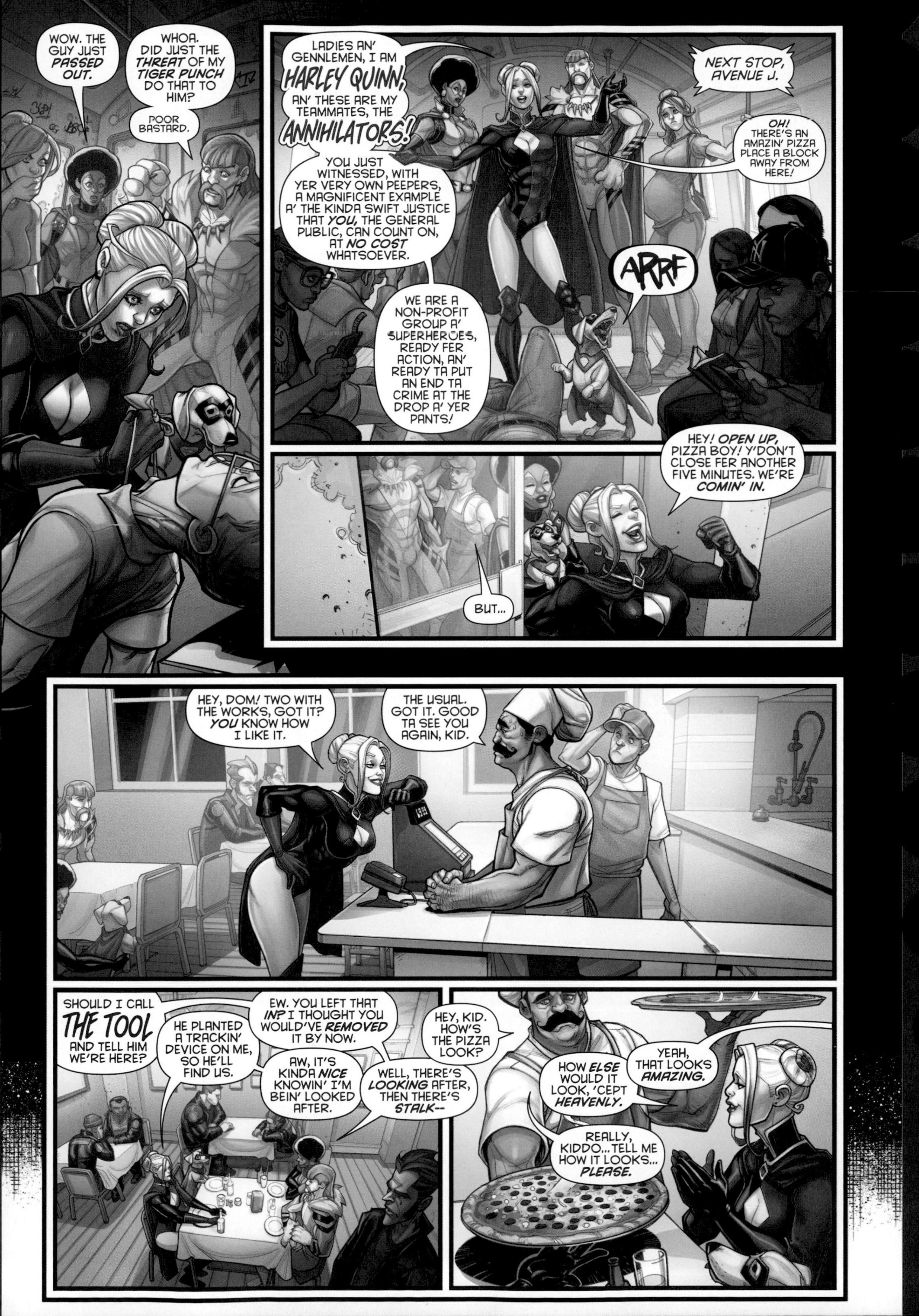
WOW. THE GUY JUST PASSED OUT.
WHOA. DID JUST THE THREAT OF MY TIGER PUNCH DO THAT TO HIM?
POOR BASTARD.
LADIES AN' GENNLEMEN, I AM HARLEY QUINN, AN' THESE ARE MY TEAMMATES, THE ANNIHILATORS!
YOU JUST WITNESSED, WITH YER VERY OWN PEEPERS, A MAGNIFICENT EXAMPLE A' THE KINDA SWIFT JUSTICE THAT YOU, THE GENERAL PUBLIC, CAN COUNT ON, AT NO COST WHATSOEVER.
WE ARE A NON-PROFIT GROUP A' SUPERHEROES, READY FER ACTION, AN' READY TA PUT AN END TA CRIME AT THE DROP A' YER PANTS!
ARRF
NEXT STOP, AVENUE J.
OH! THERE'S AN AMAZIN' PIZZA PLACE A BLOCK AWAY FROM HERE!
BUT...
HEY! OPEN UP, PIZZA BOY! Y'DON'T CLOSE FER ANOTHER FIVE MINUTES. WE'RE COMIN' IN.
HEY, DOM! TWO WITH THE WORKS, GOT IT? YOU KNOW HOW I LIKE IT.
THE USUAL. GOT IT. GOOD TA SEE YOU AGAIN, KID.
SHOULD I CALL THE TOOL AND TELL HIM WE'RE HERE?
HE PLANTED A TRACKIN' DEVICE ON ME, SO HE'LL FIND US.
EW. YOU LEFT THAT IN? I THOUGHT YOU WOULD'VE REMOVED IT BY NOW.
AW, IT'S KINDA NICE KNOWIN' I'M BEIN' LOOKED AFTER.
WELL, THERE'S LOOKING AFTER, THEN THERE'S STALK--
HEY, KID. HOW'S THE PIZZA LOOK?
YEAH, THAT LOOKS AMAZING.
HOW ELSE WOULD IT LOOK, 'CEPT HEAVENLY.
REALLY, KIDDO... TELL ME HOW IT LOOKS... PLEASE.

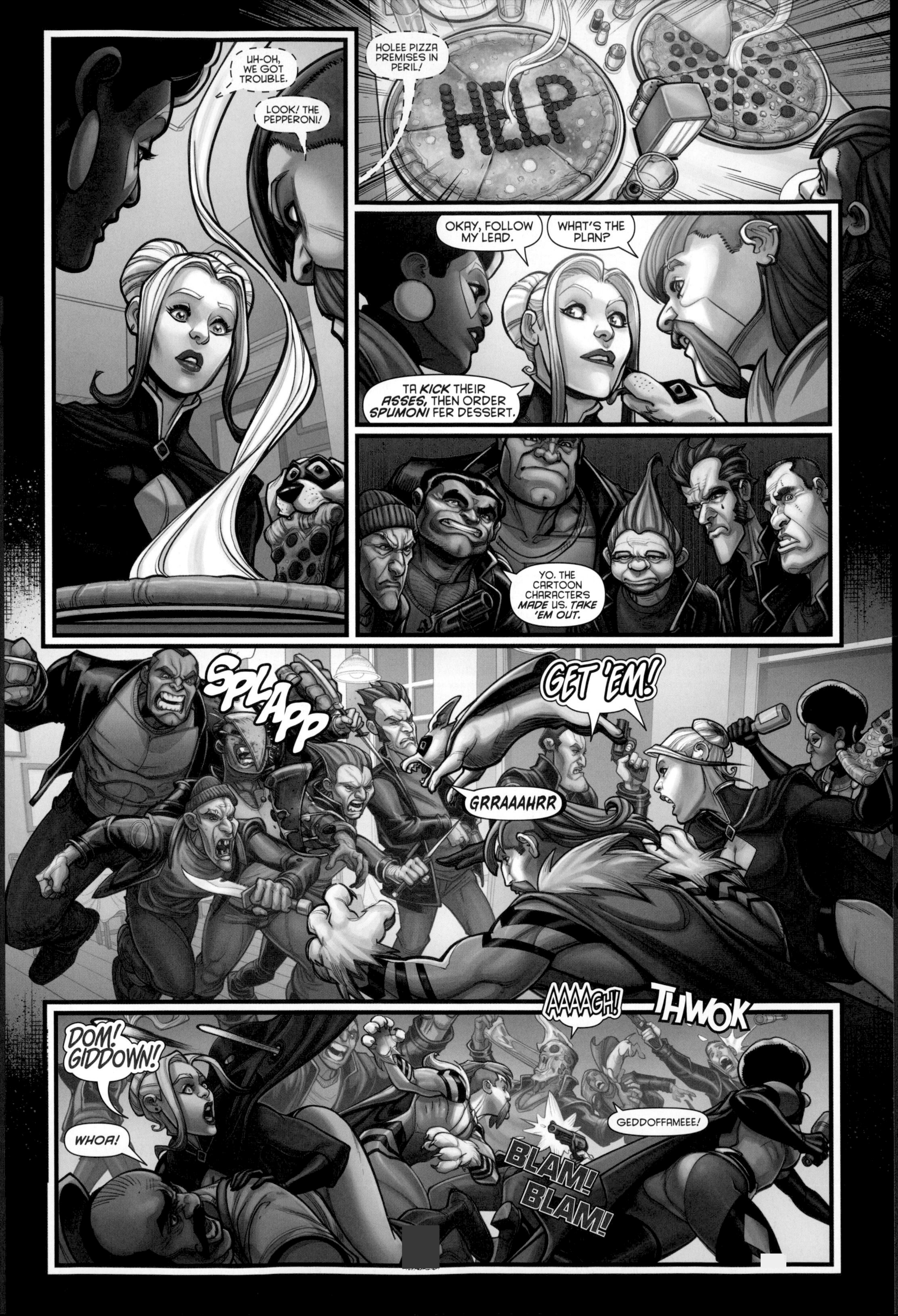
UH-OH, WE GOT TROUBLE.
LOOK! THE PEPPERONI!
HOLEE PIZZA PREMISES IN PERIL!
HELP
OKAY, FOLLOW MY LEAD.
WHAT'S THE PLAN?
TA KICK THEIR ASSES, THEN ORDER SPUMONI FER DESSERT.
YO. THE CARTOON CHARACTERS MADE US. TAKE 'EM OUT.
SPLAPP
GET 'EM!
GRRAAAHRR
AAAAGH!
THWOK
DOM! GIDDOWN!
WHOA!
GEDDOFFAMEEE!
BLAM! BLAM! BLAM!

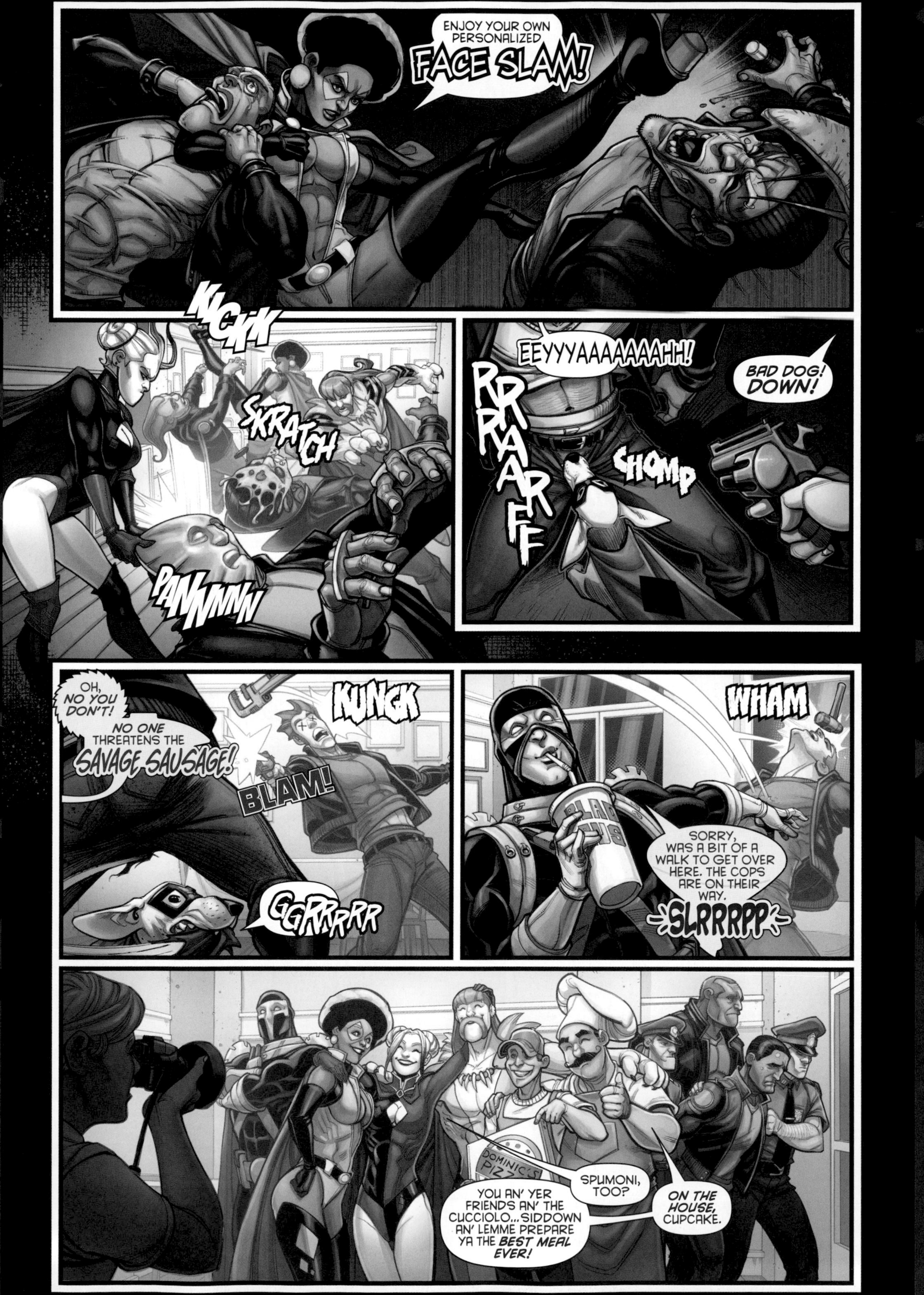
ENJOY YOUR OWN PERSONALIZED FACE SLAM!
KICKK
SKRATCH
PANNNNN
EEYYYAAAAAAAHH!
RRRAARFF
CHOMP
BAD DOG! DOWN!
OH, NO YOU DON'T!
NO ONE THREATENS THE SAVAGE SAUSAGE!
KUNGK
BLAM!
GGRRRRRR
WHAM
SORRY, WAS A BIT OF A WALK TO GET OVER HERE. THE COPS ARE ON THEIR WAY.
SLRRRPP
DOMINIC'S PIZZ
SPUMONI, TOO?
YOU AN' YER FRIENDS AN' THE CUCCIOLO... SIDDOWN AN' LEMME PREPARE YA THE BEST MEAL EVER!
ON THE HOUSE, CUPCAKE.

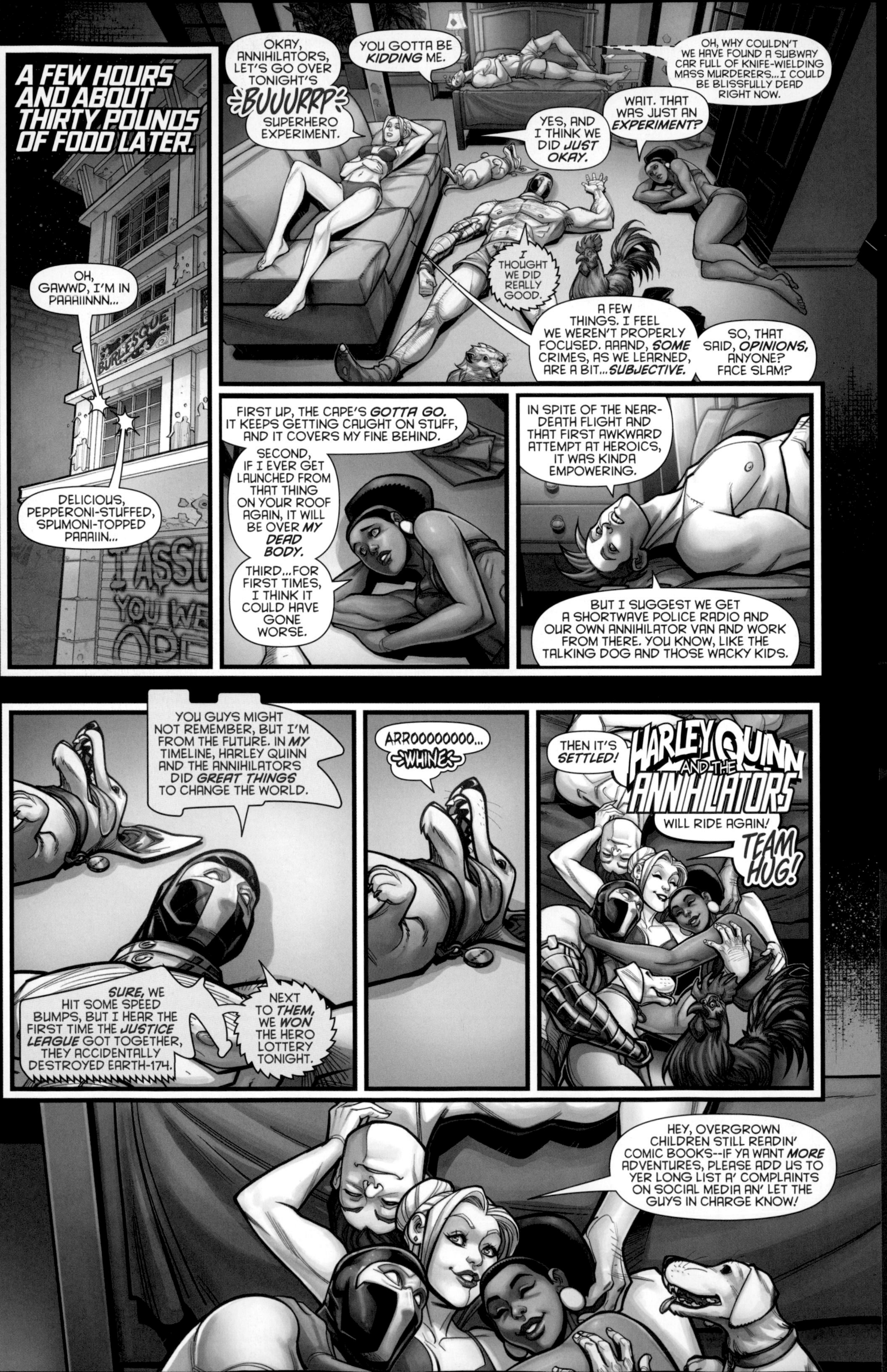
A FEW HOURS AND ABOUT THIRTY POUNDS OF FOOD LATER.
OH, GAWWD, I'M IN PAAAIIINNN...
DELICIOUS, PEPPERONI-STUFFED, SPUMONI-TOPPED PAAAIIN...
BURLESQUE
OKAY, ANNIHILATORS, LET'S GO OVER TONIGHT'S BUUURRP SUPERHERO EXPERIMENT.
YOU GOTTA BE KIDDING ME.
OH, WHY COULDN'T WE HAVE FOUND A SUBWAY CAR FULL OF KNIFE-WIELDING MASS MURDERERS...I COULD BE BLISSFULLY DEAD RIGHT NOW.
YES, AND I THINK WE DID JUST OKAY.
WAIT. THAT WAS JUST AN EXPERIMENT?
I THOUGHT WE DID REALLY GOOD.
A FEW THINGS. I FEEL WE WEREN'T PROPERLY FOCUSED. AAAND, SOME CRIMES, AS WE LEARNED, ARE A BIT...SUBJECTIVE.
SO, THAT SAID, OPINIONS, ANYONE? FACE SLAM?
FIRST UP, THE CAPE'S GOTTA GO. IT KEEPS GETTING CAUGHT ON STUFF, AND IT COVERS MY FINE BEHIND.
SECOND, IF I EVER GET LAUNCHED FROM THAT THING ON YOUR ROOF AGAIN, IT WILL BE OVER MY DEAD BODY.
THIRD...FOR FIRST TIMES, I THINK IT COULD HAVE GONE WORSE.
IN SPITE OF THE NEAR-DEATH FLIGHT AND THAT FIRST AWKWARD ATTEMPT AT HEROICS, IT WAS KINDA EMPOWERING.
BUT I SUGGEST WE GET A SHORTWAVE POLICE RADIO AND OUR OWN ANNIHILATOR VAN AND WORK FROM THERE. YOU KNOW, LIKE THE TALKING DOG AND THOSE WACKY KIDS.
YOU GUYS MIGHT NOT REMEMBER, BUT I'M FROM THE FUTURE. IN MY TIMELINE, HARLEY QUINN AND THE ANNIHILATORS DID GREAT THINGS TO CHANGE THE WORLD.
SURE, WE HIT SOME SPEED BUMPS, BUT I HEAR THE FIRST TIME THE JUSTICE LEAGUE GOT TOGETHER, THEY ACCIDENTALLY DESTROYED EARTH-174.
NEXT TO THEM, WE WON THE HERO LOTTERY TONIGHT.
ARROOOOOOOO... WHINE
THEN IT'S SETTLED! HARLEY QUINN AND THE ANNIHILATORS WILL RIDE AGAIN!
TEAM HUG!
HEY, OVERGROWN CHILDREN STILL READIN' COMIC BOOKS--IF YA WANT MORE ADVENTURES, PLEASE ADD US TO YER LONG LIST A' COMPLAINTS ON SOCIAL MEDIA AN' LET THE GUYS IN CHARGE KNOW!

DC

BLACK
LABEL

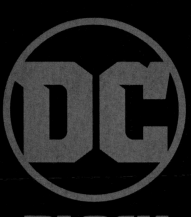